ecpr PRESS

Democratic Reform and Consolidation

The Cases of Mexico and Turkey

Evren Çelik Wiltse

ecpr PRESS

First published by the ECPR Press in 2015

Cover: © Evren Celik Wiltse (2014) 'Mexican Mural on Revolution'

The ECPR Press is the publishing imprint of the European Consortium for Political Research (ECPR), a scholarly association, which supports and encourages the training, research and cross-national co-operation of political scientists in institutions throughout Europe and beyond.

ECPR Press
Harbour House
Hythe Quay
Colchester
CO2 8JF
United Kingdom

Typeset by Lapiz Digital Services

Printed and bound by Lightning Source

British Library Cataloguing in Publication Data

A catalogue record for this book is available from the British Library

ISBN: 978-1-907-301-67-4
PDF ISBN: 978-1-785-521-36-2
EPUB ISBN: 978-1-785-521-35-5
KINDLE ISBN: 978-1-785-521-34-8

www.ecpr.eu/ecprpress

ECPR Press Series Editors

Dario Castiglione (University of Exeter)
Peter Kennealy (European University Institute)
Alexandra Segerberg (Stockholm University)
Ian O'Flynn (Newcastle University)

More books from the ECPR Press on democracy

Agents or Bosses?: Patronage and Intra-Party Politics in Argentina and Turkey
ISBN: 9781907301261
Özge Kemahlioğlu

Between-Election Democracy: The Representative Relationship After Election Day
ISBN Hardback: 9781907301988, ISBN Paperback: 9781910259399
Peter Esaiasson and Hanne Marthe Narud

Conditional Democracy: The Contemporary Debate on Political Reform in Chinese Universities
ISBN: 9781907301698
Emilie Frenkiel

Consultative Committees in the European Union: No Vote – No Influence?
ISBN: 9781910259429
Diana Panke, Christoph Hönnige, Julia Gollub

Democratic Institutions and Authoritarian Rule in Southeast Europe
ISBN: 9781907301438
Danijela Dolenec

Is Democracy a Lost Cause?: Paradoxes of an Imperfect Invention
ISBN: 9781907301384
Alfio Mastropaolo

Parties, Governments and Voters in Finland: Politics under Fundamental Societal Transformation
ISBN: 9781910259337
Lauri Karvonen

Please visit http://www.ecpr.eu/ecprpress for information about new publications.

Dedicated to Dave and William Selim

Contents

List of Abbreviations

AKP	*Adalet ve Kalkınma Partisi*, Justice and Development Party of Turkey
AMLO	Andrés Manuel López Obrador
ANAP	*Anavatan Partisi*, Motherland Party of Turkey
AP	*Adalet Partisi*, Justice Party of Turkey
BoP	Balance of Payments
CEDESA	*Centro de Desarollo Agropecuario*, Center for Development in Agriculture
CHP	*Cumhuriyet Halk Partisi*, Republican People's Party of Turkey
CKMP	*Cumhuriyetçi Köylü Millet Partisi*, Republican Peasant and Nation Party of Turkey
CMHN	*Consejo Mexicano de Hombres de Negocios*, Mexican Council of Businessmen
CONCAMIN	Confederation of Industrial Chambers of Mexico
CONCANACO	The Confederation of Chambers of Commerce of Mexico
CROM	Regional Confederation of Mexican Workers
CTM	*Confederacion de Trabajadores de Mexico*, Confederation of Workers of Mexico
DGM	*Devlet Güvenlik Mahkemeleri*, State Security Courts in Turkey
DISK	*Devrimci İşçi Sendikaları Konfederasyonu*, Confederation of Revolutionary Workers' Unions in Turkey
DP	*Demokrat Parti*, Democrat Party of Turkey
DPT	*Devlet Planlama Teşkilatı*, State Planning Organisation of Turkey
DTP	*Demokratik Toplum Partisi*, Democratic Society Party of Turkey
EU	The European Union
EZLN	*Ejército Zapatista de Liberación Nacional*, Zapatista National Liberation Army
FDI	Foreign Direct Investment
FDR	Franklin Delano Roosevelt
GATT	General Agreement on Tariffs and Trade
GDP	Gross Domestic Product
IFE	*Instituto Federal Electoral*, Federal Electoral Institute of Mexico
IMF	International Monetary Fund
IMSS	*Instituto Mexicano de Segura Social*, Mexican Social Security Institute

IS/ISIS	Islamic State, Islamic State of Iraq and Syria
ISI	Import substitution industrialization
MGK	*Milli Güvenlik Kurulu*, National Security Council of Turkey
MHP	*Milliyetçi Hareket Partisi*, National Action Party of Turkey
MNP	*Milli Nizam Partisi*, National Order Party of Turkey
MSP	*Milli Selamet Partisi*, National Salvation Party of Turkey
MUSIAD	Independent Industrialists' and Businessmen's Association of Turkey
NAFTA	North Atlantic Free Trade Agreement
NATO	North Atlantic Treaty Organization
OAS	Organization of American States
OPDA	Ottoman Public Debt Administration, (*Düyun-u Umumiye*)
OYAK	*Ordu Yardımlaşma Kurumu*, Turkish Armed Forces Assistance and Pension Fund
PAN	*Partido Accion Nacional*, National Action Party of Mexico
PEMEX	*Petroleos Mexicanos*, Mexican national oil company
PNR	*Partido Nacional Revolucionario*, National Revolutionary Party of Mexico
PP	People's Party, later became the Republican People's Party of Turkey
PR	proportional representation system
PRD	*Partido de la Revolución Democrática*, Party of Democratic Revolution of Mexico
PRI	*Partido Revolucionario Institucional*, Revolutionary Institutional Party of Mexico
PROCEDE	*Programa de Certificación de Derechos Ejidales y Titulación de Solares,* Certificate program for Mexican collective land owners.
PRONASOL	National Solidarity Program of Mexico for social assistance (later PROGRESA)
SEE	State Economic Enterprise
SSK	Turkish Social Security Institution
TAF	Turkish Armed Forces
TEB	*Türk Eczacılar Birliği*, Pharmacists' Association of Turkey
TEKEL	Turkish tobacco and alcohol monopoly
TGNA	Turkish Grand National Assembly
TIP	*Türkiye İşçi Partisi*, Worker's Party of Turkey
TMMOB	*Türk Mühendis ve Mimar Odaları Birliği*, Union of Chamber of Turkish Engineers and Architects
TOBB	*Türkiye Odalar Borsalar Birliği*, The Union of Chambers and Commodity Exchanges of Turkey

TRT	Turkish Radio Television, state-owned broadcasting agency of Turkey
TUSIAD	Turkish Industry and Business Association
TUSKON	Turkish Confederation of Businessmen and Industrialists
Türk-İş	Turkish Labour Confederation
UNAM	National Autonomous University of Mexico
VAT	Value added tax
YÖK	*Yüksek Öğrenim Kurumu*, Higher Education Council of Turkey

List of Figures and Tables

Tables

Acknowledgements

Extending from Mexico to Turkey and back to the US, it took a global village to complete this book. This makes it harder to express my heartfelt thanks to all of my colleagues, advisors, friends and family members that helped me along this journey, but I will try my best.

First and foremost, I would like to thank Professor Howard J Wiarda, who was my advisor at the University of Massachusetts-Amherst, and then a lifetime mentor. As an international student trying to master both the rigorousness of the academic world in the US, as well as the peculiarities of life in Massachusetts, it was an honour and privilege to work with Dr Wiarda. During my graduate studies, Dr Wiarda's insights pushed me outside the proverbial box. Instead of specialising solely on my home country, his encouragement and support sowed the seeds of a unique cross-regional comparison with Turkey and Latin America. His strong pedagogy in comparative method and democracy provided great inspiration for this work. I am also deeply appreciative of the fact that his mentoring continued years after I received my PhD. Probably the crowning point for me was during a workshop in Istanbul in the winter of 2014, where we had three generations of comparativists around the same table: Professor Wiarda, myself and one of my graduate students from Ankara. Both Dr Wiarda and his wife, Dr Ieda Siqueira Wiarda have set the bar extremely high on academic mentorship. I hope I can measure up to those standards during my own career.

I received financial assistance from various institutions for language training and field trips to Mexico. I would like to thank the University of Massachusetts, Amherst College of Social and Behavioral Sciences, Center for Latin American, Caribbean and Latino Studies, as well as the Political Science Department for multiple travel and summer research grants. I also would like to thank the American Research Institute in Turkey (ARIT) for their dissertation writing grant.

My visits to Mexico were far from cut-and-dried research trips. Rather, they became invaluable opportunities to peek into this incredibly sophisticated society and make lifetime friends. First, I would like to thank the Jimenez family in Cuernavaca, who were my hosts in my first trip. Their sons, who were the producers of the documentary *Los últimos zapatistas, héroes olvidados*, and the rest of the family showed enormous generosity and patience despite my endless questions in broken Spanish. In San Miguel de Allende, I would like to thank the Center for Global Justice, and particularly Bob Stone, Cliff DuRand, Betsy Bowman, Yolanda Milan and Norma Suarez, for providing me a welcoming research home.

While conducting research on the civil society, land-tenure system and *ejidos* in rural Mexico, I met some of the most inspiring people. In Dolores Hidalgo, I would like to acknowledge Teresa and Graciela Martinez (a.k.a. Tere y Chela) of Centro de Desarrollo Agropecuario (CEDESA). The weeks I spent with them at CEDESA were among the most memorable moments of my research. I am grateful for having a chance to witness their struggle for democratic empowerment of women and rural communities with such intimacy.

This research would probably not have gone as smoothly as it did without institutional support. At the Mexican Embassy in Turkey, I would like to thank Ambassador Martha Bárcena Coqui and the Chief of Mission, Mr Héctor Rodriguez, for their continuous encouragement and logistic support. Similarly, the Turkish Ambassador in Mexico, Hon. Ahmet Acet, was extremely generous and supportive. At *El Colegio de México*, I would like to especially thank Professors Fernando Escalante and Celia Toro for taking their time to help me make sense of this comparative endeavour. At the Mexican Council on Foreign Relations (COMEXI), I would like to thank its Director Dr Claudia Calvin for an extremely productive workshop. Overall, Mexicans from all walks of life, ranging from *campesinos* in dusty villages of Guanajuato to ex-President Ernesto Zedillo – with whom I had a chance to have a short interview in Connecticut – helped me tremendously with their heartening attitude and candid views. I hope my work accurately reflects their insights.

Two universities in Turkey probably provided the greatest intellectual support for my work: my *alma mater*, Bogazici University in Istanbul and TOBB University of Economy and Technology in Ankara. It is difficult to name everyone but I want to express my deepest gratitude to my professors and colleagues, who supported and cherished my work and provided an intellectual home for me to grow. They were the ones who took me to observe the famous protests in the summer of 2013, and they were the ones who helped me get out unharmed. I also want to thank all of my students, who made teaching such a joy during the hottest summer months and Ramadan. Some of them ventured into their own academic explorations in Latin American Studies. My advice to them is not any different than Garrison Keillor's classic line: Be well, do good work, and keep in touch […]

Also in Ankara, I would like to thank my beloved veterinarians, the Özdemir-Yilmaz family. They not only put up with my endless questions about the agricultural policies of Turkey but also arranged interviews with the leading experts in the sector and essentially offered free room and board and excellent childcare during my summers in Ankara. I doubt there is any way to reciprocate such levels of unconditional care and support.

My current home institution, South Dakota State University, provided the seed grant to travel to Mexico for my most recent interviews and funds to disseminate my work in regional and international conferences. I would like to thank the Provost of SDSU for multiple dissemination grants, and the Dean of College of Arts and Sciences for the seed grant. My Department Heads – past, interim and present – provided consistent support and encouragement, for which I am deeply grateful. Academic writing is a rather lonely enterprise. Especially during the long winters, it could be rather taxing. I doubt I would have survived the South Dakota winters without the cameraderie and sage advice of my colleagues at SDSU. They provide a sense of community of which I am deeply appreciative.

The European Consortium for Political Research (ECPR) General Conferences were critical outlets for disseminating my early research and receiving feedback.

I am proud that the ECPR Press accepted my manuscript for publication. I would like to thank my editors Peter Triantafillou and Dario Castiglione, and the anonymous reviewers for their help and constructive suggestions. Laura Pugh and Kate Hawkins from the ECPR Press were extremely kind and generous throughout the process. I am deeply appreciative of their patient support.

On the home front, I would like to thank my parents for their brave efforts to combine east and west of Turkey through their marriage, and thereby helping me grow a keen pair of comparativist's eyes early on. I want to thank my father for all those fishing trips to remote villages when I was a little girl, for taking me to his barber for haircuts, and for the awkward timing of his compulsory military service that coincided with the 1980 military coup. All of these experiences influenced my perception of social reality immensely, and made a unique mould in which my character was shaped. I want to thank my mother for her support and for being a feisty working mom committed to her business as a pharmacist. Much later in life, I realised the importance of having strong women role models around as I was growing up. I am happy to be the torch-bearer for my mother and my caring and equally feisty aunts.

Lastly, I want to thank my husband Dave for his never-ending support. He was a competent father, who could take care of our little son during my extended trips to Mexico and Turkey. He is an incredibly tolerant partner who endured all the difficulties life threw in our way, and a fantastic editor, who definitely improved the quality of my work. Refuting the Huntingtonian predictions, we have had hardly any 'culture clashes' after more than a decade-long marriage. Life with him is a happy journey that took me from Massachusetts, to Zimbabwe, Pennsylvania, Minnesota, Turkey, Norway, Iowa and to South Dakota. I am so glad he interrupted my incessant lecturing on inequality with a ring in Zimbabwe and I am so glad Willie came to our lives. That is why this book is dedicated to both of them.

Evren Celik Wiltse
April 2015

Preface

Why can some nations experience rapid democratisation and consolidation while others remain partly democratic for decades? What are the conditions for democratic improvement and consolidation? How do societies with some degree of development and democratic opening create free and open regimes? Which types of historical institutions and state–society relations help foster this? Finally, what is the role of international actors? Which forms of international engagement enhance the prospects of democratic progress and consolidation and which ones hinder it?

These and similar questions made me think about countries that are stuck in a democratic grey-zone. As a long-time observer of democratic progress in Turkey, I wanted to expand beyond a single case study and find out more systematic, institutional reasons that help or hinder democratic progress. It is also important to note that my coming of age as a political scientist took place simultaneously with multiple US interventions in the Middle East. The policy and punditry circles at the time, particularly in the US, were trumpeting democracy as the panacea for all ills, and were advocating elections as the gateway to a glorious future.

Contrary to these cheerleaders of fast-track democracy, many countries that already had the basic minimum qualities of a democracy, such as regular elections, were stuck in limbo. Essentially, my research tries to tackle this question of democratic inertia. It challenges the short-term wishful thinking that assumes democracy would 'spring up' in an authoritarian society after a single mass protest and subsequent elections. Instead, this book highlights the importance of the long-term historical and institutional legacies that shape the bedrock of a democratic polity, including rule of law and civil society.

This book addresses the perplexing democratic underperformance question by looking at two key emerging economies: Mexico and Turkey. This duo offers significant insights on institutional structures and state–society relations that help or hinder democratic progress. The book analyses the democratic-consolidation process from a comparative historical perspective. Secondly, given the extensive engagement of Mexico and Turkey with the US and the EU respectively, this study also sheds light on the efficacy of different forms of international engagement with democratisation. Both Mexico and Turkey are pivotal countries in their respective regions. They are also significant partners and allies with the Global North. This solid partnership notwithstanding, the US–Mexican engagement is very different from that of the EU–Turkey one. Given the topicality of the subjects addressed, it is my hope that this book will be a relevant contribution to both academic and policy-making circles on democratic consolidation.

E.C.W.
Brookings, South Dakota
December 2014

Chapter One

Introduction

Democratic progress has been a perennial subject of inquiry for the social sciences. Particularly since the end of the Cold War, a significant amount of ink has been used in discovering the factors that help or hinder democratic progress. Despite the unceasing efforts of both domestic and international pro-democracy actors, the global outlook does not resemble a rose garden. While scholars relish the fact that since 1989 the number of democracies has exceeded the number of authoritarian regimes,[1] the picture becomes more blurred when the borders between types of political regime are painted with less broad strokes. According to the 2014 Freedom House Annual Survey, which uses a three-part classification of states, only 40 per cent of the world population lives in 'free' and democratic countries. Nearly as many (35 per cent) live in 'partly-free' societies, while 25 per cent live in undemocratic, or 'not-free' states.[2]

This book targets a specific group of countries that occupy a halfway position between full-fledged democracies and closed, authoritarian regimes. These 'partly free' countries, which make up 59 cases out of the 185 states that Freedom House classifies, pose an interesting challenge to scholars of democratic progress. Even though the bulk of the literature seems content with democratic progress once countries have achieved a certain degree of electoral competition, certain countries seem to be stuck in the grey zone of semi-democracy for decades. After their initial departure from blanket authoritarianism, they achieved limited political opening with somewhat competitive elections. At this stage, though, it seems that a significant proportion of them, some 35 per cent according to the Freedom House, end up in a perpetual struggle for democratic consolidation. While most do not slide back to authoritarianism, they do not advance to the ranks of full-fledged free and democratic countries either. Their lacklustre democratic reforms are occasionally interrupted by military coups and democratic breakdowns and eventual restorations. Important questions that this book tries to tackle are the following: *why* do certain countries get stuck in the halfway house of 'partly free' status for decades? What are the main factors that hinder their graceful promotion to the premier league of full-fledged, mature democracies? Which factors facilitate

---

1. C. W. Haerpfer *et al.*, 'Introduction', in C.W. Haerpfer *et al.* (eds), *Democratization*, New York: Oxford University Press, 2009, pp. 1–7.

2. *Freedom in the World 2014*, report by Freedom House. Online. Available at http://www. freedomhouse.org/report/freedom-world/freedom-world-2014#.UuQW0hZ6gy4 (last accessed 25 January 2014).

the consolidation of democratic regimes in these relatively fragile, partly free societies?

Since it would be rather challenging to conduct an in-depth comparative analysis of all 59 countries that are classified as partly free, this book will zoom in on two particular cases. When we look at the group of partly free countries that have for decades failed to achieve democratic consolidation, two countries from two regions particularly stand out: Mexico and Turkey. These two countries are important test cases, since both are fairly large countries with sophisticated economies and also with significant experience in electoral competition. They are key players in their respective regions, for they stand between the advanced capitalist economies of the North and the lesser-developed economies of the Global South. This geographic proximity of Mexico and Turkey to established economies can also help us test the democratic contagion hypothesis.[3] A comparison of bilateral relations between Mexico and the US *versus* Turkey and the EU would offer important clues as to if/how prosperity and democracy travel from the advanced North to the Global South.

Pairing Turkey and Mexico in a single comparative framework might sound counter-intuitive at first glance. Yet, a closer look would reveal that the socio-political and development trajectories of these countries have important similarities. First, both countries have launched massive economic restructuring packages since the 1980s, similar to many other developing countries. The import-substitution–industrialisation (ISI) model of development in the 1950s and 1960s paved the way to massive fiscal imbalances. By the 1980s, both countries had embarked on an economic overhaul under the auspices of international power-brokers such as the International Monetary Fund (IMF) and the World Bank. As in many other parts of the developing world, the state began to withdraw from the economy through privatisation and deregulation. The private sector became the new locomotive of economic growth, replacing the state and the public sector.[4] In terms of the basic structures of their state–economy and state–society relations, Mexico and Turkey had much in common, as is discussed in the following chapters. However in recent decades, the gap between Mexico and Turkey regarding their performance in democratic consolidation has been widening. More strikingly, Mexico began to be classified as a liberal democracy and the *Freedom House* survey updated Mexico's democratic status after the momentous Presidential elections of 2000. However, Turkey continues to be ranked in the 'partly-free' category, despite the series of democratic reforms that have been made. It is also the purpose of this book to uncover some of the causal factors that contribute to this democratic performance gap between the two countries.

---

3. P. Schmitter, 'The influence of international context upon the choice of national institutions and policies in neo-democracies', in L. Whitehead (ed.), *The International Dimensions of Democratization: Europe and the Americas*, Oxford and New York: Oxford University Press, 1996, pp. 26–54.

4. C. Gore, 'The rise and fall of the Washington consensus as a paradigm for developing countries', *World Development* 2000, 28(5), pp. 789–804.

For most scholars of democratisation, Mexico was the less likely candidate of the two to improve its democratic credentials. After all, it was Mexico that was labelled as the 'perfect dictatorship', for having single-party rule for seven decades. Turkey, on the other hand, had held competitive multi-party elections since the 1950s, although democratic politics was periodically interrupted by military coups. In the end, Mexico seems to have beaten the structural odds by improving its democratic credentials; Turkey, however, has underperformed, despite having decades-long experience with competitive elections and despite its long-term engagement with the EU – a quintessentially democratic union. This book attempts to grasp the mechanisms that led to the deepening of this democratic performance gap between Mexico and Turkey.

There has been a growing literature on recent socio-economic transformation and democratisation in Turkey and Mexico;[5] however, this book differs from the existing literature on democratic progress mainly in two aspects. First, most studies of democratic consolidation in Turkey or Mexico are single-case studies that gauge democratic progress from a temporal comparative framework. That is, they compare the democratic progress in a single country over time. This book adds a spatial dimension to that comparison by using a second case as a comparative benchmark. Things might have improved over time, but by how much? A paired-comparison will help shed light on the pace of democratic progress in both contexts.

The second important aspect of this book is the way in which it incorporates domestic and international factors in the analysis of democratic consolidation. In the post-Cold-War era, and particularly after the traumatic experience of September 11 2001, the world became acutely aware of the global democratic gap. Impoverished and authoritarian regions could no longer be neglected, thanks to the neck-breaking pace of globalisation. Subsequently, advanced democracies, particularly the US, began a campaign of aggressive democracy-promotion in the Global South. North-American and European engagement in Afghanistan, the Middle East, North Africa and Eurasia – despite the protracted economic recession since 2008 – seems unlikely to disappear any time soon. In a far-reaching speech delivered in Cairo before the events of the 'Arab Spring', then US Secretary of State Condoleezza Rice lamented that her country had preferred stability to

---

5. *See* S. Haber, *et al.*, *Mexico Since 1980*, Cambridge: Cambridge University Press, 2nd edition, 2011; J. Dominguez *et al.* (eds), *Consolidating Mexico's Democracy: 2006 presidential campaign in comparative perspective*, Baltimore, MD: Johns Hopkins University Press, 2009; Z. Öniş, 'Sharing power: Turkey's democratization challenge in the age of the AKP hegemony', *Insight Turkey* 2013, 15(2), pp. 103–22; E. Özbudun, *Contemporary Turkish Politics: Challenges to democratic consolidation*, Boulder, CO and London: Lynne Reinner Publications, 2000. Two important recent works analyse Turkey in a comparative framework. Sultan Tepe compares religious politics in Israel and Turkey in S. Tepe, 'The perils of polarization and religious parties: the democratic challenges of political fragmentation in Israel and Turkey', *Democratization* 2013, 20(5), pp. 831–56; Ayşe Zarakol compares and contrasts modernisation and civil–military relations in Thailand and Turkey in A. Zarakol, 'Revisiting second image reversed: lessons from Turkey and Thailand', *International Studies Quarterly* 2013, 57(1), pp. 150–62.

democracy for far too long. She continued by pledging solid US support for the democratic aspirations of all peoples.[6] Years later, President Obama delivered a similar pro-democracy speech in the very same venue.

When we look at the democracy-promotion record of the EU, comparative studies of democratisation state that the 'leverage of the EU' has been the 'single best tool' for promoting democracy in Eastern Europe.[7] Potential EU membership remains an attractive 'carrot' for political regimes that are willing to put their houses in democratic order. Currently, the EU is expanding into the Balkans and possibly further to the East, while the US is simultaneously engaged in two nation-building projects (Afghanistan and Iraq). Last but not the least, the Arab Spring phenomenon is rapidly changing political dynamics in the Middle East and North Africa (MENA) region. The MENA region was long considered an 'exception' to democratisation theories, since these social and political systems looked rather static, entrenched in various forms of authoritarianism. However, the avalanche of change since the Arab Spring has brought the possibility of a democratic opening-up to the MENA region as well.

Given the vast number of cases where parties and elections exist, yet the goal of democracy without qualifiers is still unattained, it might be timely to look at Turkey and Mexico. The experiences of these two cases can provide significant insight into the perennial questions of 'what to do' and 'what not to do' to achieve open, liberal and democratic regimes. Due to their decades-long socio-political and economic reform experiences, and their centuries-long interactions with Europe and the US, Turkey and Mexico can be crucial cases that illustrate the virtues and drawbacks of particular approaches to democratic consolidation.

Why Mexico and Turkey? Some notes on methodology

There has been a proliferation of single-case studies on democratic progress in Mexico and Turkey since the late 1990s, when both countries launched a series of political and economic reforms.[8] Despite the ample amount of in-depth knowledge produced by these studies, the theme of democratic progress inevitably begs another question: *progress according to what criteria?* Certainly, Mexico and Turkey went through immense changes that addressed substantive aspects of their democratic regimes in the last decades. But exactly how much have they changed and, compared to their peers, have they done enough?

In their seminal book on comparative method, Dogan and Pelassy state that 'we gain knowledge through reference'.[9] By comparing Turkey and Mexico, then,

6. C. Rice, 'Remarks at the American University in Cairo', 20 June 2005, http://www.2001–2009.state.gov/secretary/rm/2005/48328.htm (last accessed 28 January 2014).

7. M. A. Vachudova, *Europe Undivided: Leverage and integration after communism*, Oxford: Oxford University Press, 2005, p. 247.

8. Haber *et al.* 2011; Dominguez *et. al.* 2009; Oniş, 2013; Özbudun, 2000.

9. M. Dogan and D. Pelassy, *How to Compare Nations: Strategies in comparative politics*, Chatham, NJ: Chatham House Publishers, 1990, p. 3.

we can simultaneously use each country as a benchmark for the other. This will help us better gauge the scale and significance of the democratic progress in each context. Studies that focus exclusively on a single case will very likely be rich in detail. However, a comparative perspective will force us to develop stronger analytical arguments that can explain democratic progress in multiple contexts. Addressing multiple cases in a single analytical framework will also help us grasp shared trends at the systemic level.

Some of the earliest comparative studies were intensive, two-case comparisons. *Democracy in America* by Alexis de Tocqueville is among the most influential works that used this method. Tocqueville developed a compelling study of liberal democracy, by juxtaposing the centralised and statist French model to the decentralised, pluralist US model, in which the state remained relatively weak. A foremost advocate of cross-regional comparisons, French historian Fernand Braudel, says: 'Live in England for a year and you will not get to know much about England. But through comparison, in the light of your surprise, you will suddenly come to understand some of the more profound and individual characteristics of France, which you did not previously understand because you knew them too well.'[10] Thus, Braudel tells us that factors which could be overlooked or taken for granted in a single-case study might receive their due attention in a comparative framework.

Especially after the quantitative turn in the discipline, area studies came increasingly under attack for being too descriptive and for lacking methodological and theoretical rigor. Monographs and small-N studies were particularly criticised for parochialism and for being insufficiently sophisticated. Despite these harsh critiques, a survey of leading comparative-politics journals reveals that approximately 70 per cent of the articles still fall under the category of area studies. Among those, nearly 70 per cent look at a single region.[11]

Muck and Snyder argue that it would be misleading to dismiss all area studies research as 'merely descriptive', since there is significant variation within area studies and it is still the dominant form of research in comparative politics. Yet they also highlight the pitfalls of concentrating on small-N, single-region studies.[12] This 'balkanisation' of comparative politics could mean either that the knowledge produced about one region is not transferable to another region or simply that comparativists with different regional specialties could not speak to one other. This lack of inter-regional dialogue would be detrimental to democratisation studies, since it would mean that accumulated wisdom from one regional context would not be transferable to another. Hence, each time the wheel needs to be invented anew and all the potential hurdles and mistakes had to be overcome again.

---

10. F. Braudel, 'History and social science', in *Economy and Society in Early Modern Europe: Essays from Annales*, P. Burke (ed.), New York: Harper & Row, 1972, p. 24.

11. G. Muck and R. Snyder, 'Debating the directions of comparative politics: an analysis of leading journals', *Comparative Political Studies* 2007, 40 (1), pp. 5–31, p. 14.

12. Muck and Snyder, p. 25.

An in-depth, comparative study of Mexico and Turkey would probably find a strong methodological advocate in Sidney Tarrow. Without mincing words, Tarrow argues that a 'paired comparison' would have distinct advantages. He lists the advantages of the paired-comparison method in the following way:

> First, it provides an intimacy of analysis that is almost never available to large-N analysis. Second, it draws on – and indeed insists on – deep background knowledge of the countries being examined. Third, it facilitates what Brady and Collier call 'causal-process analysis,' in contrast to the 'data-set observations that are the basis of correlational and regression analysis.[13]

When it comes to epistemological rivalries in the discipline, there is a progressively widening gap between area specialists and the more generalist, quantitatively and deductively oriented scholars. Rudra Sil highlights the potential 'mediating role' of small-N, *cross-regional* comparisons.[14] The pivotal role that cross-regional comparisons can play was also underscored by the then-chair of the comparative politics section of American Political Science Association, Evelyn Huber. However, she laments that comparativists rarely take this tool out of their methodological toolbox. Out of the 30 books that she examines, only four of them include cross-regional comparisons.[15] Understandably, the practical difficulties of acquiring language skills and conducting fieldwork in separate regions play a role in this preference. But a fruitful dialogue is hardly possible among comparativists if the field gets methodologically *and* regionally balkanised.

Regional comparisons and generalisations on Latin America or the Middle East certainly carry important heuristic value. However, by confining their comparisons strictly within these geographic contexts, researchers run the risk of over-emphasising regional similarities and underestimating potentially diverse trends in the same region. Some of the recent works on the so-called Arab Spring can be considered examples of these excessively broad regional generalisations. More seasoned experts on the region argue that lumping together a variety of political regimes simply because they happen to be next to each other is akin to making the 'comparing-apples-to-oranges' mistake.[16]

Last but not the least, a cross-regional comparison of two countries from the Global South would also illustrate the systemic forces that shape the contemporary world-system. Most small-N comparative studies conceptualise their cases as two distinct entities that are either significantly similar to each other (most-similar-cases comparison) or are significantly different from each other (most-different-cases

---

13. S. Tarrow, 'The strategy of paired comparison: toward a theory of practice', *Comparative Political Studies* 2010, 43(2), pp. 230–59, p. 243.

14. R. Sil, 'Area studies, comparative politics and the role of cross regional small-N comparison', *Qualitative & Multi-Method Research* 2009, Fall, pp. 26–32.

15. E. Huber, 'The role of cross-regional comparison (letter from the president)', *APSA-CP: Newsletter of the APSA Organized Section in Comparative Politics* 2003, 14(2), pp. 1–6.

16. L. Anderson, 'Demystifying the Arab Spring', *Foreign Affairs* 2011, 90(3), pp. 2–54.

comparison). However, this book does not conceptualise its cases as two separate, unit-level observations that collide with each other like billiard balls. Rather, it emphasises the spatial similarities between the two cases, specifically with respect to their position in global capitalism.[17]

Mexico and Turkey might be located on different continents but, particularly since the early 1980s, important developments have placed them in the same boat. During the 1980s, both Mexico and Turkey faced very similar challenges and both tried hard to survive the choppy waters of neo-liberal reform. Economic reforms in both countries were nearly identical since it was the same global financial powerhouses that dictated the terms: that is, privatisation of state-owned industries and utilities, de-regulation, liberalisation of financial and capital markets, elimination of price controls and subsidies and so on.

In an eloquent speech delivered in Istanbul, Immanuel Wallerstein mentioned the temptation to every researcher of looking at 'smaller and more familiar' subjects. However, 'in order to make sense', he added, one needs to place all these individual pieces of information in a larger context.[18] This way, we might better trace the causal mechanisms and general patterns that unite seemingly isolated social reality.

In sum, juxtaposing this distant pair of countries could be a worthy enterprise for a number of reasons. Analysing Turkey and Mexico together might reveal some of the important factors that shape democratic progress and consolidation, regardless of the cultural context. Such information could be relevant for a significant number of countries across Latin America and the Middle East that currently have some attributes of democracy but still in need to grapple with a deficient form of democratic regime.

A fellowship of regional outliers/exceptions

Generally speaking, Mexico and Turkey are somewhat exceptional cases in their respective regions. Turkey (along with Israel) stands out as a significant outlier in the Middle East. More often than not, researchers find it difficult to pigeonhole Turkey, a secular republic with hotly contested elections and no substantial oil or natural resource income. Similarly, Mexico strays from the general socio-political trends in Latin America. The post-1980 literature on development and democratisation usually refers to 'Mexican exceptionalism', for the stable civilian rule of a one-party-dominant political system that cannot be easily categorised as either authoritarian or properly democratic.[19]

17. C. Chase-Dunn, *Global Formation: Structures of the world-economy*, Cambridge: Basil Blackwell, 1991.

18. I. Wallerstein, speech delivered at a special conference on World-Systems School and Faruk Tabak, 7 March 2008, Bilgi University, Istanbul.

19. D. Levy and K. Bruhn, *Mexico: The struggle for democratic development*, Berkeley, Los Angeles, London: University of California Press, 2001, pp. 105–6; J. Rosenberg, 'Mexico: end of party corporatism?', in C. S. Thomas (ed.), *Political Parties & Interest Groups: Shaping democratic governance*, Boulder, CO: Lynne Reinner, 2001, p. 247.

Mexico differs from the rest of Latin America on several major issues. Like most countries in Latin America, Mexico has a federal system. However, until recently, Mexico was also among the most centralised countries in the region. Until the 1990s, the federal government of Mexico controlled, on average, 80–90 per cent of public revenues, allowing less than 5 per cent of public revenues to be controlled by its more than 2000 municipalities.[20] As a result, it would be safe to argue that until the recent reforms for decentralisation and devolution of power, federalism was a nominal rather than an actual characteristic of the Mexican political system.

Another related characteristic of this strong centralist state tradition in Mexico is the issue of super-presidentialism. The amount of executive power that is concentrated in the office of presidency is a distinguishing feature of Mexico. Comparatively speaking, Mexican presidents enjoy significantly more powers, 'more than any military president in the Southern Cone', according to Brazil's prominent sociologist-cum-President, Fernando Henrique Cardoso.[21] Widely referred as 'king for six years', Mexican presidents probably have more in common with the Aztec kings and Spanish viceroys than their contemporary peers in Latin America.

Mexico deviates significantly from the regional trends when it comes to church and state division as well. Unlike most Latin American nations, the state in Mexico retains a passionately secular character, despite the fact that an overwhelming majority of its citizens self-identify as Catholic.[22] Since the electoral success of centre-right National Action Party (*Partido Accion Nacional*, PAN) in 2000, religion has become somewhat less controversial and more visible in the public realm. However, Mexican politics retains a unique tension between the state and Catholicism.

Last but not least, Mexico shares its longest border with the US, the global superpower. This geographic proximity has been a mixed blessing for Mexico, summarised by its long-time autocrat Porfirio Diaz in the following way: 'Mexico, so far from God, so close to the US'. The social, political and economic complexities of a 2000-mile border and intensifying integration between the US and Mexico since the inauguration of the North American Free Trade Association (NAFTA) in 1994, contribute to the unique status of Mexico among its peers in

---

20. OECD, *Decentralisation & Local Infrastructure in Mexico*, OECD Publications, 1998, p. 22.

21. F. H. Cardoso, 'On concentration of authoritarian regimes in Latin America', in D. Collier (ed.), *New Authoritarianism in Latin America*, Princeton, NJ: Princeton University Press, 1979, pp. 42–3.

22. Nearly 90 per cent of Mexicans define themselves as Catholic, yet political elites during decades-long single-party rule maintained a rigid church–state separation. Hostility towards the Catholic Church was so pronounced in the PRI in the 1960s that President Gustavo Díaz Ordaz refused to enter the church for his son's wedding (A. Zarembo, 'Second coming: Vicente Fox's religion,' *Newsweek International*, 8 Jan, 2001, p. 48).

Latin America. Mexico offers some rare puzzles to social scientists, and thus is particularly worth paying attention to in comparative studies.

By a similar token, Turkey is an exceptional case in comparative politics in the Middle East – usually seen in the company of Israel and Iran. Having been categorised as a *partly free* country by Freedom House for decades now, Turkey also stands in the twilight zone between authoritarianism and democracy.[23] Even though there have been competitive multi-party elections since the 1950s, democratic politics in Turkey has taken place under close surveillance from the military and bureaucratic elites. Since the 1960s, the Turkish military has directly intervened in politics three and a half times (the 'half coup' being the 'post-modern' intervention of February 1997, which caused the elected government to step down but without the military directly intervening), although the soldiers have never remained directly in charge for more than two years.

Other prominent characteristics of the Turkish system that deviate from regional trends are laid out in its constitution. The Constitution of Turkey describes the republic as a democratic, secular, social state that upholds the rule of law. Political rights and civil liberties have been progressively expanding, especially since Turkey committed itself to gaining EU membership. Important progress in democratic reforms has been achieved, thanks to successive EU harmonisation packages. However, it is also evident that there remains a gap between translating the legal reforms and pro-democracy 'governmental rhetoric' into 'effective and irrevocable' patterns in everyday practice.[24] Turkey has definitely moved away from the club of military-authoritarian nations. But the jury is still out on whether it has made it to the league of the advanced democratic regimes.[25]

Probably among of the most important differences between Turkey and its neighbours in the Middle East is the nature of its domestic economy. In his classical work on *rentierism*, Giacomo Luciani classifies the states in the region as either 'production' states and 'allocation' states. While production states acquire most of their revenues from a diverse array of economic activities, in allocation states, most state revenue is generated from oil royalties. Under these circumstances, allocation states have a relatively free hand in distributing this wealth, without leaving much room for popular bargaining, concession or demands for 'voice'.

---

23. O. Matthews and S. Kohen, 'Strong army democracy', *Newsweek International*, 4 November 2002, p. 30.

24. R. Falk, 'Foreword', in Z. K. Arat (ed.), *Human Rights in Turkey*, Philadelphia, PN: University of Pennsylvania Press, 2007, p. xvi.

25. Periodic democratic regressions and breakdowns also make it difficult for quantitative analysts to categorise Turkey. In Przeworski *et al.*, the period from 1950 to 1990 was divided into four different categories: 1950–60: bureaucratic (authoritarian); 1961–79: parliamentarism; 1980–82: autocracy; 1983–1990: parliamentarism (A. Przeworski, *et al.*, *Democracy and Development: Political institutions and well-being in the world, 1950–1990*, Cambridge: Cambridge University Press, 2000, p. 68).

According to Luciani, oil rents are distributed in exchange for loyalty at home and international protection abroad.[26]

The high level of external revenues alters state–society relations in a fundamental manner. It enables the state to purchase the loyalty of its citizens, rather than being accountable to the people in a taxation–representation type of relationship. Turkey does not share in the mixed blessing of oil, nor is it so strategically important a partner of the superpowers as to enjoy substantial amounts of foreign aid (as in the cases of Israel, Iraq and Egypt).[27] Without readily available natural resources or foreign aid for populist spending sprees, the Turkish state needs to generate the bulk of its revenues from citizens, through taxes.

Unlike Turkey, Mexico does have significant oil reserves, as well as a national oil company, PEMEX. Nonetheless, revenues from PEMEX fall short of enabling a nation-wide payroll in a country of more than 100 million people. Non-tax revenues constitute only 11 per cent of total state revenues in Mexico and 17 per cent of total state revenues in Turkey (a non-oil economy). In this aspect, the share of non-tax revenues in both Mexico and Turkey is very different from, say, Egypt (37 per cent) or the United Arab Emirates (48 per cent). The average for non-tax state revenues for the Middle East and North Africa region is 30 per cent.[28] Consequently, it would be safe to argue that neither Turkey nor Mexico has the characteristics of a *rentier* state, despite the proximity of the former to the Middle East and the vast oil reserves in the latter.

Last but not the least, there is the issue of secularism, which makes Turkey stand out from its neighbours to the east. Turkish elites have associated development, modernisation and progress with the West for a very long time. This tendency grew even stronger as the new Turkish Republic emerged from the ashes of the Ottoman Empire in the twentieth century. Both the military and bureaucratic elites of the time shared a mindset that blamed Ottoman conservatism for Turkey's humiliating defeat by the European powers. Henceforth, they became staunch advocates of modernisation and westernisation, in order to catch up in the civilisational race.

The modernisation project of Turkish elites inevitably included important Western values and ideals. Consequently, secularism was included among the

---

26. G. Luciani, 'Allocation vs. production states: a theoretical framework', in G. Luciani (ed.), *The Arab State*, London: Routledge, 1990, pp. 65–84. On the concept of economic rent, *see* A. Richards and J. Waterbury, *Political Economy of the Middle East*, 3rd edn, Boulder, CO: Westview Press, p. 16: 'Economists define *rent* as the difference between the market price of a good or factor of production, and its opportunity cost. Owners of certain assets [...] may enjoy a strategic position in the markets that allow them to set prices well above the opportunity cost [...] In addition, rents have allowed governments to avoid heavily taxing their citizenries, thereby breaking that vital, often adversarial link between governments and the people they tax. Out of such links governmental accountability may flow; in their absence governments may ignore their citizens'.

27. According to USAID, the top five US aid (combined military and economic aid) recipients are Afghanistan, Israel, Iraq, Pakistan and Egypt ('US Overseas Loans & Grants', FY2011). Online. Available http://www.gbk.eads.usaidallnet.gov/data/fast-facts.html (last accessed 05 February 2014).

28. World Bank, *World Development Report*, New York: Oxford University Press, 2002, pp. 252–524.

pillars of the new republic during the 1920s. Turkey was a pioneer among the majority-Muslim countries in the region in endorsing a rather strict interpretation of secularism. In this regard, it is no surprise that the country has been trying to become a formal member of the European 'club' since the 1960s. Even though Turkey has not reached its final destination on the road to membership, certain values and principles it endorses, in particular secularism, set it significantly apart from other Muslim majority nations in the Middle East and North Africa.[29]

Conceptual framework and plan of the chapters

Scholars of democratic progress are trying to hit moving targets particularly in the last decades. At the time of writing, military and authoritarian regimes are collapsing from Thailand and Indonesia to Ukraine and Tunisia. Societies mobilise and take to the streets with election fever from Iran to Egypt, and popular movements achieve historic victories in a wide range of countries, from Brazil to Mexico and Turkey. The cases are diverse, spread across Europe, Asia, Latin America, Middle East and Africa; each of them has a different culture, historical background and level of economic development. However, there is some convergence too, as the empirical evidence keeps accumulating. Researchers acknowledge that there is no single path to democracy and the process is neither universal nor irreversible (as the Iranian Revolution forcefully demonstrated). Moreover, with the breakneck pace of globalisation, it is becoming increasingly difficult to separate the impact of domestic and international factors.[30]

This book dips into multiple approaches when explaining the historical trajectory of democratic progress and consolidation in Mexico and Turkey. This is not an attempt to hedge one's bets, or to appeal simultaneously to multiple constituencies. Rather, it is a practical necessity when the research question at hand covers such a wide geographical and temporal span. When explaining the historical weakness of bottom-up demands for democracy in Mexico and Turkey, both civil society paradigms[31] and structural paradigms are used. For instance, Barrington Moore's emphasis on the historic experience of capitalism, emerging hand-in-hand with a strong middle class and ushering in a democratic polity[32] provides an invaluable theoretical framework for understanding the difficulties of democratic consolidation in Mexico and Turkey. The strong centralist state traditions that the modern-day Mexican and Turkish republics inherited from their

---

29. H. Yilmaz, 'Introduction', in H. Yilmaz (ed.), *Placing Turkey on the Map of Europe*, Istanbul: Bogazici University Press, 2005, pp. 1–22.

30. H. Wiarda, *Non-Western Theories of Development*, Fort Worth, TX: Harcourt Brace College Publications, 1999.

31. A. de Tocqueville, *Democracy in America*, trans. Harvey C. Mansfield, Chicago, IL: University of Chicago Press, 2000; R. Putnam, *Making Democracy Work*, Princeton, NJ: Princeton University Press, 1993.

32. B. Moore, *Social Origins of Dictatorship and Democracy*, Boston, MA: Beacon Press, 1967.

imperial past left little breathing space for the emergence of an autonomous socio-economic sector. Thus, the relative weakness of organised society vis-à-vis the state became an important handicap that stalled democratic progress for decades.

Chapter Two, on the Spanish and Ottoman imperial legacies, highlights the importance of historical institutions for democratic progress. Colonial political and administrative structures and economic institutions (land tenure, mercantilist trade policies and so on) are covered in this chapter. In many ways, the chapter tries to articulate a historical-institutional narrative of the colonial era, similar to the works of Acemoglu and Jameson.[33] Centralist and state-dominant political traditions, limitations on the emergence of economically autonomous propertied classes and the lack of inclusive political structures are discussed.

Chapters Three and Four are dedicated to the twentieth-century revolutions and the emergence of modern republican regimes in both countries. These two chapters focus on the emergence of modern nation-states, development efforts and state–society relations. They highlight a preference for corporatist forms of interest-mediation instead of pluralism in both Mexico and Turkey.

Chapter Five looks at post-1980 developments and socio-economic transformation in Mexico and Turkey. Despite siding with the Western capitalist bloc during the Cold War, both countries had highly protectionist and statist economies until the 1980s. However, these closed economic structures went through a radical transformation with the arrival of the neo-liberal era. Class divisions also began to intensify as both countries adapted to the competitive pressures of global capitalism. This chapter analyses the changing class dynamics in the post-1980 era, and the political consequences of the new economic and redistributive order.

For a comprehensive analysis of democratic progress in contemporary Mexico and Turkey, this book incorporates the international dimension. While covering socio-economic changes, Chapter Five also takes regional and international dynamics into consideration. In particular, US–Mexican relations are systematically compared with EU–Turkish relations. The difference in democratic consolidation between Turkey and Mexico could, in part, be explained by variation in these patterns of bilateral relations. Finally, Chapter Six concludes by summarising the findings of this research.

---

33. D. Acemoglu and J. Robinson, *Why Nations Fail? The origins of power, prosperity and poverty*, New York: Random House, 2012.

Chapter Two

The Legacy of the Empires

The Spanish Viceroys and the Mexican Presidents are successors of the Aztec rulers [...] [T]here is a bridge that reaches from *tlatoani* to viceroy, viceroy to president.[1] (Octavio Paz)

As institutions influence behavior and incentives in real life, they forge the success or failure of nations [...] Different patterns of institutions today are deeply rooted in the past because once society gets organized in a particular way, this tends to persist.[2] (Acemoglu and Robinson)

There are times when nations try to shed their historical and institutional baggage violently. Usually, those are revolutionary moments and both Mexico and Turkey have had their fair share of such extraordinary turning points in their respective histories. However, despite their deliberate attempts to leave the past behind and begin again from scratch during such moments of rupture, both countries have strong imperial legacies that cast long shadows on their modern collective psyches.

Today, scholars who analyse the factors that give rise to democracies and autocracies are realising that the only way to proceed '[...] is by going back – back to the origins of institutions and conditions gave rise to them'.[3] The underlying assumption in this line of thinking is the following: there is an intimate relationship between the *political institutions* of a society and its long-term *structural-economic characteristics*.[4]

To claim that the imperial legacy of the Castilian Crown and the Ottoman Sultanate left lasting imprints on contemporary Mexico and Turkey would be an understatement. The political and administrative structures, socio-economic systems and land-tenure practices of both empires had unique characteristics. All of these continued to shape the modern republican regimes that inherited this imperial legacy. Despite deliberate efforts to distance themselves from this past, neither the Mexican nor the Turkish republic has managed to radically eradicate its lineage.

---

1. O. Paz, *Labyrinth of Solitude*, New York: Grove Press, 1985, p. 315 and 324.

2. D. Acemoglu and J. Robinson, *Why Nations Fail: The origins of power, prosperity and poverty*, New York: Crown Business, 2012, pp. 43–44, italics mine.

3. T. Iversen, 'Capitalism and Democracy', *Oxford Handbook of Political Science*, New York: Oxford University Press, 2009, pp. 841–42.

4. Acemoglu and Robinson, 2005; Boix, 2003.

Unlike most countries of the Global South, in which the post-colonial state usually had to struggle to establish itself almost from scratch, Mexico and Turkey inherited strong 'state traditions' from their imperial ancestors[5] that remained resilient in the face of attempts to eradicate them.

The blueprints of the modern Mexican and Turkish states and their bureaucratic and administrative structures, as well as the predominant patterns of state–society relations, owe a great deal to these imperial traditions. Therefore, in order to reach a thorough understanding of contemporary democratic progress in Mexico and Turkey, it is crucial to incorporate this historical-institutional legacy into our analysis. However, it would not be feasible to cover the socio-economic structural dynamics of both empires throughout their entire lifespans. Consequently, this chapter focuses on the most typical institutions and practices of both empires during their heyday, before they began to deteriorate in the seventeenth century.

Despite their geographic and cultural differences, the Spanish and the Ottoman Empires displayed remarkable similarities during their heydays. From the fifteenth century onwards, they were the two most formidable powers in the Mediterranean. At a time when the rest of Europe was struggling with deep internal divisions and the destructive centrifugal forces of feudalism, the Spaniards and the Ottomans were enjoying the fruits of their strong, unified and centralised empires. For example, the unification of Castile and Aragon united 82.4 per cent of Iberian territory and 85 per cent of its population. Along with the unified territory came strong standing armies and the successful, centralised taxation regimes that were necessary to finance this military might. With such newly acquired powers of unification and centralisation, the Spanish Crown put an end to the seven-century-long Moorish presence on the Iberian Peninsula and ventured out to colonise the Americas. The Ottomans, too, displayed skill in terms of centralising and strengthening their political and military power. The Ottomans expanded their imperial boundaries from Vienna and the Balkans all the way across Egypt and North Africa.

The successful expansion of the Spanish Empire to the Americas and the Ottomans towards Eastern Europe, Asia Minor and North Africa were by no means accidental developments. In fact, this progress would be traced back to their successful evolution from small city-states to massive global empires. During the fourteenth century, for instance, the Crown of Aragon, which together with the Crown of Castile later established the formidable Spanish Empire, was merely centred around Barcelona and Valencia. The famous Byzantine Empire in the east 'consisted almost entirely of the extended suburbs of two cities, Constantinople and Salonica'.[6] By the end of fifteenth century, however, these small and decentralised forms of political power became too precarious to sustain. Constantinople (1452, to the Ottomans)

5. M. Heper, 'The strong state as a problem for the consolidation of democracy: Turkey and Germany compared', *Comparative Political Studies* 1992, 25(2), pp. 169–94; C. Veliz, *The Centralist Tradition of Latin America*, Princeton, NJ: Princeton University Press, 1980.

6. F. Braudel, *The Mediterranean and the Mediterranean World in the Age of Philip II*, translated by Sian Reynolds, London: Harper Collins Publishers, 1992, p. 459.

and Barcelona (1472) and Granada (1492 to the Kingdom of Spain) all fell under the control of much larger political entities that were capable of mobilising stronger standing armies and had much larger fiscal resources at their disposal.

According to Braudel, the Spanish and the Ottoman Empires were among the first to take advantage of this dramatic historic shift, which favoured larger and more centralised political entities at the expense of smaller ones. Braudel calls this development the 'rise of the Leviathans' and he highlights the distinctiveness of the two empires in the following way:

> [...] Spain under Ferdinand and Isabella was no 'mere nation-state': it was already an association of kingdoms, states and peoples united in the person of sovereigns. The sultan too ruled over a combination of conquered peoples and loyal subjects, populations which had been subjugated or associated with the fortunes.[7]

The next two sections of this chapter will provide more detailed account of the administrative structures and socio-economic institutions of both empires. This chapter will conclude with a comparative synthesis of both empires.

Imperial administrative legacies

The political and administrative structures of Imperial Spain

Imperial Spain projected a hierarchical, bureaucratic and centralised style of administration in its new colonies across the Atlantic. Naturally, there existed a long-established pedigree of philosophical and theoretical background for these top-down structures of political power. The political traditions of Latin America 'draws from Aristotle, Plato, Roman Law, Augustine, Thomas Aquinas, Spanish medievalism, sixteenth century neo-scholastics such as Suarez, Rousseau, Comte, Rodo, Hispanismo and corporatism', according to Howard Wiarda.[8] One common theme in many of these political philosophers is their emphasis on *order, discipline* and the importance of *hierarchy* in a given polity. Furthermore, they project an 'organic' view of society, a characteristic particularly pronounced in the works of early Christian thinkers such as Saint Paul and Saint Augustine. Accordingly, different sectors or classes in a society are conceptualised as integral parts of a living organism that all need to function in harmony for the long-term survival of that organism. This conceptualisation implies an intrinsic order and hierarchy, for not all parts are of equal importance. Some parts form the brain while others form the limbs. While the organism can continue to function with amputated limbs, it would not survive without the brain.

---

7. Braudel, 1994, p. 462.
8. Wiarda, H. J., *The Soul of Latin America: The cultural and political tradition*, New Haven, CT: Yale University Press, 2001.

Other scholars look at the political and historical experiences of the Iberian Peninsula for the roots of Spanish political tradition in the colonies. In particular, they focus on the role of the seven-century-long Moorish occupation. According to Veliz, the fact that it took seven centuries for the Spaniards to dislodge the Moors made a tremendous impact on the military, political and religious institutions of the Spanish Empire. It also left deep rather marks on the Spanish psyche.

Veliz displays the impact of the Moorish invasion eloquently, by comparing and contrasting the two kingdoms of Iberia: Castile and Aragon. The Kingdom of Aragon, which included Valencia, Aragon and Catalonia, was the first to expel the Moors. Consequently, they recovered faster, established a lucrative trade in the Mediterranean and prospered rapidly. The growing importance of the commercial classes eventually compelled acceptance of the idea of contractual obligations in society, including contractual obligations between ruler and ruled. Under these circumstances, the Catalan Cortes emerged as a uniquely Catalan institution that protected the rights of its subjects and effectively limited the powers of the king.

However, the scenario was rather different in the case of Castile. Here, the wars against the Moors were too numerous and lasted for too long. Constant military campaigns against an entrenched enemy hindered the commercial prospects of the region. It remained a stagnant, peasant-based economy, embroiled in centuries-long conflict. Nominally there was a Cortes but its powers were by no means comparable to that of the Catalan Cortes. In Castile, the Crown alone would rule, without much contribution from the nobility.

During their long occupation of the Iberian Peninsula, the Moors exercised political power in a somewhat tolerant fashion. This enabled Muslims to coexist with Christians and Jews without much friction or widespread proselytising. In fact, significant numbers of Jewish community members held important positions in the political, economic and cultural/intellectual spheres under Moorish rule.[9] However, after the Castilians finally expelled the Moors, they were highly intolerant of heterogeneity and non-conformity. After all, the primary purpose of the Castilian campaign of *Reconquista* (reconquest) was to 'purify' the Peninsula of all these 'foreign' elements.

The protracted confrontation with the Moors strongly influenced the political traditions of the Castilian Crown. They preferred centralised political power, as well as the unification of religious and political authorities. Instead of the feudal mercenaries with divided loyalties, who dominated armies in the rest of Europe, under the skilful leadership of Queen Isabella, Castile established a conscripted army that was loyal solely to the Crown.

The landed classes and nobility were also under the strict control of the centre, and hence could not enjoy autonomous powers. In fact, Isabella eventually eliminated the pensions of the nobility, forbade them from erecting fortresses without her specific authorisation and even prohibited them from duelling.[10] All of these policies kept the nobility on a rather tight leash and allowed the Crown to

---

9.   Wiarda, 2001, pp. 52–53.

10. Veliz, 1980, pp. 34–37.

exercise power in a centralised fashion. When Castile and Aragon were united by the marriage of Isabella and Ferdinand, it was the centralist tradition of the larger party, Castile, rather than the relatively egalitarian and pluralist institutions of the smaller party, Aragon, that charted the course for a new and unified Spain.

The religious zeal that expelled the Moors from the Iberian Peninsula did not go unnoticed by the Catholic Church. The successful military campaigns of the Castilian Crown gave significant prestige to Isabella. She capitalised on this by seeking concessions from the Holy See. Pope Sixtus IV issued a series of Bulls that granted the Castilian Crown the right to nominate the staff of all churches and monasteries in reconquered Granada. Finally, with a Bull of Julius II, called *Universalis ecclesiae regimini*, the Pope granted the Spanish Crown all the rights and privileges of establishing new churches in its overseas territories in perpetuity.[11]

In practice, this meant that no priest could cross the Atlantic without a specific royal permit. No church, monastery or hospital could be built in the Americas without the Crown's authorisation. As such, the Spanish Crown had secured control over secular and ecclesiastical domains, both in Iberia and in the colonies.

Following the centuries-long military struggle with the Moors, political structures in Castile evolved into an efficient central government with a well organised bureaucracy. The settlement of church and state relations in favour of the state also fortified the powers of the political centre. When Columbus 'discovered' the Americas in 1492, this political tradition was transplanted to the colonies wholesale. As C. H. Haring states, 'the laws and institutions of Spanish America were modelled on those of Castile, often modified in form and in function to meet local needs, but always emanating from the crown and kept under royal control.'[12]

The political power structure in the colonies imitated that of the motherland. It was hierarchical, as displayed in Figure 2.1. On top of the pyramid was the viceroy (vice-king), who was directly appointed by the king. All in all, there were four viceroys across north and south America, in Mexico, Peru, Rio de la Plate (Argentina) and New Granada (Gran Colombia). The Crown appointed these viceroys directly. The viceroys were followed by the captain-generals, who governed smaller territories. Political authority in cities and small towns rested in *alcalde mayores* and councils called *cabildos*.

Even though the viceroy was at the top of the pyramid representing the Spanish Crown, 'the ultimate authority rested with the monarchy in Madrid.'[13] Among the important characteristics of Spanish rule in the Americas was the fact that, despite his seemingly absolute status, the powers of the viceroy were significantly curtailed by another institution, the *Audencia*, the supreme court for the Spanish Empire. The absolute rulers, Ferdinand and Isabella, were extremely wary of concentrating too much power in the hands of a strong colonial ruler. This was evident even at the earliest stages of the conquest.

---

11. Veliz, 1980, pp. 39–40.
12. C. H. Haring, *The Spanish Empire in America*, Oxford: Oxford University Press, 1947, available online through ACLS History E-Book Project at http://www.humanitiesebook.org.
13. Wiarda, 2001, p. 98.

Figure 2.1: Pyramid of Spanish colonial political and administrative hierarchy

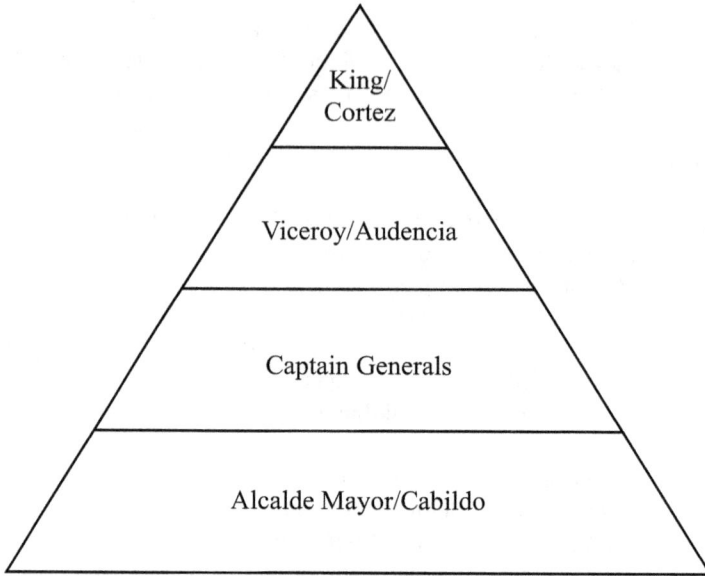

King/
Cortez

Viceroy/Audencia

Captain Generals

Alcalde Mayor/Cabildo

The letters of Hernán Cortés reflect the anxiety of this great *conquistador* towards the Spanish Crown. Despite the vast distance and the limited lines of communication, Cortés was eager to get the approval of Ferdinand and Isabella at every major step. He was aware of the fact that his legendary reputation as the man who conquered a continent with 500 men and 16 horses depended solely on the continuous support and approval of the Spanish Crown. Shown below are excerpts from his letters in which he tries to counter allegations of disobedience and embezzlement:

If these people were to look at my acts impartially, they would judge them quite differently; for until now there has not been, nor shall there ever be whilst I live, a single letter or command from Your Majesty which has not been, or is not, or will not be obeyed and fulfilled in every detail [...]

[F]or the short while that I have been in this land, I believe more wealth has been remitted to Your Majesty than from all the Islands and the mainland which was discovered more than thirty years ago at great expense to the Catholic Monarchs [...] Not only have I sent to Your Majesty all that is yours by law but also some considerable amount of my own and of those who helped me, taking no account of all that we have spent in Your Royal service.[14]

---

14. A. Pagden, (ed. and transl.), *Hernan Cortes: Letters from Mexico*, New Haven, CT: Yale University Press, 2001, pp. 438–9.

The absolute monarchs of Spain deliberately designed a system that divided the authority and responsibility of the viceroy, making him share those powers with a council whose members were direct royal appointees from Spain.[15] The *Audencia* in Mexico City was the highest court of appeal in the Americas. It was a constant reminder to the viceroy that supreme authority laid in Madrid. Symbolically, the *Audencia* was the extension of the justice that the king had to deliver to its subjects. Therefore, complaints against the viceroy could be brought before this court and its decisions were binding.

The *Audencia* also met for *Acuerdos*, which were consultative sessions held jointly with the political administration. Thus, it had an advisory function along with its judicial one. Despite his participation in the *Audencia*, the powers of the viceroy were limited in many ways. When the *Audencia* met for a judicial decision, the viceroy could not intervene unless he was a *letrado* (law graduate). In many cases, the authority of *letrados,* who were of modest background and were educated in elite Spanish universities to staff the imperial bureaucracy, outraged the patrician administrators of New Spain. They were upset that a *letrado*, who was 'not even a son of *hidalgo*', had so much clout in public administration. Yet, precisely because of their elevated social status as government officials, 'the services by these humble men devoted to the prince cannot be gainsaid.'[16] Similarly to the Ottoman Sultans, who created a separate class of bureaucrats of humble origins, the Spanish Crown counted on the skills and loyalty of these low-born *letrados* over the nobles.

Viceroys could not issue their own writs either. They needed the signatures of the *oidores* (advisors who could judge in crown's name) in order to pass such orders.[17] At the end of their term (five or six years) the viceroys had to have a judicial review (*juicio de residencia* or 'judgment on his term of office'), which also kept them on their toes. There were also inspectors (*visitadores*) sent periodically from Spain, should the Crown feel the need to further investigate the actions of the viceroys. Finally, on religious matters viceroys were constrained by the Church and the Archbishop.[18]

In short, the Spanish Crown made sure that the viceroys never gained autonomous power and were under constant surveillance by Madrid through this set of institutional restraints. Holders of all the important offices in the colonies, such as the *Audencia*, were appointed and removed from Madrid, which, in turn, eliminated the chance of viceroys establishing loyal bureaucracies of their own. Such arrangements fortified the centralised and hierarchical aspects of the political

---

15. A. Cañaque, *The King's Living Image: The culture and politics of viceregal power in colonial Mexico*, New York: Routledge, 2005, pp. 53–4.

16. Braudel, 1992, pp. 483–5.

17. Cañaque, 2005, p. 58.

18. E. Krauze, *Mexico: Biography of power 1810–1996*, translated by Hank Heifetz, New York: Harper Collins Publishers, 1997, p. 63.

power in the Americas and effectively hindered the progress of centrifugal forces that tried to share power in a more horizontal fashion.

Unlike in Continental Europe, feudalism could never take firm root in the Spanish Americas. The Spanish king was never merely 'the first among equals'. Both administrative structures and the actual practices demonstrate that even the highest authorities in the colonies were by no means on a par with the king. The Spanish Crown jealously guarded its absolute authority and denied feudal titles and privileges to those who ruled the colonies in its name.

'As early as the 1570s, the political and administrative stability that would characterize post-Conquest New Spain until the nineteenth century was firmly established',[19] thanks to the unequivocal structure of the colonial administrative pyramid. The Conquest was an attempt to establish *unity* out of a diverse palette of ethnicities, races, religions and political and economic interests. Octavio Paz praises the strength of the Spanish institutions in the following way: 'Despite the ambitions of its military commanders, the infidelities of its judges, and rivalries of every kind,' Spaniards accomplished this task with the 'solidity of the social edifice [they] constructed'.[20]

During the reign of Philip II (1556–98), Spain enjoyed the pinnacle of its power in Europe. The Spanish Crown had full control over the political, ecclesiastical and economic domains and the cargo of the galleons of gold and silver from Veracruz kept rolling into Seville to sustain this vast empire. From the 1620s, however, Spain started to descend to the status of a secondary European power. An important reason for this regression was the shortcomings of the economic policies Spain had employed early on in its trade relations with her colonies. As will be discussed in more detail later, mercantilism, which was a protectionist doctrine that prioritised politics over economy, did not deliver a dynamic, efficient and productive economy for Spain. The massive amounts of bullion transported to the motherland depreciated the value of gold and silver, weakening the financial power of the empire. Spain also undertook extended military campaigns against other European powers, particularly against the Dutch, most of which ended in Spanish defeat. These military defeats, combined with the economic problems, undermined the status of the Spanish Crown both in Europe and in the colonies.[21]

While Spain was struggling with succession conflicts, military campaigns and economic stagnation, across the Atlantic, the Spanish colonies were growing prosperous at a rapid pace. The lack of war, political stability, economic prosperity and a growing population turned the tables in favour of the colonies, particularly of New Spain (today's Mexico).

In order to ease its economic difficulties, the Spanish Crown started to sell administrative offices in the colonies. This was not an uncommon practice at the

---

19. M. Burkholder, 'An Empire Beyond Compare', in M. Meyer and W. Beezley (eds), *Oxford History of Mexico*, New York: Oxford University Press, 2000, p. 115.

20. Paz, 1985, pp. 100–101.

21. Veliz, 1980, pp. 70–72.

time. Selling offices – particularly of tax collectors – was also becoming fashionable among the Ottomans. As the economic pressures increased, the Spanish Crown put up more and more offices for sale in order to collect more revenue. In 1633, the offices at the Treasury were sold. In 1677, provincial administrative positions were also included among the offices for sale. Finally, in 1687, positions in the *Audencia*, the most powerful colonial administrative body, went up for sale.[22]

The sale of administrative offices had important repercussions for both the colonies and the motherland. First and foremost, this practice signalled the declining power of the central authority *vis-à-vis* the periphery, even though certain term limits were imposed on the purchased offices. Second, it undermined the strict racial hierarchy in the administration of the colonies. It provided the native-born elites (*criollos*) the opportunity to buy their way into the upper echelons of the political establishment, which used to be reserved exclusively for the *peninsulares*.[23] Third, because many of these new office-holders had paid significant amounts for their positions, they resorted to aggressively exploiting the people within their jurisdictions in order to recoup their expenses and make a profit. In short, towards the end of the seventeenth century, deep cracks were opening in the political and administrative structures of the Spanish colonial empire.

The political and administrative structures of the Ottoman Empire

Earlier studies by Turkish historians and western Orientalists have highlighted both religious fervour and military might in explaining Ottoman success. The nationalist inclinations of numerous early Turkish historians tended to portray the Ottomans as an efficient conquering force with a strong spirit of *gaza* (holy war) that sought to expand Islam to Christian lands. Orientalists, on the other hand, depicted an excessively militaristic Ottoman nature that portrays them as 'a nomadic war-band [...] carried from one triumph to the next by a ruthless dedication to conquest and predation.'[24] From this point of view, the Ottomans had a 'demonic religion' and their 'savage nomadic ways' imprisoned Europe under the 'Turkish yoke' for several centuries.[25]

Both of these approaches employed religion as their central explanatory variable, and both have significant flaws in grasping the sophisticated nature of the politics of the Ottoman Empire. Firstly, the *gaza* argument cannot explain why the Ottomans also spent so much time, effort and manpower fighting against their Muslim rivals in the East (such as numerous other ethnically Turcoman

---

22. Burkholder, 2000, pp. 122–123.

23. Cañaque, 2005, p.75.

24. P. Coles, *The Ottoman Impact on Europe*, London: Thames and Hudson, 1968, p.77.

25. D. Goffman, *The Ottoman Empire and Early Modern Europe*, Cambridge: Cambridge University Press, 2002, pp. 5–6; Goffman's work provides excellent examples of this Eurocentric view of the Ottomans. His research refutes most of these arguments by providing first-hand accounts of the diversity, tolerance and sophistication of the Ottoman Empire and by placing the Ottoman experience within the larger European historical context.

principalities and the Safavids in Persia). Secondly, both approaches disregard the pragmatic and flexible nature of Ottoman rule, which used strategic marriages and political alliances with Muslim *and* Christian principalities in order to expand its sphere of influence. The Ottomans capitalised on the fragmented and chaotic state of the Balkans at a time when 'Byzantines, Serbs, Bulgars, Albanians, Venetians and Genoese fought among themselves'.[26] In fact, the first Ottoman foothold in the Balkans was gained when an over-ambitious Byzantine feudal lord from Gallipoli invited them across the Dardanelles. The Byzantine strongman was seeking Ottoman help in order to claim the throne of Constantinople and the early Ottoman rulers were pragmatic enough to enter into such coalitions regardless of the religious affiliations of the corresponding party. Thirdly, the arguments that either champion the role of religion (the '*gaza* school'), or condemn it as a 'demonic' yet powerful catalyst for Ottoman expansion do not hold against more recent archival research.

As Ottoman archives under the Turkish government's control became more accessible and historians with less ideological baggage delved into these newly available resources, monolithic notions of the Ottomans as an 'Islamic empire' began to crumble. These later studies uncovered strong evidence for religious heterodoxy, both at the state level and in the astonishingly diverse Ottoman society. *Sharia* (Islamic law) was an important component of the Ottoman political and judicial system but it was not the only one. Moreover, *Sharia* was interpreted and implemented in such a way that it protected non-Muslim subjects from forced conversions to Islam.[27] It is true that a certain section of the Christian population was forced to convert because of the *devşirme* system, which will be discussed in detail below. But the practice of *devşirme* (also called the child levy) affected a very limited sector of the Christian population – a certain portion of young boys – and did not amount to a massive Islamisation of the conquered lands by the threat of the sword. In the Balkans, for example, 'the inhabitants of towns which submitted voluntarily [to Ottoman rule] were left unmolested; if inhabitants resisted they were forced to leave their towns to the Turks. The Ottoman government encouraged Turks from Anatolia, sometimes by forcible deportation, to settle the newly conquered lands.'[28] The Ottomans officially recognised the Orthodox Church and granted certain privileges to its clergy, such as tax exemption. Finally, the fact that the Greek, Bulgarian, Serbian, Jewish and Armenian communities co-existed and retained their distinct identities after more than four centuries of Ottoman rule further challenges the studies that focus solely on religion to explain the Ottoman expansion.

Braudel, Inalcik and many other prominent historians of the region argue that more than any other variable, one should look at Ottoman *statecraft* in order to

---

26. Braudel, 1992, p. 468.

27. D. Quataert, *The Ottoman Empire 1700–1922*, New York: Cambridge University Press, 2000, p. 31.

28. H. Inalcik, *The Ottoman Empire: The classical age, 1300-1600*, Trans. N. Itzkowitz and C. Imber, London: Weidenfeld and Nicolson, 1973, p. 10.

explain the success and longevity of the empire. The following two sections look at the underlying bureaucratic structures of the Ottomans in the centre and in the provinces. These illustrate not only the exceptional administrative capacity of the rapidly expanding empire but also the importance of Ottoman efforts to centralise and consolidate that power.

Central government and the devşirme system

In the early stages of their rule (1290s–1470s), as the inhabitants of a small frontier principality, the Ottomans did not have the capacity to staff the key political and administrative positions in their new territories with a professional class of bureaucrats. Therefore, they either relied upon prominent Turcoman families from Anatolia or recruited any existing feudal lords who were willing to co-operate with the Ottomans. Because of this, their control over the provincial administration was relatively indirect, hence weak.

Immediately after the conquest of new territories, government commissioners would record the revenue sources of these areas and divide them into taxable units (*timars*). Each *timar* had to provide for a cavalryman and his horse, which formed the reserve military force of the Ottomans. The *timar* system was the core institution that determined the basis of the Ottoman taxation system, military order and overall socio-political structure. It classified the land as the Sultan's property, divided it up and taxed it according to the state's priorities, and essentially placed significant limitations over private property rights.

From the fifteenth century onwards, major socio-economic cleavages emerged around the question of land tenure. Initially, when the Ottoman state granted *timars* to Turcoman families, it did not legally transfer the title of these properties to individual families. Similar to the exclusive property rights the Spanish Crown had in the colonies, the Ottoman sultans retained ultimate property-ownership. While they distributed *timars* to Turcoman families, they were reluctant to grant them freehold right. Meanwhile, however, as more and more families acquired these privileges from the state, they wanted to keep these properties within the family and pass them from father to son. Initially, they gained some foothold due to the new and relatively weak nature of Ottoman central rule.[29] However, subsequent sultans took important measures to curb this trend and fortify what Kafadar calls the 'centralizing thrust' of the Ottoman Empire.[30]

The expansion of this small frontier principality to a large empire required the Ottoman rulers to establish more assertive central power structures and create a professional class of military and bureaucratic administrators. The state was sceptical of the growing powers and aspirations of the local nobility and therefore

---

29. S. J. Shaw, *History of the Ottoman Empire and Modern Turkey*, vol. I, Cambridge: Cambridge University Press, 1976, pp. 25–7.

30. C. Kafadar, *Between Two Worlds: The construction of the Ottoman state*, Berkeley, CA: University of California Press, 1996, p. 121.

wanted to create a loyal class of subjects that would defend and perpetuate the interests of the state without being tempted by their own parochial ambitions. The institutional arrangement for achieving this goal was called the *devşirme* system.

The origin of the *devşirme* practice goes back as early as the reigns of Sultans Murat I (1362–89) and Bayezit I (1389–1402). Under this system, which is also referred as the 'child levy', the Ottoman state went out and collected the best and the brightest of the boys among its Christian subjects. One in every 40 Christian families had to give up their son. The recruits would then be assigned to Muslim families and go through an extensive training that also included a rigorous study of Islam. This large class of converts (the root of the word *devşirme* comes from 'conversion') would then fill up the military, administrative and scholarly ranks of the empire.[31] As Quataert describes, these children

> [...] received the best mental and physical education the state could provide, including, as a matter of course, conversion to Islam. The crème de la crème of this group entered the state elites, becoming commanders and grand viziers and playing a distinguished role in Ottoman history. The others became the famed Janissary corps, an extra-ordinarily well-trained, fire-armed infantry center of armies that won many victories in the early Ottoman centuries. The Janissaries for centuries were technologically the best-trained, best-armed fighting force in the Mediterranean world.[32]

As opposed to the reservist cavalry (*timarli sipahis*), the Janissaries were a standing infantry force, well trained and equipped, and received regular salaries from the state. Unlike the cavalry that depended on *timar* lands for income and mobilised only in time of war, the sole occupation of the Janissaries was the military service. The Janissaries were not allowed to marry or engage in economic activities during active duty.

Along with the military, there were also civilian career paths for the *devşirmes*: as bureaucrats and *ulema* (students of Muslim theology). Those who chose the route into the bureaucracy formed the privileged class of high-ranking administrators (viziers, governors, judges and so on) and civil servants of the empire. They were recruited to all levels of the Ottoman administration, including the second-highest position after the sultan, the grand viziership. As Braudel reports, 'of the forty-eight grand viziers between 1453 and 1623, five were of Turkish birth [...] thirty-three were renegades, including six Greeks, eleven Albanians or Yugoslavs, one Italian, one Armenian and one Georgian'.[33] The remaining ten grand viziers were of unknown origin.

Such facts about the Ottoman military and administrative structure raise certain questions. Why did the state go at such lengths to create this type of a military and

---

31. K. Barkey, *Bandits and Bureaucrats: The Ottoman route to centralization*, Ithaca, NY: Cornell University Press, 1994, chapter 2.

32. Quataert, 2000, p. 30.

33. Braudel, 1992, p. 483.

bureaucratic force? What was the rationale behind the *devşirme* system? What were the socio-political dynamics that lead to such an establishment?

In *A History of the Arab Peoples*, Albert Hourani classifies the Ottoman Empire as a multi-religious state, which gave 'a recognized status to [its] Christian and Jewish communities'.[34] However, despite their legitimate status within the empire, non-Muslims were excluded from military and administrative positions. They were also required to pay a poll-tax (*cizye*) to compensate for their exemption from military service. This system could have been sustainable had the Ottoman Empire remained static with a predominantly Muslim population.

As the Ottomans expanded their territory, particularly deep into the western frontier, it was faced with two important problems: Firstly, the Turcoman elites, who were settled in the newly acquired territories and were given titles by the central government, were gradually becoming more powerful. They owned substantial amounts of land either as free holdings (*emlak*) or as religious foundations (*wakfs*). They wanted to keep those privileges rather than submitting them to Ottoman central authority. Secondly, the Ottomans were depriving themselves of a major source of human capital by excluding all non-Muslims from public service. Thus, the centre's scepticism of ambitious local elites and the appeal of tapping into this vast non-Muslim talent pool paved the way for the establishment of the *devşirme* system.[35]

Quataert, Kafadar and many other prominent Ottoman historians agree that political concerns superseded religious ones in the establishment of the *devşirme* system. The Ottoman state was expanding at a rapid pace and the political establishment in the centre was growing wary of the emerging power of local Turcoman elites. A major cleavage in the Ottoman polity was opening up between the centralising state and an aspiring local aristocracy that had a tendency to assert their local and regional autonomy. Thus, the state tried to nip these efforts in the bud by introducing a whole new elite whose members had no provincial or familial ties. Because the individuals who filled the *devşirme* ranks lacked strong ties to their families and localities, the assumption was that they had absolute loyalty to the Sultan himself. By recruiting children at a young age and rigorously training them as a loyal military and bureaucratic elite, the Ottomans established an autonomous class that identified itself solely and strongly with the interests of the state.[36] The system provided social mobility to talented non-Muslim children, even to those from very humble backgrounds, which, in turn, created a vast pool of manpower in the hands of the state to be used for critical government functions. This privileged class became one of the most important means through which the Ottoman sultans extended central control and kept the local nobility on a very short leash.

---

34. A. Hourani, *A History of the Arab Peoples*, Cambridge: The Belknap Press of Harvard University Press, 1991, p. 207.

35. Inalcik, 1973, pp. 18–19.

36. Quataert, 2000, pp. 30–32; Barkey, 1994; H. Inalcik and D. Quataert (eds) *An Economic History of the Ottoman Empire*, 1300–1914, New York: Cambridge University Press, 1994, pp. 16–27.

The power of the *devşirmes* was firmly established during the rule of Sultan Mehmet II the Conqueror (1444–6, 1451–81). After the conquest of Istanbul, Mehmet II discharged and executed his powerful grand vizier, Çandarlı Halil Paşa, who was of Turcoman origin and was known to be a committed representative of the most powerful families in Anatolia.[37] In the remaining 28 years of his sultanate, Mehmet II picked all of his grand viziers from among the *devşirmes*. Moreover, he confiscated the privately owned properties of approximately 20,000 *wakfs* (religious endowments), which belonged to prominent Muslim families.[38]

The *devşirme* system had its heyday during the period of the sultans of the Classical era (1300–1600), particularly during the reign of Suleiman the Magnificent (1520–66). It was highly meritocratic and was strongly associated with the imperial power of the Ottomans. After the Classical era, however, as the empire stagnated and started to decline, so did the *devşirme* system. New generations preferred to pass their posts to their sons or relatives, rather than to other, more qualified *devşirmes*. Nepotism and corruption started to undermine this core institution of the Ottoman Empire and severely handicapped its administrative capacity in the centre and in the provinces.

The legal structure and the 'circle of justice'

In many ways, the reign of Mehmet II marks the consolidation of Ottoman central power. His legal and administrative reforms strengthened the central state and established stringent controls over the periphery. Mehmet II enacted laws based on the sultanic law (edicts and decrees of previous sultans) (*kanun*) and traditional regulations (*örf*), rather than *Sharia*. He systematised the sultanic body of law into two *kanunnames*. The Second Kanunname (1476) '[...] strongly reflects the concept of the sultan as the centre of government and the source of all authority within a system of protocol based on the degree of proximity to the sultan as its framework'. The basic principle of Ottoman sultanic law was that the population (*reaya*) '[...] and the land belonged to the sultan'. No one had any right or could exercise any authority over the land and the peasantry without specific mandate from the sultan. This principle essentially terminated all seigniorial privileges, allowed the state to distribute the land as *timar* and even permitted the sultans to extend their authority over private freeholds and *wakfs*.[39]

Sultanic law was based on rational rather than religious principles and dealt primarily with public administration. In some cases sultanic laws directly contradicted the teachings of the Qur'an and *Sharia* but they became the laws of the land nonetheless. Among the most famous of these was the fratricide law of Mehmet II. Unlike their European counterparts, the Ottomans did not have an established system of succession by male primogeniture. Technically, all his sons

---

37. Inalcik, 1973, p. 26.
38. Barkey, 1994, pp. 28–30.
39. Inalcik, 1973, pp. 72–3.

could claim the throne when the sultan died. While this system encouraged the 'survival of the fittest' during the contentious succession rivalries, it also had the potential to create lasting divisions at the top of the imperial administration, when the support of palace elites was split between various brothers. Because of this, Mehmet II skilfully employed the *raison d'état* argument when he ordered that 'for the welfare of the state, the one of my sons to whom God grants the sultanate may lawfully put his brothers to death'.[40] This was completely at odds with the teachings of Qur'an but the supreme religious authority of the Empire (*Şeyh-ül-İslam*) accepted it as legitimate, henceforth making fratricide the official imperial policy.

In his typology of political systems, Weber classifies most Eastern and Asian political regimes as regimes of 'sultanic rule'. By their nature, political power in these systems is vested in a single person, the sultan, who tends to operate in a rather arbitrary fashion. Weber places sultanic regimes in stark opposition to rational-bureaucratic ones. In rational bureaucracies, political power is exercised through institutional channels, which operate in an elaborate system of impartial rules and regulations. This is a more advanced form of political organisation and Weber considers it as the cornerstone of a stable, successful and long-lasting state.[41]

The Ottoman empire can also be classified as a pre-modern regime of 'sultanic rule' according to Weber. This classification defines the regime as a personalistic, nomadic and frontierist entity that lacked a rational institutional structure, that is, a modern and rational bureaucracy that could execute political power in a consistent, efficient and impersonal manner. Most contemporary Ottomanists, however, reject this Weberian classification. They assert that one of the most important reasons behind the success and longevity of the Ottoman Empire was its advanced bureaucratic and administrative structures. The absolute powers of the sultans notwithstanding, 'the Ottoman Empire was a bureaucratic state', which was based on a group of people appointed for the purpose of managing state affairs and drawing salaries to do so. According to Haim Gerber, this is the fundamental reason why the Ottoman Empire was not just a frontier entity that sparked and died down like a wildfire but persisted for centuries and emerged as a world empire.[42]

Karen Barkey also rejects the descriptions of the Ottomans as oriental despots '[...] with little institutional development of state'. 'The greatest achievement of the Ottomans by the time of Classical Age', she argues, 'was building an empire with a bureaucratic administration that extended beyond the immediate patrimonial realm'. Ottoman civilian and military bureaucracy of the empire

40. *Ibid.*, p. 59.

41. M. Weber, 'The types of legitimate domination', in G. Roth and C. Wittich (eds) and Ephraim Fischer *et al.* (trans.), *Economy and Society: An outline of interpretive sociology*, vol. I, Berkeley, CA: University of California Press, 1978, pp. 212–300.

42. H. Gerber, *State, Society and Law in Islam: Ottoman law in comparative perspective*, Albany, NY: State University of New York Press, 1994, pp. 18–20.

not only infiltrated into all corners of the empire but also had an 'unchallenged allegiance' to the centre and to the Ottoman sultan.[43]

At the top of the Ottoman central government were the sultan and his imperial council (*Divan*). The function of the *Divan* was very similar to that of the Cortes in the Spanish Empire. It served both as a cabinet and a high court. The viziers were responsible for the political decisions while the judicial issues were referred to the *kazaskers* (highest imperial judges), and the financial issues to the *defterdar* (head of the treasury). The Sultan was present in person during *Divan* meetings and the most important political, economic and judicial decisions of the empire were taken in this imperial court. The Council also heard complaints from the subjects of the empire and received foreign dignitaries. Throughout the Classical period, the sultans were actively engaged in the *Divan* meetings and delegated their political and executive powers only to their viziers. Among them, the grand vizier was the military commander and the sultan's top-ranking deputy in civilian administration.

The central administrative structure also had built-in mechanisms of checks and balances, especially upon the powers of the grand viziers. Being the commander of the military forces and only second to the Ottoman sultan did not grant him immunity from institutional scrutiny. He had to consult the *Divan* for major decisions. All of his financial transactions had to go through and get the approval of the head of the treasury (*defterdar*). Even though the grand vizier was the top military commander, he did not have absolute powers in this area either. The main branch of the military, the Janissary corps, had their own representative in the *Divan*, who was appointed directly by the sultan.

The Ottoman Empire consolidated its power with the help of these administrative and legal structures and managed to establish effective central control over its core provinces, namely, Anatolia and the Balkans (*Rumeli*). The supremacy of sultanic law over the *Sharia* increased the powers of the central political authority and the embedded checks and balances in the imperial bureaucracy ensured the undivided allegiance of the military and bureaucratic elites to the state.[44]

The political culture of the Ottoman Empire further buttressed the role of the state and its central authority. Its core assumption was the protection of subjects from abuse (such as over-taxation, exploitation and so on), which ultimately depended upon the existence of a strong ruler who could establish law and order. To become a strong ruler, one needed a strong military. The strength of the military, in turn, depended upon a rich treasury and an economically prosperous population. To be prosperous, society needed just laws and the means of their effective enforcement. In order to achieve this, there had to be a strong ruler who could enforce just laws.[45]

As Heper eloquently states, the logic of this 'circle of justice' established a rather peculiar political culture in the Ottoman polity, wherein the welfare of the

---

43. Barkey, 1994, pp. 24–8.
44. *Ibid.*, pp. 30–4.
45. Shaw, 1976–7, p. 112.

public ultimately depended upon the welfare of the state. Therefore, the critical question for the ruling elite was 'how can we maintain and strengthen the state?'[46] From this perspective, the overall well-being of the society became a function of the strength and vitality of the state. Needless to say, this was a state-centric political culture, rather than a society-centric one. It also helped nourish a particular type of political elite which considered itself a higher order of guardians, ensuring the perpetuity of the state for the greater good.

The 'circle of justice' argument and its state-centric political culture served the Ottomans well, until they were challenged by Western ideas of popular sovereignty and representative democracy. Especially after the French Revolution, Ottoman elites had a hard time reconciling their statist habits with increasing pressures for democratic participation coming from all sections of society. As will be discussed in subsequent chapters, this dilemma continued to plague the modern elites of the new Turkish Republic, who had very much been socialised within the Ottoman political tradition. Like their predecessors, the modern Turkish elites also had a strong state-centric bias, which became a significant handicap to democratic progress.

Provincial government

The strict division between the *askerî* (government officials) and the *reaya* (civilians) in the Ottoman empire shaped the predominant structures of provincial governments as well. The top-down framework of the imperial administration was successfully implemented in Anatolia and the *Rumeli*, which were under the 'direct rule' of the imperial centre. Those provinces that joined the empire later and were geographically far from the capital (such as Egypt, Baghdad, Moldavia and so on), were relatively more autonomous and therefore were under 'indirect rule'. For the purposes of this volume, we will concentrate on the 'direct-rule' provinces, for they embodied the standard Ottoman practices of provincial government and they were the territories from which the modern Turkish Republic emerged. It was these institutions that left deep marks on the state tradition and political culture of modern Turkey.

The chief administrative unit of the Ottoman Empire was the *sanjak*. The size of *sanjaks* varied but, in general, they were organised around a capital to which numerous small towns and villages were administratively connected. The provincial government was composed of two centrally appointed authorities: the *sanjakbeyi* (governor of the *sanjak*) and the *kadi* (judge). Both were of the *askerî* class, but the *sanjakbeyi* came from the military and represented the executive authority, while the *kadi* was a member of the *ulema* and was the legal authority in the *sanjak*. There was a deliberate effort to divide the powers of the provincial authorities, which provided an effective mechanism of checks and

---

46. M. Heper, 'The Ottoman legacy and Turkish politics', *Journal of International Affairs*, 2000, 54(1), pp. 63–82.

Figure 2.2: Pyramid of Ottoman political hierarchy

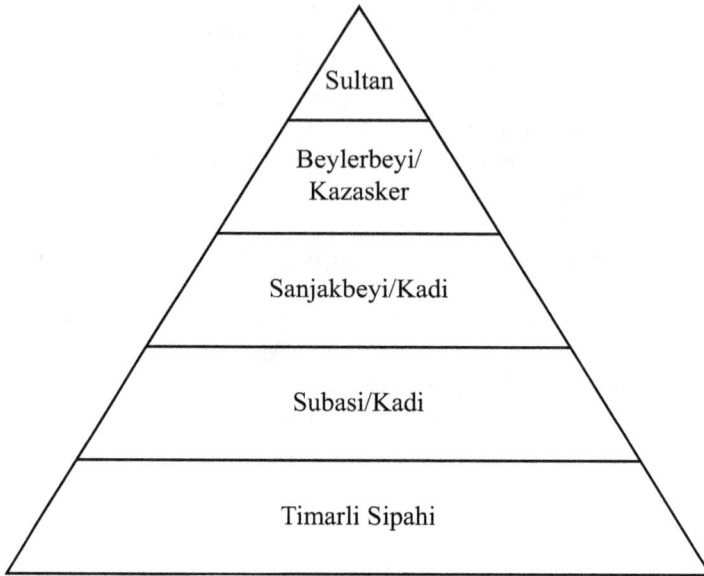

balances in the periphery. The *kadi* implemented both *Sharia* and sultanic law but needed the *sanjakbeyi* in order to execute his sentences. On the other hand, this did not compromise his judicial authority, since the position of the *kadis* were independent of the *beys* (governors), and the former were directly linked to the sultan.[47] Similarly to the policy of Spanish rule in the Americas, the Ottomans were suspicious of concentrating power in the hands of local administrators. This is why they designed strong mechanisms of checks and balances that deliberately divided the powers of provincial authorities.

The highest-ranking provincial administrators were the two *Beylerbeyis* (heads of the governors, *see* Figure 2.2). The *Anadolu Beylerbeyi* was in charge of all the *sanjaks* in Anatolia, while the *Rumeli Beylerbeyi* did the same for the *sanjaks* in the Balkans. They came from the highest ranks in the military and, in time of war, all the troops from the Anatolian and Balkan provinces united under their command.

As mentioned above, division of power was the preferred principle of Ottoman rule in the provinces. This is why the system gave overlapping powers to military/political administrators and religious/judicial ones. Encouraging competition and power struggles among the provincial elites was an important strategy employed by the state to prevent potential challenges to central rule. There were two parallel

---

47. Inalcik, 1973, chapter 13, pp. 104–20.

structures of authority in the provinces, one controlled by a member of the military and another by a member of the *ulema* (doctors of Muslim law and theology). All provincial officials rotated regularly, approximately every three years. After the Classical Age of the Empire, these terms got shorter, due to increasing complaints about bribery and abuse.

In the provinces, the last link in the Ottoman chain of command was the *timarli sipahi*. The *Timarli sipahi* was the cavalryman who 'resided in the village that was itself his source of income'.[48] The *timar* lands were allocated to *sipahis* in exchange for military service during war times. They utilised part of the land to provide for themselves and collected taxes from the villagers who lived on and worked the rest of the land. Unlike in feudalism, the villagers were not the vassals of the *sipahis* and sultanic law explicitly protected them from abuse by *timar*-holders. The more successful a cavalryman was, the larger plots of *timar* he would be granted. The security and policing of the area were also under his responsibility. If his performance was not satisfactory, the *sipahi* would lose his *timars* to a more accomplished peer.

In their early years, the Ottomans granted *timars* to prominent Turcoman families. As the empire expanded and the state wanted to consolidate its central control over these newly acquired territories, *timars* were increasingly granted to loyal *devşirmes,* rather than the established local families. Starting under Murad II, *devşirmes* were systematically preferred to Turcoman families, who were too eager to by-pass state control and transform *timars* into private properties.[49] The *timar* system was one of the most fundamental institutions of the Ottoman Empire, encompassing critical military, economic and administrative functions. As long as it stayed under rigorous state control, as was the case during the Classical Period, it became one of the institutional strongholds of the Ottoman Empire. When it deteriorated in later periods and turned into a corrupt and abusive system of tax-farming, it undermined both the administrative capacity and the socio-economic fabric of the empire.

The *timar* system was a typical example of Ottoman political structures that sharply divided the ruler and the ruled. The Ottomans did not want any fluidity between these two categories and therefore restricted the access of civilians to provincial administration by gradually excluding them from the *timar* system. As a result, the dividing-line that separated the state and the society was a very pronounced one in the Ottoman Empire. The *askerî* class was in charge of the military, bureaucratic, academic and judicial functions, while the rest of the civilian population, both urban and rural, formed the *reaya* class (*reaya* literally meaning 'the flock'). In this highly segregated system, administration at the central and provincial levels was the duty and privilege of the *askerî* class. Power was consolidated in the political 'centre' and the rest of the society was designated of 'peripheral' status.

---

48. Inalcik, 1973, pp. 107–8.

49. Shaw, 1976–7, p. 27.

A leading scholar of Ottoman state–society relations, Mardin underlines the fact that the social forces of the periphery had only *de facto* autonomy in the Ottoman Empire.[50] In the Anglo-American political tradition, city and town councils composed of civilians had significant power and autonomy *vis-à-vis* the central state. Even the Spaniards had a partial council tradition with the *cabildos*, albeit under the close scrutiny of the central authority. On the contrary, the Ottomans did not include any civilian elements in the governance of their provinces, cities and towns until the nineteenth-century administrative reforms that hastily tried to modernise the empire.

This hierarchical style of local administration, its centralising reflexes and sharp divisions between the state-affiliated class and the rest of the society carried significant implications for the institutional fabric of modern Turkey. As will be discussed in subsequent chapters, such institutional baggage made the transition to democracy all the more difficult. Having their roots deep into the Ottoman political tradition, military and bureaucratic elites in Turkey proved to be particularly reluctant to relinquish their position as the guardians of the state. This created periodic clashes between them and the elected members of the government, some of which ended in military coups. The existence of such a strong class of state elites became a serious impediment to democratisation, since it kept elected political actors under tutelage and undermined the democratic preferences of large sectors of Turkish society.

Imperial economic legacies

Land tenure and trade in Imperial Spain

The land-tenure system

In 1501, Fray Nicolas de Ovando was appointed as the governor of Hispaniola (today's Haiti and Dominican Republic), which was the first Spanish settlement in the Indies. His mission was to establish effective central control in this island, which was torn by factions among the settlers and suffering a severe labour shortage. In order to overcome the labour problem, Ovando recommended that the Crown adopt a forced-labour system, by which the native population could be allocated to the Spanish land- and mine-owners as workers. By 1503, the Crown had approved the distribution of Indians as forced-labourers in the Indies. Those who were the recipients of this royal favour were then responsible for the care and religious instruction of their Indian labour force. Eventually, the right to collect tribute was also added to the right to use the native labour, hence the institution of *encomienda* was established in the Americas.

---

50. Ş. Mardin, Türk Siyasasını Açıklayabilecek Bir Anahtar: Merkez-Çevre İlişkileri, *Türkiye'de Toplum ve Siyaset –Makaleler 1*, İstanbul: İletisim Publications, 1994, p. 37; originally published as 'Center-periphery relations: a key to Turkish politics?', *Daedalus*, December 1973, 102, pp. 169–91.

A prominent historian of Latin America, J. H. Elliot, states that '[m]any of the practices and institutions that were later to be transported to the mainland of America were the direct product of the Ovando regime in Hispaniola [today's Haiti and Dominican Republic], which in turn drew on the experiences of the *reconquista* in Spain and the conquest of the Canaries'.[51] Interestingly, this early system of distribution of Indians to landowners as free labour was inspired by a practice that was once common in the Moorish villages of medieval Spain. The assignment system, as it was called, had a slightly different purpose though: it allocated land and rents to the successful members of the Moorish military. Yet, the same idea of assigning the land to privileged members without transferring legal property rights appears in both contexts. In this regard, the Moorish practice was certainly a strong point of reference and inspiration for Ovando's proposal.[52]

The *hacienda* is the stereotypical economic structure that comes to mind in the Latin-American context, mainly because of its vast productive lands, great walls, brutal landlords (*hacendados*) and the indentured Indian workforce. However, the *hacienda* was significantly different from the early colonial institution of *encomienda*. While a *hacienda* was a privately owned grand estate, *encomienda* was a tribute-collection institute owned by the state. Proprietorship of these large estates was not a trivial matter, especially in the extremely legalistic political tradition of imperial Spain.[53] Furthermore, whether these grand estates were owned by the government or by private individuals gives us important cues about the distribution of wealth and political power in the New Spain. Therefore, it is important to understand their particulars and trace their evolution as one gradually decays and gives way to the other.

Encomienda was the earliest form of land tenure in the Spanish colonies and its characteristics demonstrate the underlying economic logic of the Spanish Empire. Driven by the then popular ideology of mercantilism, the Spanish Empire considered the economic domain subordinate to politics. From this perspective, economic activities were valued as long as they contributed to immediate state interests. Consequently, it was imperative for the state to establish direct control over economic assets and activities, especially in the lucrative colonial lands.

The establishment of *encomienda* was driven largely by these mercantilist concerns. The initial arrangement recommended by Governor Ovando and eventually implemented by the colonial government was similar to a tribute system. It did not transfer the legal property rights to the *encomienda*-holders (*encomenderos*). Hence, the Spanish Crown remained the legal owner of the

---

51. J. H. Elliot, 'The Spanish conquest', in L. Bethel (ed.), *Colonial Spanish America*, Cambridge: Cambridge University Press, 1987, p. 164–5.

52. *Ibid.*, p.17.

53. The earliest work to refute the direct evolution of *haciendas* from *encomiendas* was L. B. Simpson, *The Encomienda in New Spain: Forced native labor in the Spanish colonies, 1492–1550*, Berkeley, CA: University of California Press, 1929. For a current discussion of the encomienda–hacienda debate, *see* J. Lockhart, 'Encomienda and hacienda', in *Of Things of the Indies*, Stanford, CA: Stanford University Press, 1999, pp. 1–26.

property and the *encomendero* was granted only the right to native labour and tribute. The concessions were never given in perpetuity; nor were the grantees rewarded with any seigniorial title or jurisdiction.[54] Even though this right could be revoked at the discretion of the Crown, though, in general, *encomiendas* tended to remain within the same family.[55] Essentially, *encomienda* '[...] was an administrative concession [...] which evidently resulted in the creation of economic privileges and military duties'.[56] The recipients of this concession were the patriarchs of the time. In the early decades of colonial expansion, for example, '[...] the councils of most cities consisted exclusively of *encomenderos*'.[57] They provided the vital link between the cities and the countryside. Moreover, they were important instruments in the hispanicisation of the pre-Colombian cultures. Each *encomienda* had an ecclesiastical staff member, called a *doctrinero*, who was both the private chaplain of the property and priest for the natives living and working on the estate.[58]

Technically, the Indians working on *encomienda* grounds were not slaves or debt peons but free men and subjects of the Crown, with certain rights and duties. Among the duties was the tribute owed to the Crown. Indians paid this either in kind, with their labour or with gold and silver. The *encomenderos* were only the intermediaries in this process. They were required to treat the Indians in a humane way and ensure their physical and spiritual well-being. Royal and ecclesiastical attempts to protect the Indians notwithstanding, there was significant mistreatment and abuse by the *encomenderos*, who typically considered the natives 'naturally lazy and vicious, melancholic, cowardly and in general a lying and shifty people'.[59] The degree of exploitation and mistreatment reached such unacceptable levels that Father Bartolomé de Las Casas of the Dominican Order took up the issue personally and started a through investigation in the colonies. His final report was so compelling that Charles V finally abolished the institution of *encomineda* with the New Laws of 1542.[60]

This act of Charles V was by no means motivated solely by his humanitarian concerns. As Fuentes states, Father Bartolomé 'was the Crown's most useful tool

---

54. Veliz, 1980, p. 57.
55. Lockhart, 1999, p. 11.
56. Quoted from M. Góngora by C. Veliz, 1980, p. 26.
57. Lockhart, 1999, p.11.
58. *Ibid.*, p.13.
59. Quoted from L. Hanke, by Veliz, 1980, p. 53.
60. On the issue of protection of the Indians, the efforts of Bartolomé de las Casas were particular noteworthy. The following is the full title of his report to the King: *An Account of the first voyages and discoveries made by the Spaniards in America: Containing the most exact relation hitherto publish'd, of their unparallel'd cruelties on the Indians, in the destruction of above forty millions of people: with the propositions offer'd to the King of Spain to prevent further ruin of the West-Indies*, London, printed by J. Darby for D. Brown, 1699. Accessed online through the University of Massachusetts Libraries, EEBO-Early English Books On-line service.

in attacking the feudal pretensions [of the conquistadors]'.[61] He was appealing for the right cause at the right time. Historical records of the period also show that anonymous advisors in Spain recommended that the king prefer well paid governors over *encomenderos*. They pointed out that while governors served in the Americas and came back to the motherland after their term, *encomenderos* were permanently settled in the colonies and argued that because of this, the former would have unwavering loyalty to the Crown while the latter might well become all too consumed by their privileges and undermine the interests of the Crown. In fact, one such advisee used the example of the Ottoman imperial system to make the case for tighter state control over colonial lands: '[...] the Turks keep all their territories in safe subjection [...] by refusing to grant city, village, or fief to anyone'.[62]

These strong centralising reflexes of the Crown combined with the strategic mistakes of *encomenderos* brought about the decline of the *encomienda* system. Furthermore, increasing market pressures made this form of land-tenure highly untenable. The population in the colonies was growing, urban centres were expanding and there was an increasing demand for more efficient forms of agricultural production in order to feed the growing urban population. It was the combination of these factors that favoured another form of grand estate, the *hacienda*, in Spanish America.

Eric Van Young described the emergence of the *hacienda* as a 'complex symbiotic relationship' between the landlords and the labourers; between Indian villagers and the hacienda stores; and between urban markets and rural producers. It was not solely the outcome of greedy colonists aspiring to wealth and status. As the initial hurdles of the conquest were resolved and the populations gained a steadier outlook, the value of land, as well as the intensity of its use, increased. Mining towns and colonial urban centres also prospered, expanding the markets for agricultural products and livestock.[63]

This progress of *hacienda* however, came at the expense of the *ejidos*, which were communally owned lands of indigenous peasants. Contrary to the common perception about *haciendas* being grand estates dating back to the early decades of the conquest, the actual *hacienda* deeds show that these properties emerged much later and were acquired by gradually incorporating adjacent *ranchos* (small family farms) and *ejidos*. Most *hacienda* deeds are bundles of smaller deeds, through which the story of expansion can be traced. These records also debunked the myth of centuries-old *hacendado* dynasties. The deeds showed that bankruptcy was not uncommon, especially in years of crop failure, and *haciendas* rarely remained in the hands of the same family for more than three decades.

---

61. C. Fuentes, *The Buried Mirror: Reflections on Spain and the New World*, New York: Houghton Mifflin Company, 1999, p. 132.

62. S. Zavala, *New Viewpoints on the Spanish Colonization of America*, New York: Russell & Russell, 1968, pp. 72–3.

63. E. Van Young, *Hacienda and Market in Eighteenth Century Mexico*, Berkeley: University of California Press, 1981, pp.1–8.

The increasing rate of population growth, particularly in urban centres, and certain policies endorsed by the colonial administration to guarantee food supplies for urban residents generated a convenient economic environment for *hacienda*-owners. *Hacendados* had plenty of farm labour when the population of the indigenous communities finally stabilised after long decades of pandemics. There were steadily expanding urban markets for their grain, cattle and sheep. Moreover, government policies inadvertently favoured larger estates over smaller ones. The implementation of the *abasto de carnes* (city meat monopoly) was a practice intended to provide the cities with constant supply of meat at a stable price. The *abasto* contracts were granted in a public auction to the lowest bidder. Afterwards, a single contractor had a monopoly of supplying meat to the city at that set price throughout the term of his *abasto*. Needless to say, only the largest estates that could operate economies of scale could compete in the auctions for this meat monopoly. As Van Young's study shows, between 1687 and 1815 the meat monopoly for Guadalajara switched between only a handful of contractors who were, incidentally, the largest *hacienda* owners in the region.[64]

Later works on the rural history and economy of Latin America employ more of a contextual reading of the institution of *hacienda*, rather than isolated analyses that focus merely on certain characteristics of the *hacienda* and *hacendados*. These later studies place *hacienda* in its rightful place within the larger network of market relations in these progressively expanding and developing colonial lands. As a result of this, *hacienda* emerges as the interesting by-product of tension between Spanish mercantilism and its constant efforts to bring economic forces under centralised government control, on the one hand, and progressively advancing market forces trying to break free from this tight centralist grip on the other. Furthermore, the institution of *hacienda* shows the close linkage, and even dependence, of economic elites on political structures. As later chapters will illustrate, this was an important characteristic that carried over to state–society relations in contemporary Mexico. In this regard, far from being an ancient artefact with expansive feudal powers and autonomy, *hacienda* was the 'modern' solution the Spanish Empire adopted to the problems of the economic needs of her colonies and the political need of the Crown to prevent the emergence of a strong, autonomous bourgeoisie. The reluctance of the Crown to grant nobility status to *hacendados*, the precariousness of their land titles and the extensive government control over the trade and prices of essential foodstuffs were all deliberate attempts to keep economic elites under the surveillance of state.

Trade

The economic policies of the Spanish Empire were guided by mercantilism during most of its colonial rule in the Americas. As early as 1503, the House of Trade was established in Seville in order to closely monitor and control nearly all aspects of colonial trade. The House of Trade licensed the ships and the passengers to

---

64. *Ibid.*, pp. 43–58.

the New World, oversaw loading and unloading of the ships, and collected duties from the goods that arrived in Spain. Mapping the new routes and coastlines and handling commercial disputes also fell within the jurisdiction of this body. The Crown established two treasury offices in the Americas (one in Mexico City and one in Veracruz) and appointed mostly Spanish-born bureaucrats to these important posts.[65]

Any type of trade to and from the colonies had to be conducted via Spain, by Spanish vessels and under the close surveillance of Spanish authorities, for the Spanish Crown 'considered New Spain its private property and tried to prevent any direct contact between the colony and other European countries'.[66] All transactions had to take place through the mother country, even if this lead to some economically unsound practices. The colonies could not sell their products directly to the highest bidder, nor could they import from the cheapest supplier. A good example for this was the burgeoning trade between Manila and Acapulco that started in the 1570s. There was a strong demand in New Spain (Mexico) for cheap Asian silks and spices. As the volume of trade between New Spain and Asia increased, Spanish merchants became more and more anxious. They requested the Spanish Crown to prohibit the trade with Asia. In 1634, the Crown officially severed the trade links between Asia and the colonies.[67] After the royal ban, some contraband trade continued between Asia and New Spain but its volume could never reach the previous levels and Spain remained as the sole trading outlet for the colonies.

By all measures, precious metals were the largest export item from the colonies to Spain. Between 1551 and 1560, a total of 43 tons of gold arrived in Seville from the New World.[68] First Peru, then Mexico became the greatest supplier of silver for the imperial coffers (*see* Figure 2.3) Unfortunately, these vast quantities of gold and silver that arrived in Spain in sealed ships were not used to set up new and profitable domestic enterprises. Successive Spanish monarchs failed to establish a national bank and almost always lost their battles against the skilled *hombres de negocios* of international finance. In explaining this phenomenon, Fernand Braudel draws a parallel between the situation of Philip II and the resource-rich countries of contemporary South America. In both cases, there was enormous richness from the mines and the plantations, but both were '[...] helplessly out of depth in the world of international finance'. In fact, the abundance of precious metals had created a false sense of security and fuelled unreasonable expenditures, particularly military campaigns against the rest of Europe, while Spain was on the brink of bankruptcy.[69]

---

65. More than 75% of all treasury officials were born in Spain (Burkholder, 2000, p. 122).
66. *Ibid.*, p. 134.
67. *Ibid.*, pp. 131–2.
68. Braudel, 1992, p. 334.
69. *Ibid.*, pp. 362–364.

Figure 2.3: Registered bullion production in Spanish colonies*

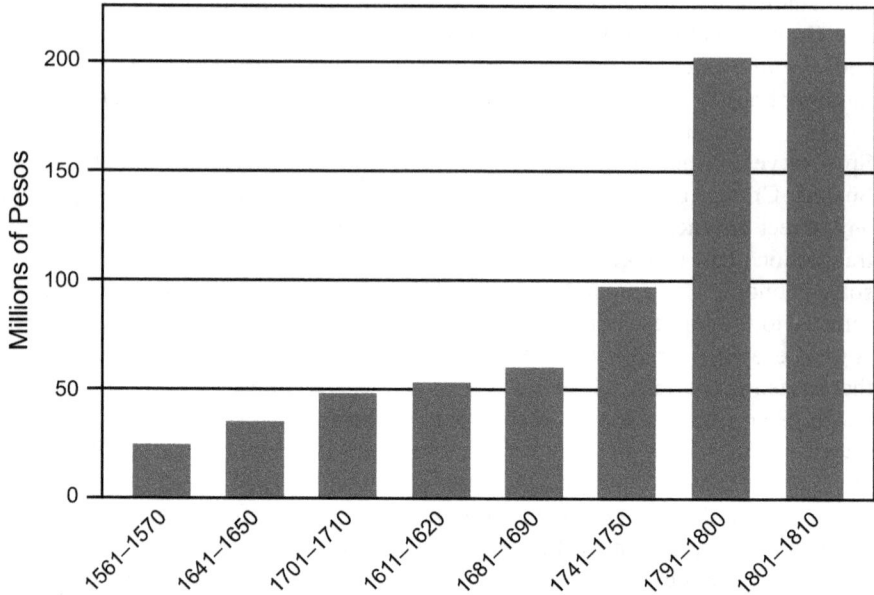

*Actual production was greater than these numbers suggest.
Source: Mark A. Burkholder, 'An empire beyond compare', in M. Meyer and W. Beezley (eds) *The Oxford History of Mexico*, New York: Oxford University Press, 2000, p. 130

The economic downturn of Spain took place at a time when the economy of New Spain began to flourish. From the 1660s on, the overall trade volume of New Spain increased continuously. It was producing more bullion and more goods and the lucrative contraband network was gaining a significant foothold, particularly with increasing imports of British textiles. The Spanish Crown desperately tried to eradicate the smuggling but, in 1701, the country succumbed to political turmoil during the War of the Spanish Succession. The French and the British did not lose any time in taking advantage of Spanish vulnerability and gained access to the port of Veracruz during this period.[70] It became clear that the tide had turned away from the large empires in favour of more moderately sized political entities (such as Britain, France and The Netherlands), which could keep their economic houses in better order.

Spain's power in its colonies was now in rapid decline, due to the unproductive nature of its mercantilist economy, the ineffectiveness of its colonial administration and its excessive defence spending. When the Bourbon kings took control of the

---

70. Burkholder, 2000, p. 141.

Spanish Crown, they initiated comprehensive administrative and economic reforms in order to reverse this trend. The first problem the Bourbon monarchs addressed was the increasing authority and prosperity of *criollos* (colonial-born people of Spanish heritage). They tried to strengthen central rule by appointing Spanish-born local governors who were responsible directly to the crown and by eliminating the practice of office sales, which became a lucrative path for the creoles to buy their way into power and prosperity. The second important set of reforms during the Bourbon era addressed the power of the church. In a rather bold fashion, Charles III (1759–88) expelled the Jesuits from the Americas, confiscated all their wealth and auctioned off their best properties to generate revenues for the royal coffers. In order to increase the revenues from the colonies, the Bourbons allowed some liberalisation in the trade routes and commercial relations between the colonies and Europe. Lastly, they tried to modernise the military by establishing local militias, which could also serve as a 'source of prestige for the status-hungry creoles'.[71]

The progressive reforms undertaken by the Bourbon dynasty to tighten control of the colonial administration and increase revenue antagonised the local elites. In fact, the Spanish-born appointments of the Bourbon era and Bourbon efforts to re-centralise the empire increased the discontent and the creole-staffed militias emboldened pro-independence subjects against colonial rule. Bourbon re-centralisation sowed the seeds of the idea of independence among the disgruntled colonial elites.[72] However, the fate of Spanish rule in the Americas was really sealed in Old Europe. The Napoleonic invasion of the Iberian Peninsula in 1808 demonstrated the weakness of Spain and encouraged mobilisation in support of popular sovereignty and independence in the colonies.[73]

Land tenure and trade in the Ottoman Empire

The land-tenure system

The Ottoman economy was predominantly agrarian, with 90 per cent of the population living in rural areas and working the land. In the pre-capitalist agrarian economy of the empire, the main social division was between those who produced the value added (*reaya*) and those who collected taxes from it (*askerî*). The small peasant family farm (*çift-hane*) was the basic economic unit of production.[74] It corresponded to a plot of land that could be ploughed with a pair of oxen and its income could provide for one family. The Ottomans favoured small family farms over large estates because they wanted to diminish the chances of large estate-owners gaining political clout and challenging the central state.

---

71. T. Skidmore and P. Smith, *Modern Latin America*, New York: Oxford University Press, 5th edn, 2001, pp. 26–7.
72. C. Fuentes, 1999, pp. 234–8.
73. Skidmore and Smith, 2001, pp. 28–9.
74. H. Inalcik, 'The çift-hane system and peasant taxation', in H. Inalik (ed.), *From Empire to Republic: Essays on Ottoman and Turkish social history*, Istanbul: ISIS Press, 1995 pp. 61–72.

The land-tenure system in the Ottoman Empire was interwoven with the provincial administration. The *timar* system brought almost all agricultural lands under state control. After a rigorous survey and registration of the arable lands, the state distributed them to government officials, based on their merit and ranking. The cavalrymen received *timars*, the smallest plots of land, while higher-ranking bureaucrats and soldiers received *has* and *zeamet*, which were larger estates that yielded higher income and tax revenues. The *timar* holders had term limits and when they underperformed, those plots were taken away and re-assigned to other government officials. Until the end of the sixteenth century, the cavalry force that was raised through the *timar* practice was the most powerful unit in the Ottoman military. According to 1527 numbers, 'there were 37,521 *timar* holders in the empire [...] [which] formed a cavalry force of some 70,000 to 80,000 men in all, as opposed to the *kapikulu* [full-time soldiers who received salaries directly from the treasury], which still had, at best, no more than 27,900 men.'[75]

Starting with Murad II, and particularly with the centralising reforms of Mehmet II, the Ottoman rulers increasingly assigned *timar* lands to government officials rather than to prominent civilian families. With similar wariness towards the accumulation of private property in the hands of local nobility to that of the Spanish Crown, the Ottomans also wanted to restrain the economic power of the locals by keeping the most important economic asset, arable lands, under strict state control. As a result, the wealthiest members of the society were not the business-owners, merchants or large landowners but government officials. In the 1500s, for example, the average annual income of a *sanjakbeyi* (governor) could reach up to 12,000 gold ducats, while at the same period the richest merchant or money-changer in the city of Bursa could not make more than 4,000 gold ducats per year.[76]

The *timar* system was implemented throughout the Ottoman Empire, except in Egypt, Mesopotamia and Crimea, where they already had long-established systems of land tenure before the Ottomans arrived. In these non-*timar* provinces, the Ottomans only collected an annual tribute and did not intervene in the existing system. According to Barkan's research into the 1527–8 Ottoman budget, approximately 88 per cent of the value added in the Ottoman Empire came from publicly owned lands while only 12 per cent came from privately owned property. Throughout the Empire (excluding Egypt), only one-fifth of the land belonged to private individuals and the *wakfs* (privately run religious foundations) and the rest belonged to the government.[77]

The *timar* system was an important institutional pillar of the Ottoman imperial system. It served multiple critical functions, helping the empire militarily, administratively and financially. From the perspective of state–society relations,

---

75. Shaw, 1976–77, p. 127.

76. Inalcik, 1973, p. 115.

77. Ö. L. Barkan, "*Tımar*", *Türkiye'de Toprak Meselesi*, (*The Land Issue in Turkey*) Istanbul: Gözlem Publications, 1980; Egypt was excluded from this calculation since *timar* was never established there.

the *timar* system was extremely effective in preventing the rise of a strong and autonomous nobility by keeping property rights strictly within the state. From a military perspective, it enabled the Ottomans to maintain a large body of armed forces (cavalrymen) at almost no cost to the state treasury. Administratively, the *timar* system was one of the most efficient ways to control the expansive imperial territory with centrally appointed bureaucrats and soldiers. Lastly, from an economic perspective, the *timar* system closely documented the revenue sources in the periphery and kept them under state control.

The Ottoman land-tenure regime differed significantly from the feudal practices of Europe. In many ways, it was similar to the state-controlled *encomienda* estates of the Spanish Empire. Both in the *timar* and *encomienda* lands, the sultan and the king were the ultimate title-holders and all the agricultural land was considered to be their property. Private property rights were granted to certain individuals but strictly at the discretion of the sultan or king and these could be revoked at any time. The *timar* holder, much like an *encomendero*, was not a landlord but a government official, enforcing land laws and collecting a fixed amount of revenue from the peasants on that land. There was no bond vassalage or serfdom on these lands. At least in theory, Ottoman peasants and indigenous *campesinos* were free individuals and the subjects of the sultan and the king, respectively. They were owed just treatment from the *timar* holders and the *encomenderos*, and could not be bought and sold along with the land.[78]

At the end of the sixteenth century, Ottoman central control over agricultural lands began to weaken. On the one hand, corruption started creeping into the system, wherein the local administrators started granting *timars* to unqualified civilians (*reaya*) in exchange for bribes. On the other, the power of private landlords was progressively strengthening as they used the religious law (*Sharia*) to protect their *wakf* lands from being confiscated by the state. These two developments reduced the total amount of land available for new *timars* and created a large number of poor and dispossessed soldiers, who then resorted to domestic unrest and revolts in Anatolia.[79] When the economic crisis of the seventeenth century made the Ottoman treasury desperate for cash, the state sought refuge in the taxation of farming instead of rehabilitating the broken *timar* system. This was the final blow to this crucial institution and many Ottoman writers and historians of the time highlighted the degeneration of the Ottoman land-tenure system as one of the most important reasons behind the decline of the Empire.[80]

The land-tenure practices of the Ottomans had enduring institutional and socio-cultural implications for modern-day Turkey. They fortified the economic power of the state and contributed to a weak culture of private property rights in the new republic. In his meticulously researched book, Timur Kuran demonstrated that many of the institutional structures of the Empire, including the *wakf* system,

---

78. Goffman, 2002, pp. 81–2.

79. Inalcik, 1973, pp. 114–16.

80. Anon, *Koçi Bey Risalesi*, Ankara: Akçağ Publications, 1998 (original publication date 1654).

proved to be harmful for the long-term prospects of capitalist accumulation and economic efficiency. Weak property rights and a weak civil society undermined the relative strength of economic actors *vis-à-vis* the state.[81]

Despite all the recent privatisation efforts, the state is still the largest landlord in Turkey and private property rights are still not fully protected by the legal system. The Ottoman land-tenure system also amplified the role of the state in the economy and created a political culture that was more conducive to state-lead economic development models, such as import-substitution–industrialisation (ISI). It took decades for Turkey to finally shed this heritage and bring more dynamic private economic actors to the forefront in its long struggle for economic development and progress.

Trade

The trade practices of the Ottoman Empire were in many ways similar to those of their Spanish counterparts. Like the Spaniards, the Ottomans were primarily concerned with political matters, such as military achievements and the overall strength and stability of the empire. From the Ottoman perspective, the economy, especially the regulation and manipulation of trade, was yet another means of pursuing these political goals. The most prominent example of this attitude happened during the reign of Mehmet II, after his conquest of Constantinople in 1453. Sultan Mehmet II granted commercial and other privileges to Italian merchants, primarily due to political considerations. Following this precedent, other sultans also granted such 'capitulations', as they were commonly referred to: to the French in the sixteenth century and to the British and the Dutch in the seventeenth century.

Probably the most important purpose of the Ottomans in granting these capitulations was to create divisions within the Christian world and establish alliances against their powerful Catholic rival, the Habsburgs. As Goffman states, these extended trade privileges given to certain European powers were, in essence, 'anti-Habsburg rapprochements'. Through these economic incentives, the Ottomans wanted to reward the enemies of the Habsburg Empire. The capitulations were considered simply as economic favours to foreign merchants in exchange for political leverage; the Ottomans never considered them as treaties between equals.[82]

The sheer size of the Ottoman Empire made it a vast trading area and a great revenue source for the imperial treasury. The state took important measures to secure these trade routes, which stretched from the Indian subcontinent to Western Europe. Having a robust economy was crucial for the empire as it enabled a steady flow of revenues into the state coffers and helped sustain its military power and bureaucratic structures. The strength of Ottoman central authority and its success

---

81. T. Kuran, *The Long Divergence: How Islamic law held back the Middle East*, Princeton, NJ: Princeton University Press, 2010.

82. Goffman, 2002, pp. 183–4.

in establishing public order brought bourgeoning long-distance trade across the Ottoman territories. Moreover, the population growth in the sixteenth century, both in urban centres and in rural areas, further contributed to the increase in the volume of trade.[83]

The composition of those engaged in trade and commerce activities is illustrative of the critical social, economic and political aspects of the empire. Until the conquest of Constantinople in 1453, trade in the southern (Islamic) Mediterranean basin was mostly controlled by European merchants. According to Goffman, this was largely because European merchants could easily reside in Muslim lands because they were considered to be the 'People of the Book'. From 1453 on, as the political clout of the Ottoman Empire amplified in the region, Ottoman merchants became more visible figures in the Mediterranean and European trade. These merchants, however, were rarely Muslim. Most of them were Armenian, Jewish and Greek Orthodox subjects of the Empire. These non-Muslim communities of the Ottoman Empire had a unique opportunity to establish commercial links between the Islamic and Christian worlds. They were well adjusted to their host society, were conversant in multiple languages and were also familiar with the commercial techniques of Western Europe. The diasporas of each community were helpful in facilitating trade links as well. These trading networks 'helped produce a uniform commercial method throughout the Mediterranean and European worlds, a technological and cultural interplay between the Ottoman Empire and the rest of Europe, and a new people – the Levantines – who eventually became the principal communicators between the two zones'.[84]

Muslim merchants were not completely absent from the commercial sphere, however. They dominated the land and seaborne trade in Egypt and Syria but further to the West, in Anatolia and south-eastern Europe, non-Muslim communities had a much stronger presence.[85] Two other factors also contributed to the weak Muslim presence in the commercial world within the Ottoman Empire. First, as discussed in more detail above, the highest level of the social ladder in the Ottoman polity (positions in the military and bureaucracy) were exclusively open only to Muslims. This policy practically closed channels of social mobility for ambitious non-Muslim subjects of the Empire; as a result, these communities concentrated their energies in other profitable endeavours, such as trade, commerce and banking. The second point was related to the intensely agrarian character of the Empire. About 90 per cent of the population lived in rural areas and the Ottoman state placed great importance on maintaining Muslims as the prominent agriculturalists.[86] In fact, a tax penalty (*çift bozan*) was imposed upon those who quit their farms and moved to urban areas. Policies like these were major disincentives for Muslim and Turkish populations to engage in trade and commerce.

---

83. Hourani, 1991, pp. 231–3.
84. Goffman, 2002, pp. 15–16.
85. *Ibid.*, pp. 90–1.
86. *Ibid.*, p. 89.

The economic and trade policies of the Ottomans reflected the interests of the dominant social classes. The state elites were at the top of the social ladder and their priorities in many ways shaped the economic outlook of the empire. Because of this, government intervention and regulation were fairly common practices in commodity markets and long-distance trade in order to secure a steady supply of goods for the palace, the military and urban residents.[87] The government would set price-ceilings (*narh*) for staples in urban markets, which were then enforced by the local judges (*kadi*). Price-gouging would be punished severely and in most cases publicly, in order to discourage potential exploiters in the future. Commodity exports were particularly discouraged in such an economy, for they would undercut supplies to urban areas and increase the price of urban consumption. The solidly established guild system self-regulated and protected domestic production from outside competition. There were also state-granted monopolies, particularly for provisioning meat to Istanbul and other urban centres. Very similar to the *abasto de carnes* practice of the Spanish Empire, the Ottomans would have annual bids among the meat suppliers (*celep*), and the winner would have the responsibility of supplying the meat for the whole city at the set price. As in the Spanish case, the system favoured large merchants over smaller ones and the fixed-price aspect of it would have the potential to financially ruin even the richest of *celeps*.[88]

In general, Ottoman trade policies carried strong elements of mercantilism. The predominance of political concerns over economic ones, intense state intervention and regulation and strong restrictions on exports were all part of this mercantilist predisposition. Çizakça argues that these mercantilist practices undermined the domestic economy in numerous ways. Because of the capitulations, manufactured goods gradually started flooding into Ottoman markets and destabilised the local guild system, which used to be the backbone of the urban economy. Despite the restrictions on exports, merchants found innovative ways to take raw materials to European markets for higher prices. This situation further worsened the conditions of local manufacturers as they started competing with European markets over raw materials and ended up being priced out.[89]

The seventeenth century saw the beginning of a steep decline in Ottoman economic power. The empire gradually lost its pivotal position in the Mediterranean trade after new geographic discoveries. The massive influx of gold and silver from the New World changed the dynamics of the international monetary system. These developments had serious destabilising effects in the Ottoman Empire, exposing it simultaneously to grave fiscal and monetary problems. On the one hand, state revenues kept shrinking, due to the decline in the volume of

---

87. Ş. Pamuk, *A Monetary History of the Ottoman Empire*, Cambridge: Cambridge University Press, 2000, pp. 9–19 and pp. 225–6.

88. İ. Ortaylı, *İstanbul'dan Sayfalar (Pages From Istanbul)*, İstanbul: İletişim Publications, 1995.

89. M. Çizakça, 'Fiyat Tarihi ve Bursa İpek Sanayii: Osmanlı Sanayiinin Çöküşü Üzerine Bir İnceleme' ('Price history and silk industry in Bursa: a study on the decline of Ottoman industry'), *Toplum ve Bilim (Society and Science)* 11, 1980.

trade. On the other, the country was plunged into an inflationary spiral as the Ottoman currency continuously depreciated. The Ottomans resorted to currency debasement in order to pay the salaries of their soldiers and finance costly military campaigns. This turned out to be an ill-fated strategy since it instigated armed rebellions among the discontented soldiers (*Celali isyanları*), which consequently destabilised the agricultural lands in Anatolia and further reduced state revenues. Without a decent banking and credit system, the Ottoman turned to domestic and international borrowing, in which the non-Muslim subjects of the Empire played a critical role. These economic problems severely undermined Ottoman power as one by one they chipped away the fundamental institutions of the Empire, such as the military, guilds, land-tenure regime (*timar*) and the tax system. Unfortunately, these Ottoman difficulties in reconciling international economic dynamics with the domestic structures continued to plague the modern Turkish Republic as well.

A comparative synthesis

> The more one thinks about it, the more convinced one becomes of the striking similarities, transcending words, terminology and political appearances, between East and West, worlds very different it is true, but not always divergent.[90] (Fernand Braudel)

Three centuries of Spanish imperial rule left lasting political, economic and cultural imprints on Latin America, including modern-day Mexico. The institutional and cultural legacies of the Spanish colonial administration significantly shaped the political culture and the socio-political and economic structures of Mexico after independence. Across the Mediterranean, the six-century reign of the Ottomans in many ways framed the political and economic development goals of modern Turkey. Similarities in the political and economic institutions of these two empires provide equally challenging problems for Mexico and Turkey in their pursuit of democratic development.

When trying to establish strong connections between weak economic and democratic performances and imperial traditions, one needs to be wary of the slippery slope towards ethnocentrism. Earlier culturalist explanations too easily accused centuries-old imperial rule (Iberian or sultanic) and world religions (Roman Catholicism or Islam) of being unfit for economic development and democracy. However, more recent scholarship is wary of this and tends to seek answers about the authoritarian legacies of the past by grounding their arguments upon (i) particular *formal structures* and *institutions* inherited from the past; and (ii) socio-cultural and psychological manifestations and *mentalities* as remnants

---

90. Braudel, 1992, p. 485.

of an authoritarian past.[91] Consequently, the attributes of authoritarian legacies are carefully specified in the following way:

> Authoritarian legacies are those rules, procedures, norms, patterns, practices, dispositions, relationships, and memories originating in well defined authoritarian experiences of the past that, as a result of specific historical configurations and/or political struggles, survive democratic transitions and intervene in the quality and practice of post-authoritarian democracies.[92]

Even when countries try to break away from their pasts through revolutionary ruptures, the lingering impact of the authoritarian past can be traced in the new formal and institutional structures that are created. Moreover, certain psychological attitudes, such as feelings of distrust and alienation towards political authority, internalisation of hierarchy or anxiety towards the state, may persist in the society. Past historical traditions cannot outright determine modern political cultures but they can certainly work their way in, by tacitly influencing the new formal and institutional structures or by shaping the perceptions and mentalities of citizens about political authority.

The purpose of this chapter was to highlight some of the key formal and institutional structures of the Spanish and Ottoman empires, as well as the predominant forms of state–economy and state–society relations. In this process, important similarities emerged in the imperial legacies of Mexico and Turkey, which later turned out to be unconducive to the emergence of horizontal, open, pluralistic and democratic regimes in both contexts. A synthesis of the most significant similarities in authoritarian imperial legacies of Spanish and Ottoman Empires could include the following aspects:

Synthesis of similarities between Spanish and Ottoman authoritarian legacies

A loyal bureaucratic class

Braudel underlines the importance of *letrados* as a separate class of imperial civil servants dedicated to serve the interests of the Spanish Crown in the Americas. Rather than granting authority to the local nobility in New Spain, the Crown deliberately gave significant political, judicial and administrative powers to these law graduates of humble origin.[93] It was assumed that, given their background, the *letrados* would have a stronger devotion and allegiance to the prince. Later, when this system was penetrated by the locals, the Bourbon reformists also tried

---

91. P. Cesarini and K. Hite, 2004, 'Introducing the concept of authoritarian legacies', in K. Hite and P. Cesarini (eds), *Authoritarian Legacies and Democracy in Latin America and Southern Europe*, South Bend, IN: University of Notre Dame Press, 2004, p. 2.

92. Cesarini and Hite, 2004, p. 4.

93. Braudel, 1992, pp. 483–4.

to strengthen the control of the central authority by appointing loyal, Spanish-born administrators. Similarly, the Ottoman sultans created a separate class of state elites with the *devşirme* system. Recruited from among non-Muslim subjects at a young age and rigorously trained at palace schools, this class also associated itself strongly with the state and dedicated itself to perpetuating imperial interests. In both cases, the imperial rulers managed to check the feudalising tendencies of local elites and strengthened central rule in their expanding territories, with the help of their loyal bureaucratic classes. These imperial legacies, however, saddled both Mexico and Turkey with strong state traditions and authoritarian bureaucracies that became significant hurdles on the path to democratisation. The legacy of a separate and fairly autonomous class of state elites, which functioned almost as the *guardians* of the nation, made it rather difficult for the rest of the society, particularly for the middle classes, to penetrate into decision-making mechanisms and establish an open, democratic and accountable polity.

Close surveillance of provincial administration

The vast territories of both the Spanish and the Ottoman Empires presented a unique challenge to their administrative capacities. Yet, both empires managed to establish significantly strong centralist regimes by denying seigniorial titles and privileges to local elites and by establishing rigorous mechanisms of checks and balances over provincial authorities. These measures proved to be highly effective in preventing regional social forces from counterbalancing the powers of the centre. This top-down style of provincial administration created a weak culture of power-sharing between the central government and the rest of the society. It amplified the strength of the central government at the expense of local governments and, for a very long time, hindered the prospects for popular participation at the local level. Thus, the new republics inherited a political culture with little or no experience in democratic self-government. Both empires chose their local administrators from a very small pool of loyal bureaucrats (Spanish-born *peninsulares* and palace-trained *devşirme* Muslims) and did not encourage the emergence of horizontal and deliberative means of decision-making, even at the local level.

Land tenure

The Spanish and the Ottoman empires considered land to be royal property and were very reluctant to grant exclusive property rights to private individuals. Their land-tenure systems were structured in such a way that access to land was tied directly to access to public office. Both *encomienda* and *timar* holders were, at the same time, government officials with only limited rights over the properties that they managed. Because of this, it was difficult for them to exploit the long-term potential of their estates in the most commercially effective manner. Strict term-limits and the threat of confiscation kept these officials on their toes and strengthened state control over key economic assets. These land-tenure practices fortified the notion of the state as the largest economic actor in both the Mexican and Turkish context.

They undermined the establishment of a strong culture of private property rights and limited the prospects for the emergence of a vibrant middle class in both countries. As the volatility and tenuousness of estate titles demonstrate, an insecure class of estate-holders that were operating at the whim of the state could hardly be transformed into assertive agents of political freedoms and democracy.

Mercantilism and strict regulation of trade

The Spanish and the Ottoman empires were both very late in discovering the profitable nature of free trade and commerce. For centuries, they focused primarily on political and military achievements and channelled a greater part of imperial economic resources to these ends. This state-centric and mercantilist predisposition was carried out by heavily interventionist and protectionist policies in the economic realm. Trade restrictions, price ceilings for staples and the arbitrary treatment of commercial activity by the state left domestic economic sectors weak and subservient. Having these characteristics in their institutional and cultural heritage, it is no surprise that the political elites of Mexico and Turkey found state-led development programmes highly attractive. Their mercantilist pasts and scepticism towards free trade railroaded both countries towards state-centric models and thwarted the emergence of middle classes that were autonomous (in both economic and political terms) from the state. Despite brief periods of experimentation with economic liberalism, both countries waited until the 1980s to gradually eliminate their protectionist barriers and open up their markets to free trade.

Absence of civil society and intermediary institutions

In both the Spanish and Ottoman empires, military and bureaucratic posts were the most prestigious in the eyes of their status-conscious elites. Economic activities, trade and commerce did not constitute the top choices for their best and the brightest. The persistence of mercantilist doctrines further undermined the development of free trade, as well as the growth of a 'self-reliant middle class of independent farmers and entrepreneurs that might have served as the basis for moderation and stability'.[94] In both empires, social status and capital accumulation were strongly tied to the political centre, making it very difficult for a separate and autonomous class to exert bottom up pressure for political representation. The Ottoman polity consisted of essentially two classes, *askerî* (military-bureaucratic class) and the *reaya* (civilians), with no intermediary sector or even a rudimentary civil society in between. Likewise, the socio-racial rigidities and corporatist privileges of the Spanish Empire did not facilitate horizontal forms of associations among individuals. As a result, instead of an emerging civil society with a dense network of intermediary institutions, republican Mexico and Turkey inherited these rigidly hierarchical traditions and exclusionary forms of social stratification from their imperial pasts.

---

94. Wiarda, 2001, p. 82.

Chapter Three

Nation-Building through Corporatism: The Turkish Republic until the 1980 Crisis

For analysing Turkish and Mexican politics up until the 1980s, corporatism proves to be one of the best devices in the social scientist's toolbox. The corporatist paradigm has significant advantages for explaining state–society relations, as well as the predominant economic development models of the time. First of all, both Turkey and Mexico carried strong imperial heritages, as discussed in the previous chapter, which tipped the balance in the state–society scale in favour of the former. Neither strong individual civil liberties nor an autonomously organised civil society existed, due to the overpowering strength of the Turkish and Mexican states.[1] Given the strength of state institutions *vis-à-vis* the society, liberal or pluralistic paradigms that focus on individuals or social groups have limited explanatory power for our particular cases.

Secondly, both Mexico and Turkey had experienced large-scale traumas at the beginning of the twentieth century – the Mexican Revolution and the Turkish War of Independence. After decades of war, civil strife and turmoil, both countries undertook the task of rebuilding their nations, during which process the state took the leading developmental role in order to bring peace, tranquillity and prosperity.[2] The ideological climate of the interwar years also helped the elites nurture this type of interventionist, controlling state. In the 1930s, there was a reverse global tide against liberal and individualistic political systems, which culminated in a variety of corporatist systems and the fascist regimes of Germany and Italy. Even though the Mexican and Turkish regimes did not take this sharp turn towards fascism, they too placed a strong emphasis on national solidarity and favoured the collective over the individual. As will be discussed in detail below, both countries established single-party regimes to unite all social classes under a single, national umbrella, with the ultimate goal of creating *republican, secular* and *modern* nations.

Lastly, despite the strength of the central state, neither of these societies chose to establish full-fledged socialist or communist regimes. It is true that Marxism and its

---

1. On the high degrees of *stateness* and weak culture of civil society in Turkey, *see* M. Heper, *The State Tradition in Turkey*, Walkington: Eothen Press, 1985. For Mexico, *see* D. Levy and K. Bruhn, *Mexico: The struggle for democratic development*, Berkeley, CA: University of California Press, 2001, especially pp. 73–86 and chapter 4. For a classical work on the comparative weakness of civil society in Mexico, *see* G. Almond and S. Verba, *The Civic Culture: Political attitudes and democracy in five nations*, Princeton, NJ: Princeton University Press, 1963.

2. B. Lewis, *The Emergence of Modern Turkey*, New York: Oxford University Press, 2002, L. Bethell, (ed.) *Mexico Since Independence*, New York: Cambridge University Press, 1991.

variants gained a certain following in both societies, especially among intellectuals, university students and working classes. This sympathy notwithstanding, the cornerstone of the socialist agenda (that is, land redistribution), was implemented only half-heartedly in both countries.[3] Once they entrenched themselves in the power structures, the state elites paid only lip service to revolutionary ideals. Especially from the 1950s on, redistributive and egalitarian ideals were further abandoned in the midst of short-term political manoeuvring. Consequently, due to historic, institutional and ideological reasons, these two societies were very hospitable to corporatist state–society structures at the beginning of the twentieth century. Needles to say, this institutional baggage cast strong shadows on their future prospects of establishing genuinely democratic regimes.

This chapter and the following one (Chapter Four) discuss the establishment of corporatist regimes in Turkey and Mexico. These chapters describe the modernisation processes and the predominant patterns of state–society relations in Turkey and Mexico until the 1980s. An accurate assessment of the democratic transition and consolidation in both societies is not possible without clearly plotting out the state–society dynamics in the pre-1980 era. The first section of this chapter will look at the dynamics of state–society relations in corporatist regimes. After this brief conceptual and theoretical section, it will discuss the Turkish case. The establishment of Turkey's single-party regime, its efforts to unite all sectors of the society under a single umbrella and the eventual breaking up of this system are all covered in the remaining sections.

The adoption of import-substitution industrialisation (ISI) as the preferred economic development model of this corporatist state is also discussed in this chapter. ISI had been a common strategy many developing countries have used to jump-start a home-grown industrial sector, by providing incentives and shielding their infant industries from international competition. This is also a suitable alternative in corporatist regimes since the state would not be capable of co-opting every group without an economic model that caters to all its constituencies. In this regard, the ISI model was the perfect match for the political agenda of the corporatist state.

Chapter Four will discuss similar developments over the same period for the Mexican case (from the 1910 Mexican Revolution to 1980s). While bearing in mind a comparative-historical perspective with the Turkish case, Chapter Four will cover the emergence and consolidation of single-party regime in Mexico. Political-economic choices of the era and their subsequent consequences will also be highlighted. The substantial similarities as well as the differences between these two cases will be summarised in the last section of Chapter Four.

---

3.   On land reform in Turkey, *see* C. Keyder and S. Pamuk, 'Çiftçiyi Topraklandırma Kanunu Üzerine Tezler', [Thesis on the Land Reform Law] *Yapıt,* 8, December–January, 1984–1985, pp. 52–63. W. Cornelious and D. Myhre (eds) *The Transformation of Rural Mexico: Reforming the ejido sector*, La Jolla, Center for U.S.–Mexican Studies, University of California, San Diego, 1998.

Corporatism as the third way

The intellectual origins of corporatism

Non essent omnia, si essent aequalia.[*] (St Augustine)

The twentieth century was marked by competition between the liberal-democratic-capitalist regimes of the West, and the Marxist-socialist-communist regimes of the East. These were the two major alternatives or, in Wiarda's words, the two 'great isms' of the modern world. Yet, for several reasons, neither of these paradigms could be a snug fit for developing countries like Mexico and Turkey. In the case of liberalism, its promise of economic prosperity sounded highly attractive but the liberal emphasis on the individual seemed too atomising and unrealistic.[4] Those who criticised liberalism in favour of more solidaristic models argued that the rampant individualism of capitalism was creating 'moral anomie' and therefore weakening 'public morality'.[5] Certain societies were group–rather than individual-centred and group-oriented thinking was embedded in their political cultures.[6] Parla and Davison highlight the 'third way' characteristic of corporatism in the following way:

> Corporatism's distinction lies in its view of society as an organic whole, consisting of mutually interdependent and functionally complementary parts. The major units, the molecules of society, are the occupational groups. Corporatism, therefore, opposes the central categories of liberal and Marxian models of society.[7]

Corporatism has a distinct way of viewing society. Instead of considering individuals or social classes as building blocks, corporatism takes occupational groups as the primary units of a given polity. Political and administrative elites are located at the top, functioning like the 'brain' in a body. Doctors, lawyers, academics and other professional classes perform mid-level critical functions, much like our inner organs. Industrial and agricultural workers perform manual tasks, which are very similar to what the 'limbs' do in our body. All told, the vision of society from a corporatist perspective is very similar to that of a live organism. It highlights the functional utility and complementary role of each sector (corporation) for the preservation of the whole society but, at the same time,

---

[*]   'If all things were equal, they would not exist'.

4.   T. Parla and A. Davison, *Corporatist Ideology in Kemalist Turkey: Progress or order?*, New York:, Syracuse University Press, 2004, pp. v–viii.

5.   Quoted from positivist sociologist Emile Durkheim, in Parla and Davison, 2004, pp. 26–28.

6.   H. J. Wiarda, *Corporatism and Comparative Politics: The other great 'Ism'*, New York and London: M.E. Sharpe, 1997, pp. 13–15.

7.   Parla and Davison, 2004, p. 28.

implies the inherent hierarchy among them (that is, the brain is clearly superior to the feet).

This organic conception of society has roots in both the Ottoman and Spanish tradition. In the case of the Ottomans, the very nature of economic organisation (the guild system) was probably the quintessential corporatist arrangement of its times. Almost all economic activities were organised around guilds that enjoyed a monopoly over their designated sector. Individuals who were members of these vocational associations were entitled to certain rights and privileges, as well as subject to duties. While guilds were mostly autonomous in regulating their internal affairs, relations between them were administered centrally by the state. In fact, given the strengths of the control mechanisms over manufacturing and trade, İnalcık considers the Ottoman system a great attempt to establish a centralised division of labour throughout the Empire.[8]

The Ottoman *Weltenschaung* was very static and did not permit much social mobility among classes either. The order of the world, or *Nizam-ı Alem*, depended on everyone's consent and respect for this hierarchical order. The fundamental division between *askerî* (military and civilian bureaucracy) and *reaya* (all the civilians) was almost impregnable. The popular Turkish expression '*haddini bilmek*' ('knowing your limit or place') goes back to Ottoman times, when the socio-economic system established clear hierarchical stratification both within and between corporate groups.[9]

The origins of an organic conception of society in Spanish and Latin American political culture can be traced back to the early Christian thinkers. Most of these political philosophers emphasise order, discipline and the importance of hierarchy in a given polity. They projected an 'organic' view of the society, which was inspired particularly by the writings of the early Christian thinkers such as Saint Paul and Saint Augustine. According to this political tradition, different groups (usually separated along occupational lines) were conceptualised as integral parts of a living organism that functioned in harmony. This harmony, however, came at the expense of a rigid hierarchy, wherein social mobility was undesirable and next to impossible.[10]

Aside from intellectual inclination, a second important political heritage that promoted corporatist structures in Latin America was the institution of *fueros*. These were rights and privileges granted to members of a certain group, such as the military, bureaucracy or clergy. *Fuero* entitled members of a group to special treatment, to which they would not have access had they been ordinary individuals. Separate tribunals for the military, or tax-exempt status for the clergy

---

8.   H. Inalcik, 'Capital formation in the Ottoman Empire', *Journal of Economic History*, 1969, I, pp. 98–106.

9.   C. Imber, *The Ottoman Empire, 1300–1650: The structure of power*, Basingstoke and New York: Palgrave Macmillan, 2002.

10. H. J. Wiarda, *The Soul of Latin America: The cultural and political tradition*, New Haven, CT: Yale University Press, 2001, p. 345.

are examples of these group-based rights/privileges. These historic institutions of group privileges organised along occupational lines made Latin America a highly conducive environment for the establishment of modern corporatist regimes.[11]

The predominant political traditions of Mexico and Turkey are also far from being fertile grounds for the emergence of liberal principle of individualism. On the one hand, corporate groups had much more prominence as the basic building blocks of society than solitary individuals. On the other, the fundamental class-conflict thesis of the Marxist paradigm was unsuitable for these societies, especially after the traumas of the early twentieth century (the Mexican Revolution and the Turkish War of Independence). Both societies at the time were engaged in the process of re-emerging from the ashes of their previous incarnations. During this modernisation and nation-building stage, solidaristic social theories had much more appeal to the elites of the time, rather than the antagonistic discourse of Marxist theories. Even after the Mexican Revolution – which carried strong overtones of class conflict, hence the subsequent attempts at land reform – the party that 'institutionalised' the revolution aspired to invite *all* sectors of society into its big tent. Certain elements of socialism, particularly its call for a planned economy and equitable income distribution, appealed to the modernising elites. However, neither of these nations established a full-fledged socialist system. As Parla and Davison note for the Turkish case, the radicalism and class-based politics of socialism were considered too divisive by the founding elites of modern Turkey. Even in the Mexican case, the scale and scope of land reform was limited and, after a few decades, political enthusiasm for socialist ideals within the PRI waned. Thus, corporatism resembled a happy medium, as a political ideology that pursued capitalist modernity but rejected the individualism of liberalism and the class-based confrontations of socialism.[12]

For all these reasons, corporatism's promise of functional harmony and social order proved to be an extremely attractive alternative for the political elites of both Mexico and Turkey in the early twentieth century. Corporatism was the 'happy medium' option between too-individualistic liberalism and too-antagonistic socialism. Thus, leaders in both countries wasted no time in establishing single-party regimes to institutionalise corporatist forms of state–society relations. The political and economic foundations of modern Mexico and Turkey were organised around the corporatist paradigm and were carried on under single-party-dominant political systems. As will be discussed below, opposition parties did exist in both contexts (hence the 'semi-open' nature of these regimes) but the official party and the state merged in such a way that, for decades, it became impossible to distinguish where the party ended and the state began. That is why it took decades for the opposition in both countries – precisely seven decades in Mexico – to take down the state 'Goliath' through democratic means.

---

11. H. J. Wiarda, 2001.
12. Parla and Davison, 2004, chapter 1.

State–society relations in corporatist systems

> [...] corporatism may coexist with, not totally replacing the political party system, which has now become subordinate to corporative interests, or it may be implemented by a single-party regime, whose associations are made organs of the party.[13]

Certain characteristics are common to regimes that display strong corporatist elements. Despite the heated debates over different types of corporatism (neo-corporatism; liberal corporatism; state *vs.* societal corporatism; solidaristic corporatism; fascist corporatism and so on), shared characteristics still allow us to speak of a corporatist type of regime. Certainly there are variations in the degree to which each characteristic is pronounced in any particular sub-category. For example, liberal corporatist regimes might have fewer restrictions over interest-group activity than more statist or solidaristic ones. Yet, it would be safe to say that the three main points listed below would be mostly sufficient to identify regimes that operate according to corporatist principles.

Strong state

Without exception, corporatist regimes develop in places where the state is significantly more powerful than social groups or individual citizens. The resilience of patrimonial imperial legacies can be further incentives for these states to establish strong interventionist and corporatist structures.[14] The state has significantly more authority and capacity to organise the socio-economic realm in such societies.

Restrictions on interest-group activity

Unlike liberal, pluralist systems, where there are few or no restrictions on the free-association rights of citizens, interest-articulation is highly regulated in corporatist regimes. In such systems, interests are aggregated along functional lines (in corporate groups) and the state sanctions, licenses and closely monitors these corporations. In most cases, the state grants monopoly of representation to its preferred group, which significantly hinders group competition and pluralism.

---

13. Parla and Davison, 2004. p. 32.

14. Er. Ozbudun, 'The Ottoman legacy and the Middle East state tradition', in C. Brown (ed.), *Imperial Legacy: The Ottoman imprint on the Balkans and the Middle East*, New York: Columbia University Press, pp. 133–57.

Figure 3.1: State–society relations under corporatism

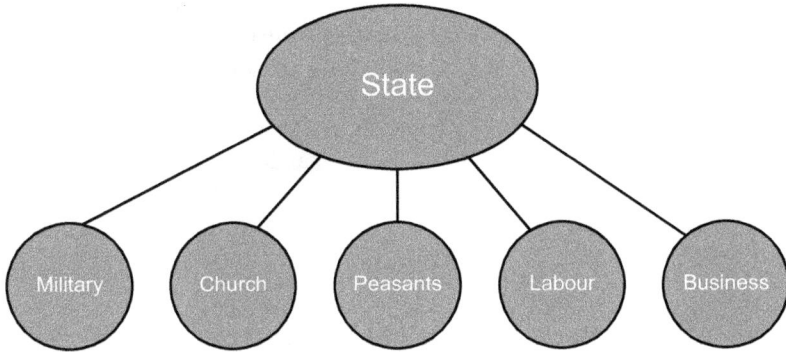

State

Military   Church   Peasants   Labour   Business

Connections between corporate groups and the state

In corporatist systems, the state acts as the primary mediator between corporate groups. Grievances between groups (such as between labour and business over wages and benefits) are not directly addressed by the relevant parties. Instead, both parties take the issue to the state and expect the state to mediate inter-group relations. Hence, there are almost no horizontal connections between corporate groups, whereas all are vertically tied to the central state apparatus (*see* Figure 3.1). In most cases, corporate groups are formally incorporated into the state, which makes them quasi-governmental institutions, rather than expressions of the autonomous voice of civil society.[15]

While the above-listed criteria define corporatism in broad strokes, there is significant variation between the countries that implement this model. On the one end of the spectrum, corporatism can have rather authoritarian interpretations, as seen in the case of Italian fascism under Mussolini during the 1930s. On the other hand, corporatism can also flourish in some of the most open and democratic regimes, as the *neo-corporatist* models of Scandinavia illustrate. For the cases we have at hand, there has been extensive debate over whether they should be classified as state-corporatism (Schmitter), solidarist or fascist corporatism (Parla), or historical-societal corporatism (Wiarda).[16]

It is beyond the scope of this book to settle the debate over corporatist typologies. However, one important issue that is common to most regimes identified as corporatist is the longevity of corporatist structures and their

---

15. Wiarda, 1997.
16. P. C. Schmitter, 'Still the century of corporatism?', in Schmitter and Lembruch (eds), *Trends Toward Corporatist Intermediation*, California: Sage Publications, 1979, pp. 22–4; T. Parla, *Ziya Gökalp, Kemalism and Corporatism in Turkey,* Istanbul: İletişim, 1989, p. 53; Wiarda, 2001.

evolutionary resilience. In many cases, corporatism might have been deliberately constructed by elites or the state might have had a rather active role in establishing, licensing and monitoring corporate groups. Yet, an historical perspective would also illustrate that some societies have certain institutional baggage (that is, hierarchical and group-oriented thinking, strong guild traditions and so on) that, in turn, make them particularly susceptible to the growth of corporatist types of state–society relations. Finally, the same nation can experience different versions of corporatism at different times. As Ahmet Makal discusses for the Turkish case, the quintessentially corporatist decades of the single-party era display rather fascist characteristics at times, whereas at other times there were genuine attempts to liberalise.[17]

The emergence and consolidation of a single-party regime in Turkey (1923–46)

The traditional historiography of the Turkish Republic – the *official* or Kemalist historiography, as the more critical schools call it – makes the case for a clean break from the Ottoman past. This school tends to portray the Ottoman Empire and its institutions at the end of the nineteenth century as *passé*, decayed or completely in ruins. On this reading, the Sultan in Istanbul had resigned himself into the hands of the Western powers and, had it not been for the resistance of Anatolia, this part of the world would have been parcelled into colonies of the European powers. Utmost importance is attributed to the mobilisation of Anatolia, which included meetings at Samsun, Erzurum and Sivas to galvanise resistance to European occupation. All of these took place despite the complacency of the Sultan in Istanbul. Since there was nothing left from the old regime to build upon, the emergence of the Republic under Ataturk's leadership is seen as nothing short of a miracle. In fact, the new Turkish Republic declares a city in the heartland of Anatolia, Ankara, as its capital. This was not a random choice, but an important symbolic gesture to highlight the rupture from the centuries old imperial tradition and its capital, Istanbul. One of the canonical writers of Turkish modernisation, Feroz Ahmad, for instance, praises the new Republic for its 'youthful vigour of the new' as opposed to the decay of the old.[18]

From the 1950s on, a new school of historiography emerged which 'acknowledges the debt of the republic to its immediate predecessors'. This 'revisionist' historiography conceptualised the Kemalist reforms as part and parcel of the late-Ottoman reforms (1808–39). Prominent scholars of Ottoman

---

17. A. Makal, 'Türkiye'de Tek Parti Dönemi ve Korporatizm Tartışmaları' ['The single party era and the corporatism debates in Turkey'], *Toplum ve Bilim* [*Society and Science*], 2002, 93, pp. 173–99.

18. F. Ahmad, *The Making of Modern Turkey*, London: Routledge, 1993: Ahmad also considers the destruction of the Empire a 'blessing' for the Turks, as it meant abandoning a 'decadent' past to make a 'fresh start' (p. 77).

and Turkish history carefully traced the institutional linkages between the 'old' and the 'new'.[19] As Zürcher states, 'a picture of almost total continuity emerges' here. He lists the substantive areas of this continuum, such as the military, civilian bureaucracy, education and even the religious establishment.

The New Republic relied upon the state elites of Ottoman times, who were trained either in the western-style military academy or in the civil service academy (*mulkiye*) in Istanbul. Particularly in the religious sphere, Zürcher argues that the very reason that the clergy remained largely docile under the new Republic – despite radical reforms (including the abolition of the Caliphate, the closure of *medreses*, and the replacement of *Sharia* law with European-style family law) – shows 'the degree to which the Ottoman religious establishment had already been bureaucratized and brought under state control in the Ottoman Empire'.[20] If the most important institutions of the Republic were largely inherited from the Empire, then, what was the 'unique contribution' of Kemal Atatürk?

According to Zürcher, the People's Party – created in 1923 – unequivocally emerges as the single most important means of institutionalising the regime in Turkey. Certainly, the institutions and the cadres of the new Republic had much in common with their imperial predecessors. But the entire organisation of a party, with its ideology, rank and file and nation-wide outreach, were all novel developments.

At the time, the term *party* had rather negative connotations. It was associated with special interests, factionalism and bickering. That is why the word was carefully avoided throughout the Independence War, when unity was much needed. The organisation that co-ordinated national mobilisation during war time and its immediate aftermath called itself the Society for the Defence of National Rights (*Müdafa-i Hukuk Cemiyeti*). 'Society' (*cemiyet*) was preferred to 'party' (*firka*), because it sounded more inclusive and neutral.

When Mustafa Kemal announced his intention to establish a political party, he made a linguistically strategic move by including the word 'people' (*halk*) in the party name.[21] It was meant to reflect the party's goal of embracing all sectors of society, particularly the urban and rural working classes. Yet this did not mean that the People's Party (*Halk Fırkası*) would pursue a socialist path. In fact, Atatürk himself made it very clear in two subsequent speeches that the People's Party was the representative of the national will (as was the Society for the Defence of

19. Among them are: K. Karpat, *Türkiye'de Siyasi Sistemin Evrimi 1876–1980* [*The Evolution of Political System in Turkey 1876–1980*], Istanbul: Imge Publications, 2007, and S. Mardin, *Religion, Society and Modernity in Turkey*, Syracuse: Syracuse University Press, 2006, especially chapter 8, 'Continuity and change in the ideas of the Young Turks'.

20. E. J. Zürcher, 'Institution building in the Kemalist Republic: the role of the People's Party', in T. Atabaki (ed.) *Men of Order: Authoritarian modernisation under Ataturk and Reza Shah*, London: I. B. Tauris & Co., 2004, p. 102.

21. M. Tuncay, *Türkiye'de Tek Parti Doneminin Kurulması 1923–1931* [*Establishment of the Single Party Era in Turkey*], İstanbul: Cem Publications, 1989, pp. 48–9.

National Rights during the War of Independence) and would not side with any class or sector of the society at the expense of any other. In Zürcher's words:

> He emphatically stated that large landowners and capitalists were so rare in Turkey that there was no reason why improving the living standard of the peasants should be at their expense. Industrial workers, he said, did not number more than 20,000 in all of Turkey, so they could not form the basis of a political party either. The new party would be a party for all sections of society, preaching harmony and not class struggle.[22]

Thus, Atatürk announced the futility of class antagonism, for the material conditions that could create and sustain robust class relations did not exist in Turkey. Hence, the new party would be a 'big tent', embracing all in a harmonious way. In the summer of 1923, the People's Party (PP) declared itself the only legitimate heir to the Society for the Defence of National Rights and 'it took over all of its assets'.[23] During the remaining part of the decade, the PP and its permanent chairman, Mustafa Kemal, institutionalised a regime of a single-party monopoly.

From June 1925 onwards, the PP became the only legal party in Turkey after effectively eliminating its liberal and socialist competitors. Even though elections were held for the Turkish Grand National Assembly (TGNA), only the PP could nominate candidates. Between 1925 and 1929, the Parliament passed most of the reforms that laid the groundwork for the westernised and secular outlook of the new Turkish Republic.

The authoritarian and centralising tendencies of the PP did not continue unopposed. In fact, even before the Party was established, there were First and Second Groups in the Parliament. Mustafa Kemal and his friends formed the First Group. The Second Group was a more heterogeneous entity and was accused of being anti-secular or reactionary (*mürteci*) by the First Group. Contrary to this accusation, there were well known generals, journalists and intellectuals in the Second Group who were united in their opposition to Mustafa Kemal. In late 1924, they established the Progressive Republican Party (*Terakkiperver Cumhuriyet Fırkası*), which, according to its programme, endorsed liberalism both politically and economically.[24] Here, the catch was, however, the party's open statement on their 'respect for religion'. Because of this, the progressive credentials of the Progressive Republican Party were always suspected by the Kemalist elites. Thus, when a religious upheaval broke out in eastern Turkey (*Şeyh Sait İsyanı*), they wasted no time in using it as an excuse to close down the Progressive Republican Party.

---

22. Zürcher, 2004, p. 104 (*author addition*).

23. Zürcher, 2004, p. 105.

24. C. Koçak, 'Siyasal Tarih (1923–1950)', ['Political history (1923–1950)'], in S. Aksin (ed.) *Çağdaş Türkiye 1908–1980*, [*Modern Turkey 1908–1980*], İstanbul: Cem Publications, 1997, pp. 98–9.

The Şeyh Sait Rebellion was a turning point in the establishment of authoritarian single-party rule. The secular, modernising elites perceived the uprising of the conservative-religious sectors as an existential threat. Soon after the revolt, the Law on the Maintenance of Order (*Takrir-i Sükun Yasası*) was enacted, martial law was declared in most of the Eastern provinces and special tribunals with extraordinary powers were established. Subsequent to this crisis, a plot to assassinate Atatürk in İzmir was revealed. Organised opposition was associated both with the religious rebellion and with the assassination plot. Their leaders – among them six active generals and a few members of the parliament – were arrested and brought in front of special courts. This was a serious blow to any attempt to organise dissent, particularly one with conservative and religious overtones. After this heavy-handed suppression, the already feeble debate and deliberation capacity of the Parliament altogether disappeared and single-party rule made its presence felt in all aspects of Turkish political life.[25]

Consolidation of the People's Party (after 1935, the Republican People's Party, [*Cumhuriyet Halk Partisi*,], henceforth CHP) rapidly resumed after these incidents. First, the political influence of prominent military figures was terminated when they were forced to choose between their military and parliamentarian roles. Some chose to return to barracks, albeit with diminished political clout. Others remained in parliament but devoid of the prestige that came with the uniform. Secondly, the CHP switched to a two-stage election system.[26] From 1927 on, Mustafa Kemal became the permanent Party Chairman. The top leadership of the Party consisted of the chairman, the vice-chairman and the general-secretary. Only these three figures could nominate candidates for the parliamentary elections. When the statist and authoritarian wing of the party became dominant in the 1930s, the fusion of party and state became more apparent. The hardliner General-Secretary Recep Peker announced that 'the principles of the party will now be the principles of the new Turkish state'. From then on, governors (centrally appointed top civilian administrators in provinces) became the heads of the CHP organisations in each province and the general-secretary of the party became the Minister of the Interior.[27] Supporting the continuity thesis between the late Ottoman and early Republican eras, Owen describes the predominant ideological outlook of the Republican elites during the 1930s with the following words:

> [T]he statist tradition inherited from the Ottoman period was eagerly continued by Turkey's civilian bureaucratic elite. In these circumstances there was no great problem in presenting the state as a single, coherent, autonomous enterprise, the more so as rival social forces, like the landowners, remained weak.[28]

---

25. Koçak, 1997, p. 102.
26. R. Owen, *State Power and Politics in the Making of the Modern Middle East*, London: Routledge, 2000, p. 23.
27. Ahmad, 1993, pp.19–20; Koçak, 1997, pp.115–16.
28. Owen, 2000, p. 24.

The new Republic was the child of a coalition that included the military and civilian bureaucracies, merchants, businessmen, workers, rural landlords, and a new class of professionals – teachers, lawyers, journalists – who jointly resisted the foreign occupation of the motherland. Therefore, until the mid-1920s, the Turkish Grand National Assembly (TGNA) reflected this plurality. Even though the CHP tried to cast a wide-enough net to capture all these groups, there was definitely tension between the state-centric, radical group and the state-sceptic, conservative one. For decades, this division determined the main cleavage in Turkish politics: *centre* versus *periphery*. The military and civilian bureaucracy, together with the modern professional sector, formed the centre, while urban and rural economic interests with strong religious sensitivities constituted the periphery.[29]

The bureaucratic-revolutionary elite envisioned a more active state both in the economy and in social areas. From their perspective, the ultimate goal of the Kemalist revolution was to transform the whole nation into a modern one. Their belief in the revolutionary principles (the '*six arrows*' of the CHP, *see* below) were unwavering. Despite popular discontent and resistance (particularly against secularism), the elites were persistent in their tutelary attitude. If enough effort was dedicated to education and propaganda, they believed a majority of the population would definitely embrace the Party's modernisation message.[30]

The opposition, however, was far less enthusiastic about these goals. As the possessors of substantial private wealth, they were sceptical of the benefits of too much state involvement in the economy. Secondly, most of them had vast amounts of land in rural parts of the country, tied to some not-so-modern titles. When 80 per cent of the population lived in rural areas, any radical change – such as an extensive land reform, or education programmes to enlighten the peasantry – meant an immediate threat to the privileges of these rural elites.[31]

The international environment of the 1930s put the statist groups in a decidedly advantageous position, however. The new Republic could not remain isolated from the devastating effects of the Great Depression. Global commodity prices fell dramatically and severely undermined the economic elites, who were largely dependent on the agricultural sector. This brought about a long-anticipated opportunity for the bureaucratic elites of the time. They highlighted the relative success of the state-controlled, planned economies of the Soviet Union and Germany and advocated a similar model for the socio-economic development of Turkey. Also, in 1929, the liberal economic provisions of the Treaty of Lausanne[32]

---

29. S. Mardin, 'Center-periphery relations: a key to Turkish politics?, *Daedalus* 1973, 102(1), pp. 169–91.

30. Zürkher, 2004, p. 109.

31. F. Ahmad, *Demokrasi Sürecinde Türkiye 1945–1980* [*Turkey in the Process of Democratization*] Istanbul: Hil Publications, 1996, pp. 20–21. For a more detailed analysis of the Turkish elites until the 1950s, *see* F. Frey, *The Turkish Elite*, Cambridge: MIT Press, 1965.

32. The Treaty of Lausanne was signed in July 1923 between Turkey and the Allies. It marked the end of the War of Independence and established the borders of modern-day Turkey.

had expired, which meant that the country could now switch to a more protectionist trade regime.[33] Even though Atatürk was not all that convinced about the success of a state-sector-dominated economy, the global economic dynamics of the 1930s discredited the *laissez-faire* model and made İsmet İnönü's vision of state-led economic development look more promising.[34]

The tightening of single-party rule and the stifling of dissident voices during the 1930s can also be observed from the decision-making patterns of the parliament. In the early 1920s, the TGNA was a more diverse and representative body. After the establishment of the People's Party, however, the top leadership realised that it needed a docile legislature in order to implement the modernisation agenda. Therefore, the party weighed in more and more in the nomination process and made sure that 'friendly' candidates were placed in electable spots in every province.

In general, the first two parliaments were thought to be more democratic and representative than subsequent ones. Recent research provides strong empirical evidence in support of this. In her meticulous study of the voting records of representatives, Meral Demirel had sifted through over a hundred thousand pages of parliamentary proceedings, from 1920 to 1946. As seen in Table 3.1, unanimous decisions were rather infrequent (2.5 per cent of all decisions) during the first parliament. In the second parliament, 31.8 per cent were unanimous, which still implies a certain level of diversity and deliberative capacity within the legislative body. Starting from the third general election however, we can observe the tightening grip of the single-party over the TGNA. Unanimous decisions jump to over 90 per cent and stay that way until the 1940s. For some two decades, the Party operated the legislative branch unopposed. After the late 1940s, however, we observe the fracturing of its rule. The economic elites split from the military-bureaucratic elites and established their own party (the Democrat Party or DP) during this era. In the 1950 elections, the DP finally managed to end single-party rule.

The 'six arrows': Principles of the single-party regime

The 1930s was a fertile decade for the flourishing of authoritarian regimes in Europe. Upon occupying the top political seats in their countries, it was not uncommon for charismatic leaders to claim titles that declared their omnipotence. The *Fuhrer* in Germany and *Il Duce* in Italy were trendsetters in this regard. Spain too had its *Jefe del Estado* after 29 September 1936, when Franco set up his dictatorship following the bloody civil war.[35] Mexico saw the triumph of President Plutarco Elias Calles as *Jefe Maximo* between 1924 and 1934. In the Turkish case, Kemal

---

33. C. Keyder, *Türkiye'de Devlet ve Sınıflar*, İstanbul: İletişim Publications, 2000, pp.133–7.

34. Koçak, 1997, pp. 117–18.

35. LIBRO, The Library of Iberian Sources Online, chapters 13 and 14 of *Spanish History* by Richard Herr.

Table 3.1: Unanimous decisions of Turkish Grand National Assembly, 1920–1946

Period	Number of unanimous decisions	Per cent of unanimous decisions	Number of non-unanimous decisions	Per cent of non-unanimous decisions	Total number of decisions
1920–3	7	2.5	270	97.5	277
1923–7	241	31.8	516	68.2	757
1927–31	316	96.6	11	3.4	327
1931–5	449	93.9	29	6.1	478
1935–9	564	98.9	6	1.1	570
1939–43	464	99.1	4	0.9	468
1943–46	284	95	15	5	299

Source: M. Demirel, "'Oybirlikli Demokrasi" Açısından 1920–1945 Arasında TBMM "deki Oylamalar"' ['TGNA votes between 1925–1945 from the 'unanimous democracy' perspective'], in M. Alkan, T. Bora and M. Koraltürk,(eds) *Mete Tunçay'a Armağan [Tribute to Mete Tunçay]*, İstanbul: İletişim Publications, 2007, p. 739.

Atatürk was declared the Eternal Chairman of the Party. In 1938, the Second Man, İnönü adopted the title 'National Chief'(*Milli Şef*). The famous slogan of the times characterised the regime in a nutshell: '*One Party, One Nation, One Leader!*'

The fourth General Party Congress in 1935 listed the principles that the Party and the Republic would embrace. Also called the 'Six Arrows of Kemalism', these principles determined the general characteristics of the new Republic. Later, in 1937, they were all included in the Constitution, with an amendment to Article 2. However, only the names of these principles were listed in the Constitution. Their content was explained in party documents, especially in the Party Programme of 1935. According to the Programme, the regime in Turkey was republican, nationalist, populist, statist, secular and revolutionist.[36]

The literature on Turkish modernisation and Kemalism discusses all six of these principles extensively. The six arrows have both symbolic and practical utility as they embodied the fundamental characteristics of the new regime and pointed at the direction it aspired to achieve. While the debate is almost endless over the original intentions of the republican elites at the time they adopted these, and the actual implementation of each principle over time, for the purpose of this study, a general perspective on them may suffice. The short definitions below might appear rather barren, given the intensity of arguments over them. Nonetheless, these are the definitions taken from the original 1935 party programme, which reflects the authentic form and wording of the principles.

Republicanism: This first principle was about the type of regime that was established subsequent to six centuries of sultanic rule. It clearly and unequivocally

---

36. Ahmad, 1996, p. 17; L. Köker, *Modernizm, Kemalizm ve Demokrasi*, İstanbul: İletişim Publications, 1995, p. 133.

states that the Turkish nation has rebelled and taken sovereignty in its own hands. The new state will be republican, and the Party is there to defend this regime under all circumstances.

Nationalism: While the Republic openly sets the goal of achieving Western levels of development, it also highlights the importance of keeping distinct national culture, values and other characteristics.

Populism: One of the most debated principles, populism, was the most extensively defined principle in the party programme. 'Sovereignty belongs to the people' was the initial statement. After this came the declaration on the equality of all citizens, irrespective of their family, class or communitarian affiliations. This article strongly emphasised the egalitarian character of the new nation and defined populism as a principle that united all sectors of the society in harmony. 'The purpose of our party with this principle is achieving social order and solidarity instead of class conflict'.[37]

Statism: Another later-added and much-disputed principle, statism, was included largely due to the Great Depression of 1929. Having witnessed the collapse of the global markets and the inadequacy of the national bourgeoisie as the locomotive of economic development, the elites now turned to the state. Without completely eliminating the private sector, this principle declared the state to be in charge of economy. The public sector was going to lead the way to development and therefore the state would be a crucial and integral actor in the economy.

Secularism: 'Religion is a matter of conscience', said this item. This meant that it is a private and subjective matter. Therefore, all the laws and regulations in government affairs would be based on the objective, scientific and technological principles that civilised nations embrace. Underneath this principle lay decades-long debates among the elites over why the Ottomans lagged behind Europe. Here, religion appeared to be the main culprit. It was considered the biggest obstacle to rationality and progress. By strictly constricting the religious domain, the Republic declared its intention to organise public life (education, the legal system, rights of citizens and so on) according to secular and not sacred rules.

Revolutionarism: This last principle states the Party's willingness to adhere to a revolutionary transformation of the Turkish state and society. It also mentions the commitment of the Party to protect these principles (each of them perceived as a revolution) when needed.[38]

These six principles generated a great deal of debate in the 1930s, when they were included in the Constitution. They continue to be the subjects of ideological debate in contemporary Turkey. While they seemed radical for the times, these

---

37. Ahmad, 1996, p. 18.

38. Köker, 1995, pp. 134–5. For a detailed analysis of each of the six principles, *see* L. Köker, 1995, pp. 133–209. In the last principle, the similarities with Mexico are striking. It seems like both regimes were trying to institutionalise their revolutions, either by making it a core principle of the Republic, as in the Turkish case, or by establishing a political party (PRI) as the embodiment of an 'institutionalised' revolution.

principles – mostly inherited from the reformist cadres of the late Ottoman elites – had a strongly conservative element, due to their embedded elitism. Instead of being the collective demands of the general public, emerging after a process of deliberation and negotiation, they were articulated by the elites of the time with their own vision of what was good for the general society. The elites had a self-assigned role as the guardians of the society, with a duty to enlighten the nation according to these ideals. In this regard, even the populism (*halkçılık*) principle did not have a genuinely participatory, democratic content.[39] For the elites, the top priority was to disseminate these principles to the rest of the society in the fastest and most effective way possible. Therefore, the direction of the six arrows was from the top to the bottom.

State–society relations during the single-party era: For the people, despite the people!

In order to spread the principles of Kemalist revolution and its modern-secular agenda, the Party wanted to establish more direct linkages with the rest of the society. Rather than building upon existing societal organisations, they preferred to start from scratch. 'From the early 1930s onwards, the PP government organised a drive to eliminate all forms of civil society organisations that were not directly linked to the party'.[40] Among them were the Turkish Women's Union, Free Masons, some professional organisations, like the teachers union, and the associations of journalists. Even the nationalist educational organisations, such as the Turkish Hearths (*Türk Ocakları*), were not spared.

> These independent organisations were replaced with new ones, which, however, were completely under party control: the women's branch of the PP replaced the women's union and the People's Houses (*Halkevleri*) were founded in February 1932 as successor to the Turkish Hearths and took over the latter's assets, primarily its buildings. The People's Houses soon became by far the most significant vehicle for mobilization of the party. The aims of the People's Houses were summarized by the party leadership as follows: to build national unity through the spread of culture and ideals, to bring villagers and town dwellers closer together, and to explain the principles of the People's Party to the masses.[41]

A total of 478 People's Houses and 4,322 People's Rooms were established between 1932 and 1950.[42] Their purpose was to re-educate the whole nation, inculcating the core ideals of the Republican regime. Given the 80 per cent

---

39. S. Mardin, *Jön Türklerin Siyasi Fikirleri 1895–1908* [*The Political Ideas of the Young Turks*], Istanbul: İletişim Publications, 1983, p. 35.
40. E. J. Zürcher, 2004: p.106.
41. *Ibid.*
42. C. Koçak, 1997, p. 115.

illiteracy rate in the country, activities were geared towards speeches, lectures, films, theatre, puppet shows, posters and concerts. The emphasis on art with a populist agenda shows strong similarities with the muralist movement in Mexico around the same time. Enlightenment and modernisation would disseminate through these venues. Needless to say, the educated middle classes (teachers, civil servants, officers and so on) were the natural agents of the process. Membership of these places was free to all but 'those higher up in the social scale were as good as obliged to take up membership'.[43]

Similarly to their late Ottoman counterparts, the Republican intelligentsia was also drawn to Auguste Comte's principles of *order* and *progress*. They wholeheartedly embraced positivism and its belief in transforming the social reality using objective, scientific methods. A natural consequence of this worldview was the desire of 'enlightened' individuals to be in charge of administration, in order to 'show the way to the masses'. Thus, the elitism of the Ottoman reformers and the Kemalist ones was rather similar. Despite their frequent references to populism and the popular classes, what they projected was an elite-driven social-transformation programme.[44]

With the establishment of People's Houses and People's Rooms, the CHP was creating a new public space, separate from workplace and homes, through which they could establish closer contact with society.[45] The Houses were the most concrete examples of the revolutionary elite's desire to leave their imprint not only on political life but also on culture and daily life as well. Dance, music, theatre and public lectures were mechanisms for spreading Kemalist ideals to the rest of the society. The concerts and ballroom dances at the People's Houses, for example, were great venues for women and men to get together in public space for entertainment. Their gymnasiums were dedicated to training a healthy and disciplined young generation. The use of traditional musical instruments (*ney*, *kanun*, and so on) was banned in these places. Instead, the western musical canon, particularly polyphonic music, was introduced to the people though the People's Houses. The party elites were especially impressed by the indoctrination capacity of theatre. They calculated that 'a play with a message' could reach out to 136,000 citizens in just a couple of days, through the means of 136 People's Houses.[46]

The purpose of People's Houses and Rooms was not limited to indoctrination. They also provided practical skills through vocational training. Courses on reading and writing, civics, foreign languages, typing, basic accounting, sewing, hat-making, gardening and so on were also offered regularly across the country. While the art departments of the Houses were providing the ideological components of westernisation, courses on vocational training equipped citizens with skills that

---

43. Zürcher, 2004, p. 108.

44. Köker, 1995, pp. 222–3.

45. N. Yeşilkaya, 'Halkevleri' ['People's Houses'], in *Modern Türkiye'de Siyasi Düşünce: Kemalizm (II)*, [*Political Thought in Modern Turkey: Kemalism*] İstanbul: İletişim Publications, 2001, p. 113.

46. Yeşilkaya, 2001, p. 115.

a modern lifestyle demanded. The village branches were critically important in offering literacy courses to peasants and providing them with some basic social services, such as healthcare. The ultimate goal was to 'unify' the nation through these institutions and create a 'people's nation', free of class conflict and based on Kemalist principles.[47]

Despite their overtly ideological agenda, the People's Houses and Rooms made numerous positive contributions to society. First, they were the secular alternatives to the mosques as public spaces for socialisation and collective action. Second, they had a critical role in increasing literacy through their reading and writing classes for adults. Third, they promoted gender equality by offering visibility and opportunity for women in public space. These contributions notwithstanding, they were still the mechanism by which the revolutionary elites sought to disseminate a new and westernised culture to the masses. Moreover, they were very much associated with the Party, despite the leaders' efforts to maintain formal autonomy. Thus, when the opposition party (DP) came to power, one of the first things it did was to close down the Houses and Rooms and confiscate their assets.

Economic policies of the single-party era

The economic situation of the Ottoman Empire before the republican era was rather bleak. Even though the Ottomans were not formally colonised by the Western powers, the economy was, by and large, under the control of foreign economic actors, be they Western countries, multinational companies or foreign merchants. This is why Korkut Boratav, the eminent Turkish political economist, referred to the late-Ottoman economy as *semi-colonized*.[48] He and other scholars of Ottoman economic history list numerous reasons for this. Firstly, there was the changing structure of Ottoman imports and exports. At the beginning of the nineteenth century, for example, the Ottomans were self-sufficient in textiles. This was not surprising since the empire had numerous provinces, such as Egypt, Bursa and Denizli, with strong textile industries. By the end of the nineteenth century, however, almost 90 per cent of domestic consumption was met by imported textiles.[49] This meant that the strongest sector in Ottoman economy was taken over by foreign competition in less than a century. 'The Ottoman economy was increasingly transformed into an exporter of primary products and an importer of manufactures'.[50]

Secondly, there was the deepening financial dependence of the Ottoman Empire. The scale and scope of foreign borrowing had been expanding exponentially since the Crimean War (1853–6). As the Empire continued to slide deeper and deeper into

47. Yeşilkaya, 2001, p. 116.
48. K. Boratav, *Türkiye İktisat Tarihi 1908–2002* [*Turkish Economic History 1908–2002*], İstanbul: İmge Publications, 2004.
49. Boratav, 2004, p. 20.
50. S. Pamuk, 'The evolution of fiscal institutions in the Ottoman Empire, 1500–1914', paper presented at the Thirteenth International Economic History Congress, Buenos Aires, 2002, p. 32.

foreign debt, it kept granting more economic privileges, known as capitulations, to foreign economic actors. These privileges turned the whole territory of the Empire into a wide-open market with virtually no barriers to entry and exit.

Finally, there was the Ottoman Public Debt Administration *(Düyun-u Umumiye)*, the iconic institution of Ottoman financial dependence. When the Empire encountered difficulties in servicing its mounting debt, lenders offered to become directly involved in the process. Thus, the OPDA was established in 1881 under the control and supervision of foreign lenders. The purpose of this institution was to collect government taxes and channel them directly to the lenders. 'For the following three decades until the outbreak of World War I, a sizable share of government revenues were controlled by the OPDA and applied to debt payments'.[51] This meant that the Empire could not exercise control over some of the most basic functions of government, such as tax-collection and fiscal policy.

The Turkish economy before the Great Depression (1908–29)

It would not be an overstatement to call this a period of wars, turmoil and rebellions. Between 1912 and 1922, much of the economic infrastructure was destroyed. Only in 1929 did the country regain its 1913 levels of GDP per capita.[52] Despite the predominantly agrarian character of the economy, the largest cities of the Empire, such as Istanbul and Izmir, had to import flour and other staples from abroad. During the war years, the country had to struggle with all the predictable economic evils: shortages, a black market and profiteering. The group that benefited the most from the economic hardships was the Muslim merchants. They accumulated large sums of wealth due to speculation in food prices and also due to their political connections.

The elites of the time were trying to replace the broken economic models of the past with new and successful ones. Having achieved political independence after a long and arduous struggle, they began to seek economic independence as well. Consequently, the Young Turk and Kemalist leadership wanted to establish a national bourgeoisie that could replace exploitative foreign capitalists. Just as the Mexicans nationalised the railroads, mines and oil sectors after the Revolution, their Turkish counterparts also expelled international capital. It was assumed that a native bourgeois class would keep their investments in the country and help bring prosperity. In such a climate, Turkish-Muslim merchants with political connections filled their coffers and began to form the nucleus of a newly emerging national bourgeoisie. Certain political elites took advantage of their status and established lucrative business careers as well.[53]

---

51. Pamuk, 2002, p. 30; *see also* S. Pamuk, 'The evolution of the financial institutions in the Ottoman Empire, 1600–1914', *Financial History Review* 2004, II(1), pp. 7–32.

52. S. Pamuk, 'Dünyada ve Türkiyede İktisadi Büyüme' ['Economic growth in the world and in Turkey'], *Uluslararası Ekonomi ve Dış Ticaret Politikaları*, [*International Economic and Trade Policies*] 2007, 1(2), p. 16.

53. A. Buğra, *Türkiye'de Devlet ve İşadamları*, [*State and Business in Turkey*], 2nd edn, İstanbul: İletişim Publications, 1997, pp. 67–74.

In the last decades of the Ottoman Empire, some intellectuals promoted a liberal economic regime but the majority still supported the statist 'national economy' (*milli iktisat*) model. They were, by and large, inspired by the German school, which advocated active state involvement in the economy in order to cultivate a national industrial bourgeoisie. Among the leading figures of the national economy model were, Ziya Gökalp, Yusuf Akçura and Tekin Alp. This model pledged rapid development and modernisation with the help of the state and was therefore particularly appealing to elites who already had substantial nationalist inclinations.

When the new Republic was established in 1923, the nationalist economic philosophy shaped the political-economic direction of the nation. It placed strong emphasis on the necessity of a strong national bourgeoisie as a prerequisite of a modern, developed nation. In the İzmir Economy Congress (1923) the main economic policies of the Republic were discussed and accepted. The Congress was composed of key economic actors, including farmers, merchants, industrialists and workers. Each group had bloc votes but the industrialists and workers were represented mostly by high-ranking bureaucrats. The format of this Congress, the modalities of representation and the role of state bureaucracy as the ultimate mediator are good examples to illustrate the highly corporatist character of the Republic from the very beginning.

The Economic Principles (*iktisadi esaslar*) endorsed by the Congress could be classified as developmentalist and mildly protectionist. Subsequent to the Congress came a series of nationalisations: from 1924–8, railroads were nationalised; in 1925 the tobacco industry was nationalised by establishing a public monopoly, TEKEL; and, in 1926, a law that required shipping to and from Turkish ports to be done solely in Turkish vessels was passed (*Kabotaj kanunu*). Regarding domestic–foreign joint ventures, Mustafa Kemal welcomed foreign investment to the country, as long as investors played by the same rules as national companies and did not seek special treatment.[54] As is discussed in the next chapter, the Revolutionary Constitution of Mexico (1917) also urged foreign companies operating on Mexican soil to abide by Mexican laws and *not* to seek favouritism or intervention from their home countries.[55] Thus, in the first quarter of the twentieth century, both countries shared a certain level of mistrust and scepticism towards the intentions of foreign capital.

---

54. Atatürk's Opening Remarks at İzmir Economy Congress, February 17, 1923. Accessed online through the Historical Archives of İzmir Economy University, Research Institute for İzmir Economy Congress, TBS No: 2006/01.

55. Article 27 of Mexican Constitution specifies the ownership of lands, waters, natural and subsoil resources and utilities. Among other restrictions, it includes the following statement regarding foreign property owners: 'Only Mexicans by birth or naturalization and Mexican companies have the right to acquire ownership of lands, waters, and their appurtenances, or to obtain concessions for the exploitation of mines or of waters. The State may grant the same right to foreigners, provided they agree before the Ministry of Foreign Relations to consider themselves as nationals in respect to such property, and bind themselves *not to invoke the protection of their governments* in matters relating thereto [...]' (*author addition*). Full text of the Mexican Constitution available at https://www.constituteproject.org/constitution/Mexico_2007 (last accessed 25 November 2014).

This was an important transitional period for both the Turkish economy and Turkish society. It was largely an agrarian and a raw-material-exporting economy (60–72 per cent of all exports were raw materials). Moreover, the economy was largely in the hands of foreign actors. Despite the revolutionary character of the new regime, it could not eliminate these twin problems right away. The first major obstacle was the lack of a national bourgeoisie with sufficient capital and knowhow to spearhead industrialisation. Political elites tried to resolve this by turning blind eye to the profiteering activities of Muslim entrepreneurs during the war years. Capital accumulation in native hands would eventually form the seed money for a national industry. The second economic problem, however, had a legal aspect to it. The economic clauses of the Lausanne Peace Treaty (1923) restricted the manoeuvres of the Republican elites. According to Lausanne, Turkey had to pay some of the Ottoman debt –two-thirds of it, to be specific – and had to maintain rather low tariff levels. On the one hand, this debt burden drained valuable state assets that could have been used for industrialisation. On the other hand, the 12.9 per cent overall tariff for imported goods further diminished the money that was going to the state coffers.[56] In short, until the end of 1920s, Turkey could not be as protectionist as it wanted. International economic and political developments after 1929, however, would turn out to be just the right context to fortify corporatism and implement a state-sector-dominant economic-development model.

On the eve of the Great Depression, the Turkish state was trying to create a suitable environment for the emergence of a national bourgeoisie. And it was partly successful in doing this. In less than two decades, a Muslim-Turkish bourgeoisie had sprung up.[57] The state was also maintaining an open-door policy towards foreign capital. But still, there was no major progress towards industrialisation. Even though the annual growth rate of industry was 10.2 per cent between 1924 and 1929 (the economy in general grew by 8.6 per cent in the same period), this was still inadequate because industry contributed only 11 per cent to GNP.[58]

The impact of the 1930s: The statist turn in the Turkish economy

The economic policies of the 1930s were the reverse of the model since 1908. While protectionism and state involvement in the economy had existed before (for example, the nationalisation of the railroads and the establishment of public monopolies in the 1920s), the 1930s marked the advent of import-substitution industrialisation (ISI) in Turkey. Immediately after the Great Depression, international conditions created an environment wherein the state could play a 'more encompassing role [...] in investment decisions, the generation of capital and ownership of enterprises'. In many ways, these attempts to industrialise

---

56. Boratav, 2004, p. 45.

57. Boratav, 2004, p. 61-61.

58. T. Çavdar, *Türkiye Ekonomisinin Tarihi (1900–1960)* [*The History of the Turkish Economy (1900–1960)*], Ankara: İmge Publishers, 2003, pp. 198–220.

through protectionism and replacing imports with domestic production 'paralleled the actions taken by Latin American countries'.[59]

As the shock waves of the Great Depression hit the world markets, prices of raw materials bottomed out in comparison to prices of manufactured goods. The price of wheat, for instance, dropped by 68 per cent.[60] Thus, it became next to impossible for underdeveloped nations to continue their free-trade policies. The West had clear dominance in manufactured goods. Peripheral economies, however, were, without exception, vested in agricultural goods and raw materials. Almost all of them, responded to this crisis with protectionism and, subsequently, realised the absolute necessity of industrialisation. Despite the protectionist barriers, the private sector in most countries did not have sufficient capital accumulation to finance the industrial development of the whole nation. Consequently, the state had to take on the locomotive role in import-substitution industrialisation until the 1960s.[61]

Leaders of the single-party regime in Turkey were not of one mind in their opinions on the economy. There was the more liberal wing, represented by Atatürk and Celal Bayar (Prime Minister 1937–8). This group saw the role of the state in the economy only as a temporary phenomenon, until the national bourgeoisie was strong enough to function on its own. In fact, Atatürk himself supported the establishment of a second party, largely to challenge the state-centric economic policies of the RPP. The Free Party (*Serbest Fırka*) experience (August–November 1930) was cut short, however, when it became a magnet for reactionary groups who were overwhelmed by the secular reforms of 1920s.

A prominent leader of the Free Party, Ağaoğlu, moved to academia after the closure of the party. On the issue of the weakness of private sector in Turkey, he too agreed with the state-centric wing of the party. However, contrary to them, Ağaoğlu insisted that all the state needed to do was to protect and support the private sector, not replace it. He claimed that, by its nature, the state sector could not be as productive as private enterprise because bureaucrats could never be experts in running profitable businesses. Economic development could only take place when private entrepreneurs took initiatives in a liberal environment. To make his point, Ağaoğlu gave Ford as an example:

> Having started as labourers, Fords are now creating and accumulating vast sums of wealth with the experience and other innovative qualities they acquired from their environment [...] This is something, and in fact, a very important thing.[62]

According to him, the reason why eastern societies lagged behind in economic terms was because the state put authoritarian pressure on private

59. H. J. Barkey, 'State autonomy and the crisis of import substitution', *Comparative Political Studies* 1989, 22(3), p. 297.
60. Boratav, 2004, p. 67.
61. Barkey, 1989, pp. 297–8.
62. M. Türkeş, *Kadro Hareketi*, İstanbul: İmge Publications, 1999, p. 164.

entrepreneurs. The solution he offered was to establish a genuine parliamentary democracy in the country and support private entrepreneurs.[63] Unfortunately, the extraordinary economic conditions of the 1930s did not create a suitable environment for the implementation of these ideas. With the overall collapse of the world markets, the statist wing in the party began to dominate national economic policies.[64]

Almost all developing countries, including the Latin American ones, saw this as the crisis of the world capitalist system and perceived it as a window of opportunity to develop their national industries. They initiated the first attempts at industrialisation through large-scale public investment in manufacturing.[65] As the dominant paradigm in international political economy of the time, the 'dependency school'[66] emphasised that the economic exchange between the West and the underdeveloped rest happened on a very unequal basis, with the former dominated the high-value-added manufacturing sector while the latter was confined to exporting agricultural and raw materials.

This dependency argument was also mentioned in the first Five Year Development Plan (1933) of Turkey. Given the unequal terms of trade with the advanced Western nations, it deemed industrialisation an absolute necessity for the country. The state started to expand its role in the economy as investor, manufacturer and regulator. From the 1930s on, a set of legal reforms consolidated this new economic role.[67] Government gained authority to regulate exports and placed quotas on imports. Remaining enterprises still owned by foreigners were nationalised. The banking system was brought under state control. Price controls were imposed by the state on most staples. State monopolies were declared in many sectors, such as steel, energy, and municipal services. In other sectors and mining, there were no government monopolies but the state was still the locomotive of economic activity.[68]

Despite the rapid industrial growth and capital accumulation of the 1930s, the country did not have a chance to enjoy it due to the outbreak of World War II. Even though Turkey did not formally join the war, it suffered all the related economic hardships during the 1940s. There was a significant decrease in production followed by enormous surges in inflation. Wheat production, in particular, decreased by 50 per cent when most of the adult male population was called to take up arms

---

63. Türkeş, 1999, pp. 165–8.

64. Ahmad, 1996, p. 21.

65. V. Bulmer-Thomas, *The Economic History of Latin America Since Independence*, Cambridge: Cambridge University Press, 2003; *see especially* chapter 7, 'Policy, performance, and structural change in the 1930s' and chapter 9, 'Inward-looking development in the postwar period'.

66. The dependency school originated the idea that colonialism was to blame for the underdevelopment of the Third World. Among the leading scholars of the dependency school are Raul Prebish, A. G. Frank and P. Baran; since it emerged in the Latin American context, they are often called *dependistas*.

67. Pamuk, 2007, p.16, K. Boratav, 2004, pp. 65–6.

68. Boratav, 2004, p. 70.

and its price shot up by 200 per cent.[69] There were chronic food shortages in large cities and black markets emerged in virtually every sector. Under such desperate circumstances, the government imposed strict price controls, distributed staples by ration and imposed two extraordinary taxes in order to supplement dwindling state revenues.

The first of the extraordinary taxes came in November 1942. The Wealth Tax (*Varlık Vergisi*) was a one-time-only tax that was calculated on all the assets of a citizen. The payment was due in one month and there could be no objections to the amount. Individuals were compelled to sell or give up their properties and businesses in order to meet this overwhelming financial burden. Many businesses changed hands, from non-Muslim to Muslim owners, during this process.[70] Those who could not pay were sent to labour camps in the East. They had to work off their debt under notoriously harsh conditions. Most perished either on the way, or in the labour camps, where they were largely forgotten.[71] Statistics later revealed the discriminatory nature of this tax. More that half of it came from the non-Muslim citizens. It did, however, provide significant income for the state. In 1943, 38 per cent of state expenditure was financed from the Wealth Tax.[72]

The second extraordinary tax was imposed on agricultural goods. It was a 10 per cent tax on all agricultural production, very similar to the Ottoman tax of tithe (*aşar*) that was abolished during Ataturk's progressive reforms. Needless to say, this placed an enormous burden on the rural sector. The single-party regime of the CHP was gradually alienating itself from most sectors of society. Its wartime economic measures were distancing the party from both rural and urban working classes. Price and wage controls, imposed to curb the soaring inflation, were disproportionately hurting workers and peasants. Added to this was a regressive and *ad hoc* taxation policy, which fuelled public discontent even further.

When the extraordinary measures of the war economy were finally over in 1946, the Muslim bourgeoisie was much better off in comparison to all the other classes. They had secured vast amounts of wealth due to both profiteering

---

69. Boratav, 2004, pp. 83–4.

70. The Sabancı Group began its evolution as an industrial giant when its founder, Haci Ömer Sabancı, purchased a factory in Kayseri from a Russian Jew who hastily had to sell the place in order to pay his Wealth Tax; *see* Buğra, 1997, pp. 123–4. Today, Sabancı Group is the second-largest conglomerate in Turkey, having partnerships with Aviva, Bridgestone, Carrefour, Citi, Philip Morris and many other global corporate giants. In 2013, the consolidated revenue of Sabancı Holdings was US$ 12.7 billion, with an operating profit of $2.6 billion: *see* http://www.sabanci. com (last accessed 10 April 2015).

71. Very few resources exist on the tragic consequences of the Wealth Tax. According to Buğra, most of the non-Muslim business elites who survived the ordeal are treating it as a nightmare they try to forget, hence are reluctant to rehash the old memories; *see* Buğra, 1997, pp. 169–70. One of the best accounts of the time is actually a novel called *Salkım Hanımın Taneleri*. It was written by a Muslim bureaucrat turned businessman, who was born in the 1930s. The book was later made into a television movie by the state-owned channel TRT and created significant public debate.

72. Boratav, 2004, p. 85.

and the effect of the state's deliberate policies of transferring the wealth of non-Muslims to Muslims. Yet, even the Muslim bourgeoisie was critical of the CHP's economic policies. First, they were unhappy about the *ad hoc* taxation policies. Even though they benefited significantly from the Wealth Tax, they also became resentful towards the state. Essentially, they had to stand on the sidelines as the state confiscated the lifetime wealth of established people and let them perish in labour camps. This was a valuable lesson for the emerging bourgeoisie. They realised that they should not 'rely upon the good will of the [CHP] government or its leader and the President of the country, İsmet İnönü'.[73]

The second issue that disturbed the Muslim bourgeoisie, particularly the landed elites, was the CHP's land-reform proposal. On 1 January 1945, the statist wing of the CHP came up with a bill that proposed large-scale reforms to provide land and other agricultural means to landless peasants. According to the proposal, all properties larger than 500 acres would be nationalised and distributed to the landless, along with idle treasury and public lands. Furthermore, the government was going to provide agricultural machinery and credit to the rural sector in order to increase its productivity. It was assumed that some 5 million citizens would be affected when the land reform was implemented, hence Turkey would transform into a nation of small family farmers.[74]

After long and heated discussions in the parliament, the CHP managed to push through the land-reform legislation with unanimity. It became clear to the economic elites (urban and rural) that if they wanted to steer the economic policies towards their preferred routes, they needed to sever ties with the CHP and establish an independent political party.[75] Thus, the four most vocal leaders of opposition within the CHP split from the party on the grounds that the party did not operate under democratic principles.

The end of the single-party regime (1946–50)

Four prominent dissidents from the CHP established the Democrat Party (DP) in January 1947. It endorsed the Six Arrows of Kemalism, which were already incorporated into the Constitution. However, it differentiated itself from the ruling CHP on three grounds. First, the DP argued that as their name implied, democracy was the most crucial issue on their agenda. They promised to promote a democratic regime by means of curbing the excesses of the government and expanding individual liberties. Second, the party claimed to be a bottom-up political movement, receiving its strength and vigour from the people. This was particularly appealing to the masses who felt they had been subjugated by

---

73. E. Kalaycioglu, *Turkish Dynamics: Bridge across troubled lands*, New York: Palgrave, 2005, p. 70.

74. B. Lewis, *The Emergence of Modern Turkey*, New York: Oxford University Press, 2002, pp. 474–5.

75. Ahmad, 1996, pp. 14–15.

the top-down reform agenda of the CHP's bureaucratic elites for far too long.
Having sensed this public resentment, the DP elites trumpeted populist messages
throughout their campaigns. The last point of differentiation was in the economy.
Contrary to the entrenched statism of the CHP, the leaders of the DP emphasised
their belief in the importance of the private sector for economic development and
prosperity.

The first multi-party elections in Turkey were held on 21 June 1946. They
turned out to disgrace the reputation of single-party rule because of a too-blatant
and amateurish attempt to rig the election results. According to the election rules,
voting was to be done *openly* while the counting of the ballots was in *secret*. The
CHP had mobilised all the resources at its discretion to block the electoral success
of the DP. With the state apparatus solidly backing the CHP, it got 390 of the 465
seats in the Parliament while the DP could only get 65 seats.[76] Nonetheless, this
was the very last breath of the single-party regime. It could no longer maintain the
corporatist network that simultaneously catered to and controlled multiple sectors
of Turkish society. The relations of the two dominant groups, the state-centric
bureaucratic elites and the urban and rural economic elites, were strained in an
irreconcilable way after six years of wartime mobilisation and economic distress.
Moreover, the decades-long ideological bombardment that the CHP had carried out
in the name of modernisation had alienated a large majority of the society, which
was resistant to abandoning its traditional values. Secularism was the ideological
cornerstone of the Kemalist regime. While the concept implied a separation of
religious matters from that of state, in the Turkish context, it was employed in
such a way as to exert central state control over all aspects of religious life. This
became a major cause of discontent in society that was 80 per cent rural and deeply
attached to traditional values and symbols.[77]

After the rigged elections of 1946, the first free and fair elections were held in
14 May 1950. Under Adnan Menderes' leadership, the Democrat Party declared
its victory and ended the single-party chapter in Turkish history. Sixty per cent
of the electorate who went to the ballot box cast their vote *against* the CHP. The
National Chief, İnönü, could barely get elected from his hometown, Malatya.[78]
The leader of the DP, Adnan Menderes, was a large landowner from the Aegean
region. Despite having been operating within the CHP ranks until its break-up, the
socio-economic roots of top DP leaders were significantly different from those of
the CHP.

In his book *State and Class in Turkey*, Çağlar Keyder provides a lucid,
class-based analysis study of this momentous transition in the late 1940s and
early 1950s. He argues that after the collapse of the Ottoman Empire, it was the

---

76. Ahmad, 1996, pp. 32–3.

77. B. Toprak, *Islam and Political Development*, Leiden: Brill, 1981, pp. 46–53.

78. In the 1950 general elections, the DP received 53.35% of the votes and 408 seats (out of 487) and
the CRP 39.78% of votes and 69 seats; M. Tunçay, *Çağdaş Türkiye 1908–1980* [*Contemporary
Turkey 1908–1980*], Istanbul: Cem, 1989, p. 182.

bureaucratic class – not the bourgeoisie – that was in charge of the new nation-state.[79] By the 1950s, discontent with the economic policies and ideological agenda of the bureaucratic class had reached epic proportions. Particularly the domestic bourgeoisie – sceptical of the statist economic policies of the CHP and concerned about its *ad hoc* taxation regime and socialist-leaning land-reform programme – wanted to flex its own political muscles in national politics. The key to the success of the bourgeoisie and the DP leaders, in terms of offering a viable alternative to single-party rule, was their populist discourse. Rather than articulating their opposition solely in economic terms, they emphasised universal freedoms. Because of this, not only did conservative sectors of society flock into the DP but other ideological groups threw their support behind the party too. In the 1950 elections, even the Communist Party of Turkey wholeheartedly supported the DP.[80] In short, according to Keyder, the political transformation of the 1950s was a bourgeois revolution and, because of this very nature, it brought the country liberal economic and political measures.

The peaceful transfer of power from single-party rule marks the first important step towards democracy in Turkey. In fact, a leading scholar of democratisation in Turkey, Ergun Özbudun, states that, '[t]echnically, Turkey is not a third wave democracy but a second wave democracy'.[81] Because of this peaceful democratic transition and the multi-party experience until the 1960 military intervention, it is plausible to separate Turkey from the 1970s 'third wave' and place it amongst the second-wave democracies. The growing power of the opposition during the single party regime, culminating in the electoral success of the DP, had managed to usher Turkey into an era of relative democratic freedom.

Many scholars of Turkish political development mention the importance of the international context when they look at the political transition in 1950. It has been well documented that during the early part of the 1940s, Turkey had disturbingly close relations with Germany. There were economic agreements between the two countries to facilitate trade and, in 1941 a ten-year friendship and non-aggression pact was signed. Throughout WWII, Turkey tried to remain neutral, despite significant pressures from the Allies – and particularly from Churchill – to join the war against the Axis powers. However, the official neutrality policy was not reciprocated by actual practice at all times.[82] Turkish–German relations experienced their heyday in 1941, especially when Turkey started selling chrome to Germany, which, no doubt, was used in arms production.[83]

---

79. C. Keyder, *Türkiye'de Devlet ve Sınıflar*, [*State and Classes in Turkey*] 6th edn, İstanbul: İletişim Publications, 2000, p. 9.

80. Keyder, 2000, pp. 169–70.

81. E. Ozbudun, *Contemporary Turkish Politics: Challenges to democratic consolidation*, Boulder, CO and London: Lynne Rienner Publishers, 2000, p. 6 .

82. S. Deringil, *Turkish Foreign Policy During the Second World War: An 'active' neutrality*, New York: Cambridge University Press, 1989.

83. A. C. Edwards, 'The impact of the war on Turkey', *International Affairs*, 1946, 22(3), pp. 389–400.

Turkey was hesitant to enter the war alongside the Allies for two reasons. First, Turkey almost always felt an imminent Soviet threat due to the suspicion that the Soviets had an eye on the Bosphorus and Dardanelles Straits. Consequently, it was reluctant to see the Soviets expand their military power by defeating the Germans. Second, some influential generals in the Turkish military were under the impression that the Germans had an invincible army. Thus, the military establishment was reluctant to join the war on the side of the Allies. Consequently, Turkey played a delicate diplomatic game by maintaining its neutrality on the one hand and by demanding military equipment from the Allies who were pressuring them to take sides.

The power balance during the war suddenly started to change after the Japanese attack on Pearl Harbor in 1941. The US entered the war as a fresh and strong military power. Furthermore, the Soviets defeated the Germans on their own and were now more assertive. Thus, the Soviets did not want or need Turkey as an ally any more. In fact, after the war, Stalin pursued a rather hostile policy towards Turkey, demanding cession of territory in eastern Turkey and asking for extensive rights of passage along the Straits. Fortunately, the UK and the US sided with Turkey. Both the Truman Doctrine (1947) which provided military aid to Greece and Turkey to bring them closer to the US sphere of influence, and Turkish membership in NATO (1952) anchored Turkey solidly to the Western bloc, and thereby averted the Soviet threat.[84]

The international political climate after WWII was clearly favourable to liberal Western democracies. The authoritarian and totalitarian regimes in Germany, Italy and Japan were defeated and discredited. Moreover, Stalin's hostility was pushing the Turkish government into the arms of Western powers, who did not seem to harbour any territorial ambitions towards Turkey. In light of these developments, the Turkish rapprochement with the democratic Western bloc accelerated. The pro-German Turkish Joint Chief of Staff, Fevzi Çakmak, was sent into retirement and a more neutral figure, Kazım Orbay, replaced him. When the US stepped up its efforts to claim superpower status, Turkey was included in the Truman doctrine, along with Greece, and received significant amounts of military aid as a member of the Western bloc. When accounting for the end of the single-party era in Turkey and the liberalisation of the domestic political climate, it is also important to take into account these international power dynamics of the time.[85] Both the class arguments and the international dynamics arguments offer compelling reasons to explain the demise of the single-party regime in Turkey.

---

84. F. A. Vali, *The Turkish Straits and NATO*, Stanford, CA: Hoover Institution Press, 1972.

85. H. Yilmaz, 'Democratization from above in response to international context: Turkey 1945–1950', *New Perspectives on Turkey* 1997,17, pp. 1–37. A celebrity in social sciences, Samuel Huntington also refers to the Turkish transition in the 1950s as an example of how US victory in WWII had impressed other nations and encouraged them to switch to democracy. 'No one copies a loser', says Huntington, and quotes extensively from the Turkish Premier Menderes praising the victory of the free world (S. P. Huntington, 'American ideals versus American institutions', *Political Science Quarterly* 1982, 97(1); reprinted in, J. Ikenberry (ed.) *American Foreign Policy*, 5th edn, New York: Pearson, 2005, p. 242.

However, other scholars argue that these were necessary but not sufficient factors to trigger democratic transition in Turkey. In the case of class arguments, Özbudun states that certainly the economic stratification of the country was more pronounced towards the end of the 1940s. However, the CHP had the option to modify itself and incorporate the rising economic classes. This way, the story would have been very similar to the PRI experience in Mexico, and the single-party regime in Turkey could have survived for many more decades:

> Turkish society had reached a somewhat higher level of social differentiation and complexity by the end of single-party rule, but the RPP [CHP] had other options, such as broadening its elite recruitment base to include pro-business groups or mobilizing poor peasants with the help of land reform. The experience of the Mexican Institutional Revolutionary Party [PRI] suggests that a pragmatic single party can show sufficient adaptability to accommodate newly emerging groups [...] Consequently, the main reasons for the Turkish transition should be sought in the nature of the RPP authoritarian regime.[86]

On the issue of international support for regime-change in Turkey, certain prominent scholars argue that all the West (or the US) did was create a favourable atmosphere. There was no direct meddling in the domestic affairs of Turkey, nor explicit back-peddling after the democratic elections in 1950. According to Bernard Lewis, '[t]he rulers of Turkey were not likely to change their form of government and surrender power to an opposition, merely to please a foreign state'.[87] Moreover, the standard US foreign-policy position was more concerned with the loyalty of its allies than with the characteristics of their political regimes. Especially in a region like the Middle East, stability was a much higher priority than democracy or multi-party competition.

The end of single-party rule in Turkey has more to do with the nature of the Party and its leadership than class dynamics or international pressures. Here, a comparative analysis of the Turkish experience would illustrate two crucial points. First, despite its attempts to spread the Kemalist reforms and reshape the nation according to the 'Six Arrows', the CHP remained largely a *cadre* party. Consequently, it could never enjoy the mass appeal of the Mexican PRI or other successful single-party regimes that capitalised on mass mobilisation and popularity. The CHP remained the party of the 'small, westernized, educated elite'.[88] Second, this elite cadre had positivist, rational and pro-Western commitments. They perceived the move towards a multi-party regime as a natural stage of development.[89] Thus, they tried to facilitate it when the time was right. Consequently, when the global liberal tide was on the rise after the WWII, the National Chief himself led the

86. Ozbudun, 2000, p. 21 (italics in original).

87. B. Lewis, *The Emergence of Modern Turkey*, 3rd edn, New York: Oxford University Press, 2001, p. 315.

88. Ozbudun, 2000, p. 23.

89. D. A. Rustow, 'Atatürk as a founder of a state', *Daedalus* 1968, 97(3), pp. 793–828.

way to the multi-party era. Below is an excerpt from a *New York Times* article that captures the dynamics of the moment succinctly:

> Real authority in the country rests with the leadership of the dominant People's Republican Party. It has managed to establish firm control of economic resources in this *étatist* state, nominate candidates, supervise elections and regulate the strength of the opposition [...] But this is changing [...] President İsmet İnönü, who actually has occupied a position comparable to that of a dictatorship despite parliamentary trappings, seems to be deliberately fostering the drive toward more real democracy, using his authority to impose the concept from above while other elements work for it from a base below [...] At this stage in history, there is no doubt that leaders of the regime are seriously seeking to push this country at a more than gradual rate toward democracy.[90]

Turkey on the multi-party roller coaster (1950–1980)

The 'İnönü factor' was a critical determinant when the CHP handed over political power to the opposition in 1950. As the President and the most revered military commander of the War of Independence, İnönü was at the top of the political hierarchy and enjoyed a great deal of respect from the military. His decision to respect the landslide electoral victory of the opposition party in 1950 is very much comparable to the role that Ernesto Zedillo played in the Mexican elections of 2000. Zedillo did not manipulate the state machinery to tilt the election results – as happened under his predecessor, Salinas, when the government computers 'broke down' while tallying the votes, and worked again a few days later, showing a comfortable margin favouring the PRI.[91] Unlike Salinas, Zedillo decided that he would respect the outcome of a democratic race. Thus the seventy-one-year-reign of the single party ended in Mexico. Likewise, İnönü also made a historic choice and let the democratic process unfold rather than resorting to ballot-burning or instigating a military intervention.

Large sectors of Turkish society were also tired of the single-party regime and its failed economic policies. Associated with the military-bureaucratic elites, the CHP had largely abandoned the rural masses as well as the merchants and private-business-owners. Even modestly well off urban constituents were discontented. The priority given to public servants in the food-rationing system alienated many people who did not have direct links to the bureaucracy. The DP and its leader Menderes took advantage of these convenient resentments. Soon after coming to power, Menderes unlocked significant amounts of credit for the agricultural sector.

---

90. 'Turkey is advancing toward western democracy: President İnönü spearheading the campaign', *The New York Times*, 29 March 1950, p. 24 (*author addition*).

91. Mexicans used the expression *el sistema se cayó*, referring to the incident when the computer system crashed. But the expression has a dual meaning, since the word *el sistema* is also used to describe the PRI regime. When President Salinas needed to openly resort to fraud to determine his successor, the popular perception was that the PRI system was seriously in trouble.

Thus, he marked the definitive character of the DP as the party of the rural sector for decades to come. Below is an excerpt from an oral history study conducted in central Anatolia in recent years. The statements of this old woman about the scarcities and religious repression during the single-party era and subsequent prosperity that came with the DP, reflect the popular perceptions on both parties that still linger among the rural population:

> [The state] did not take care of us at all. Then came working in road construction. Those with five children could be excused from it. Those without five children would grab their bread and for ten–fifteen days work on roads, in snow and winter. They would make roads for the villages [...] Then Menderes came. He didn't have us work on the roads, he brought us the roads, the [drinking] water. But they hanged him in exchange. We used to read the old script [...] They took that from us. They burnt the books of imams, hanged them as well. God forbid, even imams were scarce [...] After that came tithe. Can one person be enough for ten tasks? We could find neither soap, nor salt or pots, we suffered so much [...] Came Menderes, and we were relived. God is our witness [...][92]

In many ways, the 1950 elections caused the 'bifurcation of the elites' in Turkey.[93] From then on, the CHP became associated with state-centric military and bureaucratic interests, whereas the DP gained a more popular following from among the sectors that felt subjugated by the former elites. Heper refers to this as the 'state elite' versus the 'political elite' division. In this elite competition, the state elites considered themselves as the guardians of the Republic and its modernisation and secularisation agenda. The political elites, however, positioned themselves squarely against these issues, by catering to the traditional constituency in exchange for electoral support. Democracy and respect for the will of people were popular notions among the political elites, for they wanted to capitalise on the failures of the state elites to win the hearts and minds of the ordinary people.

Once in power, however, the DP proved to be not much of a champion of democracy. On the one hand, it tried to appease its conservative constituency by making religion more visible in the public sphere. In many cases, this amounted to the use and abuse of religion for political ends. The DP also doled out substantial resources to its rural constituents, in the form of agricultural subsidies. On the other hand, Menderes himself and the top leadership of the DP considered the state bureaucracy and other prominent public institutions as the bulwarks of CHP rule. Thus, they mounted an extensive campaign against the bureaucracy, military, universities, national radio and television (TRT), and against the CHP itself.

---

92. S. Aydın, *'Amacımız Devletin Bekası': Demokratikleşme Sürecinde Devlet ve Yurttaşlar* [*'Our Goal is the Longevity of the State': State and citizens in the democratization process*] İstanbul: TESEV Publications, 2006, p. 41.

93. M. Heper, 'The Ottoman legacy and Turkish politics', *Journal of International Affairs* 2000, 54(1), pp. 63.

Below is a list of some of the DP policies that aimed at appeasing the conservative constituency and stifling the opposition:

- Purging of the high command of the Turkish Armed Forces: Menderes was suspicious of their 'too close' relations with the CHP, and was wary of a military coup.
- Legal moves to confiscate CHP assets: the purpose was to weaken the opposition party financially.
- Banning political activities of university professors through amendments to the University Law: Protests on campuses were suppressed heavy-handedly, rectors dragged around by police.
- Purges in the bureaucracy: compulsory retirement for high-ranking judges, bureaucrats and professors.
- Compulsory religion classes in public schools.
- Return to Arabic calls to prayer: previously, calls to prayer were done in Turkish. Broadcasting of Arabic prayers on public radio, TRT (Turkish Radio Television).
- Increasing the number of religious vocational schools training imams and preachers: this eventually created a highly problematic dualism in the Turkish education system: national-secular schools *versus* parochial-clerical schools.
- Censoring the press: the new Press Law threatened journalists with imprisonment if their writing 'harmed the prestige of the members of the government or the private citizen'. It denied journalists the right to defend themselves.
- Purging the opposition within the DP: Menderes became rather intolerant of dissent and periodically purged critical voices from his own party rank and file.[94]
- Anti-communist rhetoric and practice: the DP systematically intimidated left-wing intelligentsia by firing academics, closing their journals and taking legal action against them. The CHP was also the target of this anti-communist fury. Menderes accused the political campaigns of the CHP of being 'just like the Moscow radio'.
- Establishing the Patriotic Front (*Vatan Cephesi*), a proxy organisation for compelling citizens to join the DP. The names of new and existing members of the PF were continuously read on public radio in order to intimidate those who had not yet joined.[95]

The majoritarian character of the Turkish electoral system amplified the electoral success of the DP in parliament. With slightly more than 50 per cent of the votes, the DP could control more than 90 per cent of parliamentary seats.

---

94. F. Ahmad, *Bir Kimlik Peşinde Türkiye*, İstanbul: Bilgi University Publications, 2007, pp. 131–8, published in English as *Turkey: The quest for identity*, trans. C. S. Karadeli, London: Oneworld Publications, 2000.

95. F. Ahmad, 2007, p. 140.

Victories in consecutive elections plus their overwhelming majority in the TGNA emboldened the party leaders. When they split from the CHP, 'democracy' was the number-one agenda item in their political campaign. Because of this, they could appeal to a large but heterogeneous constituency. However, once in power they '[...] considered any opposition to them as intolerable, reprehensible and illegitimate'.[96] This was largely because the DP leaders had spent a sizable portion of their political careers within the CHP. Despite all their initial pledges for democracy, their political socialisation was not very conducive to pluralism or dissent. They interpreted democracy as *majoritarianism* and were further emboldened by their electoral victories, which they considered as an unequivocal mandate from the people. When Prime Minister Menderes survived a deadly plane crash near Gatwick Airport in London, the incident was quickly turned into a political campaign attributing miraculous qualities to Menderes and thereby affirming his destiny to lead the nation.[97]

The excesses of DP rule eventually brought the first military coup in Turkey, on 27 May 1960, and the junta terminated the political careers of the DP troika, including Menderes himself, at the gallows. From then on, the military became a rather dominant actor in Turkish politics, looming over the competition between the civilian political parties like an elephant in the room. More importantly, the DP experience and subsequent military coup sharpened the centre–periphery division in Turkey, which has still not been bridged. In Kalaycioglu's words:

> A paradox started to take hold in Turkey ever since: The military trusted the [CHP], the party of the Center, which the people have not usually been inclined to trust or support at the polls, while the people tended to trust the parties of the periphery, such as DP, and support them at the polls, which in turn have been viewed with great suspicion by the Center, the [CHP] [...] and the military.[98]

The 1961 Constitution and the fragmentation of the Turkish party system

The new Turkish Constitution was prepared by the leading academics of the country under the auspices of the military. After the experience of the 1950s, which almost amounted to a *tyranny of the majority*, the 1961 Constitution tried to establish institutional checks on elected governments. Even though it granted extensive individual rights and liberties, the right-wing and populist parties à la DP never really approved of the 1961 Constitution. First, they considered the constitution a by-product of the military coup that deposed and executed their legendary leader Menderes. Second, they considered the institutional checks that were adopted by this constitution as a nuisance or bureaucratic barrier against the 'popular will'. Lastly, they disliked the liberal

---

96. Kalaycioglu, 2005, p. 89.
97. Ahmad, 2007, p. 139.
98. Kalaycioglu, 2005, p. 90.

spirit of the Constitution. For them, the constitution granted far too many rights and liberties to a people who were not yet ready for such 'luxuries'. Thus, it was not uncommon to hear the right-wing politicians of the time referring the Constitution as 'two sizes large for Turkey'. The following are some of the key aspects of the 1961 Constitution:

- It created a bicameral legislative system. The upper chamber (Senate) was expected to put the brake on the decisions of the directly-elected lower chamber.
- It established a Constitutional Court to bring the legislative functions of the Parliament under judicial review.
- It established the autonomy of certain public institutions, such as the universities, and public radio and television, in order to insulate them from direct political pressure.
- It expanded social rights and civil liberties.
- It granted independence to the judiciary and provided certain protections for the rest of the civilian bureaucracy.[99]
- It established the State Planning Organisation (*Devlet Planlama Teşkilatı, DPT*) for economic planning and monitoring of the economic policies of the elected governments.
- It established the National Security Council, NSC (*Milli Güvenlik Kurulu -MGK*).

The NSC consisted of the President, the Prime Minister and the Ministers of the Interior and Foreign Affairs, the Joint Chiefs of Staff and the heads of each branch of the armed forces. It would supposedly advise the cabinet over national security matters. However, the numerical majority of the military members, as well as later constitutional amendments that elevated the function of the Council to *notification*, made the NSC the foremost institution in determining the direction of Turkish politics.[100]

When the military regime closed down the Democrat Party, the confounded voters of the periphery split their votes between two parties, each claiming to be the true successor of the DP. According to Sayarı, '[t]he DP's unnatural death, coupled with the switch from a plurality to a proportional representation (PR) system in the 1961 elections, increased the level of party fragmentation in the early 1960s.'[101] In Kalaycıoğlu's terms, smaller and more ideological parties 'came out

---

99. Ozbudun, 2000, pp. 53–6.

100. Kalaycıoğlu, 2005, p. 94. As will be discussed in Chapter Five, the NSC proved to be one of the biggest obstacles to the democratic consolidation of Turkey. By increasing the civilian members of the NSC, democratic reforms under EU auspices tilted the numerical balance in favour of civilians. Nevertheless, the military still carries a significant weight within the NSC. At times, by imposing its own 'red lines' over the NSC agenda, it frames the issues and determines the boundaries of legitimate debate.

101. S. Sayarı, 'The changing party system', in S. Sayarı and Y. Esmer (eds) *Politics, Parties and Elections in Turkey*, Boulder, CO and London: Lynne Reinner Publishers, 2002, p.12.

of the closet' during this period. The CHP benefited from the confusion and won a plurality of the votes in the first post-coup election.

From the 1960s on, the Turkish political spectrum became a lot more diverse, fragmented and polarised. Extreme-right, extreme-left and religious revivalist parties joined the mainstream electoral race. The first party with a strong ideological component was the Turkish Workers Party (*Türkiye İşçi Partisi* or TIP), established in 1961. Then, in 1964, came the ultra-nationalist party of Colonel Alparslan Türkeş (a leading figure in the 1960 coup), the Republican Peasant and Nation Party (CKMP), later named the National Action Party (*Milliyetçi Hareket Partisi* or MHP). The religiously conservative and Islamist elements were united under Prof. Necmettin Erbakan's National Order Party (*Milli Nizam Partisi*) in 1970, which was later renamed the National Salvation Party (*Milli Selamet Partisi* MSP).[102]

In order to prevent the excessive majoritarianism of the previous era, the 1961 Constitution had adopted the proportional representation (PR) principle. This way, political divisions in society would be better reflected in Parliament. It was also assumed that the PR principle and the multi-party system would be strong incentives for the parties to trim their excesses, negotiate and compromise, if they wanted to win a governing majority in the Parliament. Once again, Turkish politics would prove these expectations wrong.

Military, politics and the perils of constitutional engineering

The 1961 Constitution introduced the coalition phenomenon into Turkish political culture. For the next two decades, no party could win a governable majority in the Parliament – except for the two decisive elections in 1965 and 1969.[103] The combination of strict proportional representation with a multi-party system resulted in a series of weak coalition governments (*see* Table 3.2). Even though institutional constraints were compelling the parties to join forces, politics was still considered to be a zero-sum game. Despite the medley of parties in the parliament, political culture was not hospitable to negotiation and compromise. These were considered 'weaknesses' especially by the political leaders of the time.

Coalition governments could be formed when the party leaders agreed upon the partitioning of the ministries among the parties. Afterwards, each ministry was run solely by the party that controlled it, as if it were completely autonomous from other parties in the coalition. Each ministry was treated as a key asset for doling out patronage to the loyal party constituency. When the AP controlled the Ministry of Education, for example, it would only hire and promote AP sympathisers and the services of the Ministry of Education would be channelled almost exclusively to provinces known to be AP strongholds. Likewise, other parties would run their

102. E. J. Zürcher, *Turkey: A modern history*, London and New York: I. B. Tauris, 1994, pp. 259–70.
103. Sayarı, 2002, p. 13.

Table 3.2: Prime Ministers of Republic of Turkey, 1920–80

Year		Name	Dates
1920–5	1	Mustafa Kemal Atatürk	3 May 1920 – 24 January 1921
	2	Fevzi Çakmak	24 January 1921– 9 July 1922
	3	Rauf Orbay	July 12, 1922 – August 13, 1923
	4	Fethi Okyar	August 14, 1923 – October 27, 1923
	5	İsmet İnönü	November 30, 1923 – November 21, 1924
	6	Fethi Okyar	November 21, 1924 – March 2, 1925
1925-1930s	7	İsmet İnönü	March 4, 1925 – October 25, 1937
	8	Celal Bayar	October 25, 1937 – January 25, 1939
1940s	9	Refik Saydam	January 25, 1939 – July 8, 1942
	10	Şükrü Saraçoğlu	July 8, 1942 – August 5, 1946
	11	Recep Peker	August 5, 1946 – September 9, 1947
	12	Hasan Saka	September 9, 1947 – January 14, 1949
1950s	13	Şemsettin Günaltay	January 15, 1949 – May 22, 1950
	14	Adnan Menderes	May 22, 1950 – May 27, 1960
1960s	15	Cemal Gürsel	May 28, 1960 – November 20, 1961
	16	İsmet İnönü	November 20, 1961 – February 21, 1965
	17	Suat Hayri Ürgüplü	February 21, 1965 – October 22, 1965
	18	Süleyman Demirel	October 27, 1965 – March 19, 1971
1970s	19	Nihat Erim Ferit Melen (interim)	March 19, 1971 – April 17, 1972 April 17, 1972 – April 29, 1972
	20	Suat Hayri Ürgüplü	April 29, 1972 – May 13, 1972
	21	Ferit Melen	May 15, 1972 – April 7, 1973
	22	Naim Talu	April 12, 1973 – January 25, 1974
	23	Bülent Ecevit	January 25, 1974 – November 17, 1974
	24	Sadi Irmak	November 17, 1974 – March 31,1975
	25	Süleyman Demirel	March 31, 1975 – June 21, 1977
	26	Bülent Ecevit	June 21, 1977 – July 21, 1977
	27	Süleyman Demirel	July 21, 1977 – January 5, 1978
	28	Bülent Ecevit	January 5, 1978 – November 12, 1979
	29	Süleyman Demirel	November 12, 1979 – September 12, 1980

Source: S. Shaw and E. K. Shaw, *Osmanlı İmparatorluğu ve Modern Türkiye* [*History of the Ottoman Empire and Modern Turkey*] Vol: II, 2nd edn, Istanbul: E Publications, 2006, pp. 514–15

ministries with this 'distributing the spoils' mentality. Ultimately, however, this political attitude created a system in which each ministry was like an island in and of itself. It fragmented the executive branch, as well as the political party system itself. Inevitably, the political system was unable to sustain such a divided executive with so many conflicting agendas in each ministry.[104] The coalition governments kept crumbling, one after another, leaving the impression among the people that coalitions are inherently flawed and unstable (for the frequent changes of governments during the 1970s, *see* Table 3.2.).

The short lifespan of coalition governments made it even less likely that party leaders would find common grounds for compromise. They expected the coalition to fail and give them their chance to form a government and be in charge of the executive power. Once in power, it would be their turn to deliver patronage. The success rate of coalition governments was very low, given the fact that the coalition partners' political agendas and priorities were never in sync with each other. The likelihood of consolidation of party system was also very low, for each party knew the coalitions would fail sooner than later and that they had a real chance to be in the next one, no matter how small they were. When it became clear that the two of the largest parties on the centre-right and centre-left could not reconcile their differences to form a grand coalition, small and extremist parties began to enjoy disproportionate power as the key partners of ruling coalitions.[105] Needless to say, these were extremely perverse incentives that undermined the institutionalisation of the party system, and political party identities in Turkey.

Political instability and the escalating mobilisation of students and workers in the late 1960s triggered another intervention by the Turkish armed forces in March 1971. A bipartisan technocratic cabinet lead by Nihat Erim was then established under the auspices of the military coup leaders. Subsequently, there was a serious overhaul of the political regime that included party closures (the religious MNP and socialist TİP were banned); the execution of leading student activists; and lawsuits against labour unions, professional and youth organisations and other representatives of civil society.[106] There were also a series of constitutional amendments that tried to curb the liberal aspects of the 1961 Constitution. Some of the most prominent changes were:

- Restrictions on basic rights and liberties.
- Extension of detention period from 7 days to 15 days.
- Banning unionisation rights of civil servants.

---

104. F. Tachau, 'An overview of electoral behavior: toward protest or consolidation of democracy', in S. Sayarı and Y. Esmer (eds) *Politics, Parties and Elections in Turkey*, Boulder, CO and London: Lynne Reinner Publishers, 2002, p. 46, and endnote 25.

105. I. Sunar, *State Society and Democracy in Turkey*, İstanbul: Bahçeşehir University Publications, 2004, pp. 84–6; Zürcher, 1994, pp. 275–6.

106. H. Ozdemir, 'Siyasi Tarih 1960-1980', in *Türkiye Tarihi 4* [*History of Turkey* Volume 4], Sina Akşin *et.al.* 9th ed, İstanbul: Cem Publications, 2007, pp. 260–267.

- Establishing the State Security Courts (*Devlet Güvenlik Mahkemeleri*, or DGM), which were extraordinary tribunals to prosecute crimes committed against the Turkish state.
- Abolishing the autonomous status of Turkish Radio and Television (TRT).[107]

Economic crisis and the failure of the ISI

During the 1950s, the leaders of the DP had identified the agrarian sector and urban and rural merchants as their primary constituency. Thus, the DP catered to the needs of these groups and did not initially prioritise industrialisation. When the polarising effects of the Cold War began to be felt in the post-WWII era, Menderes received significant amounts of foreign aid from the US but spent it largely in a populist fashion. Progressively increasing inflation and sluggish economic growth began to hurt the waged sectors, including industrial workers, state employees and, most importantly, the military.[108] The 1960 coup left reformist officers in charge. Important measures were taken to improve the status of the waged sectors and industrial joint-ventures were established with foreign auto companies (Renault) and the military owned corporations (OYAK). Among other things, the coup leaders were in favour of an orderly industrialisation drive.[109]

In late-developing countries, the state needs to play a more active role in economic modernisation and industrialisation. In fact, one of the foremost economic historians, Alexander Gerschenkron, states that the more backwards a nation is, the more intervention in the economy is necessary. Thus, in late-developing countries the state acquires the role of a compensator. Because the private sector is heavily burdened by its insufficient capital accumulation and inadequate entrepreneurial knowhow and technological sophistication, the state has to move in both as a large economic entrepreneur and as a benefactor of the private sector. Under these circumstances, the industrial sector that emerges under the wings of the state is heavily dependent upon imported technology and is oriented towards the domestic market.[110] The Turkish case of modernisation and economic development concurs with all the major assumptions of the Gerschenkronian paradigm.

The rejuvenation of the import-substitution strategy in the 1960s and its state-centric approach to economic development brought the CHP back into the driver's seat. Given its statist background, the CHP became a natural candidate for implementing the economic policies of the 1960 military coup. With the establishment of the State Planning Organisation (DPT), the country was ready for an industrialisation drive through five-year development plans. The protectionist policies of the ISI and its orientation towards domestic markets resembled the

---

107. Ozdemir, 2007, p. 265.

108. Ahmad, 2007, p. 138–40.

109. Barkey, 1989, pp. 297–8.

110. A. Gerschenkron, *Economic Backwardness in Historical Perspective*, Cambridge, MA: Harvard University Press, 1962.

1930s, but its sectoral preferences were different. Now that Turkey had become more urban and middle class, the new focus was on consumer durables.[111]

From 1961 to 1974, Turkey experienced the 'easy phase' of ISI. Protectionist barriers were raised, in order to produce simple consumer goods domestically.[112] The Turkish currency remained overvalued so that the import-substituting-industrialists could import their machinery and intermediary goods more cheaply. Even though these artificial manipulations of the currency regime hurt exporting sectors (mainly agriculture), the state was committed to assisting industrialists. Prospering in this artificially created heaven, it became even more difficult for domestic industries to step up to the more risky stages of ISI. The second and third ISI stages require the gradual lifting of protectionist barriers and letting domestic industry face international competition. However, insulated from competition, Turkish ISI sectors were far below international standards.[113] Moreover, they had secured significant privileges (economic rents) through intricate political ties to the government, which, in turn, made it very difficult for the state to have any leverage over business. In this regard, the state in Turkey (*and* Mexico) differed significantly from East Asian counterparts. In the case of South Korea, for example, the state maintained a principled stance towards the domestic business sectors. It imposed strict international competition requirements and implemented 'carrot and stick' policies to reward the successful ones and penalise underperformers.[114]

The ISI regime had created winners as well as losers. Expansion of socio-political liberties with the 1961 Constitution had improved the lot of the working classes significantly. While the burgeoning urban-industrialists and the working classes benefited from the new direction of the economy, rural and commercial interests were put on the back burner. An artificially inflated exchange rate hurt rural exports. There was also a growing rift between commercial and industrial interests. While the industrialists accused the former of being 'opportunistic merchants', the President of the Istanbul Chamber of Commerce criticised the state-nurtured and uncompetitive industrialists in the following way: 'no industry which surrounded itself with protective customs barriers of the magnitude of 150 per cent could ever hope to export its output.'[115]

By the end of the 1960s, Turkish industry had achieved some level of development and could now produce consumer durables.[116] Yet the problems

---

111. Boratav, 2004, p.118–19.

112. Hirschman, 'The political economy of import-substitution industrialisation in Latin America', *A Bias for Hope*, New Haven, CT: Yale University Press, 1971, pp. 85–123.

113. Hirschman, 1971, pp. 119–20.

114. P. Evans, 'State structures, government-business relations and economic transformation', in S. Maxfield and B. R. Schneider, (eds) *Business and State in Developing Countries*, New York: Cornell University Press, 1997.

115. H. Barkey, *The State and Industrialisation Crisis in Turkey*, Colorado: Westview Press, 1990, pp. 114–18.

116. Barkey, 1989, p. 299.

related to the ISI were mounting. These were not unlike the problems faced by many other developing nations, particularly in Latin America. The output of the ISI sector was poor in quality, expensive and by no means exportable. Rather than striving for a share in the global market place, domestic industry was comfortably in the habit of enjoying the benefits of protective barriers and exploiting domestic market expansion.[117] In Barkey's harsh words, they were nothing more than 'glorified assembly operations'. After decades of ISI, the auto industry, for example, absorbed 20 per cent of all the nation's non-oil imports (1978 numbers) while not a single car it produced could be exported.[118] Moreover, according to the DPT measures, the domestic component share of the ISI sector still hovered around 20 per cent.[119]

The ISI sector in Turkey had an insatiable appetite for foreign currency. Yet the artificially overvalued exchange rates hindered other sectors' ability to export and earn hard currency. The effects of this bottleneck notoriously caused by ISI were postponed until the mid 1970s, thanks to the consistent flow of remittances from Turkish workers in Europe. Unfortunately, the global oil shocks of the 1970s dried up these remittances and emptied the foreign currency reserves of the Turkish Central Bank. The situation was so dire that a cheque drawn in Europe on the Central Bank for only 70 cents bounced,[120] creating the infamous political narrative of 'those days when we needed 70 cents' which remained in the political memory for years to come.

The policies of ISI caused significant fragmentation within the business sector as well. The corporatist structure of the Union of Turkish Chambers (better known by its Turkish acronym: TOBB) – a quasi-governmental body representing the business sector, established in early 1950s – could no longer withstand the growing cleavage between the commercial and industrial sectors. While the Chambers of Industry enjoyed significant economic clout, they were concentrated mostly in the developed western cities (particularly in Istanbul and Izmir). The Chambers of Commerce had a greater numerical advantage and a wider geographic appeal. Growing discontent within the business sector began to manifest itself in the late 1960s. The first sign was the victory of Necmettin Erbakan in the TOBB elections in 1969.[121] Erbakan presented himself as the representative of the small- and

---

117. M. Sönmez, *Türkiye Ekonomisinde Bunalım [Depression in the Turkish Economy]*, İstanbul: Belge Publications, 1980, pp.79–81.
118. Barkey, 1989, p. 307.
119. The industrialists were consistently lobbying for a reduction in domestic component requirements, while they proudly– and selectively – announced the products with higher percentage domestic components, such as refrigerators (90 per cent domestic components), and vacuum cleaners (89 per cent domestic). Yet in the same period, the State Planning Organization measures revealed that in overall domestic production, domestic components constituted only 23 per cent of finished products (Barkey, 1990, pp. 114–15).
120. E. Çölaşan, *24 Ocak: Bir Dönemin Perde Arkası [January 24th: Behind the Scenes of a Period]*, İstanbul: Milliyet Publications, 1983, p. 74.
121. Buğra, 1997, pp. 330–1.

medium-size entrepreneurs of the Anatolian heartland. Later he became the leader of the MSP, the right-wing party with very strong religious overtones. Erbakan accused the mainstream centre-right party (AP) of being the instrument of foreign capital, big business, Zionists and Freemasons, and presented himself and his party as the representatives of small businesses.[122]

After the execution of its charismatic leader (Menderes) during the 1960 coup, Süleyman Demirel had become the new leader of the centre-right. He was trying to hold together a very difficult and even contradictory set of interests. The AP constituency included industrialists, small traders and artisans, peasants and large landowners, religious reactionaries and western-oriented liberals. He tried to use a rather crude anti-communist rhetoric to keep his electoral base united but eventually, lost the conservative elements to Erbakans's MSP and the overzealous nationalists to the MHP, when the AP sided with industrialisation and big business[123] (*see* Figure 3.2 for the distribution of political parties on a left–right scale).

From political fragmentation to political polarisation

The expansion of political liberties with the 1961 Constitution paved the way for the emergence of a number of more ideological parties on Turkish political landscape, as illustrated in the Figure 3.2. The first party to take advantage of this new era was the Turkish Workers Party (*Türkiye İşçi Partisi*, TİP), which was established in February 1961. According to Zürcher:

> [T]he importance of [TİP] lay not in its political power or the votes it attracted. It never managed to attract more than 3 per cent of the vote in a general election and never entered a governing coalition – but rather in the fact that it was the first really ideologically based party to compete in elections. By its existence, it forced other parties to define themselves more clearly in ideological terms.[124]

No matter how severe an economic crisis it brought upon the country, the import-substitution strategy did achieve certain levels of economic development and industrialisation. An important sign of this was the rural exodus and the increasing urban populations of major western cities from the 1950s onwards. Turkey was experiencing rapid demographic changes side-by-side with the political changes consequent to the 1961 Constitution. Changing socio-economic dynamics and the emergence of new political actors on the party scene generated heated discussions within the elite about the direction of the centrist parties as well. Progressive magazines, such as *Yön* [*Direction*], Forum, and *Ozgür İnsan*

---

122. Zürcher, 1994, p. 270.

123. Zürcher, 1994, pp. 263–4.

124. Zürcher, 1994, p. 259.

Figure 3.2: Turkish Political Landscape, 1923–80

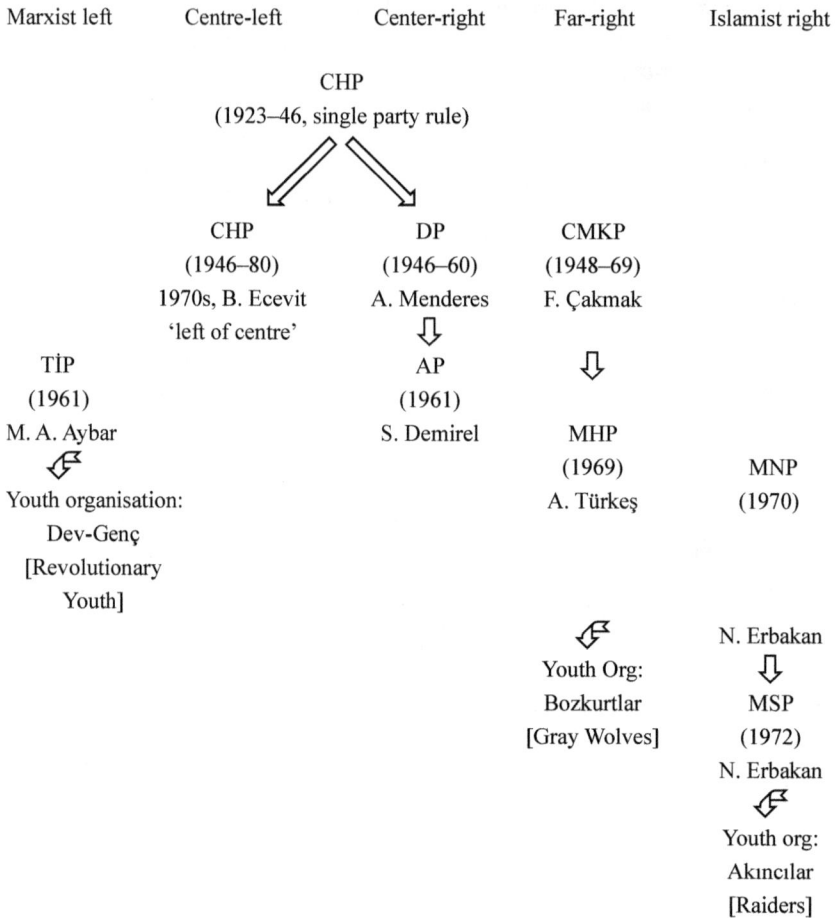

Marxist left	Centre-left	Center-right	Far-right	Islamist right

CHP
(1923–46, single party rule)

CHP	DP	CMKP
(1946–80)	(1946–60)	(1948–69)
1970s, B. Ecevit	A. Menderes	F. Çakmak
'left of centre'	⇩	

TİP   AP   ⇩
(1961)   (1961)
M. A. Aybar   S. Demirel   MHP
                                          (1969)   MNP
Youth organisation: A. Türkeş   (1970)
  Dev-Genç
  [Revolutionary
    Youth]

Youth Org: N. Erbakan
Bozkurtlar   ⇩
[Gray Wolves] MSP
                 (1972)
                 N. Erbakan

Youth org:
Akıncılar
[Raiders]

[Free Man] became important venues for debates over justice, equity, freedoms (personal and associational) and democratisation.[125]

From the 1970s on, the CHP acquired a new vision under the young leadership of Bülent Ecevit, who envisioned a left-of-centre model similar to the social-democratic parties of Europe and Scandinavia. This 'left turn' in the party provoked a strong reaction from the old guard and even caused the resignation of İnönü. Nonetheless, it also marked the populist turn of a party that had been strongly associated with the military-bureaucratic establishment. Throughout the 1970s, the CHP gained a mass following among the newly urbanised working

---

125. A. G. Ayata, 'The Republican People's Party', in B. Rubin and M. Heper (eds) *Political Parties in Turkey*, London: Frank Cass, 2002, p. 103.

classes, university circles, young urban professionals and even among the 'market-oriented small peasantry,' who used to be the bastion of conservative, right-wing parties in Turkey.[126]

Labour activism

An important characteristic of corporatist regimes was the management of state–society relations through quasi-governmental peak organisations. In compliance with this pattern, formal state–labour relations in Turkey were mediated largely through the national labour confederation, called Türk-İş. Türk-İş enjoyed a semi-official status and close clientelistic ties with the government in exchange for 'cooperation in reducing working class demands and promoting social peace'.[127] Yet close connections between the largest labour confederation and the state did not mean strong social rights or a dense social safety net for the working classes. In fact, the Labour Law of 1947 defined the unions not as organisations that defend the rights of the working classes but as organisations that work for the collective/public good. It also restricted union activity, including the rights of collective bargaining and striking.[128]

The corporatist character of state–society relations in Turkey created a hierarchical structure in which the labour market was also stratified and fragmented. In such a system, health and pension benefits were provided only to the 'formally employed heads of household according to their status at work',[129] leaving the unpaid family labour and informal sectors completely outside the social safety net. Furthermore, due to the fragmented nature of the welfare system, employees were subject to separate health and pension regimes with various degrees of coverage and benefits. State employees were covered by *Emekli Sandığı* (Retirement Pension), the workers by SSK (Social Insurance Institution) and the self-employed by *Bağ-Kur*.[130] Comparatively speaking, the state employees received better coverage than the rest of the working population.

The representational cartel of the Türk-İş labour confederation was challenged with the expansion of social and political rights after the 1961 Constitution. The 1961 Constitution had defined the Turkish state as a 'social state' and thereby granted significant benefits as well as collective bargaining rights and the right to strike to the working classes. The political stance of the corporatist labour association was extremely docile, due to its self-defined status as a federation 'above party

---

126. Ayata, 2002, pp. 104–5.

127. R. Bianchi, *Interest Groups and Political Development in Turkey*, Princeton, NJ: Princeton University Press, 1984, p. 212.

128. Law on Business and Labour Unions and Associations, passed in 1947 (no: 5018).

129. A. Buğra and C. Keyder, 'The Turkish welfare regime in transformation', *Journal of European Social Policy* 2006, 16(3), p. 212.

130. *Bağ-Kur* is the shortened name of the Social Security Institution of Merchants, Artisans and other types of Self Employed.

politics'. In practice, this meant a rather muted and impotent labour movement. Türk-İş leaders preferred to maintain 'good relations' with the governing parties in order to secure worker's rights (and cushy post for themselves), rather than organising and mobilising an assertive class movement.[131] In February of 1967, an alternative labour organisation emerged from the ranks of five labour unions that decided to pursue a more radical path.

The Confederation of Revolutionary Workers Syndicates (*Devrimci İşçi Sendikaları Konfederasyonu* – DİSK) became the representative of a more vocal labour movement. It became a formidable public actor through out the 1970s, until it was closed down by the 1980 military coup. Even though it was organised mainly in the private manufacturing sector and its activities were systematically hampered by the state and the corporatist unions (organised under Türk-İş), DİSK managed to expand its base when it became clear that it was securing better terms for its members (*see* Table 3.3) Large numbers of unionised workers shifted their affiliations to DİSK when they saw higher pay rises and better working conditions in factories organised under the DİSK banner. Soon, its membership increased from 30–40,000 to half a million.[132]

Along with effective job-site activism (strikes, sit-ins, factory occupations and so on) the 1970s was also marked by large-scale public demonstrations and pro-democracy meetings organised by DİSK. On 15 and 18 June 1970, DİSK organised one of its largest public demonstrations in order to protest against the government's attempts to restrict union activities. Their most famous meeting, however, was the May Day celebrations of 1977. On 1 May 1977, members from 99 unions and 53 civil-society organisations gathered around Taksim Square in Istanbul under close surveillance by the military and police. The participants numbered around 100,000 according to the official records but other sources claimed much higher numbers. Despite heavy monitoring by the security forces, the crowd was targeted by random gunshots coming from the Intercontinental Hotel that looked over Taksim Square. The gunfire and the subsequent panic left 34 demonstrators dead and numerous others wounded. This incident became one of the most notorious events in Turkish democratic history.[133] Despite all the evidence from eyewitnesses and recordings of news media covering the events, as well as from state intelligence sources, the perpetrators were never captured. The perception about the May Day tragedy that still lingers in public is that the state was complicit in the events.

Labour activism did bear its fruits when one looks at the increase in real wages. Despite the inflationary environment during the 1970s, real wages

131. K. Sülker, *15–16 Haziran: Türkiye'yi Sarsan İki Uzun Gün* [*June 15–16: Two long days that shook Turkey*], 3rd edn, İstanbul: İleri Publications, 2005.

132. F. Pekin, 'Farlı Olmanın Adı: DİSK' ['The name of difference: DİSK'], *Sosyalizm ve Toplumsal Mücadeleler Ansiklopedisi 1960–1980* [*Encyclopedia of Socialism and Popular Resistance Movements*] vol. 7, Istanbul: İletişim Publications, 1988, pp. 2290–1.

133. *Sosyalizm ve Toplumsal Mücadeleler Ansiklopedisi* [*Encyclopedia of Socialism and Popular Resistance Movements*] vol: 7 (1960–1980), İstanbul: İletişim Publications, 1988, pp. 2280–81.

Table 3.3: Distribution of membership in rival union organisations, by economic sector, 1975 (%)

	Conservative Unions	Social-Democratic Unions	Socialist Unions
Public manufacturing and mining	37.0	15.4	5.1
Private manufacturing and mining	31.4	32.1	42.4
Transport, communication and public utilities	12.0	26.7	9.0
Construction	8.7	24.1	2.4
Private services	3.3	0.7	16.3
Public services	4.8	1.0	24.5
Agriculture	2.8	0	0.3

Source: R. Bianchi, Interest Groups and Political Development in Turkey, Princeton, NJ: Princeton University Press, 1984, p. 231

continued to increase until 1977. There was also a certain level of improvement for the workers in private industries. Between 1970 and 1974, for example, the share of wages in value added was around 32 per cent. In the next four years, it increased to 34.1 per cent. This meant that the lot of the workers was improving at the expense of the industrialists.[134] Overall, political economists who analyse this period highlight the relative progress in the economic status of labour. This is generally attributed to the populist, redistributive policies of the ISI model, the expansion of political liberties with the 1961 Constitution and effective mobilisation of the workers.

On the eve of the 1980 military coup

Explanations of why another military coup happened on 12 September 1980 fall into two camps. The political-institutional school focuses on the domestic political environment, institutional gridlocks and the irreconcilable attitudes of party leaders. They point to the escalating political violence that paralysed the country and the incapacity of political mechanisms to resolve these problems peacefully. Here, one also needs to take into account the incapacity of corporatist structures of interest-representation to absorb the growing socio-economic and political discontent. Thus, in the late 1960s and throughout the 1970s, Turkey witnessed the emergence of more autonomous organisations, some of which became rather radical in their defence of the interests of their members.

---

134. K. Boratav, 'Iktisat Tarihi 1908–1980' [Economic History], in S. Akşin et al. (eds) Türkiye Tarihi 4 [History of Turkey], 9th edn, İstanbul: Cem Publications, 2007, pp. 369–70.

Paralysis in legitimate political venues served as a catalyst for the agitated and radicalised political groups in the country. Political violence among the extreme rightist, leftist and Islamist militants reached intolerable proportions by the end of the 1970s. Journalists, university professors, student leaders, mayors, ex-ministers, union leaders and even random citizens increasingly became targets of political violence. Growing insecurity and turmoil reached epic proportions twice, when rightist militants created riots in two cities: Kahramanmaraş, in December 1978 and Çorum, in July 1980. For a few days, neither the police nor the armed forces could regain control of the situation and almost 200 people were killed, according to the official records. In both incidents, the *Alevis* (a heterodox Muslim sect usually associated with the left) were targeted and hundreds of homes, businesses and even CHP party buildings were vandalised.[135]

The second group of explanations could be categorised as the political economy school. Political economists who study the contemporary Turkish system argue that the failure of the ISI model in Turkey is the main culprit behind the military coup of 1980. They emphasise the dependent development thesis, which claims that development in the periphery is limited and externally induced. In that sense, the national bourgeoisie in Turkey did not have the capacity to produce self-generating wealth. The particular nature of the ISI regime in Turkey made the capitalist classes highly dependent on the state and on the economic rents it created through protectionist policies. The industrialists were at the mercy of the state, for their high-priced, low-quality products could exploit domestic markets only as long as the state kept the protective barriers up. The commercial sectors also relied on the state, since their import privileges and excessive profit margins were the direct result of political choices. This kind of weak and dependent capitalist class could not be the midwife of a transparent and accountable state, nor could it effectively promote strong and democratic political institutions. The democratic demands of other groups and classes, such as students and workers, could easily be crushed by the state in the absence of a larger class alliance for democratic reform. According to Boratav, the shortcomings of an economically weak and dependent bourgeoisie condemned Turkey to oscillate between populism and military politics.[136]

Highlights of the Turkish case

This chapter has plotted out significant developments in Turkish politics and the general characteristics of state–society relations from the early days of the Republic until the 1980 military coup. This period started with state-led development and modernisation of Turkey under single party rule during the 1920s and 1930s. The 1940s was a stressful interim era for Turkey, marked by wartime mobilisation and delicate diplomatic manoeuvring to stay out of WWII.

135. T. Çavdar, *Türkiye'nin Demokrasi Tarihi: 1950'den Günümüze* [Democratic History of Turkey: From 1950s On], 3rd edn, Ankara: İmge Publications, 2004, pp. 248–51.

136. Boratav, 2007, p. 370.

From the 1950s on, subsequent to its alignment with the liberal Western bloc and NATO, Turkey established a multi-party regime and achieved a certain degree of political liberalisation. State–society dynamics could not break free from the old corporatist framework, however. As discussed in the previous chapter, the Ottoman and Turkish political traditions 'historically have tended to support corporatist policies and structures, while inhibiting the emergence of pluralist policies and structures'.[137] These corporatist forms of interest-representation remained unchallenged until the late 1950s. However, with growing functional cleavages as a result of rapid development and urbanisation during the 1960s and 1970s, new groups with new demands began to emerge. Again, the Turkish state tried to organise the new economic actors under the semi-official, compulsory associations of the corporatist network.

The state's strategy of co-opting new groups under the existing corporatist umbrella turned out to be only partially successful. Critical economic and political developments had created an environment wherein a new generation of private and voluntary associations began to emerge. The ISI strategy had created strong constituencies of industrialists and labour unions. Their organisations, TÜSİAD and DİSK respectively, were spearheading new and relatively autonomous forms of organised interest. Further more, the expansion of basic rights and freedoms by the 1961 Constitution also contributed to the emergence of a more active and diversified political arena. Workers, university students, professional organisations, as well as other forms of organised interest were all becoming more assertive.

The emerging seeds of social pluralism during the 1960s had a corresponding impact in political arena as well. Turkish party politics experienced a major boom with the establishment of numerous new parties anchored in class- or identity-based politics. As discussed in detail above, rather than paving the way to a democratic polity, the proliferation of parties further fragmented and polarised the political system, while the weakening of corporatist structures resulted in rivalry between organisations, deepening cleavages and rampant violence towards the end of the 1970s. The levels of political agitation and social unrest reached unbearable points when political killings occupied the headlines every single day and famous journalists, academics and activists became walking targets.

Political institutions failed to resolve the problem of social and political polarisation. Coalition governments crumbled one after another, leaving a vast political vacuum behind. Compounding this political crisis, the economy was also in dire straits as the ISI strategy yielded a colossal failure. Finally, on 12 September 1980, the Turkish armed forces stepped in to take charge of the deteriorating political situation. This was the third direct intervention of the military in politics since the establishment of the modern Turkish Republic. While it brought an abrupt end to rampant political violence, the coup itself caused significant trauma for the nation and hindered democratic progress for years to come. The impact of the 1980 coup and subsequent attempts to revitalise Turkish democracy will be discussed in Chapter Five.

---

137. Bianchi, 1984, p. 339.

Chapter Four

Mexico After 1910: Revolution, Modernisation and Corporatist Nation-Building

This chapter is a companion to the previous one and will discuss similar developments over the same period for the Mexican case, from the 1910 Mexican Revolution to the 1980s, bearing in mind a comparative-historical perspective with the Turkish case but identifying the aspects that distinguish Mexico. Thus there is a particular focus on the emergence and consolidation of single-party regime in Mexico. The first section gives a brief background on the pre-revolutionary period and identifies the consequences of President Porfirio Diaz's experiment with liberal political-economy that Mexican revolutionaries were determined to avert in the regime they established. It also offers a comparison between the revolutionary leaders of Turkey and those of Mexico, which points to some interesting similarities between them. The following section analyses the emergence and establishment of a political regime of 'institutionalised revolution' dominated by a single party, the PRI. Then the discussion moves on to state–society relations, examining first how the revolution's secularism and vision of a modernised national culture informed its anti-clerical, educational and cultural policies. The section then looks at Mexican corporatism and in particular how the 'triangle' of business, labour and agriculture were brought into an all-encompassing structuring of state–society relations. The focus then turns to the economic sphere, with sections on the pillars of the 'Mexican miracle' and the reasons why the miraculous model subsequently failed. The substantial similarities as well as the differences between the Mexican and Turkish cases are summarised in the last section.

The *Porfiriato* and the Mexican Revolution

Mexico had a rather eventful start to the twentieth century. The revolutionary energy that sparked in 1910 was fuelled by a desire to replace the *ancien régime*, which was a peculiar mix of a liberal economy and repressive, authoritarian politics. During his 34 years in power, President Porfirio Diaz (1876–1910) had been the architect of a liberal economy in Mexico. Between 1877 and 1910, 'the volume of foreign trade increased nine times.'[1] Despite his adherence to a liberal economic model, however, Diaz ruled the country with an iron fist. His *order*

---

1.   P. Smith, 'Mexico since 1946: dynamics of an authoritarian regime', in L. Bethell (ed.), *Mexico Since Independence*, New York: Cambridge University Press, 1991, p. 323.

and progress dictatorship subdued the chaotic social forces of Mexico and reorganised socio-economic life according to the principles of *positivism*. Like many other 'order and progress' dictators of the era, Diaz had faith in the science, rationalism, new discoveries and technologies of his times. He tried to reorganise the society along these principles, and achieved a certain degree of economic growth. However, this relative progress came at great human cost. While foreign entrepreneurs (predominantly from the US) were reaping the benefits of Porfirian order and progress, the vast majority of Mexicans were living in dismal conditions. Unionisation efforts by labour were harshly suppressed in order to please foreign capital. Land collectively owned by peasants (*ejidos*) was privatised in the name of productivity and efficiency.

By 1910, the US had accumulated considerable oil, mining and utility interests in Mexico, amounting to an estimated value of $1 billion.[2] At the turn of the twentieth century, almost 90 per cent of Mexican industry was controlled by foreigners. In agriculture, out of 485 million total acres, 150 million belonged to foreigners.[3] Because of his vast concessions to foreign capital, Diaz was commonly referred as 'the father of foreigners, stepfather of Mexicans.'[4]

Despite all the efforts of the Porfirian *scientificos* to industrialise Mexico, the country's most important export items were still minerals and agricultural products. Agricultural production was geared towards cash crops for export. The northern and central states of Mexico produced grains and cattle, mainly for the US market. When the domestic-use agriculture could no longer feed the growing population, Mexico resorted to importing food. Thus, a predominantly agricultural economy became dependent on food imports in order to feed itself. Under such dire conditions, any sign of organised dissent in the countryside was put down by Diaz's menacing *rurales* (rural police). *Porfiriato* lasted almost four decades and, towards the end, the accumulation of grievances had turned the country into a pressure cooker.[5]

During the Revolution (1910–20), two groups with two different visions for Mexico joined forces against Diaz. On the one hand, there were moderate reformists, who came largely from middle- and upper-class backgrounds. These moderates, led by Francesco Madero, were unhappy with the increasing foreign

2.   M. Kryzanek, *U.S.-Latin American Relations*, New York: Praeger, 1996, p. 54.

3.   J. M. Hart, 'The Mexican Revolution', in M. Meyer and W. Beezley (eds), *The Oxford History of Mexico*, New York: Oxford University Press, 2000, p. 436.

4.   D. Levy and K. Bruhn, *Mexico: The struggle for democratic development*, Los Angeles, CA: University of California Press, 2001, p. 183.

5.   On the state of labour *see* F. Katz, 'Labour conditions on haciendas in Porfirian Mexico', *Hispanic American Historic Review* 1974, 54(I), pp. 1–47. On rural conditions *see* B. Tenenbaum, *Mexico and the Royal Indian: The Porfiriato and the national past*, College Park, Latin American Studies Center, University of Maryland, 1994. On the economic policies of *Porfiriato see* J. H. Coatsworth, *Growth Against Development: The impact of railroads in Porfirian Mexico*, DeKalb, IL: Northern Illinois University Press, 1981 (also available online through the University of Michigan, History E-book Project).

control over the Mexican economy; and they were excluded from Diaz's narrow political circle. This group envisaged a democratic Mexico following a nationalist-capitalist path to development. They proposed a land-reform agenda for greater social justice but it was gradualist and legalistic; they did not intend to change the overall capitalist orientation of the Mexican economy. The revolutionary motto, 'effective suffrage, no re-election!' summarised the political demands of this group.[6]

Fighting side by side with the moderates were revolutionary hardliners. Under the leadership of the legendary Emiliano Zapata, the radical wing of the coalition had more drastic plans for land reform. Most of these revolutionaries were from impoverished agrarian regions, which had probably suffered the most during the three decades of the *Porfiriato*. The difficulties caused them by the commercialisation of communal lands (*ejidos*), the export-orientation of agriculture, an increase in the number of *haciendas* and more exploitative landlords were compounded by population expansion in rural areas. During the *Porfiriato*, the share of total agricultural lands held by *ejidos* dropped from 25 per cent to 2 per cent.[7] The combination of these developments created what Tutino calls 'the agrarian compression' in rural Mexico. Finally, in the 1900s, discontented elites under Madero joined forces with Zapata and his revolutionary peasants. It was this coalition that seriously challenged the Diaz regime and, in 1910, the 'compressed agrarian grievances exploded'.[8]

Most scholars concur that the Mexican Revolution was a heterogeneous phenomenon. In a sense, 'there were several revolutions within the Revolution.'[9] The economic and class backgrounds as well as the political visions of groups varied significantly. As a result of this, after the Diaz regime was toppled, there followed almost a decade of in-fighting. During this time, the Revolution swallowed many of its own children, including the legendary leaders Emiliano Zapata and Pancho Villa.

The political turmoil between 1910 and 1920 had a great cost for Mexico. It depleted the nation demographically, politically and economically. Death, migration (particularly to the US) and famine during the war years left a smaller and poorer population. Moreover, the country had huge amounts of debt – some $1 billion in overdue interest payments. In this regard, in the immediate aftermath of the revolution Mexico's condition was not very different from Turkey's after the War of Independence: tired, depleted, and saddled with a huge amount of foreign debt.

The post-revolutionary elites of Mexico were faced with the monumental task of reconstructing a new nation based on the ideals that they fought for. They

---

6. J. Tutino, *From Insurrection to Revolution in Mexico: Social bases of agrarian violence, 1750–1940*, Princeton, NJ: Princeton University Press, 1986, chapters 1 and 8.

7. Hart, 2000, p. 436.

8. Tutino, 1986, p. 279.

9. J. Meyer, 'Revolution and reconstruction in the 1920s', in L. Bethell (ed.), *Mexico Since Independence*, New York: Cambridge University Press, 1991, p. 201.

promoted radicalism, anticlericalism and nationalism, as well as egalitarian and solidaristic ideals. In this respect, Mexicans also display strong similarities with their Turkish revolutionary counterparts. The particular circumstances of each country certainly account for significant historic and socio-political differences. Yet some of the similarities in the characteristics of the leadership cadres and revolutionary ideals in both cases are striking.

Revolutionary leaders: Similarities between Turkey and Mexico

Military backgrounds

The leaders of the Mexican and Turkish Revolutions who presided over the post-revolutionary reconstruction period in each country had rather similar military backgrounds.[10] They were generals with proven track records and had scored vital victories for the Turkish and Mexican nations. Neither country placed civilians in their top executive positions until the mid twentieth century: Miguel Alemán became the first civilian President of Mexico in 1946 and Adnan Menderes the first civilian Prime Minister of Turkey in 1950. Another interesting shared characteristic is that post-revolutionary leaders in both countries came largely from the more developed western and north-western regions of their countries. Compared to their peers, they had more exposure to Western socio-political and economic systems. This aspect became critical in their respective campaigns to modernise and develop their nations.

Nationalism

Whether it was due to their military backgrounds or not, both sets of leaders resented the economic and political control that foreign nations and nationals exercised over their homelands. They shared a strong commitment to nationalism and national pride. Once in power, they nationalised foreign-owned industries, railroads and utilities in order to assert domestic control over the key economic assets of their countries. Exerting national sovereignty in economic and political realms was an important priority for the revolutionary leaders of both nations.

---

10. Oddly enough, President Calles, the victorious revolutionary general and the architect of Mexico's single-party regime, was the son of Ottoman immigrants. His father left the Mediterranean port-city of İzmir (Smyrna) to seek his fortune in the New World. Because he travelled on Ottoman papers, President Calles came to be known as 'El Turco', an expression used to describe immigrants from Asia Minor. For more information on the family roots of President Calles, see the interview with the Mexican Ambassador in Turkey, Hon. Salvador Campos Icardo, published in *Today's Zaman* (a Turkish daily) 4 September 2007. *See also* E. Krauze, *Mexico: Biography of Power: A history of modern Mexico, 1810–1996* (transl. Hank Heifetz) New York: HarperCollins Publishers, 1997, pp. 412–3.

Authoritarian, not totalitarian

Post-revolutionary Turkey and Mexico were far from being open and democratic political systems. Yet, the overall scale and scope of each state's central control and political suppression fell short of allowing us to classify these regimes as fascist or totalitarian. Even though the most important sectors of the society (labour, peasantry, business, popular sectors, church and so on) were subjugated under single-party regimes, there was still a small breathing space for dissent. In Mexico, the regime did 'permit a considerable amount of individual and group freedom'.[11] In both cases the single-party regimes held regular elections and tried to expand their electoral support. Opposition parties also existed – albeit generally with very limited resources and short lifespans – and were allowed to compete in elections. Societal repression was limited and usually balanced with the extensive co-optation mechanisms of a corporatist state.

Modernising ethos

Both sets of elites visualised modern, developed and prosperous nations. Development, modernisation, and westernisation were central concerns of the leaders who shepherded their respective nations into the twentieth century in both Mexico and Turkey. To achieve this goal, both regimes launched massive education campaigns and adult-literacy programmes, especially in rural and underdeveloped parts of their countries. They used art as a means to 'educate' and 'enlighten' the masses. This functionalist approach to art is exemplified in the giant murals on the public buildings of Mexico and in the classical music concerts at the Village Institutes of Turkey. The purpose of these public education and art campaigns was largely to transform their ignorant and illiterate 'subjects' into patriotic and educated citizens.

Secularism and anti-clericalism

Part of the modernising agenda of the revolutionary elites in both countries was to shed the conservative, parochial and backwards institutions of the past. Here, religion stood out as the largest obstacle on the way to creating a modern and rational society. Thus, both regimes attacked organised religion with almost equal relentlessness. Churches in Mexico and mosques, *medreses* and religious brotherhoods in Turkey were stripped of their privileges, their properties confiscated and educational facilities shut down. Organised religion did not turn the other cheek against these assaults from the state. Therefore both countries encountered massive religious rebellions (*Cristeros* in Mexico and *Seyh Sait* in Turkey) during the 1920s. Mexican and Turkish laws imposed strict dress codes on

11. H. J. Wiarda and C. Guajardo, 'Mexico: the unraveling of a corporatist regime', *Journal of Interamerican Studies and World Affairs* 1988, 30(4), pp. 1–28.

clergy, thereby banning the use of religious garb outside houses of worship. Civil codes were accepted in both countries, which eliminated the principal ceremonial powers of organised religion at births, deaths and marriages.

Land reform

The issue of equitable distribution of land was a concern for both Mexican and Turkish revolutionary elites, although the intensity of the problem and the commitment of political leaders varied considerably between the two cases. In Turkey, the phenomenon of large landlords and landless peasantry was mostly confined to the eastern and south-eastern provinces. Still, the single-party leaders considered this issue significant, for it created political problems due to powerful and over-zealous regional strongmen. Moreover, turning a blind eye to this issue would be perceived as a betrayal of their promise of social justice. Thus, they kept land reform on their agenda and pushed for it when the inner-party dynamics were suitable. In Mexico, the scale and scope of land reform was much larger and the issue was also one of the key motives behind the Mexican Revolution. Consequently, land-reform attempts in Mexico were more comprehensive than in Turkey. These differences notwithstanding, it is important to note that both elites considered land reform an effective means to curb the economic and political powers of regional strongmen.

'Institutionalising revolution': The emergence of a single-party regime

> The Mexican regime that emerged after ten years of fighting was broad-based and viable [...] The exclusivist Porfirian oligarchy, rival provincial elites, industrial and urban workers, and peasants were all defeated at various points in the struggle and reincorporated into the new regime through subordinate organizations that recognized the supremacy of the new state [...] Each defeated group – peasants, industrial workers, and capitalists, and later the church – [...] [was] forced to concede ultimate power to the state-building elite. (John Mason Hart)[12]

After years of revolutionary warfare, the delegates of the 1917 Constitutional Convention assembled to draw the contours of the new regime. They placed the burning questions facing Mexico on the table. The more liberal-leaning delegates had moderate views on issues like land reform and anticlericalism. Among them, Venustiano Carranza tried to put the brakes on the extreme anticlericals by stating that

---

12. J. M. Hart, *Revolutionary Mexico*, Berkeley: University of California Press, 1987, p. 270.

[...] the customs of a people do not change overnight; for a people to stop being Catholic, the triumph of the Revolution is not sufficient; the Mexican people will continue to be just as ignorant, superstitious and attached to their ancient customs until one educates them.[13]

The radical wing, however, was more ambitious in their plans to change Mexico for the better. They claimed that such statements about the innate backwardness of ordinary Mexicans were often times used to '[...] disguise privilege and oppression'.[14]

The revolutionary leaders agreed upon a new constitution in 1917, despite all their differences. As the embodiment of the revolutionary spirit, the 1917 Constitution was determined to undo the economic structure established during the *Porfiriato*. It promoted the ideals of nationalism, egalitarianism, solidarity and anticlericalism. It provided substantial rights for workers and reinstated the institution of communal lands (*ejidos*) in rural areas. True to its nationalistic spirit, the Constitution also prohibited foreign ownership of the country's critical economic sectors, such as oil, railroads and utilities.[15]

Implementation of the new Constitution, however, was a different story. Revolutionary leaders, particularly the elites from the state of Sonora, decided that priority should be given to political centralisation. Given the heterogeneity of the revolution and the traditional strength of the regional leaders (*patrons, caciques, caudillos*), Mexico had too many centrifugal forces to reckon with. After the revolutionary dust settled, the leaders were left with the rather difficult task of reconciling the demands of the agitated peasantry and working classes, distraught urban middle classes, insubordinate military and regional elites.

The first constitutional President, Venustiano Carranza (1917–20) tried to rule the nation during the last years of the revolutionary decade. Even though his elderly wisdom and moderation served the nation well, some of his ambitions proved to be premature for Mexico. Carranza wanted to eliminate the political aspirations of the Mexican military by curbing the powers of generals. The generals, particularly those from Sonora, were at the peak of their political power, however. They had emerged victorious from a decade-long Revolution. General Álvaro Obregón, in particular, enjoyed enormous power and prestige as the 'undisputed *caudillo* who defeated Villa'.[16]

When President Carranza tried to name a civilian as his successor, he received a strong reaction from the military. At the peak of his power, General Obregón, another Sonoran, organised a military revolt against the President and eventually

---

13. Krauze, 1997, p. 361.

14. Krauze, 1997, p. 365.

15. On property rights, nationalisations and land reform, *see* Article 27. On labour rights, minimum wage, work hours, etc. *see* Article 123. On issues related to the Catholic Church, secular education, anticlericalism and abolition of the privileges of organised religion, *see* Articles 3, 5, 24, 27 and 130.

16. Krauze, 1997, p. 370.

took the presidency himself in December 1920. It would take one more presidential term for Mexico to address the praetorian role of the military in politics.

Obregón's successor, Plutarco Elias Calles, established the blueprint of the Mexican regime that lasted until the end of the twentieth century. Also a Sonoran, Calles became the architect of the modernisation, secularisation and centralisation of Mexican society and politics. Calles was the first President to acknowledge the problem of executive succession in Mexico and tried to come up a viable solution. His military background gave him plenty of opportunity to observe individual aspirations among high-ranking officers. Thus, throughout his term he made extensive efforts to address the problem of military meddling in civilian affairs. Above all, he was determined to institutionalise Mexican politics. In an important speech he delivered at the Congress in 1928, he stated very clearly that the military phase of the Revolution was over and the nation had 'embarked on what may be called the political or governmental phase of the Mexican Revolution'. From then on, the country had to change 'from being 'a country ruled by one man' to a 'nation of institutions and laws'. According to Calles, it was absolutely necessary that Mexico dismantled what he called 'the government of caudillos' and instead established a 'regime of institutions'.[17]

In the same speech, Calles highlighted the importance of the 'no re-election principle' as the sacrosanct legacy of the Revolution. He also warned the military in no uncertain terms that they should not harbour any political ambitions under the cloak of patriotism. It is also important to note that this speech was made after a short period of political turmoil, when President-elect Álvaro Obregón was assassinated by a Catholic zealot. Hence, the political climate was favourable for struggles to capture the vacant chief executive seat. The following excerpt is from Calles' address to the armed forces:

> Finally, in my triple capacity as revolutionary, division general, and chief of the armed forces, I will address myself to the army [...] all men who aspire to the presidency of the country, be they military men or civilians, will contend on the fields of honourable democracy [...] Anyone who, during those anxious moments, abandons the line of duty and tries to seize power by any means other than those outlined in the Constitution, will be guilty of the most unforgivable criminal and unpatriotic conduct [...] All members of the national army must be conscious of their decisive role in those moments. They must embrace the true noble calling of their military career: to give honour and fidelity to the legitimate institutions.[18]

Calles' efforts to institutionalise executive succession and curb the role of the military in politics and his overall attempts to institutionalise Mexican politics under

---

17. P. E. Calles, 'A nation of institutions and laws', speech delivered to Congress 1 September 1928, quoted in G. Joseph *et al.* (eds) *The Mexico Reader: History, culture, politics*, 2002, Durham and London: Duke University Press, 2002, pp. 422–3.
18. Calles, 1928 (2002), p. 425.

an all-embracing single party determined the trajectory of Mexican politics for decades to come. In terms of containing the military and barring it from politics, subsequent presidents followed his path. From Calles to Alemán, Mexican Presidents continued to emerge from the military ranks but, once they took the top seat, they effectively distanced themselves from the military and allocated progressively fewer funds to the armed forces. Thus, the incentive to 'civilianise' the political sphere came from political leaders who had been on both sides (military *and* civilian). The generals that governed Mexico in the 1920s and 1930s 'themselves initiated the concept of civilian control'[19] over the armed forces. Thus, Mexico became a unique case in the developing world in terms of civil–military relations. As will be discussed later, this issue is a major point of divergence between Mexico and Turkey.

Mexican presidentialism and regime stability

The seven-decade-long political stability in Mexico is largely attributed to the establishment of a single, all-encompassing political party and to its efficiency in resolving the problem of succession in a presidential regime. Because the President was considered 'the King for six years,' the stakes were high and political competition was intense. In the aftermath of the Revolution in 1910, the problem of succession claimed many lives and caused a significant regime threat. Immediately after a new President took office, leading figures in the military would start daydreaming about their turn in the Presidential Palace (*Los Pinos*). Subsequently, political cogs would turn and petty deals would be made in exchange for political office. Shortly thereafter, the system would succumb to factionalism and political instability.

President Calles (1924–8) was the first to effectively tackle this endemic problem of succession. Declaring himself *Jefe Maximo*, Calles personally chose three successive Mexican Presidents during the period known as the *Maximato*. Thus, the expression 'the President lives in this house, but the man who rules lives in the house across',[20] became a part of popular political discourse in Mexico. Calles's method showed that having the sitting President determine his successor was a rather pragmatic and effective way of dealing with the succession problem. Once the sitting President appointed his successor, the party would unite behind that candidate and launch a nationwide campaign for his election. Consequently, the institution of *dedazo*, as the process is known in Mexico, would save great amount of political energy and fend off divisive and destabilising forces.

> *Presidencialismo*: the concept that most political power lies in the hands of the president and all that is good or bad in government policy stems personally from the president.[21]

---

19. R. A. Camp, *Politics in Mexico*, New York and Oxford: Oxford University Press, 1996, p. 16.

20. '*El que vive en esta casa / es el senor presidente, pero el senor que aqui manda / vive en la casa de frente*'.

21. R. A. Camp, *Politics in Mexico*, New York and Oxford: Oxford University Press, 1996, p. 13.

Most analysts concure that the presidential regime in Mexico places too much power in the hands of the top executive. According to Roderic Ai Camp, this comes at the expense of a weak legislature and an even weaker judiciary and differentiates the Mexican from the US style of presidential regime, which places a strong emphasis on 'checks and balances' between the three branches of government. Thus, Camp uses the term *Presidencialismo* in reference to the top-heavy model in Mexico.

The difference of regime-type between Turkey (parliamentarian/unitary state) and Mexico (presidential/federal state) might easily be perceived as an important factor that could compromise the utility of a comparative study. However, a closer look at the ways in which presidentialism and federalism are institutionalised in Mexico reveals a different story. Most analysts state that, on paper, the political system in Mexico is not much different from US-style federalism, with clear separation of powers. However, despite their generous powers given in the 1917 Constitution, the Congress and local executives could not effectively curb the powers of the Mexican president. The urgency of subduing local and regional powers in the aftermath of the Revolution and subsequent establishment of the single-party in 1929 helped create an extremely centralised political system in Mexico. Political dissent became even more costly, especially due to the hegemonic status of the single party. As a result, Mexico had 'disproportionate presidentialism', along with an extremely centralised institutional network.[22] Political homogeneity and the strength of the institutional network that permeated almost every level of society created a system in which all roads led to the President. Federal units could hardly enjoy political or socio-economic autonomy from the centre. In this regard, Mexican-style presidentialism displays strong parallels with the unitary state structure and the centralised administrative system of Turkey.

In short, the executive-dominant presidential system, combined with a strong, corporatist party structure, and weak federalism contributed significantly to the longevity of the PRI regime in Mexico. The Congress could not effectively balance the executive until it achieved some degree of multi-party diversity in the 1990s. Labels aside, Turkish and Mexican regimes had more characteristics they shared than differences.

State–society relations after the revolution

Anticlericalism, education and art in rebuilding a nation

When they arrived in Oriziba, the first thing they did was attack and loot the town churches [...] The church of El Carmen was also raided and given to

---

22. R. Hernandez-Rodriguez, 'The renovation of old institutions: state governors and political transition in Mexico', *Latin American Politics and Society* 2003, 45(4), pp. 97–129.

the workers of La Casa del Obrero Mundial as living quarters. The saints, the confessionals and the altars were turned into firewood by women.[23] (Jose Clemente Orozco)

In the post-revolutionary era, the Sonoran faction from north-western Mexico had established its hegemony over other groups. These nationalist modernisers from the state of Sonora called themselves the 'Californians of Mexico'. They aspired to establish a modern and affluent nation and wanted to achieve levels of socio-economic development similar to their northern neighbour. The Sonoran elite were almost scandalised by the traditional and 'backwards' Mexico, which incidentally constituted nearly two-thirds of the nation. An ex-minister of the period describes the mentality of the Sonoran elites in the following way:

[...] when they realized what kind of a life was lead by the peasants of traditional Mexico, they decided that the peasants were not men in the true sense of the term, as they kissed the hands of the great landowners and the priests, they did not understand the logic of the marketplace and frittered away what money they had on alcohol and fireworks.[24]

The Mexican Revolution was about liberating the Mexican people not only from the chains of economic exploitation but also from the subjugating burdens of ignorance, superstition and archaism. An important ideal for revolutionary leaders was to create a *republican*, *secular* and *enlightened* nation: goals very similar to that of the modernising elites of the Turkish Republic. According to the reformers, '[...] the enemy of this modern Mexico [...] remained the country's heterogeneity and the Catholic Church.'[25] As a result, Mexico had to undertake the twin transformations of secularisation and nation-state formation.

Similar to most other Latin American countries, Mexico was deeply divided along ethnic, racial, regional and class lines. In such a divided and heterogeneous society, the allegiance of most people was to what was called one's *patria chica* ('small homeland').[26] The primary source of group identity was the small and local *patria*, rather than the large and abstract national homeland. Many communities, particularly those with indigenous and *mestizo* (mixed European and indigenous) origins, were far from the national centre, not only in geographic terms but also in terms of their ethnic, linguistic and cultural affiliations. Yet, the Catholic

---

23. Quoted from Orozco in Krauze, 1997, pp. 356–7.

24. Quoted from personal interviews with Luis L. Leon by Jean Meyer in 1968 and 1973–4, in J. Meyer, 'Revolution and Reconstruction in the 1920s', in L. Bethell (ed.), *Mexico Since Independence*, New York: Cambridge University Press, 1991, p. 202 (*author addition*).

25. T. Benjamin, 'Rebuilding the nation', in M. Meyer and W. Beezley (eds), *The Oxford History of Mexico*, Oxford and New York: Oxford University Press, pp. 467–502, p. 479.

26. H. J. Wiarda, *The Soul of Latin America: The cultural and political tradition*, New Haven, CT: Yale University Press, 2001, pp. 177–8.

Church could overarch successfully across this heterogeneity and command the loyalties of all these marginalised peoples. Peasants, for instance, would hand over the properties given to them by the state when their priests told them to do so.[27] From the perspective of the modernising elite, the Catholic Church capitalised on the weakness of the collective national identity. Furthermore, it took advantage of the ignorance of the masses and perpetuated a cycle of fatalism, superstition and lethargy among the people by controlling the critical aspects of their lives, including birth, education, marriage and death.

In order to create a modern Mexican nation, the revolutionary leaders had to fight a battle on two fronts simultaneously. On the one hand, they had to curb the colossal spiritual and socio-economic power of the Catholic Church. On the other, they had to build a modern and secular citizenry by means of a massive national education campaign. Indeed, the Sonoran faction of the revolutionary elite that was in charge of the reconstruction period in the 1920s was genuinely committed to removing the 'Catholicism obstacle' from the path of enlightenment and modernity. To this end, they included articles in the new Constitution that proposed to terminate the role of the Church in education (Article 3), confiscate all its properties other than church buildings (Article 27), secularise birth, death and marriage ceremonies and even prohibit clergy from wearing religious attire in public (Article 130).[28]

The strong anticlericalism of the revolutionary leaders meant a head-on collision with the traditional sectors of society. President Calles began to implement the Constitutional provisions with full force, and this generated significant reaction from Mexican society, particularly from the more religious rural parts. The first signs of popular discontent came from the conservative central and southern Mexico. The Cristero Rebellion – named after its battle-cry, *Viva Cristo Rey!* (Long Live Christ the King!) – began to spread across the country and soon the federal army was called upon to put down the revolt by force.

After the popular uprising in central and southern Mexico in 1926, the state tried to suppress the movement heavy-handedly. The federal army opened machine-gun fire on completely unarmed civilians. The army also burned countless acres of fields in accordance with the scorched-earth policy of the government, in order to subdue the peasants. Rather than suppressing Catholics resistance, however, these actions further spread the movement across Mexico. Bishops suspended church services and, for nearly three years, not a single church bell rang in Mexico. President Calles was not intimidated by the challenge from the Church, however. He said, 'each week without religious ceremonies will cost the Catholic religion two per cent of its faithful'.[29]

A simplistic conception of the Cristero Rebellion might be as a fanatical, reactionary movement of peasants lead by zealous priests. However, in-depth

---

27. Krauze, 1997, p. 420.

28. Organization of American States (OAS) Online. Available http://www.oas.org (last accessed 10 April 2015).

29. Krauze, 1997, p. 421.

academic studies reveal a more complicated confrontation. Jean Meyer's impressive work *La Cristada* is considered one of the most detailed and authoritative studies on the subject. Its English version is much shorter than his original 2,500-page thesis, which gives a full account of the intense power struggle between church and state in Mexico. In his analysis, one can observe the post-revolutionary Mexican state trying to establish itself as a modern Leviathan. Against this backdrop, the Catholic Church was trying to protect its economic interests, as well as its strong social and political ideology.[30] In its political confrontation with the Mexican state, the Catholic Church initially mobilised the 'rural poor, Indian *comuneros*, hacienda peons, small proprietors and sharecroppers, indeed all rural sectors except the big landowners and the *agraristas* (beneficiaries of agrarian reform)'.[31]

The Cristero Rebellion came to an end when the Church hierarchy conceded the demands of the Mexican state. The extreme secularism of President Calles had galvanised ordinary Mexicans against the state. After three years of internal strife, church bells began ringing again in the summer of 1929. In drawing the final truce between the parties, the mediating role of US Ambassador Dwight Morrow had also been critical. Still, some 70,000 lives were lost, 200,000 citizens were displaced internally and 450,000 migrated to the US between 1926 and 1930.[32] Subsequently, Mexican political leaders kept their distance from the Catholic hierarchy. In this regard, Mexico differs from the rest of the Latin America, where close regime–church relations are common, and its official anticlericalism has strong similarities to the Turkish brand of secularism.

The Mexican Revolution and the post-revolutionary regime have been analysed mostly through economic and political lenses. Aside from its characteristics as an agrarian revolution, a socialist or a bourgeois one – each depending on one's perspective – the revolution also had a strong cultural element to it. Immediately after the revolution, new elites undertook a project to 'destroy the old Mexico and erect upon its ruins a new utopian society by means of a veritable cultural revolution'.[33] Despite the bloody confrontation with the Church during *La Cristada*, the state did not stop its campaign against what it considered 'fanaticism' and 'superstition'.

In its original form, Article 3 of the 1917 Constitution 'stipulated that instruction was to be based on dialectic materialism'. Even though this radical phrase was amended in 1946, Mexican education remained nationalistic, democratically oriented and 'entirely apart from any religious doctrine'. Primary education was compulsory and all education given by the state was free, according to the

30. J. Meyer, *The Cristero Rebellion: The Mexican people between church and state 1926–1929*, (transl. R. Southern), Cambridge and New York: Cambridge University Press, 1976.

31. J. Lynch, 'Review of Jean Meyer: *The Cristero Rebellion*', *Journal of Latin American Studies* 1978, 10(2), pp. 365–6.

32. Krauze, 1997, p. 423.

33. A. Bantjes, 'Burning Saints, Molding Minds: Iconoclasm, civic ritual, and the failed cultural revolution', in W. Beezely *et al.* (eds) *Rituals of Rule, Rituals of Resistance: Public celebrations and popular culture in Mexico*, Boston & New York: Rowman & Littlefield, 1994, p. 262.

Mexican Constitution.[34] In his own words, Calles describes the cultural mission of the revolution and designates the young generation as its primary target:

> [...] we must enter and take control of the consciousness of the youth, because it does and must belong to the revolution [...] The reactionaries mislead us when they claim that the child belongs to home [...] the child and the youth belong to the community, and it is the revolution which has a compelling obligation towards the consciousness, to banish prejudice and to form the new national soul.[35]

Education became the central concern of the modernising campaign to create a new 'national soul'. Revolutionary education was, above all, scientific and materialistic. Very similar to the Village Institutes initiative during the early decades of the Turkish Republic, the Mexican state rapidly established rural schools across the nation. Initially, the 1917 Constitution had left education up to the state governments. With the 1921 Amendment, the federal government had the right to 'establish schools wherever they were needed'. From then on, the rural education programme took off and, by 1928, there were over 4,000 rural schools across Mexico. By the end of 1934, the number reached around 12,000.

The rural schools were established and operated under utilitarian and functionalist principles, which were largely inspired by the American philosopher, John Dewey. Most of the teachers themselves came from rural backgrounds and, alongside academic subjects, they provided extensive training in 'physical education, hygiene, singing, "small industries", agriculture, and educational methods'.[36] Similarly to the Turkish case, there were close ties between teachers, their unions and the Party.

> Teachers were obliged to join the municipal PNR [*Partido Nacional Revolucionario,* National Revolutionary Party, the PRI's predecessor] committees and participate in the party's Cultural Sundays. Here, they had to sign statements in which they confirmed to uphold Article 3 of the Constitution and refrain from religious teachings in schools.[37]

An important aspect of rural education was to integrate the vast majority of indigenous communities into national life. This seemed like an insurmountable task since the difficulties included not only great physical barriers – of geographic distance, difficult terrains, ethnic/linguistic heterogeneity, illiteracy and so on – but also deep-rooted sociological and psychological ones. In its attempts to remake the

34. H. Cline, 'Mexico: A matured Latin-American revolution', *Annals of the American Academy of Political and Social Science*, 1961, 334, p. 91.

35. Quoted in Bantjes, 1994, p. 265 (*author addition*).

36. H. Benjamin, 'Revolutionary Education in Mexico', *Annals of the American Academy of Political and Social Science*, 1935, 182, p.188.

37. Bantjes, 1994, p. 275.

rural Mexican population and turn peons into citizens, revolutionary education had to undo 'centuries of economic and political oppression'.[38] Mexico's first Minister of Education, Jose Vasconcelos, was personally engaged in the modernisation of the indigenous population through mass literacy and adult-education campaigns. A leading Latin Americanist and Mexico specialist, Frank Tannenbaum, was so impressed by the education campaigns of the post-revolutionary regime that he titled his first article on Mexico, which studied one of the schools in a poor Mexico City *barrio*, 'The miracle school'.[39]

Vasconcelos was a leading figure among the cultural architects of the new Mexican national identity. During the first decades of the revolution, the elites tried to combine native elements with progressive, revolutionary spirit and create a new national culture. The Department of Fine Arts (*Departamento de Bellas Artes*), which operated under the Ministry of Education, became the *locus* of state-sponsored artists and art works. World-famous Mexican muralists like Diego Rivera, Jose Clemente Orozco and David Alfaro Siqueiros were all masterminds of this era of revolutionary art.

The foremost socialist muralist, Diego Rivera, 'simultaneously portrayed themes of country life and the industrial city'. His state-commissioned murals were displayed in the most visible public spaces. Rivera skilfully portrayed scenes of the colonial invasion and oppression and the breakthrough that came with the Mexican Revolution. He used the aesthetic style of traditional Mexican folk art but combined with the modern socialist ideals of the new regime.[40] These impressive murals were to cultivate a sense of history, place and belonging among most deprived sectors of the Mexican society. *Muralismo* was art with a mission to create and convey revolutionary ideals to the least privileged sectors of Mexican society. Art was no longer a privileged enterprise exclusive to the upper echelons of society but was the vehicle through which the collective ideals of the revolution were spread across the masses.

Forging the corporatist triangle

The Institutional Revolutionary Party is not a majority political party: it is Unanimity itself. (Octavio Paz)[41]

The leaders of the post-revolutionary reconstruction period were, by and large, convinced that no class could bring growth and prosperity to Mexico *alone*. Thus,

38. Benjamin, 1935, p. 186.

39. C. Hale, 'Frank Tannenbaum and the Mexican Revolution', *The Hispanic American Historical Review*, 1995, 75(2), p. 231.

40. A. Mendez-Vigota, 'Post-revolutionary regimes in Mexico and their influence on Mexican public architecture 1920–1952', in E. Burian (ed.), *Modernity and the Architecture of Mexico*, Austin, TX: University of Texas Press, 1997, p. 70.

41. O. Paz, 'Introduction', in E. Poniatowska, *Massacre in Mexico* (transl. H. Lane), New York: Viking Press, 1975, p. x.

the state had to acquire a developmentalist role and become the locomotive of reconstruction. Under Calles, the first Central Bank of Mexico was established. New highways, irrigation projects, agricultural schools and housing projects were launched. Overall, the role of the state in the economy greatly expanded.[42] Calles finally realized his goal of institutionalising Mexican politics with the establishment of the National Revolutionary Party (*Partido Nacional Revolucionario*, PNR) in 1929. Initially, the military showed a rather hostile reaction to this development. The Sonoran generals rebelled against Calles and the PNR. Calles managed to crush this rebellion with the help of federal forces and the 47 generals involved in it were either killed or forced to resign. Eventually, with the strengthening of the PNR, Mexico managed to 'civilise' its generals and 'contained violence until it fell out of fashion'.[43]

The efforts of the political leaders to 'institutionalise' Mexican politics and incorporate all sectors of society under a single umbrella resulted in a quintessentially corporatist regime. Radical rhetoric on exploitation and class conflict during the Revolution notwithstanding, the post-revolutionary Mexican state '[...] rejected the division of society into classes'. In line with corporatist principles, it presumed that harmonising the interests of different sectors was possible when the state acted as the primary mediator in channelling their energies towards a central goal. In other words, 'the state had to accomplish everything in the name of everyone'.[44] Thus, a strong state tried to bring all major sectors of the society under its corporatist umbrella.

Corporatism seemed to be the ideal mortar to bring all the different/competing classes together. The corporatist state would form the backbone of the new political system and thus would harmonise the interests of each sector in congruence with the national interest. The organisational structure of the PNR (later PRI, *Partido Revolucionario Institucional*) was a clear indicator of the corporatist characteristics of the Mexican regime. Peasants, workers and the 'popular sector' (middle classes plus business) were all incorporated into the party apparatus (*see* Figure 4.1, below). The leaders of each of these sectors were given the chance of upward mobility and political status in exchange for loyalty and docile relations with the PRI. Eventually, this corporatist structure became the pillar of Mexican political stability.

Establishing the 'balance' among corporatist groups was of critical importance for the longevity of the system. The PRI guaranteed access for all corporatist sectors but granted supremacy to none. Second, it provided a regular flow of material benefits in the form of subsidies, wages, benefits and price controls. Finally, the state tried to ensure constant economic growth in order to meet the economic needs of this growing patronage network.[45]

---

42. Krauze, 1997, p. 416; Smith, 1991, pp. 324–5.
43. Krauze, 1997, p. 431.
44. Meyer, 1991, p. 203.
45. Smith, 1991, p. 336.

Figure 4.1: The corporatist triangle

The Corporatist Triangle in Mexico and
the Peak Representative Organisation of
Each Sector

CTM-Confederation
of Mexican Workers
(CROM until 1936)

CNC-National
Confederation of
Peasants (estab.1934)

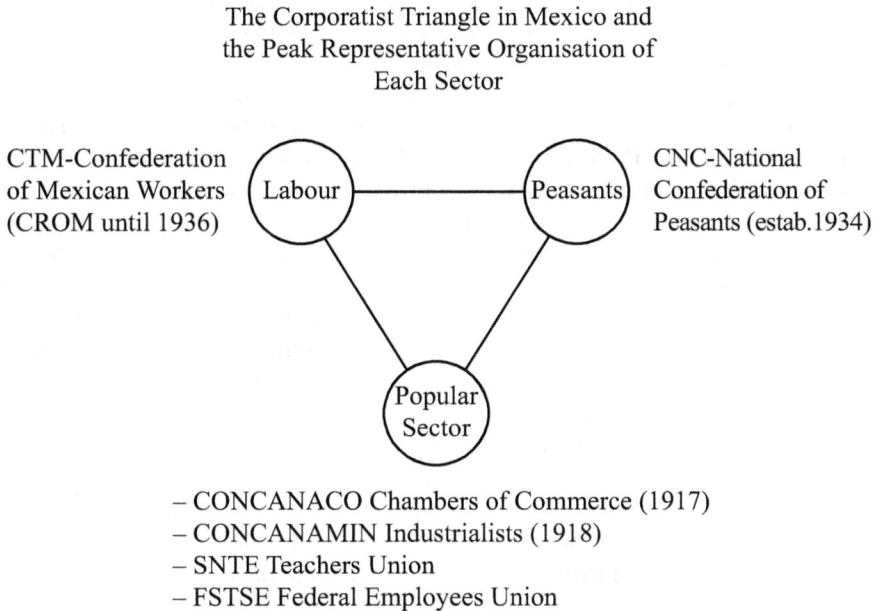

– CONCANACO Chambers of Commerce (1917)
– CONCANAMIN Industrialists (1918)
– SNTE Teachers Union
– FSTSE Federal Employees Union

Labour organisations

One of the most critical components of the corporatist triangle was organised labour. Even though the scale and scope of the labour movement was relatively small during the Revolution, the 1917 Constitution included some of the most progressive labour provisions of its era. Article 123 of the Constitution established an eight-hour workday, six-day workweek and minimum wage levels. Moreover, it placed a ban on child-labour, allowed unionisation rights for workers and even included a right to three months' maternity leave.

These progressive provisions of the 1917 Constitution could easily be interpreted as a success story for workers and unions. However, subsequent developments in state–labour relations created a rather asymmetric pattern of relations. The post-revolutionary Mexican state was interventionist and its alliance with labour was on unequal terms. Despite the relatively progressive rights of association, for instance, only the 'official' unions received significant protection and subsidies from the state. This pattern of relationships, in turn, transformed unions into mechanisms of state control over rank-and-file workers.[46] According

46. K. J. Middlebrook, *The Paradox of Revolution: Labor, the state and authoritarianism in Mexico*, Baltimore, MD and London: Johns Hopkins University Press, 1995, pp. 41–7.

to Middlebrook, 'the governing elite maintained a strong base of mass support' but, at the same time, imposed 'significant constraints on independent political mobilization, and the autonomous representation of group interests'.[47]

Traditionally, organised labour has been a stable component of the corporatist structure in Mexico and a loyal follower of the dominant party line. Support from organised labour was an important source of mass legitimacy for the PRI. Therefore, concessions were made in the form of office for politically savvy labour leaders. As early as 1938, the PRI 'formally incorporated labour as a "sector" with nominal voting rights'.[48] This organic relationship between organised labour and the Party, combined with the quasi-governmental characteristic of the party, effectively locked labour into the corporatist structure of state–society relations in Mexico. Labour unions secured votes for the party – by coercive or fraudulent means at times – in exchange for nominations for elected posts in the state.

This structure of deliberate harmonisation of interests practically eliminated worker activism, at least in the officially unionised segment of labour. The most prominent labour organisation, *Confederacion de Trabajadores de Mexico* (CTM), 'never held a general strike, preferring to resolve conflicts through negotiations with the ruling party'.[49] Labour unions and confederations did not risk severing their ties with the state; nor did they seek to challenge business directly. Rather, they preferred to channel their demands to the state by means of the Party. This form of behaviour could easily be categorised as 'corporatist' in the sense that the major organisation of a sector – the labour federation – negotiates with the state in order to improve its position, rather than directly addressing its counterpart, the business sector.

A typical personality exemplifying the nature of state–organised labour relations in this corporatist framework was Luis Morones. Morones was the president of the most powerful labour organisation of the time, the Regional Confederation of Mexican Workers (CROM), which became CTM after 1936. At the same time, he was Minister of Labour during the Calles government. Morones was famous for wild parties at his mansion, his enormous diamond rings and his commitment to fighting political battles against the enemies of Calles regime. Thus, he sided with Calles in his anticlerical campaign against the Catholic Church and also actively sought to eliminate more radical unions that were affiliated with the Communist Party.[50] The notorious contemporary case of the formidable teacher's union leader, Elba Esther Gordillo, and her expensive aesthetic surgeries and shopping sprees in the US, were not unprecedented in the context of organised labour in Mexico.

---

47. Middlebrook, 1995, p. 2.

48. J. Samstad, 'Corporatist and democratic transition: state and labor during the Salinas and Zedillo administrations', *Latin American Politics and Society* 2002, 44(4), p. 4.

49. R. L. Madrid, 'Labouring against neoliberalism: unions and patterns of reform in Latin America', *Journal of Latin American Studies* 2003, 35(1), p. 79.

50. Krauze, 1997, p. 425.

The attempts of the Mexican state and the PRI to co-opt labour were not confined to the Calles era. In fact, labour was formally incorporated into the PRI during the Cárdenas presidency; Cárdenas also provided direct material benefits to this group.[51] Later, President Alemán (1946–52) developed the art and science of labour co-optation, employing numerous methods to cajole the members of loyal labour unions and divide and intimidate (even to the extent of shooting) the supporters of dissident ones. The practice of labour leaders selling out the interests of their fellow workers in exchange for personal profit or political gain was so common that there was a special term for this type of unionism: *charrismo*.[52] When *charrismo* did not work, Alemán used other tactics, such as supporting the formation of alternative labour unions in order to weaken the established union in that sector (a divide-and-conquer strategy).

Alemán's *sexenio* (six-year term in office) coincided with the Truman Doctrine, the US's containment strategy against communism and the exertion of US hegemony in Latin America. Wary of offending US interests in Mexico, Alemán endorsed a staunchly anti-communist stance and skilfully isolated the left and organised labour. Railway and oil workers tried to establish autonomous unions but those attempts proved futile. Communists were removed from the unions and jailed and pro-government, co-opted *charro* factions were installed in their place. Co-opted leaders rationalised their situation with the following words: '[...] better a bad collective contract but which is at least honoured than a good one which remains a dead letter'.[53]

The strategy of dividing and conquering the labour movement was successfully deployed by the PRI throughout its decades-long rule. Two of the strongest labour organisations, the teacher's union and the state employee's union, were deliberately excluded from the peak labour organisation (the Labour Congress). Instead, teachers and civil servants were included in the 'popular sector', which also had the middle classes and the business as members.[54] By this means, the state reduced both the impact of the labour movement and the pressure from the business sector.

Levy and Bruhn are among the scholars who categorise state–society relations in Mexico as corporatist and they highlight the negative consequences of the state-controlled labour (and peasant) movements for democratic progress in Mexico. They argue that the PRI's capture of labour (as well as of the peasants) significantly hindered the overall democratic potential of the Mexican political

51. B. Magaloni, 'The demise of Mexico's one-party dominant regime', in F. Hagopian and S. Mainwaring (eds), *The Third Wave of Democratization in Latin America*, New York: Cambridge University Press, 2005, p. 125.

52. Smith, 1991, p. 343: originally, *charros* were the traditional horsemen in Mexico who ride in a special style on very elaborate and ornate saddles.

53. A. Knight, 'Rise and fall of Cardenismo', in L. Bethell (ed.), *Mexico Since Independence*, New York: Cambridge University Press, 1991, pp. 316–9.

54. Levy and Bruhn, 2001, p. 74.

system. In industrialised democracies, labour has a critical role as a progressive social force. Due to its size and mass-mobilisation capacity, labour can form a significant opposition bloc and exert pressure on authoritarian governments. Contrary to this pattern, however, Mexican labour was successfully enveloped by state corporatism. Because of their close links with the party apparatus and the state, the leaders 'became more responsive to the President than to their members because the state, not workers, determined who could lead unions'. The leader of the most powerful labour organisation, CMT, for example, literally kept his position for a lifetime. Fidel Velazquez was the unquestioned leader of the CMT from 1950s till his death in 1997, exemplifying the monopolistic and corrupt face of the Mexican labour movement.[55]

Peasants

Even though peasants constituted a vital constituency during the Mexican Revolution, early presidents were rather slow in acting when it came to implementing land reform and establishing formal links between the corporatist state and the rural sector. This relative neglect of peasants lasted until the Great Depression. In 1934, a separate Agrarian Department was established by the PRL. With the establishment of the National Peasant Confederation (CNC) during the presidency of Lazaro Cárdenas (1934–40), the rural sector was officially incorporated into the corporatist structure.[56]

Unlike the previous presidents, who came from the more developed northern regions, particularly Sonora, Cárdenas was from Michoacan. This made him more sympathetic to the plight of the *campesinos*. During his *sexenio*, the PRI made a sharp turn to the left, and land reform gained priority on the national political agenda. Cárdenas distributed more than 18 million hectares to some 800,000 recipients.[57] Aside from these land grants, Cárdenas also extended credit to the *campesinos* through the National Bank of Ejidal Credit. He invested in agrarian infrastructure with new irrigation projects, roads and the electrification of villages. The following table provides a summary of improvements in the rural sector by the end of Cárdenas era.

The reforms had significant impact on the living standards of the rural population. Rural productivity improved, as well as rural minimum wages. Literacy and health indicators also rose after the implementation of rural reforms. The following statement from a *campesino* summarises their overall impact: 'Before we lived like beasts. Now, at least, we are men and we increase the crop, we earn more'.[58]

---

55. Levy and Bruhn, 2001, pp. 73–5.
56. Knight, 1991, p. 257; Levy and Bruhn, 2001, p. 79.
57. Knight, 1991, p. 258.
58. Knight, 1991, p. 260.

Table 4.1: Impact of land reform during Cárdenas years

	1930	1940
Share of *ejidos* (as % of cultivated land)	15%	47%
Ejidal population	668,000	1.6 million
Landless population	2.5 million	1.9 million

Source: Alan Knight, 1991 'The rise and fall of Cardenismo', in L. Bethell (ed.), *Mexico Since Independence*, Cambridge and New York: Cambridge University Press, p. 258.

On the issue of land reform, there was an important catch. The land reform peasants wanted could only be made on a collective basis. In order to apply, peasants had to be organised into communities. Once they were granted the *ejido* by the state, their community was incorporated into the CNC. These peasant organisations later became important structures for binding peasants to the corporatist state.

The heyday of the *campesinos* did not last long. From the 1940s onwards, the economic tide turned against the agricultural sector and the policies of the PRI began to hurt. Particularly during the presidency of Alemán, the PRI experienced both a political and ideological shift. Industrialisation and providing cheap food for the urban population became the two main priorities of the party. As a result, price controls were imposed on agricultural products and state credit for peasants shrank.

Despite these unfavourable policies, peasants did not have much choice other than remaining loyal to the party. The PRI still maintained 80–90 per cent electoral support in rural Mexico. The single notable attempt to establish an independent organisation came during the 1960s under the leadership of Cárdenas but it was quickly eliminated by the PRI through the successful co-optation of some leaders and jailing of others.[59] In the end, as Tutino writes, the 'peasant communities of revolutionary Mexico received more land than autonomy'.[60] The class of landed elites in Mexico were largely undermined but this did not mean autonomy and security for the *campesinos*. Their victory and their gains from land reform were significantly compromised by their loss of autonomy to the corporatist structures of the Mexican state.

Business

In post-revolutionary Mexico, business no longer benefited from the privileged status it had enjoyed during the Diaz era. Following the Revolution in 1910 and the Great Depression in 1929, the political climate in the country was overwhelmingly statist and nationalist. During the more than three decades of

59. Levy and Bruhn, 2001, p. 79.
60. J. Tutino, *From Insurrection to Revolution in Mexico: Social bases of agrarian violence, 1750–1940*, Princeton, NJ: Princeton University Press, 1989, p. 347.

Porfirian experimentation with a liberal economy, most of Mexican society was denied the benefits of growth and prosperity. Especially after the destruction of global markets with the Great Depression, most nations had placed their faith in the state for economic development and prosperity. The new economic doctrine that carried the day was import-substitution industrialisation (ISI), which placed the Mexican state in the driver's seat. The ISI model placed a stronger emphasis on autonomous development and self-sufficiency through a state-led economy. Under ISI, most of the previously foreign-owned industries were nationalised and a domestic manufacturing and industrial sector were nurtured behind high protectionist walls. The state no longer relied on the 'invisible hand' of the market and its myth of the trickling down of wealth and prosperity. Rather, it tried to harmonise the competing interests of Mexican society by forming peak associations for labour, business, peasants and the popular sectors (mostly urban middle classes).

After the *belle époque* of Diaz, the business class, particularly landlords, were forced to adopt a defensive position. Even though only 9 per cent of Mexican land (by value) was transferred to *ejidos*, the revolutionary mentality caused great discomfort to landlords. Those who retained their lands 'did so on different terms, at greater cost'. In fact, some of them completely gave up on agriculture and transferred their capital into the urban industries and commercial sectors. This strategic shift ended up further weakening the old exploitative *hacienda* institution.[61]

The protectionist policies of the import-substitution era made Mexican business sector highly dependent upon the state for their financial wellbeing. Domestic industry benefited from tax breaks, protective tariff barriers and state subsidies in critical inputs such as oil and electricity. They were brought under the corporatist umbrella roughly around the same time as labour and the peasants; but unlike these two groups, business could never formally join the PRI. The peak organisations of business in Mexico were split into two branches, the industrial and the commercial wing. The Confederation of Chambers of Commerce (CONCANACO) was the oldest business organisation (established in 1917), followed by the Confederation of Industrial Chambers (CONCAMIN), established in 1918.[62]

The PRI was politically savvy enough to keep business at a distance, and consolidate its ties with the numerically larger constituencies, such as the rural and urban popular sectors and labour. These larger constituencies were more vital for the PRI, as they provided both electoral popularity and legitimacy for the single-party regime. The business sector itself was also rather uncomfortable with the PRI, especially during the terms of more left-leaning presidents, such as Cárdenas and Ruiz Cortines. The land-reform agenda of the PRI and its pro-labour social policies were regarded with great scepticism by the business elites.

---

61. Knight, 1991, pp. 242–3.

62. Levy and Bruhn, 2001, pp. 83–4.

This potentially hostile environment, coupled with their economic subjugation under ISI, caused business to concede an uneasy acquiescence to the authoritarian state. Schneider aptly describes the acceptance by business of a minor official role within the corporatist structure as one of 'love, hate, and exclusion'.[63]

Mexican business did not have separate formal representation in the corporate structures of the government. Nor did it receive frequent appointments within the executive bureaucracy. Unlike the US pattern of a revolving door between politics and business, business families and state bureaucracy in Mexico maintained a strict separation. Even their children went to different schools.[64] This, however, did not mean that informal links were completely out of question. During the 1970s, for example, Mexican presidents had already established a customary practice of once-a-month lunch gatherings with the *Consejo Mexicano de Hombres de Negocios* (CMHN), an exclusive business association representing the wealthiest industrialists of the country.

Despite having these informal ties with the executive, the business sector was still displeased with being lumped together with small shop-owners, teachers and civil servants under the corporatist umbrella of 'popular sector'. In fact, throughout the 1930s, in 1957, and as late as 1984, business leaders petitioned the PRI for the formal establishment of a separate business sector. They were repeatedly denied.[65] The formal participation and articulation of business interests came through compulsory membership in a handful of wide-ranging business associations. This exclusion, as Schneider notes, led to the creation and broad support of independent business organisations in the 1980s.

Beginning in the 1980s, as the internationalisation of Mexico's economy began, the old corporatist arrangements began to come unglued. As more and more sectors of the Mexican economy became export-oriented, their dependence upon the state began to wear down. The prosperity of business was no longer so heavily dependent upon government protection. Naturally, these businesses had little use for the old corporatist networks and they became resentful of state involvement in the economy. From the business perspective, government involvement in the economy only perpetuated corruption and inefficiency. As Bellin makes the case, it was at this point that the new class of economic entrepreneurs 'discovered democracy', seeking liberal reforms and essentially transforming themselves into political entrepreneurs as well.[66] Ultimately, the activities of these entrepreneurs resulted in the bankrolling of the centre-right party *Partido Acción Nacional,* (National Action Party, PAN). The details of these developments and the transition from corporatism to a more pluralistic form of state-business relations will be discussed in the Chapter Five.

---

63. B. R. Schneider, 'Why is Mexican business so organized?', *Latin American Research Review* 2002, 37(1), pp. 77–118, p. 79.

64. Levy and Bruhn, 2001, p. 83.

65. Schneider, 2002, p. 80.

66. E. R. Bellin, 'Contingent democrats: industrialists, labor, and democratization in late developing countries', *World Politics* 2000, 52 (2), pp. 175–205, p. 195.

The 'Mexican miracle': Political economy during the single-party years

The political-economic doctrine during the *Porfiriato* was a liberal one. The architects of the economic policies of Diaz were young PhD holders, mostly from the US, who placed their bets on the 'comparative advantage doctrine' of neo-classical political economy. In this model, Mexico supplied the global markets with the products in which it was most competitive (mostly raw materials and agricultural products) and then purchased its needs in the global marketplace (mostly manufactured goods).

In light of the liberal economic model, the Diaz government welcomed foreign investment, invested in the infrastructure and expanded the railway network. Northern Mexico turned into a huge quarry, with the expansion of silver, gold, copper and zinc mines. Also in the North, there were large ranches raising cattle and sheep, largely for the US market. Sugar was grown in the central and southern provinces. Overall, 'the volume of foreign trade grew nine times between 1877 and 1910' but, after three decades of intense liberalism, the Mexican economy could not graduate from being a primary-product exporter.[67]

The first quarter of the twentieth century did not bring much prosperity to most parts of the world and Mexico was no exception. Early on, Mexico was hit by the twin shocks of the Revolution (1910–20) and the Great Depression (1929). 'In 1930, Mexico's GDP fell to 12.5 per cent below its 1925 level'.[68] Most of the developing world felt the compelling necessity of industrialisation in the aftermath of the Great Depression. Hand in hand with the industrialisation drive went the general consensus that the state should have a more active role in setting the course of economy. Both of these developments coincided with the presidency of Cárdenas, who strongly favoured steering the economy away from the liberal path.

Between 1934 and 1940, President Cárdenas made critical economic decisions that would determine the political-economic blueprint of the nation for years to come. As the numbers in Table 4.1 indicate, he launched the most extensive land-reform campaign since the Revolution. Equally, if not more important than his agrarian policies were his measures against foreign capital. In a bold move, Cárdenas nationalised foreign-owned oil companies and established the state-owned petroleum company PEMEX (*Petroleos Mexicanos*).

Cárdenas could get away with nationalising oil companies because his timing was good. In the political climate of the late 1930s and early 1940s, the US could not risk severing ties with Mexico. In fact, President Roosevelt personally 'urged the petroleum companies to accept a negotiated settlement to the 1938 nationalization'. Cárdenas's timing was almost perfect, as it coincided with the non-interventionist 'good neighbour policy' of Roosevelt. In the end, FDR upheld

---

67. Smith, 1991, p. 321–3.

68. Smith, 1991, p. 324.

his pledge of non-intervention, and the expropriation issue was resolved by the World Court, when Mexico agreed to pay compensation to the US oil companies.[69]

When Germany torpedoed two Mexican oil tankers bound for the US, Mexico declared war on the Axis in 1942. By then, most other Latin American countries had already joined the Allies, except for Argentina and Chile.[70] Goods as well as workers were increasingly heading towards the US market during war years. Under the *Braceros* programme, large numbers of Mexican workers headed up to the US as a substitute for the workforce that had mobilised for war.

WWII provided further impetus to the state-led industrialisation attempts of peripheral economies. Since the US and other advanced economies were unwilling or unable to export manufactured goods, it was only logical for the rest to try producing them on their own. Consequently, the Mexican economy experienced a rapid industrialisation drive between the 1940s and 1960s. In these two decades, GDP increased on average 6.4 per cent each year, and in 1960 industry accounted for 29 per cent of the GDP.[71]

The foremost architect of the 'Mexican Miracle' was President Miguel Alemán Valdés (1946–52). Alemán's presidency marked the opening of a new epoch in Mexican history. His civilian background, flamboyant personality and American tastes were a sea change for the Mexican *nomenklatura*. Alemán was the first civilian to preside over Mexico since the Revolution. He was a lawyer by training (a Harvard graduate), fluent in English and had good looks to accompany his playboy style. He was the Businessman President who wanted 'all Mexicans to have a Cadillac, a cigar and a ticket to the bullfights!'.[72]

Alemán's economic vision energised the ISI policies of Mexico. He considered the state and private and foreign capital as partners in Mexico's industrialisation drive but conceived of the state as the main arbitrator in this collaboration. Even though he was not as hostile to foreign capital as his predecessor, Cárdenas, Alemán did not hesitate to impose high protective tariff walls (in line with ISI theory), in order to discourage imports of manufactured goods.

Alemán's presidency coincided with the emergence of a bi-polar world order. The Cold War atmosphere was beginning to be felt and Alemán used this as an opportunity to weed out left-leaning figures from the PRI. The president and his team (young, articulate, well educated, many of them his classmates from Harvard Law School) were predisposed to steer Mexico towards the US. This meant redirecting the country towards a capitalist path to development. In order to achieve this, Alemán undertook some major projects targeting infrastructure, industrial and agricultural development in Mexico.

Alemán was very much impressed by the Tennessee Valley Authority in the US, which was an expansive regional development project sponsored by

---

69. Smith, 1991, p. 337; Kryzanek, 1996, pp. 59–60

70. Kryzanek, 1996, p. 61.

71. Smith, 1991, pp. 324–5.

72. Krauze, 1997, p. 543.

the US federal government. Soon after taking power, Alemán initiated massive dam projects. Secondly, the highway network in the US left its impression on the Mexican President and thus, he invested in the Pan-American Highway, from Ciudad Juarez all the way to the Guatemalan border. By 1957, there were 15,000 miles of paved roads in Mexico.[73] The highway network was also extended to the coasts; Acapulco, in particular, benefited from this infrastructure boom and, by 1960, became a world-class tourist attraction. Four-lane highways connected Mexico City to Acapulco and Hollywood figures were now hanging out in new high-rise hotels and mixing with the flamboyant Alemán. Validating the claims of corruption under his watch, Alemán made a fortune from his properties through real-estate manipulation in Acapulco.[74]

At the heart of the Mexican Miracle was industrialisation. Industrial parks were established in the north of Mexico City during the 1950s. On average, industrial growth was 7.2 per cent annually during the Alemán years. The electricity, energy, chemicals, steel, communication and transportation sectors led the industrial drive and stimulated the 'Mexican Miracle' during Alemán's *sexenio*. Table 4.2 shows the intensity of this industrialisation drive.

President Alemán's goal of industrialising Mexico behind heavy protectionist walls, promoting tourism (which was also encouraging land speculation) and his Hollywood-style glamorous life contributed to a nationwide sense of political corruption and decay. Thus, the PRI machine came down heavily in favour of an untainted candidate as his successor.

The 'Green Revolution'

Many authors argue that, if there was anything miraculous in Mexico, it was happening in the agricultural sector. While Cárdenas had emphasised land reform in order to improve the lot of the agrarian population, Alemán emphasised the importance of productivity, profit and mechanisation. During his presidency, 30,000 tractors were imported and 'new varieties of wheat and corn were developed', with the help of the Rockefeller Foundation.[75]

Alemán also initiated massive irrigation projects and encouraged the use of fertilisers and machinery to enhance productivity. His policies, however, favoured large landholders, *haciendas*, northern ranchers and large-scale commercial farms. Alemán also tinkered with the constitutional definition of 'small properties': after a little adjustment, properties up to 100 hectares could be classified as 'small'.[76]

Alemán's 'Green Revolution' created a huge rift between the large-scale commercial agricultural operators and the communal farmers (*ejidatores*).

---

73. J. Sherman, 'The Mexican 'miracle' and its collapse', in M. Meyer and W. Beezley, *The Oxford History of Mexico*, Oxford and New York: Oxford University Press, 2000, p. 585.

74. Shennan, 2000, p. 586.

75. Krauze, 1997, p. 542.

76. Smith, 1991, p. 340.

Table 4.2: Mexican industry 1940–50

	1940	1950
Number of establishments	13,000	73,000
% of food and textiles	68%	48%

Source: Enrique Krauze, *Mexico: A Biography of Power*, New York: Harper Collins, 1997, p. 543.

Between 1950 and 1970, there was a 147 per cent increase in the per-acre output of large-scale private farms. For *ejidos*, the increase was 113 per cent. While the seemingly endless debate on the productivity gap between collective and private farms is beyond the scope of this book, it is safe to mention some concrete factors that systematically undermined the productivity of *ejidal* lands.

First, the *ejidos* had much less access to credit than commercial farms. Legally, they could not use their lands as collateral and they had very little else to offer the banks in exchange for credit. Secondly, and related to the first problem, the *ejidos* also had limited access to technology, mechanisation and fertiliser. Thirdly, the *ejidos* usually occupied lower-quality land in terms of the soil and the availability of irrigation facilities. Given these structural disadvantages, it would be unfair to argue that the *ejidos* were inherently less productive.[77] If they had better access to credit, agricultural technologies and irrigation, maybe these collective farms could have matched the productivity levels of the commercial enterprises.

The Green Revolution had a number of important consequences for the Mexican society and the economy. The enhanced productivity levels due to increased mechanisation, irrigation and fertiliser use decreased the utility of agricultural labour force and collective farms. Table 4.3 shows the increase in the amount of produce, despite the decline in the actual amount of land used in production in most parts. Yet, this came at the expense of subsistence and collective farming.

As the list of cultivated crops indicates, much agricultural production was geared towards export. Unable to compete with highly commercialised agriculture, the *ejidos* lagged behind and many eventually went bankrupt. By law, the peasants could not sell their *ejidos*, so most of them ended up perpetually renting their shares in exchange for their debts. Tragically, the peasants were still the owners of their *ejido* lands on paper, however in reality, others were harvesting these fields year after years, in some kind of a land-for-debt swap.[78] This, in turn, generated a rural exodus. Increasing rural poverty combined with the population pressure resulted in a rural exodus from 1950s onwards. In 1940, only 18 per cent of the Mexican population was living in urban areas. By 1970, this reached 35 per cent and Mexico began to suffer from the shantytown phenomenon in its large cities.[79]

This debt trap of the Green Revolution also came up during my field research in the summer of 2008. I had the chance to meet and interview numerous *campesinos*

---

77. Smith, 1991, p. 329.

78. Sherman, 2000, p. 592.

79. Smith, 1991, p. 330.

Table 4.3: Increase in agricultural production, 1946–52 (value of crop in millions pesos)

	1946	1952
Cotton	80	199
Coffee	78	283
Tomatoes	78	179
Sugar	159	292
Wheat	139	375
Corn	680	1.6 billion
Beans	94	180

Source: Enrique Krauze, *Mexico: A Biography of Power*, New York: Harper Collins, 1997, p. 542.

and rural activists in the Bajio region of central Mexico. Most of them vividly remembered the early 1970s. Those were the years of the Echeverría presidency (1970–6), who was initially perceived as a populist and a friend of the rural sector. He established the *Banco Rural*, which provided credit to *campesinos*. With these new riches, *campesinos* went out and purchased tractors, seeds and fertiliser. While most of the literature on Echeverría and his agricultural policies has a rather positive tone, the testimonies from my field research were quite critical of him. The *campesinos* of the Bajio argue that, in fact, the credit from *Banco Rural* went straight into the pockets of the tractor factories like Ford, John Deere and Massey Ferguson. In their own words, the credits were absorbed by those 'yellow' (the colour of Ford tractors), 'green' (John Deere) and 'red' (Massey Ferguson) 'monsters'. With the new machinery, the *ejidatores* became more dependent on commercial seeds and chemical fertilisers. Gradually, they all began to accumulate large debts with Banco Rural.

Technically, the *ejidos* could not be sold to pay back the debt when the *campesinos* defaulted because of the protective clause in the Constitution. Therefore, *Banco Rural* could not take over the *ejidos* themselves. Instead, the Bank made compulsory production and sales arrangements with the *campesinos*. *Ejidatores* were compelled to plant certain crops, like grapes or chillies, and sell them to the Bank for a price far below the market rate. This ended up creating another form of indentured servitude between the bank and the rural sector. They were planting maize and frijoles in a small plot for their own consumption and all the rest of the fields were harvested to service the debt to *Banco Rural*. Some of the people I spoke to told me how this burden carried over from generation to generation.

The Green Revolution also had significant environmental consequences for the Bajio region. I also learned from the *campesinos* that the purchased seeds and all the chemical fertilisers they required destroyed the organic material in the soil. This had a negative impact on the trees and the topsoil. The quality of agricultural land began to deteriorate rapidly. Due to the environmental deterioration, seasonal rains had more destructive effects. Nearly all my respondents agreed that, during the 1980s, there was a second wholesale exodus from the *campo*. Many able bodies migrated either to large cities or to the US. Among other factors, the overwhelming credit burden and environmental deterioration both played an important part in the context of globalisation and Mexico's attempts to integrate its economy with world capitalism, *via* ending the constitutional protection of *ejido* lands, allowing large, international companies to move in and so on.

The large-scale commercial farm operations came out the undisputed winners of the Green Revolution. By 1970, half of Mexican crops were produced by massive agribusinesses. The uneven nature of the Green Revolution had concentrated agricultural wealth in few hands across few Mexican States (Sonora, Veracruz and Sinaloa).[80] Their dominance in the sector has also shifted the direction of agricultural production towards export markets and middle-class tastes. As these big players produced tomatoes, strawberries, avocados, plums and such for well-off consumers, the prices of staples in Mexico went up. Subsequent administrations imposed price controls in order to provide cheap staples (corn, beans, rice), especially for the urban poor, but the Green Revolution weighed heavily on the *ejidatores*, small farmers and on the rural populations of interior and Indian-populated states.

The pendulum of Mexican politics: A key to Mexican exceptionalism

The seventy-one-year reign of a single party in Mexico might create the illusion that in the aftermath of the Revolution, politics in Mexico became dull. The unbroken rule of the PRI for seven decades, however, did not mean the absence of change in the political realm. Despite operating under the banner of the same party, Mexican presidents varied significantly in terms of their policy portfolios. While some endorsed leftist, populist options such as land reform, social security and rural credit banks, others implemented decidedly pro-business policies. Analysts of Mexican politics often invoke the pendulum metaphor in order to explain these important policy shifts from one administration to the next.

The pendulum metaphor should not be interpreted merely as the swinging of Mexican presidents from extreme left to extreme right. Such a perspective would leave numerous moderate Presidents outside the model. During the 1970s, a complex version of the pendulum analogy emerged. In this revised model, the pendulum does not make wide sweeps from extreme left to extreme right but rather moves to a central position after each of the extremes. That is, 'every first or third president stood on the extreme left or right and every second president was a centrist.'[81]

As discussed above, the corporatist structure of the Mexican polity compelled the state to incorporate or co-opt all major sectors of the society. Yet, in practice,

80. Sherman, 2000, pp. 591–2.
81. M. C. Needler, 'Metaphors, models, and myths in the interpretation of Mexican politics', *Mexican Studies/Estudios Mexicanos* 1991, 7(2), pp. 347–57, p. 349.

it was hard to accommodate all the contradictory needs of business (large *and* small), workers, peasants and the urban middle classes simultaneously. A key to the PRI's success and the much-admired political stability of Mexico was the ability of successive presidents to shift their political orientation. In Dale Story's words, the swinging of the Mexican pendulum from left to right helped accommodate excluded sectors and thereby contributed to the longevity of the regime:

> If one president is perceived to favour, even slightly, a particular group or ideology, the next president must balance the scales by leaning in the opposite direction. This shift promotes stability and a balance of forces by alternatively satisfying different interests.[82]

Along with accommodating previously excluded interests, these shifts in political orientation also represent an effort by each president to leave his own stamp on Mexican politics. In general, the incoming president tended to focus on the areas neglected by his predecessor and tried to fix the problems and failures of the outgoing president. Through new policy initiatives, new presidents tried to show that 'they are different from and better than their predecessors'.[83]

The pendulum effect can be measured by the time-series observation of several factors, such as the patterns of public spending or foreign investment flows (*see* Figure 4.2). Left-leaning governments, for instance, tend to prioritise social spending. They invest in public services such as education, healthcare and social security. Spending from the federal budget can also increase during periods of right-wing government but in these cases expenditure favours infrastructure projects such as large dams or highways.

The pendulum of Mexican politics probably experienced its most leftward swing during the presidency of Cárdenas. His land-reform initiative not only gave vast amounts of choice land to peasants but also distributed land in collective form (as *ejidos*). His nationalisation of the oil industry and the establishment of the state oil monopoly, PEMEX, gained him a legendary reputation. All these rather radical moves notwithstanding, Cárdenas decided to pass the presidential sash to the little-known moderate, General Manuel Avila Camacho.

President Camacho was by no means a radical. He continued the land-reform agenda but preferred small-scale, family farm operations to the collective *ejidos*. On the labour front, his policies and decisions also aimed at moderation. Instead of more militant union leaders, he placed the complacent Fidel Velazquez at the helm of the top labour federation. As for carrots, Camacho created the national social security agency (*Instituto Mexicano de Segura Social*, IMSS), which

---

82. D. Story, 'Policy cycles in Mexican presidential politics', *Latin American Research Review*, 1985, 20(3), pp. 139–61, p. 141.

83. Story, 1985, p. 140.

Figure 4.2: The pendulum of Mexican politics

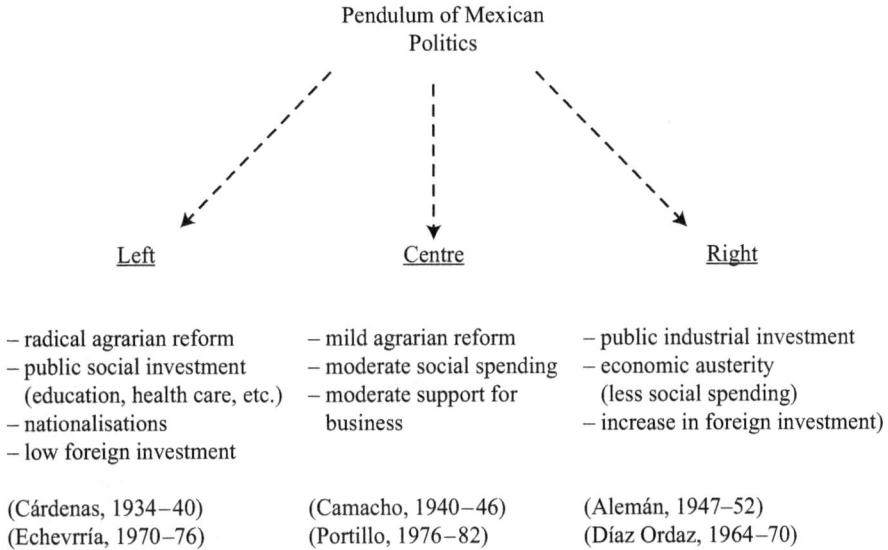

Pendulum of Mexican
Politics

Left   Centre   Right

Left	Centre	Right

– radical agrarian reform
– public social investment
  (education, health care, etc.)
– nationalisations
– low foreign investment
	– mild agrarian reform
	– moderate social spending
	– moderate support for
	  business
		– public industrial investment
		– economic austerity
		  (less social spending)
		– increase in foreign investment)

(Cárdenas, 1934–40) (Echevrría, 1970–76)	(Camacho, 1940–46) (Portillo, 1976–82)	(Alemán, 1947–52) (Díaz Ordaz, 1964–70)

provided healthcare to the formally employed workforce.[84] Thus, the pendulum of Mexican politics retreated back to the centre, after its sharp leftward swing under Cárdenas.

Mexican politics experienced a definite rightward swing during the Presidency of Miguel Alemán (1946–52). His pro-American orientation and the immediate aftermath of WWII heavily influenced the economic decisions taken on his watch. As discussed in detail above, he weighed in heavily on the side of business, invested in massive infrastructure projects that catered to the commercial interests and favoured large agricultural enterprises over small and collective farms. Despite surges in economic growth and industrialisation during the Alemán years, his flamboyant style and the growing nepotism and corruption scandals during his administration tarnished the popular image of the PRI.

President Adolfo Luis Cortinez (1952–8) came to power largely due to his honest reputation. During the formal ceremony in which the presidential sash changed hands, Cortinez did something very uncustomary. Instead of extending the usual courtesy to the outgoing president, he wagged his finger in Alemán's direction and said: 'I will not permit the principles of the Revolution nor the laws that guide us broken [...] *I will be inflexible with public servants who stray from*

---

84. T. Skidmore and P. Smith, 'Mexico: The taming of a revolution,' in T. Skidmore and P. Smith (eds), *Modern Latin America*, New York and Oxford: Oxford University Press, 2001, pp. 237–8.

honesty and decency'.[85] Well known for his professional administrative skills, President Cortinez followed conservative economic policies and brought the political pendulum back to a neutral position from its right-wing swing during the Alemán years.

After coming to a neutral position under the watch of Cortinez, the Mexican political pendulum swung all the way to the left with a new administration. The successor of Cortinez, Adolfo López Mateos (1958–64) declared that his administration would be 'on the extreme left, within the Constitution'.[86] The single-party regime needed a pro-labour and pro-*campesino* administration after more than a decade of pro-business policies in previous administrations. Therefore, the populism of López Mateos was an important strategy for reuniting these crucial corporate sectors under the single-party umbrella.

The pendulum of Mexican politics, combined with the reshuffling of the elites with each *sexenio*, provided an important degree of stability in Mexican politics. As the political leadership moved from left to right and *vice versa*, with periodic stops in the middle, these moves were accompanied by a major reshuffling of top-level elected office-holders. After more than three decades of the rule of General Porfirio Diaz, 'no re-election' became an important principle in Mexican politics. The 1933 law forbade the consecutive re-election of top-level office-holders, which includes senators, governors, deputies and municipal presidents.[87] As a result, there was a regular turnover of elites in office, no matter how well connected. From the perspective of the individual politician, it was an uphill battle to establish an opposition party and try to beat the giant PRI machine in the elections, whereas, if they were patient enough, eventually they were very likely to have their turn in office, under the banner of the PRI.

When explaining the remarkable stability of single-party rule in Mexico, these two strategies of the PRI provide significant insights. The periodic swings of the political pendulum accommodated leftist, rightist and centrist elements under the same party structure almost seamlessly for seven decades. The circulation among the elites on the other hand, provided enough openings in the top elected positions. This characteristic made the PRI highly immune to elite splintering. As discussed in the previous chapter, the single-party regime in Turkey could not protect itself from factionalism and splintering because the CHP was not as flexible as the PRI, in terms of both its ideology and institutional structure. Thus, the single party in Turkey split in 1946 and eventually the political landscape became dotted with numerous political parties.

Nevertheless, even the ever-stable PRI had to weather significant storms, especially from the late 1960s on. The 1960s, particularly its second half, was the decade of revolutionary fever around the world. Intellectuals, university students

---

85. Krauze, 1997, p. 601 (*author addition*).

86. Skidmore and Smith, 2001, p. 240.

87. Magaloni, 2005, p. 126.

and parts of the middle classes were collectively questioning authoritarian practices. They were pushing the limits of the political establishment. Mexico was no exception to this phenomenon. Similarly to their counterparts in Paris and New York, intellectuals, students and middle-class professionals took to the streets of Mexico City. Yet, the difference was in the way in which the state responded to these protests. In Mexico, the PRI overreacted to suppress the mobilisation of the 1968 generation, partly due to the pressure of hosting the 1968 Olympics. This was the first time a developing country had been given the honour of hosting the Olympics. Anxious to display a proper and orderly face to the world, the government began to crack down on popular movements with maximum force. President Gustavo Díaz Ordaz (1964–1970) was from the conservative state of Puebla. The political pendulum of Mexico clearly took a rightward swing under his watch.

The first defiance of the Díaz Ordaz administration came from the students. Between 1964 and 1965, medical interns in Mexico City went on strike. The government's reaction was harsh and 200 interns were fired. Escalating political tension in the country reached its peak in 1968. Students were again on the front lines, demanding the release of student activists who were in jail, political liberalisation and an end to police brutality. They threatened to go on strike if their demands went unheard. Díaz Ordaz had no tolerance of student activism. He declared a general lock-out of all the universities in the Federal District. Police invaded the university campuses. The rector of UNAM (National Autonomous University of Mexico) personally led a march of 80,000 students calling for the protection of the autonomy of universities. The numbers on student demonstrations subsequently grew up to 300,000.

Probably the most notorious event of the Díaz Ordaz *sexenio* was the Tlatelolco massacre. In his introduction to Elena Poniatowska's epic book, *Massacre in Mexico*, prominent Mexican author Octavio Paz describes the tragedy of Tlatelolco in the following words:

> [...] the wave of hope and generous idealism represented by these youngsters breaks against the wall of sheer power, and the government unleashes its murderous forces of violence; the story ends in a bloodbath.[88]

On 2 October 1968, only ten days before the opening of the Olympics, some 10,000 protesters gathered at the Plaza of Tlatelolco square. The security forces opened fire on the protestors indiscriminately and without warning. According to the official numbers, 32 people died. The international media and the protesters put the figure somewhere around 350. Many more than these numbers disappeared or were sentenced to jail for up to 16 years.[89]

---

88. Paz, 1975, p. viii.
89. L. Rother, '20 years after a massacre, Mexico still seeks healing for its wounds', *New York Times*, 2 October 1988.

After Tlatelolco, it became blatantly obvious that revolutionary ideals had been co-opted and destroyed by the Institutional Revolutionary Party. In Krauze's words, '1968 was both the highest point of authoritarian power and the real beginning of its collapse'.[90] Students, intellectuals and large sectors of the urban middle class were disillusioned. As a result of the massacre, intellectuals and the regime went their separate ways. Octavio Paz, who was the Mexican Ambassador in India at the time, resigned from his post in protest at the Tlatelolco incident. Carlos Fuentes also made a similar political gesture. Artists, writers, university professors and students began to question the legitimacy of the regime. Their open hostility signalled the widening cracks in the corporatist structure and the end of the 'Mexican miracle'.

The end of the 'Mexican miracle' and the decline of a 'Golden Age'

Prominent historian Eric Hobsbawm divides the Cold War era into two parts. Hobsbawm categorises the first part, which ends with the 1973 oil crisis, as the 'Golden Age'. This period is marked by significant state involvement in planning the economy, high growth rates, establishment of welfare states, rapid industrialisation, urbanisation and large public sectors around the world. According to Hobsbawm, the 'mixed economy' strategy for development was an important impetus behind this success. Most achievement stories (including France, Spain, Japan, Singapore and South Korea) are industrialisation efforts that were planned, supported and even executed by the state. Furthermore, the 'Golden Age' also coincided with 'democratisation of the markets.' Substantial progress was made in improving income-distribution, achieving full employment and providing a basic minimum level of social welfare. All of these policies expanded the pool of consumers and thereby contributed to the affluence of citizenry.[91]

In the case of Mexico, the Golden Age corresponded to the economic boom years, called the Mexican Miracle. During this era, Mexico managed to achieve an impressive 7 per cent annual growth rate for decades, despite its oversized bureaucracy, massive corruption and waste. The considerable size of its domestic market made ISI a meaningful industrialisation strategy for a long time. In Mexico, the public sector employed one-fifth of all the workforce and paid for two-fifths of the payroll.[92] As of 1970, '[...] the government controlled the principal shares in nine of the country's top ten firms, in thirteen out of the top twenty-five'.[93]

The success of Mexico depended upon the consent of an organised society and on overall economic prosperity. However, from the late 1960s on, the glitter of this era began to fade, as students and the workers began to voice their discontent. In economist's jargon, the economy 'overheated,' throwing the whole global

---

90. Krauze, 1997, p. 737.
91. E. Hobsbawm, *The Age of Extremes*, Chapter 9: The Golden Years.
92. Hobsbawm, 1996, p. 407.
93. Skidmore and Smith, 2001, p. 243.

financial system out of balance. The end of the gold standard and the decline of the Bretton Woods regime, rising commodity prices and, finally, the two oil shocks were ultimate signs of this global collapse.[94]

Under normal circumstances, the ISI model in Mexico should have run out of steam by the 1970s. The country had an outdated industrial sector that was heavily dependent upon the import of capital and intermediary goods. Since their output was not competitive in international markets, Mexico was continuously trying to finance the foreign exchange thirst of the ISI sector with exports of primary goods. Needless to say, this unsustainable policy progressively worsened the balance of payments deficit. Yet, it was the very same ISI that provided political stability and longevity for the corporatist machine of the PRI. Its protectionist policies maintained the business sector as a strong ally of the PRI, while the generous compensation of labour kept the working classes under the corporatist umbrella. Just as Mexico was approaching a financial meltdown due to its soaring trade deficit, along came the global oil crisis of 1973.

While most developing countries experienced an economic shock of historic proportions, Mexico could reap the benefits of quadrupled oil prices. As a major exporter of petroleum, Mexico's export revenues and therefore foreign-exchange reserves began to soar. Moreover, given the high price of oil and the seemingly endless reserves of oil Mexico had, international banks were suddenly eager to offer generous loans to Mexico. High oil revenues and readily available credit in a sense 'corrupted' Mexican leaders. Fuelled by the 'oil bonanza', Mexican external debt jumped from $6 billion in 1970 to $86 billion in 1982. Mexico became one of the most indebted nations in the developing world. 'In 1982, Mexico owed $24 billion in annual interest'.[95]

The second half of the 1970s was lost due to unsustainable economic policies. The huge deficit spending was financed with borrowing and an overvalued exchange rate. Rather than fixing structural problems in the system, presidents were trying to keep afloat a sinking ship.

Conclusion: Post-revolutionary Turkey and Mexico in comparative perspective

The twentieth century witnessed major transformations both in Mexico and Turkey. Modernisation, development, secularisation, industrialisation and urbanisation were all parts of this major transformation. Administrative differences between the two countries (Mexico: federalist, presidential; Turkey: unitary, parliamentarian) did not constitute important challenges for a comparative study because in both cases, centralised state power and a powerful executive branch were shared characteristics.

---

94. Hobsbawm, 1996, pp. 332–3.

95. L. Meyer, 'The second coming of Mexican liberalism: a comparative perspective', in E. Servin, L. Reina and J. Tutino (eds), *Cycles of Conflict, Centuries of Change: Crisis, reform and revolution in Mexico*, Durham and London: Duke University Press, 2007, p. 275.

In terms of their political systems, both nations started the post-revolutionary era with corporatist and single-party-dominant regimes. This situation changed in Turkey from the 1950s on, as political constituencies diversified. From then on, the country began to ride on the roller coaster of multi-party politics and oscillated between leftist and rightist coalition governments, with occasional military coups in between. Mexico, on the other hand, managed to contain this oscillation by enlarging the single-party tent. The PRI contained the often-conflicting interests of different constituencies by alternating the top executive seat between populist, left-wing and pro-market, right-wing presidents. The famous political pendulum of Mexico helped generate a significant degree of political stability and longevity for the regime.

The socio-political transformations of Mexico and Turkey until the 1980s have important similarities. The revolutionary heritages of both nations and subsequent political and economic choices about development, party organisations and social, cultural and economic policies for modernising the rural sector all have significant elements of convergence. At the same time, there are also significant points of divergence. This and the preceding chapter were an attempt to illustrate both the similarities and differences. Below, is a brief summary of these diverging and converging points.

Points of divergence

Civil–military relations

The role of the military and its relative weight in politics *vis-à-vis* other actors is one of the most important differences between Mexico and Turkey. Even though in both countries it was the upper echelons of the military who claimed the top executive positions in the aftermath of the revolutions, the situation began to change in the Mexican case from the 1930s on. Gradually, Mexico managed to tame its military and diminish its political power.

There are multiple reasons for the ascendance of civilian actors over the military in Mexico. According to Camp, 'the Revolution was critical to civil-military relations.' After the experience of revolutionary violence and a decade of turmoil, both civilian and military actors reached a consensus that violence should no longer be a legitimate political tool.[96] This was an important achievement that closed off the path towards military coups. Secondly, early Mexican Presidents, who were themselves ambitious generals before occupying the presidential palace, deliberately tried to disentangle the armed forces from politics. They praised the military at every opportunity but, at the same time, skilfully took institutional measures to undercut its strength. Establishing a strong political party and executive branch tilted the power balance in favour of civilian actors. Strong civilian political

---

96. R. A. Camp, *Mexico's Military on the Democratic Stage*, Westport, CT: Praeger, and Washington DC, CSIS, 2005, p. 5.

institutions made the military less inclined to intervene.[97] Moreover, by reducing the military budget, emphasising professionalism through modern training in military academies and strengthening the power and legitimacy of the party (PRI), Mexico succeeded in controlling the political clout of this critical institution.[98]

Early subordination of military to civilian rule in Mexico is an exception, compared to the rest of Latin America and most other developing nations. The problem of civil–military relations is also still a 'hot-button' issue in Turkey. Unlike Mexico, stability in electoral politics and strong executive institutions were rare commodities in Turkey. After the end of the single-party era in the 1950s, multi-party politics ushered in an era of polarisation and political gridlock. Combined with social violence, this polarised and ungovernable atmosphere severely compromised the legitimacy of civilian actors. This situation, in turn, created ample opportunities for the military to step in as a legitimate and trusted political actor.[99] Other reasons (such as external threats from hostile neighbours and historical and institutional legacies) certainly contributed to the powerful political clout of the Turkish military. Yet the relative weakness of civilian political actors and the subsequent compromises in their legitimacy made it even less likely that the military would retreat from the political stage.

Lifespans of the single-party regimes

Both nations embarked on the post-revolutionary era under single-party regimes and with corporatist state–society relations. The PRI and the CHP were utilised as vast networks for incorporating important sectors of the society. Most times, the party network was used as a means to control social forces such as labour, the peasantry or the urban middle classes. Many observers highlight that in both Mexico and Turkey the party and the state practically merged with each other.

Despite these characteristics during the early decades of the single party regimes, the Turkish and Mexican cases began to part ways from the 1940s on. While the PRI managed to transform into a 'mass party' and contain any splintering tendencies within the party, the CHP could not shed its 'cadre party' character. Moreover, it also suffered from elite splintering and lost the general elections in 1950 to an opposition party that emerged from within the CHP's own ranks. Later, the Turkish party system fragmented even more while the PRI in Mexico sustained its hegemonic position for seven decades.

---

97. Camp, 2005, pp. 7–9.

98. R. A. Camp, *Politics in Mexico*, New York and Oxford: Oxford University Press, 1996, pp. 128–9; *see also* R. A. Camp, *Generals in the Palacio: The military in modern Mexico*, New York: Oxford University Press, 1992.

99. Huntington argues that maximising the political power of civilians *per se* would not solve the problems, because civilian actors would compete for power among themselves: *see* S. Huntington, *The Soldier and the State: The theory and politics of civil–military relations*, Cambridge, MA: Harvard University Press, 1964, pp. 81–2.

Points of convergence

Corporatism

Both Mexico and Turkey shared a historical and cultural propensity towards a corporatist way of organising their state–society relations. Unlike a liberal model, the corporatist system requires close monitoring of interest-group activity by the state. Important sectors of society, such as labour, business, peasants, or urban professionals, were organised into state-sanctioned corporate sectors. Corporate sectors were institutionally connected to the state and interest-mediation among the groups was handled through active state involvement. Both the Mexican and Turkish states granted monopoly of representation to the peak organisations of each sector, in exchange for docile and compliant behaviour. This kind of co-optation tactic through a corporatist representation framework later turned out to be important obstacles to democratisation and political liberalisation in both countries.

Modernisation and secularisation

The post-revolutionary era in both Mexico and Turkey could be summarised as a long period of modernisation. The establishment of new schools at all levels and nationwide campaigns to reach out and educate the illiterate masses were all part and parcel of this modernisation effort. The post-revolutionary elites in both contexts also perceived the religiosity of the masses as an important factor that hindered social progress. Thus, there were systematic efforts to contain the role of religious institutions. New constitutions in both countries defined a much more limited role for religion and took away most privileges of the clergy. In modern Mexico and Turkey, the births, deaths and marriages of citizens came under the control of civilian bureaucracy. Religious institutions were banned from providing education. Their properties were confiscated and even the wearing of religious attire outside the places of worship was banned in both countries. All these secularist reforms, however, did not go unopposed. Both in Mexico and Turkey, there were important religious rebellions (*Cristeros* and *Seyh Sait*) during the 1920s. Both rebellions were suppressed by the state forces and the state and the single-parties maintained their strong secular outlooks despite the relatively more religious populations.

Land reform

The extremely unequal distribution of agricultural land in societies with large rural populations poses significant social, economic and political problems. Both Mexico and Turkey fell into this category at the turn of the twentieth century. In fact, Mexico had to fight a revolutionary war over '*Tierra y Libertad*'. Thus, both countries undertook major land-reform projects, especially during the 1930s. The agrarian reform policies provided land to landless peasants and, at the same time, provided them with credit and other kinds of assistance. The purpose was to uplift the rural sector, especially by improving the lot of the least privileged.

The Mexican and Turkish states also had a political agenda behind their agrarian reform. In both contexts, there was significant tension between the central authority of the state apparatus and local power-holders. By breaking down huge estates into smaller plots, the state also wanted to diminish the power of local elites. Land-reform efforts in Mexico were more extensive than in Turkey. Yet the priorities of both states for implementing agrarian reform, and its impact, were rather similar.

State-led development strategies

Laissez faire was not a novel phenomenon for Mexico or Turkey. Both countries had decades-long experience, particularly in the later half of the nineteenth century, with free markets, foreign investment and export-orientation. However, in both contexts, this practice proved to be rather exploitative in nature. They were exporting raw materials, importing mostly manufactured goods and whatever domestic industry they had was owned and operated by foreigners. The largest bank of the Ottoman Empire, which also functioned as the Central Bank, was owned and operated by foreigners. The Ottoman Bank, as it was called, was 'Ottoman' in name only. Likewise during the *Porfiriato*, the railroads, utilities, factories, and even most of the valuable agricultural lands of Mexico were under foreign ownership. Under these circumstances, it was no surprise that both the Mexican and Turkish revolutions ended up implementing massive nationalisation policies. Factories, banks, railroads and utilities were all brought into state ownership after the revolutions.

The international economic climate of the times also created a favourable environment for state-led development strategies. The impact of the Great Depression and World War II severely undermined faith in open markets as well as reducing the volume of international trade. Most countries in the developing world had to turn inward in order to achieve desirable levels of industrial development. Influential intellectual agencies of the time, such as ECLAC (the Economic Commission on Latin America and Caribbean), also advocated state-led and domestic-market-oriented economic development models. Thus, both Turkey and Mexico endorsed import-substitution industrialisation (ISI) and, for decades, pursued economic strategies that assigned a critical role to the state in the national economy.

The problems both countries encountered due to the ISI development model were very similar as well. Mexico and Turkey both achieved certain levels of industrial development behind their protectionist barriers and they had large enough domestic markets to sustain this strategy for decades. Yet protectionism became an important disincentive for domestic industries to upgrade themselves and become internationally competitive. While their products could not yield much foreign exchange, due to their poor quality, the ISI sector was in constant need of foreign exchange in order to import the capital and intermediary goods that were essential for their production. As a result, both countries incurred large trade deficits and tried to finance this through borrowing.

As the economic situation became more precarious, the corporatist social consensus on which this political-economic model rested also began to break down. The extraordinary outbursts of state violence against workers in Turkey during the 1977 May Day demonstrations in Taksim, and against the students in Mexico in 1968 at Tlatelolco, could be interpreted as signs of the deterioration of the ISI consensus. Finally, the inability of both countries to either mend the ISI model or to seamlessly switch to a different economic development strategy brought both of them to the edge of bankruptcy in the 1980s. The next chapter will address the political and economic changes that took place in Mexico and Turkey in the post-1980 era.

Chapter Five

Democratic Progress in Mexico and Turkey After 1980

The modernisation efforts made by Mexico and Turkey during the twentieth century were analysed in Chapters Three and Four. Despite the vast geographical difference between the two countries, both displayed rather similar state traditions (centralist), patterns of state–society relations (corporatist) and economic development models (state-centric, oriented towards import-substitution-industrialisation) during most of the twentieth century. In fact, in the first half of the century, their dominant party systems and ideologies were strikingly similar (nationalist, secular, single-party regimes).

The state-centric political and economic models endorsed by both countries for most of the twentieth century finally crash-landed in the 1980s. This infamous decade started with a military coup in Turkey in 1980 and with a disastrous economic crisis in Mexico in 1982. From then on, both Turkey and Mexico began to implement a series of reforms to open up their economic and political regimes.

Rather than making a laundry-list of democratic reforms in a descriptive manner, the purpose of this chapter is to compare and contrast the experiences of Mexico and Turkey. By using each country as a benchmark for the other, we can illustrate *how* and *why* these two countries – which were very much on a par with each other on many aspects until the 1980s (corporatist, semi-democratic and clientelistic political systems combined with state-centric economies) – gradually began to part ways. Most strikingly, in the year 2000, Mexico's status in the Freedom House Survey – one of the more respected indexes of global democratic progress – was upgraded to 'Free' and stayed that way for almost a decade (until its infamous war on drugs began), while Turkey was stuck at 'Partly Free' status and remained so at the time of writing.[1]

Since President Calderón's War on Drugs initiative in 2011, Mexico has slipped back to the 'Partly Free' category. However, the scale and scope of this novel threat to Mexican democracy remains highly controversial.[2] If anything, the issue seems to be a temporary setback impacting only a limited and distinct sector of Mexican society, rather than a wholesale and detrimental blow to the regime itself. In fact, when we look at the general statistical evidence, homicides associated with criminal activity have been systematically going down in Mexico since the 1990s.[3]

1. http:// www.freedomhouse.org, *Freedom in The World Map*, various years.
2. F. Escalante Gonzalbo, 'Homicidios 2008–2009: La muerte tiene permiso', *Nexos*, 1 January 2001.
3. F. Escalante Gonzalbo, *El Crimen Como Realidad y Representación*, Mexico D.F.: El Colegio de Mexico 2013.

If we look at the political institutional variables, democratic maturity in Mexico seems to have surpassed that of Turkey. Aside from the Freedom House rankings, domestic observers also highlight the institutional maturity of Mexican democracy, with particular emphasis on having free and competitive elections monitored by the impeccable organisation of IFE (*Instituto Federal Electoral*), achieving peaceful transitions of power from government to opposition, reaching an equilibrium amongst constitutional powers and, last but not the least, expanding civil liberties in a pluralistic political environment. While some scholars maintain a healthy critical stance, many others praise these developments as a new stage in Mexican democracy. According to Woldenberg, taken together, all of these developments illustrate that Mexico has successfully completed its democratic-transition stage.[4]

For most scholars of democratisation, Mexico's success relative to Turkey should have been less likely. While Mexico was saddled with the seven-decade-long authoritarian legacy of a single party, Turkey was considered a 'second-wave' democracy, having established competitive multi-party elections in the 1950s. Yet Mexico seems to have beaten its structural odds while Turkey has underperformed, despite certain advantages. In order to grasp the mechanisms behind this performance gap in the democratic deepening of the two countries, this chapter will place its main emphasis in two critical areas.

The first area of consideration lays in domestic politics: *changing dynamics in state–society relations*. In the Mexican case, there has been steady disintegration of the corporatist model of state–society relations. As the state (*and* the single party) was rapidly undertaking neo-liberal reforms, it began to lose the economic means to buy off a large enough clientele. Privatisation of state-owned assets, coupled with the influx of foreign capital, made it rather difficult for the Mexican political machine to use economic incentives to garner votes. Moreover, the state's loss of economic power was compounded by a steady rise of associational activism in the society. Critical moments in recent Mexican history, such as the earthquake in central Mexico on 19 September 1985, and the Zapatista rebellion of 1994, served as catalysts that spurred civil-society activism to extraordinary proportions. This expansion in civil society was diverse in terms of its class characteristics as well. It stretched from affluent and pro-market sectors to both urban and rural poor, who had disproportionately suffered from neo-liberal reforms.

Transition from a *corporatist* form of interest-representation to a more *pluralist* one, and from being *clients* to *citizens*, constitutes the locomotive of democratic progress and deepening in Mexico. As will be discussed in detail below, both the disintegration of corporatism and the rise of autonomously organised societal sectors are taking place at a much slower pace in Turkey. In the case of Turkey, corporatism seems to be alive and kicking and civil society remains weak. A similarly if not more devastating earthquake on 17 August 1999 did not generate a corresponding surge in civil-society activism. Nor was there large-scale

4. J. Woldenber, *La Transición democrática en México*, México D.F.: El Colegio de México, 2012.

civil-society activism to address the Kurdish issue in south-eastern Turkey. Last but not least, existing associational groups are highly skewed in terms of class and regional distribution, a factor that hinders the democratic progress of Turkey.

The second area of consideration in this chapter is *the international context*. As Huntington in his seminal work[5] and more recently Mainwaring and Pérez-Liñánargue state, '[...] democratization occurs in wave-like processes; what happens in neighbouring countries has a significant impact on a region'.[6] Focusing exclusively on the domestic variables would be an ill-conceived approach for explaining democratic progress. When incorporating the international context in our analysis, this chapter pays particular attention to the nexus of relations Turkey and Mexico have with advanced democracies in their geographic proximity. This takes us to Mexico's relations with the US and Turkey's relations with the EU.

This chapter argues that the predominant characteristic of US–Mexican relations was *intense economic integration*, which generated significant social and economic transformation, particularly in northern Mexico. Contrary to the scale and scope of economic relations, however, the democratic influence of the US on Mexican polity has been rather *subtle*, *indirect* and *informal*. After all, the most important treaty that binds the two countries (and Canada) together, the North Atlantic Free Trade Agreement (NAFTA), is a quintessentially economic document.

Contrary to the US–Mexican pattern, the predominant characteristic of Turkish–EU relations has been *intense political engagement*. The economic integration aspect of Turkish–EU relations lagged far behind the political engagement. Despite the customs union agreement, the scale and scope of economic relations between the parties remained limited. Often-cited evidence for the half-hearted nature of socio-economic integration is the harsh visa policies of the EU. While goods made in Turkey make their way to Europe with relative ease, Turkish business owners cannot freely follow the goods they export to the EU, due to the rigid Schengen visa requirements. According to the EU Commission on Turkey, this visa issue is not simply a 'bureaucratic hurdle' but also an important 'psychological barrier' between Turkey and Europe.[7] For each trade show or business meeting in the EU, Turkish business owners need to fill out long applications, show proofs of their assets and health coverage, verify bank accounts and business credentials, have invitation letters from the European party and apply months in advance. When they get the Schengen visa, most times it covers only the duration of that particular trip; for the next trip, the paperwork has to be repeated. Schengen procedures for Turkey are in stark contrast with the generous B2 visa policy of the US, which usually grants five to ten year multiple-entry visits for business travellers. Given

---

5.   S. Huntington, *The Third Wave: Democratization in late twentieth century*, Norman, OK: University of Oklahoma Press, 1991.

6.   S. Mainwaring and A. Pérez-Liñán, *Democracies and Dictatorships in Latin America: Emergence, survival, and fall*, New York: Cambridge University Press, 2013, p. 6.

7.   'Turkey in Europe: the imperative for change', *Third Report of the Independent Commission on Turkey*, March 2014, p. 10.

such uphill battles in socio-economic relations, it is no surprise that, as of 2013, Russia had replaced Germany as Turkey's top trading partner.

In short, despite certain problems in economic and social aspects of Turkish–EU relations, political issues – particularly democratic reforms – were explicitly on the agenda of the Union from the beginning. Political conditionality has been a defining feature of bilateral relations and it remains a tricky issue between the parties. The strong political element in the Turkish–EU relations notwithstanding, the democratic-reform agenda in Turkey seems to have produced mixed results at best.

Democracy-promotion has become fashionable, particularly in policy-oriented circles, since the latest wars in Afghanistan and Iraq.[8] Recent uprisings in the Middle East, the so-called Arab Spring, also gave momentum to enthusiasm for global democracy-promotion. Increasing number of state and non-state actors are actively trying to shape the reform processes in these fledgling democracies. On the bright side, a significant number of these countries have moved away from explicitly authoritarian regimes and began to establish electoral representative systems. However, they still are faced with long lists of political reforms necessary to establish genuinely open and democratic regimes. Given their extensive experience with democratic reforms and their long-term interactions with advanced democracies, a closer look at the Turkish and Mexican cases can be useful on several grounds. This dual comparative analysis should offer both theoretical and policy insights, in terms of hinting at which approaches to democratic reform work better, and which ones tend to backfire.

The rest of this chapter will systematically compare and contrast the reform processes in Mexico and Turkey since the 1980s. It is divided into four main subsections. The first part will cover the recent theoretical discussions in the democratic consolidation literature. This section will clarify some of the basic conceptual terminology used in the rest of the chapter, including the definitions of consolidation and civil society. Subsequent two sections will look at the neoliberal transitions in Mexico and Turkey. The chapter will conclude with a brief comparison that highlights the similarities and differences in both cases.

Democratisation and democratic consoldidation: A critical overview of theoretical debates

Social scientists across the world have been grappling with a new era of democratic transition from authoritarian regimes towards more open, democratic ones since the 1970s. As Samuel Huntington jubilantly declared, this 'third wave of democratization in the world began [...] [on] April 25, 1974, in Lisbon, Portugal, when a radio station played the song "Grandola Vila Morena"'.[9] The Portuguese

---

8. B. Obama, 'A new beginning', speech delivered at Cairo University, 4 June 2009. Online. Available, http://www.whitehouse.gov/the_press_office/Remarks-by-the-President-at-Cairo-University-6-04-09 (last accessed 23 April 2014).

9. Huntington, 1991, p. 3.

example was soon followed by Spain, Greece and Turkey. Next, the democratic wave crossed the Atlantic to Ecuador, Argentina, Bolivia, Honduras, Uruguay, Guatemala and Chile. After the collapse of the Eastern Bloc, many communist countries in Eastern Europe also jumped on the bandwagon.[10]

In their working definition of democratic transition, Juan Linz and Alfred Stepan highlight the following points as qualities of recently democratised regimes: a) *elected governments* that come to power after *free* and *competitive* elections; and b) the three main branches of the new democracies operate without having to 'share power with other bodies *de jure*'. After stating the customary warning against the 'electoralist fallacy', that is, the reductionist argument that elections are a sufficient condition of democracy, the authors claim that the transition stage is completed when there is no longer any ambivalence at the elite level, as well as at the societal level, towards democratic institutions.[11]

Subsequent to the democratic-transition drama came the efforts of 'good housekeeping'. Having completed the relatively short transition stage, the brave new performers in the democratic arena were given a long list of reforms to implement. These reforms addressed nearly all aspects of their political systems, including their constitutions; executive, legislative and judiciary branches; basic rights and liberties; civil society and state bureaucracies; civil–military relations; local and central governments; and the regulation of the economic sphere.[12]

The rapid pace of democratic reforms made it relatively difficult for social scientists to develop their theoretical and conceptual apparatus for analysing democratic transition. Some countries had disproportionally strong militaries that were reluctant to agree to the civilian leadership in a democratic polity (Spain, Chile and Turkey) whereas in others, civilians were unaccustomed to the indeterminacies of a democratic system and were nostalgic for the order and stability of one-party times (Eastern Europe and Mexico). Some had public-sector-dominant economies (ex-communist Eastern Europe) whereas others had relatively large and mighty capitalist sectors (South American countries). The cases were spread across Europe, Asia, Latin America and even Africa, with various different cultures, historical backgrounds and levels of socio-economic development.

Aside from the diversity of the cases, there was the problem of the *content* of democratic reforms. Presidential versus parliamentarian regimes, constitution-making, judicial reforms, individual rights and liberties, ethno-linguistic identity demands and numerous political and administrative concerns occupied the academic world. The content of the reform packages became highly debated within both academic and policy-making circles. Furthermore, the fact that most countries were undertaking democratisation and political liberalisation

---

10. Huntington, 1991, p. 275.

11. J. Linz and A. Stepan, *Problems of Democratic Transition and Consolidation*, Baltimore, MD: Johns Hopkins University Press, 1996, pp. 3–4.

12. L. Diamond, *Developing Democracy: Towards consolidation*, Baltimore, MD: The Johns Hopkins University Press, 1999.

simultaneously with economic liberalisation added another layer of complication to attempts to theorise about democratic progress.[13]

Part of the problem was the very fact that democratisation itself was a moving target. As soon as social scientists could come up with a basic minimum definition and a generic list of the reforms democratising countries needed to undertake, new developments from the field would challenge them, or push the democratisation bar higher. Prominent scholar Charles Tilly summarises this dilemma in the following way: 'Democratization is a dynamic process that always remains incomplete and perpetually runs the risk of reversal – of de-democratization. Closely related processes, moving in opposite directions, produce both democratization and de-democratization'.[14]

Figure 5.1, by Andreas Schedler, summarises the perpetual movement of political systems along a democratic continuum. Along this continuum, regressions toward the authoritarian end of the scale signify the erosion of democratic regimes, or 'de-democratization' in Tilly's terms. On the other hand, progress in the direction of 'advanced democracy' is usually hailed as the 'deepening' of democracy. In their initial stages, most new democracies are 'electoral democracies'. They are busy with trying *not* to relapse into authoritarianism while, at the same time, they expand political rights and civil liberties in order to become 'liberal democracies'. For those who are already at the 'liberal democracy' stage, there still is room for improvement in order to reach the 'advanced democracy' benchmark set by the European and North American models.[15]

After moving out of authoritarianism and establishing somewhat free and pluralistic systems, most countries found themselves in the conceptual jungle of 'democratic consolidation'. They are neither authoritarian nor full-fledged, mature democracies *à la* Europe; they are stuck somewhere in the grey area, struggling with the monumental task of 'deepening' their democracies.

Leading scholars on democratisation have tried vigorously to fill in the conceptual gap on 'consolidation'. Most of them tried to come up with a narrow definition, since consolidation could easily be understood as enhancing the *quality* of democratic regimes, which, in turn, is an open-ended process even in the 'advanced' democracies of continental Europe.[16] In fact, precisely because of its open-ended and boundless nature, some authors argued that the term 'consolidation' has no analytic utility.[17]

---

13. For a comprehensive study of economic reforms and democratisation, *see* A. Przeworski, M. Alvarez, J. A. Cheibub and F. Limongo, *Democracy and Development*, New York: Cambridge University Press, 2000.

14. C. Tilly, *Democracy*, New York: Cambridge University Press, 2007, p. xi.

15. A. Schedler, 'What is democratic consolidation?', *Journal of Democracy* 9(2), 1998, pp. 96–9.

16. Recently, there have been efforts to come up with systematic and analytical ways to gauge the *quality* of democratic regimes as well. One of the methods developed by this approach is 'citizen audits', which measure the satisfaction of citizens. For a quantitative introduction to the democratic-quality literature, *see* G. O'Donnell *et al.* (eds) *The Quality of Democracy: Theory and applications*, Notre Dame, IN: University of Notre Dame Press, 2004.

17. A. Schedler, 1998. pp. 91–107.

Figure 5.1: Concepts of democratic continuum

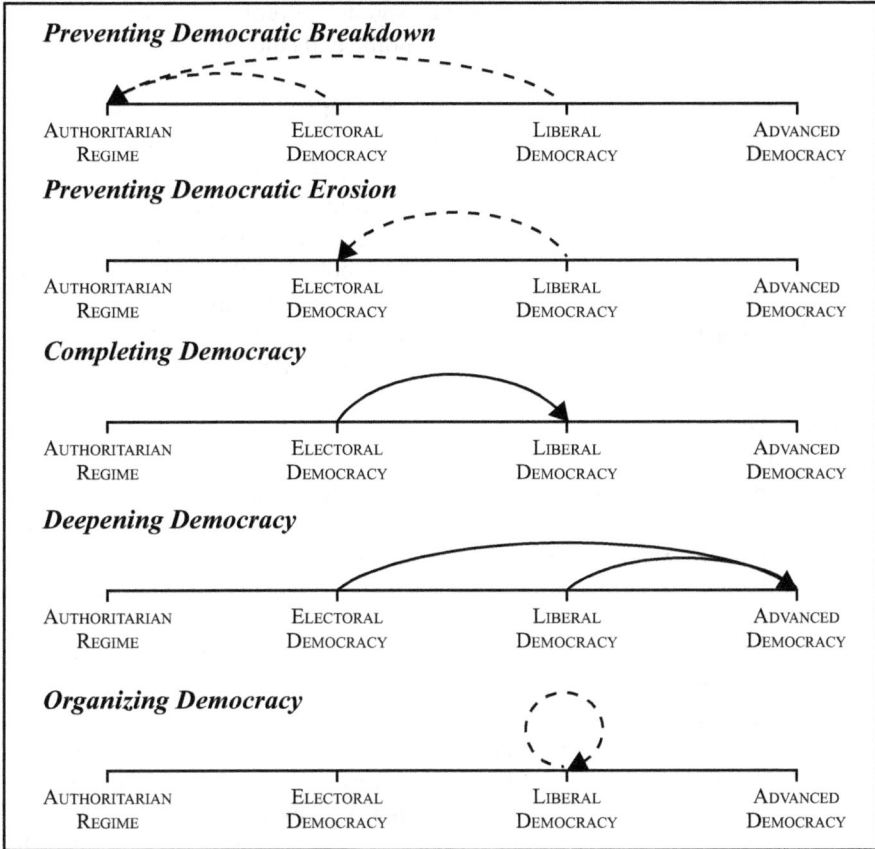

Source: A. Schedler, 'What is democratic consolidation?', *Journal of Democracy* 1998, 9(2), pp. 91–107, p. 93.

Despite the criticisms, however, prominent scholars such as Juan Linz, Alfred Stepan and Larry Diamond have tried to identify the characteristics of consolidated regimes. They came up with three key components: institutional, behavioural and cultural. The *institutional* component of democratic consolidation refers to the establishment of a coherent, capable and autonomous constitutional order, in which a responsive and accountable government caters to the needs and demands of its citizenry. *Behaviourally*, democratic deepening implies the habituation of rule of law. As a result, all political, social and economic actors are 'willing to commit to and be bound by the rules and norms'. Thus, conflicts are resolved within the rule of law without turning to violence and no significant political actor claims special treatments or 'reserved domains'. The *cultural* (or *attitudinal* in Linz and Stepan) component refers to the overall absorption of democratic principles by the majority of public opinion. It implies the existence of a vibrant civil society and the collective endorsement of the values of 'tolerance, trust, participation, and accommodation'.[18] Societies that achieved significant progress in fortifying their democratic regimes institutionally, behaviourally and culturally would henceforth be categorised as consolidated.

Tackling the theoretical aspects and substantive content of consolidation as O'Donnell, Linz, Stepan and Diamond did, was an important step in democratisation studies. Another, more empirically oriented group of scholars set out to test the most common assumptions in these theoretical works. In their analysis of 135 countries, Adam Przeworski *et al.* tried to distinguish consolidated democracies from unconsolidated ones. They looked at the factors that 'made democracies endure'. The authors tried to gauge the impact of several key variables, such as economic performance, institutional arrangements and political learning, on democratic survival. The presumption of the consolidation literature was that the more *institutionalized* the new democratic regimes are and the more *habituated* they are to democratic rules and norms, the longer they would last; and they would thus become consolidated. In Robert Dahl's words, the 'hazard rate' of new democracies would decline over time. If democracy has been around for an extended period, then it is more likely to last, and therefore be consolidated.

Unfortunately, empirical studies did not back up the conventional wisdom of the consolidation-over-time thesis. Here, a very important intervening variable was economic development. Hazard rates decline over time '*because countries develop economically*, and not because a democracy that has been around is more likely to continue being around'.[19] In fact, the hazard risk of a democracy is independent of its age. This would mean, '[...] for a given level of development, democracies are about equally likely to die at any age'. According to these empirical studies, what matters more for the durability of democracy are steady economic growth, equitable income distribution and the existence of parliamentary institutions.[20] These findings, which are based upon time-series data covering over four decades and for more than a hundred countries, carry significant policy implications for new democracies.

Most studies on democratic progress and consolidation, whether they are theoretically or more empirically oriented, tend to focus on domestic variables. Levels of economic development, institutional choices, authoritarian legacies, role of the military and the elites, strength of civil society, levels of interpersonal trust and numerous other domestic variables are taken into account while explaining the democratic progress of any given country. However, all of these are state-level and individual-level factors. Yet, as the three global democratic waves suggest, democratic progress (*and* democratic breakdowns) in any given

---

18. Diamond,1999, p. 20 and Linz and Stepan, 1996, pp. 5–6.

19. R. Dahl *et al., The Democracy Sourcebook*, Cambridge, MA: MIT Press, 2003, p. 113 (*author addition*).

20. A. Przeworski *et al.*, 'What makes democracies endure?', *Journal of Democracy* 1996, 7(1), pp, 39–55, p. 50.

country usually takes place in relation to the regional and systemic dynamics that surround it.[21]

As Schmitter refers, the 'nativist tendency' in democratisation literature is particularly striking in the 1980s. Most studies of this era assert the predominance of domestic factors. Without sparing himself some blame, Schmitter states that given the levels of 'dependence, interpenetration and even integration increasingly embedded in the contemporary world system',[22] it is highly unlikely that democratic transitions, and the subsequent choice of institutions during consolidation, are exclusively determined by domestic political forces.

Its importance notwithstanding, though, the international dimension has certain qualities that make it difficult to operationalise, when compared to domestic factors. First, international factors are usually not the prime movers in democratic consolidation (the post-WWII experiences of Japan and Germany are the only successful exceptions). Therefore, they are secondary or intervening variables that are omnipresent and can exert varying amounts of influence. Secondly, and due to this fluctuating character, the international dimension is fuzzy and difficult to measure. Finally, bringing in the international dimension to an analysis of democratic progress is difficult because this involves stepping over the paradigmatic barriers between international relations and comparative politics.[23] Among others, Yilmaz criticises this 'divorce' between the two subfields. He argues that the turf war between the two subfields significantly hurts our capacity to explain why certain countries seem to have a smooth ride to consolidation, while others with very similar domestic indicators falter. Yilmaz states that a very important effort to bridge this gap between the domestic and international dimensions was suggested by Robert Putnam. However, even Putnam himself downplayed his 'two-level-game' approach by likening it to a 'metaphor,' rather than a systematic approach to combining the two disciplines.[24]

In their efforts to combine the insights of IR on democracy with those of comparative politics, the foremost theoretical piece scholars turn to tends to be Immanuel Kant's *Perpetual Peace*. In his seminal work, Kant suggests that republican regimes, which are based upon the *freedom* of all members of society, adherence to a common set of laws (the rule of law) and *equality* of all citizens, are more prone to provide perpetual peace. This is because in republics, 'the consent of the citizenry' is necessary to wage a war, and logically, people will be reluctant to commit themselves to the risks and destructions of a war. Consequently, as the

---

21. Mainwaring and Pérez-Liñán, 2013.

22. P. Schmitter, 'The influence of international context upon the choice of national institutions and policies in neo-democracies', in *The International Dimensions of Democratization: Europe and the Americas*, L. Whitehead (ed.), Oxford and New York: Oxford University Press, 1996, pp. 26–54, p. 27.

23. Schmitter. 1996, p. 28.

24. H. Yilmaz, 'External-internal linkages in democratization: developing an open model of democratic change', *Democratization*, 2002, 9(2), pp. 67–84, p. 69.

number of republics increases, the world will become less war-prone, and more peaceful.[25]

Some of the most loyal followers of Kantian tradition in IR theory emerged from among the English School. Adam Watson, Hedley Bull and Martin Wight became the leading theorists of the 'international society' paradigm. Very briefly, they argued that states organised around the Kantian principles of individual freedom, reason and rule of law will establish a society of democratic states. Ultimately, a society of free nations that are committed to rule of law at home and at the international level will create a peaceful international society, because democracies tend not to fight each other.

Scholars who attempt to bridge the IR–comparative gap acknowledge the relative peacefulness of democratic international society. However, they tend to 'invert' the causal chain in the Kantian model. Rather than arguing the primary importance of members acquiring democratic qualities first and later advocating for peace, these scholars highlight the influence of the group (of free and democratic nations) over the individual (non- or semi-democratic) states. Thus, the free and democratic nature of immediate neighbours becomes the pull factor that attracts non-democratic actors and compels them to change their ways. Both Laurence Whitehead and Philippe Schmitter point to the regional sequencing of democratisations and claim that these could not be just haphazard developments. In the case of southern Europe, for instance, the

> complex, organizationally saturated interdependence between Spain, Portugal and Greece (and, to a lesser extent, Turkey) and the rest of Europe (the European Community in particular) did exert a powerful and positive influence upon the subsequent processes of consolidation of their respective democracies.[26]

Thus, trying to explain democratic progress in Portugal, Spain and Greece (between 1974 and 1977); Argentina, Bolivia, Uruguay, Brazil and Chile (all in a decade) and, most strikingly, in Poland, Czechoslovakia, East Germany, Hungary, Romania and Bulgaria (almost all in the same year)[27] in isolation from the international dynamics would seriously undermine the integrity of any analysis.

As it is the case with vast and diverse variables, it is rather difficult to develop a parsimonious explanation to comprehend the impact of international factors on democratic progress. In order to tackle this important handicap, Schmitter and Whitehead described four ways in which international factors influence domestic democratisation processes:

---

25. I. Kant, *Towards Perpetual Peace and Other Writings on Politics, Peace and History*, New Haven, CT: Yale University Press, 2006. *See also* the essay by M. Doyle entitled 'Kant and liberal internationalism' in the same volume.

26. P. Schmitter, 1996, p. 33.

27. L. Whitehead, 'Three international dimensions of democratization', in *The International Dimensions of Democratization: Europe and the Americas*, L. Whitehead (ed.), Oxford and New York: Oxford University Press, 1996, p. 5.

- *Contagion*: a diffusion of experience through neutral, that is non-coercive and often unintentional channels from one country to another.
- *Control*: promotion of democracy by one country in another through explicit policies backed by positive or negative sanctions.
- *Consent*: a complex set of interactions between international processes and domestic groups that generate new democratic norms and expectations from below.
- *Conditionality*: an exercise of international influence by deliberate use of coercion – by attaching specific conditions to the distribution of benefits to recipient countries – on the part of multinational institutions.[28]

In order to evaluate the impact of contagion, Whitehead develops the 'contagion through proximity' hypothesis. Very simply, he looks at the 'geographic distribution of the countries classified as democratic' and how this distribution 'changes over time'.[29] The trend of democratic expansion is analogous to an ink drop on white paper. Over time, it spreads and gradually colours the adjacent areas. However, this hypothesis cuts both ways, in the sense that democratic breakdowns and authoritarian regressions also tend to be contagious and 'colour' their neighbours. A contemporary example of the negative contagion effect could be the bureaucratic-authoritarian wave in Latin America during the 1960s and 1970s.[30]

The Global Map of Freedom, developed annually by Freedom House, can be useful when trying to highlight the contagious character of democracies. The Freedom House map illustrates heavy regional concentrations of democratic regimes. By the same token, it is also a good indicator of the regional proximity of non-democratic or semi-democratic regimes. Just by looking at the map, we can easily reach the conclusion that Mexico is in a much more 'democracy-friendly' neighbourhood than Turkey. The predominance of 'Free' regimes across the Americas certainly provides extensive *neutral* and *non-coercive* means of democratic diffusion towards Mexico. Thus, of the four modalities of international influence, *contagion* – particularly from the US – and *consent* seem to be at work for the Mexican case. The excerpt below by *New York Times* correspondents Preston and Dillion describes the early mobilisation efforts of an opposition-party candidate in a border town of Mexico. It offers a great example of how contagion can operate on day-to-day politics. Mexicans trying to articulate their discontent in the political sphere could easily resort to their northern neighbour to find effective means for democratic mobilisation:

When he threw his hat in the ring for mayor of Juarez, [Francisco] Barrio enlisted several dozen of his middle-class friends to coordinate his campaign. A real-estate agent drove across the bridge into El Paso, went to the public library, and checked out a book on U.S.-style campaign tactics. It described

---

28. Schmitter, 1996. p. 30.
29. Whitehead, 1996. p. 5.
30. G. O'Donnell, *Bureaucratic Authoritarianism: Argentina 1966–1973 in Comparative Perspective*, Berkeley, CA: University of California Press, 1988.

how to recruit volunteers, plan a campaign rally, set up precinct poll-watching committees, and other political basics. 'That book became our bible,' Barrio recalled later.[31]

Unfortunately, the Middle East and North Africa and parts of Eurasia contain a patchwork of 'Free', 'Partly Free' and 'Not Free' states on the Freedom House map. As will be discussed at the end of this chapter, the lack of a solid democratic belt surrounding Turkey tends to weaken the contagion effect. Moreover, Turkey's intense political engagement with Europe over the last four decades in an everlasting process of accession generated an atmosphere of democracy-promotion through *conditionality* and *coercion*, rather than *consent*. Although numerous studies that claim the 'leverage of the EU' as the 'single best tool' to promote democracy in the region,[32] Turkey remains curiously under-consolidated, despite having political and institutional links with the EU since the 1963 Ankara Agreement.

An important distinction in the Turkish case is the relative weakness of social contact and interaction with the EU. Even the most affluent and pro-EU business groups within Turkish society complain about their inability to freely travel and conduct business, given the tight visa requirements of EU nations. Ironically, the goods they produce can travel more freely than those who produce the goods! In 2012, the national union of chambers of commerce (TOBB), one of the leading business organisations in Turkey, began formally collecting Schengen visa complaints from its members in order to take the case to the EU. This and other differences between Mexico and Turkey regarding the patterns in which the international dimension affects democracy-promotion (that is, *contagion/consent* in Mexico–US case *versus control/conditionality* in the Turkey–EU case) and their relative effectiveness will be analysed in detail in the remainder of this chapter.

Democratic progress and society: Changes in state–society relations during consolidation

Democratic deepening cannot be achieved solely through institutional reforms or bureaucratic procedural arrangements. Those who occupy the seats of power and run the state need to be accountable and responsive towards the needs and demands of society at large. In Diamond's words, since

> democratic accountability and responsiveness are rarely achieved without concerted pressure from below, civil society (the arena of organizations and media that are autonomous from the state but concerned with public affairs) plays a central role in the process of consolidation.[33]

31. J. Preston and S. Dillon, *Opening Mexico: The making of a democracy*, New York: Farrar, Straus and Giroux, 2004, p. 125.
32. M. A. Vachudova, *Europe Undivided: Leverage and integration after communism*, Oxford: Oxford University Press, 2005, p. 247.
33. Diamond, 1999, p. 22.

The issue of civil society and its role in democratic progress has attracted considerable interest among social scientists. Since Alexis de Tocqueville's seminal work on US democracy, citizen participation in voluntary associations has come to be associated with greater political freedom and greater democracy.[34] In general, the following qualities are listed as the key attributes of civil society: 1) *open, voluntary* and *self-generating* activities of citizens; 2) possessing some degree of *autonomy* from the state; 3) occupying an *intermediary realm*, between state and individual/family; 4) expressing collective goals/interests of its members.

Unfortunately, the concept as just defined has not always been used benignly to highlight the voluntary, autonomous and pluralistic realm of collective citizen activism. Especially after the collapse of the Soviet Union, a rather disturbing trend in democratisation studies emerged. Civil society became intimately associated with the neo-liberal agenda and gained significant normative and ideological undertones. According to Beckman, it became an ideological construct rather than an analytic category; one which distinguished between a 'good' civil society organisation (one that endorsed market capitalism, the minimum state and so on) and the rest (most notably labour unions, ethnic and religious groups and the like). From these ideological viewpoints, only pro-business and pro-capitalist civil society organisations were considered part of civil society. Other organisations that endorsed workers' rights or human rights, and thus were critical of the exploitative aspects of capitalist market economy, were not as well regarded. Secondly, it created an artificial dichotomy between the state and society by *not* conceptualizing both as mutually constitutive. Third, the advocates of civil society practised a circular logic that left them with the 'chicken-and-egg' problem: you needed strong civil society for a liberal democracy and a liberal democracy for a vibrant, pluralistic civil society.[35] But which came first?

The *autonomy* aspect of the concept, and its tacit antagonism towards the state, drew particular criticism from Nordic authors. Coming from strong neo-corporatist and democratic corporatist traditions, these writers take issue with the concept's indifference to existing socio-economic inequalities and its normatively loaded deployment of 'autonomy from the state'. Both Göran Therborn and Björn Beckman argue that the state and organised society have closer ties than the liberal school presents; and that less autonomy may not necessarily be a sign of authoritarian government infringing upon the space of organised society. In particular, they give the examples of labour unions in Scandinavia. While the Scandinavian unions might have much less autonomy in the liberal, Anglo-American sense, their closeness to the state helps level the playing field in their

34. A. de Tocqueville, *Democracy in America*, translated by A. Goldhammer, New York: Library of America, distributed to the trade in the US by Penguin Putnam, 2004.

35. B. Beckman, 'Explaining democratization: notes on the concept of civil society', in E. Özdalga and S. Persson (eds), *Civil Society and Democracy in the Muslim World*, Istanbul: Swedish Research Institute, 2002, pp. 1–7.

relations with the stronger business organisations. Moreover, closer links to the state gives unions greater *capacity* in terms of influencing policy-making.[36]

The shortcomings of this concept were uncovered in Howard Wiarda's rather critical work on civil society as well. Its strong *ethno-centric* bias and the *a-historical, linear* and *universalistic* ways in which the term is deployed in the policy-making circles of Washington DC are vividly described by the author. At a time when the US government and leading international agencies were geared up to 'export' civil society across the world, from Latin America to Africa and Asia, the author gave several reasons for caution in using the concept: the ambiguity of the meaning of the term and its variation over time and place; the existence of powerful indigenous traditions at the 'receiving' end that may not always be open and conducive to the liberal/pluralist model *à la* the United States; the existence of different models of civil society (European, Scandinavian) that were not necessarily inferior to the liberal American model; and the persistence of other forms of state–society relations (such as corporatism) that seem resistant to being dislodged by the Anglo-American civil-society model.[37]

This chapter has a cautious stance towards the concept of civil society due to its above-mentioned shortcomings. However, democratic progress cannot be described solely in a minimalist sense, that is, only with reference to political institutions and procedures. 'In the absence of an active, critical and well-organized citizenry that continually pressures its country's rulers and the leaders of political parties,'[38] a country might have formal democracy but it would not mean much in the eyes of the citizens. Whether we call it civil society, social movements or grassroots activism, the organised participation of citizens in a given polity is a critical factor that greatly improves the democratic nature of political regimes. If free and fair elections, competitive party systems and just constitutions establish the *form* of democracy; the *substance* of democracy is an active, critical and organised society that voices its demands and holds this institutional framework responsive and accountable.

The last two decades of the twentieth century were critical periods in terms of democratic progress in both Mexico and Turkey. The failure of state-centric economic development models (import-substitution) in both countries also paved the way for massive economic restructuring under the auspices of international economic powerbrokers such as the IMF and the World Bank. The early 1980s (later infamously known as the 'lost decade') saw the inauguration of a neo-liberal

---

36. G. Therborn, 'Beyond civil society: democratic experiences and their relevance to the Middle East', in E. Özdalga and S. Persson (eds), *Civil Society and Democracy in the Muslim World*, Istanbul: Swedish Research Institute, 2002, pp. 4–5.

37. H. J. Wiarda, *Civil Society: The American model and third world development*, Colorado: Westview Press, 2003, *see* especially pp. 3–25.

38. S. Gomez Tagle, 'Elections in Mexico: what's the use?' *NACLA Report on the Americas*, 2008, 41(5), pp. 12–18, p. 14.

era in both contexts. During this period of massive overhaul, the state retreated from the economy through rapid privatisation and de-regulation programmes and the private sector became the new engine of the economy. Flows of foreign capital were welcomed, currency restrictions were lifted and export-promotion was the new growth strategy.[39]

These critical decades of economic reform also coincided with significant political reforms. If we take Scheduler's democratic continuum chart (Figure 5.1) as a reference point, during this period, both Turkey and Mexico moved away from authoritarian regimes. First Turkey, then Mexico, proceeded to competitive, free and fair elections. Both countries were inching towards 'liberal democracy' on the democratic continuum and both were undertaking reforms that expanded the political rights and civil liberties of their citizens. Furthermore, they were strengthening democratic mechanisms within the state apparatus through several legal and administrative reforms. Throughout these reform decades, both countries were still categorised as 'Partly Free' by the Freedom House index.

Despite these comparatively similar trends in terms of democratic progress in both countries for most of the twentieth century, the coming of a new millennium signalled a brave new era for Mexico. Subsequent to the momentous 2000 presidential elections, Freedom House upgraded the status of Mexico to 'Free', thus promoting the country into the premier league of global democracies, while Turkey remained 'Partly Free'.

The international spotlight, and a substantial amount of academic attention, focused on the 2000 presidential elections in Mexico. In fact, many analysts constructed a time-line of democratic progress based upon the presidential election cycles in Mexico. According to Beatriz Magaloni, 'Mexico became democratic sometime between the 1988 presidential election, when the PRI committed massive electoral fraud, and the 2000 presidential race'.[40] According to the author, the 1988 elections were significant for Mexican democracy, for this was the first time that a faction from the hegemonic PRI seriously challenged the party in the ballot box. The leftist opposition party *Partido de la Revolución Democrática*, or PRD, was in the lead until the government computers that counted the votes 'malfunctioned'. Two days later, when the computers were back up and running, the PRI was again leading by a large margin. Nonetheless, the blatantly fraudulent 1988 elections exposed the vulnerability of the single party, which eventually handed over the power in 2000 elections.

39. C. Gore, 'The rise and fall of the Washington Consensus as a paradigm for developing countries', *World Development*, 2000, 28(5), pp. 789–804.

40. B. Magaloni, 2005, 'The demise of Mexico's one-party dominant regime', in F. Hagopian and S. P. Mainwaring (eds), *The Third Wave of Democratization in Latin America*, Cambridge: Cambridge University Press, p. 122.

Post-1980 stabilisation and economic restructuring in Mexico

It is not a coincidence that the relatively monolithic and splinter-proof PRI could not maintain this discipline in its rank-and-file after the 1980s. As illustrated in the previous chapter, the pre-1980 PRI functioned more like a grand coalition of centre-right and centre-left parties. The presidency oscillated regularly from one end of the political spectrum to the other, accommodating the interests of on both ends. However, particularly after the 1960s, the rightward swings became more pronounced. Still, it was not until the 1982 economic crisis that the Mexico took a rather sharp right-turn towards a competitive market economy.

Realizing the darkening clouds on the economic horizon in the early 1980s, President López Portillo handpicked a successor who had strong ties with international financial powerhouses. In 1982, Miguel de la Madrid became the new President of Mexico, thanks to his connections with foreign banks and to the solid institution of *dedazo* in Mexican politics (presidents handpicking their successors). President de la Madrid (1982–8) and his technocratic team rapidly restructured the Mexican economy along neo-liberal principles. This economic reorientation excluded and alienated many left-leaning members of the ruling party. The leftist contingent was categorically against neo-liberalism, including its policies of privatisation, IMF programmes and debt-service. Needless to say, they were shut off from the top decision-making circles within the party.[41] This elite discontent within the PRI found significant mass support as well.

Throughout the 1970s in Mexico macroeconomic policy was the least of the government's concerns since the price of oil (a major export item) was high and international credit was cheap and readily available. Upon the discovery of more oil reserves in the Gulf of Mexico, which increased the nation's reserves nearly tenfold, President López Portillo (1976–82) boasted that his job was 'administering abundance'.[42] However, the international financial climate deteriorated rapidly in the early 1980s, as oil prices plummeted and interest rates went up. During López Portillo's *sexenio* the foreign debt of Mexico increased eight-fold, reaching $80 billion.[43] In economists' terms, Mexico became insolvent. Despite his ostentatious claim that he would guard the value of peso 'like a dog', the President could only stare as the peso took a nosedive. His last-minute efforts to halt the fall in the value of the peso, which included the nationalisation of banks and controls over foreign-exchange flows, just created a black market and worsened the situation.[44] At the peak of the economic crisis in 1982, the peso devalued so rapidly, it caused massive capital flight. Eventually, the 'Mexican government had to declare an

---

41. Magaloni, 2005, p. 128.
42. Preston and Dillon, 2004, p. 95.
43. J. A. Hellman, *Mexican Lives*, New York and London: New Press, 1995, pp. 4–6.
44. Preston and Dillon, 2004, p. 123.

*Figure 5.2: Exports and imports of goods and services in Mexico, 1960–2008, as %
of GDP*

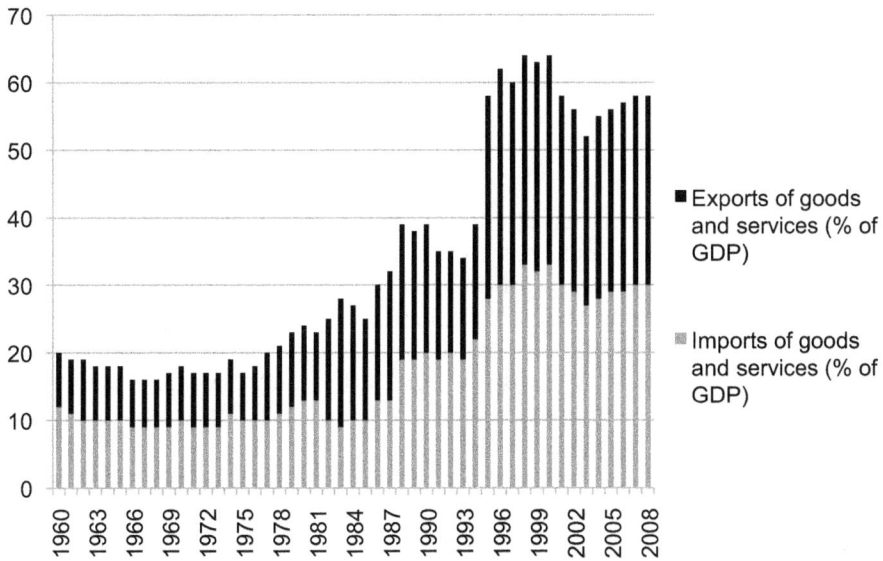

Source: Data selected from World Bank's World Development Indicators, various years.

involuntary moratorium on its debt, triggering a debt crisis that soon acquired
global proportions.'[45]

The economic policies of President Miguel de la Madrid (1982–8) sealed
the fate of the import-substitution era in Mexico. He overturned some economic
policies of his predecessor, López Portillo, in order to diminish the state's role in
the economy, and secure the ascendance of market forces and the private sector.
Thus, President de la Madrid terminated the practice of putting price ceilings on
staples and relaxed the restriction on currency movements. In 1986, he signed the
General Agreement on Tariffs and Trade (GATT), which ushered in an era of the
liberalisation of trade and commerce in the Mexican economy.[46] As illustrated in
Figure 5.2, the volume of foreign trade (imports plus exports) in Mexico had been
relatively low and steady (18–20 per cent of GDP) since the 1960s. After signing
the GATT, the volume of foreign trade nearly doubled, to 40 per cent of GDP;
the next significant jump is observed after 1994, subsequent to joining the North
American Free Trade Agreement (NAFTA). After 1994, foreign trade began to

45. N. Lustig, *Mexico: The Remaking of an Economy*, Washington DC: Brookings Institution
    Publications, 2nd edn, 1998, pp. 3–4.

46. Hellman, 1994, p. 7.

Table 5.1: State Economic Enterprises (SEEs) in Mexico, 1982–92

	1982	1986	1992
Number of Enterprises	1155	737	217
Employment	886,200	1,028,000	530,600

Source: R. Dornbusch and A. Werner. 'Mexico: stabilization, reform and no growth', *Brookings Papers on Economic Activity,* 1994, no.1, p. 261

account for nearly 60 per cent of GDP in Mexico, which demonstrates a deeper integration with global markets but, at the same time, a greater susceptibility to the effects of international economic fluctuations.

Under President de la Madrid's administration, Mexico began to restructure its debt, 'which culminated in the 1990 Brady Plan agreements brokered by then-US-Treasury Secretary Nicholas Brady'. Under the Brady Plan, the principal and interest payments that Mexico had to make were reduced in order to increase the country's ability to service its debt.[47]

To emphasise the intensity in the scale and scope of economic reforms during the 1980s, Dani Rodrik states that Mexico (along with Argentina and Bolivia) undertook more 'liberalization and privatization within five years than the East Asian countries have managed in three decades'.[48] The privatisation of state economic enterprises (SEEs) constituted a critical component of economic restructuring. In order to reduce the budget deficit, unprofitable operations were shut down and profitable ones were sold to private investors. Table 5.1 illustrates the dramatic contraction of the state sector within a decade.

The social costs of these structural adjustment and stabilisation programmes fell heavily on the poor. When price ceilings were lifted, inflation skyrocketed while real wages declined. Annual consumer price-inflation was a staggering 86 per cent between 1981 and 1988, the highest in Mexico since the 1950s.[49] 'Per capita real disposable income fell on average by 5 per cent a year between 1983 and 1988.'[50] Between 1981 and 1988, the minimum wage lost half of its value and it continued to sink until the early 1990s. President de la Madrid had secured a $4 billion loan from the IMF, with the usual austerity strings attached. Accordingly, the state began to cut back on subsidies in food, clothing, housing, health and transportation. When combined, this cut meant the loss of sizeable non-wage benefits for the urban and rural poor.[51]

---

47. R. Dornbusch and A. Werner, 'Mexico: stabilization, reform and no growth', *Brookings Papers on Economic Activity*, 1994 (1), pp. 253–315, p. 256–7.
48. D. Rodrik, 'Understanding economic policy reform', *Journal of Economic Literature*, 1996, 34(1), March, pp. 9–41, p. 18.
49. Dornbusch and Werner, 1994, p. 256.
50. Lustig, 1998, p. 2.
51. J. Hellman, 1994, pp. 7–9.

This radical switch in macroeconomic orientation and increasing exposure to international competition did not only hurt the poor. The sudden termination of protectionist policies caught even some Mexican businesses off guard. Regarding the sudden implementation of GATT, Hellman states that, 'from one day to next, the borders were thrown open to cheap Asian products, and domestic producers [...] were generally caught by surprise'.[52] While the opponents of the new economic policies criticised these reforms for undermining domestic Mexican industry, their proponents stated the necessity of allowing the 'survival of the fittest' for a healthy, modern and competitive economy. Particularly in the consumer goods sector, where average tariff levels declined from 60 per cent to less than 20 per cent, very few domestic manufacturers could compete with imports.[53] Below, a business owner in the textile sector, who had to shut down all of his production facilities and lay off 600 of his 700 workers because of cheap imports, summarises how adjustment to the new economic reality took place:

> [...] because I import, I don't have to worry about labour, about strikes, about turnover and all the other problems you have when you employ a work force. Let the Asians worry about it. Somehow their labour costs are much lower. Their governments help them to hold the price of labour down. [...] I can give you a basic equation that tells you all you need to know about the future of the domestic industrial sector: the price of an Asian product on sale in Mexico – with all the transportation and middlemen's profits figured in – is still lower than the basic cost of production of the same article manufactured in Mexico.[54]

The neo-liberal economic era in Mexico was also characterised by the ascendance of technocrats within the PRI. These *técnicos*, who were generally trained in the US and well versed in orthodox economic doctrines, have replaced the *políticos* in the top echelons of the party.[55] After the Harvard-trained de la Madrid, the Salinas cabinet signalled the 'heyday of young economists from prestigious American universities'. This was a new generation of technocratic presidents, who, in Enrique Krauze's biting words, ruled like '"enlightened despots" of the computer age'.[56] Salinas passed the torch to another Yale-trained economist, Ernesto Zedillo (1994–2000). In the homeland of neo-liberal doctrine, the standard-bearers of this particular school, like Jeffry Sachs, were calling for speedy and extensive economic reforms (employing the 'bitter pill', or 'big bang' analogies), conducted by politically insular, technocratic administrations.

---

52. Hellman, 1994, p. 29.

53. Dornbusch and Werner, 1994, pp. 261–2.

54. Hellman, 1994, pp. 30–1.

55. S. Babb, *Managing Mexico: Economists from nationalism to neoliberalism*, Princeton, NJ: Princeton University Press, 2004.

56. E. Krauze, *Mexico: Biography of power*, New York: Harper Collins, 1997, p. 772–3.

The Mexican case certainly complies with this prescription. However, whether or not this was a sound economic policy that yielded the optimum outcome is still debated, even among the mainstream economists.[57]

Reforms in the agricultural sector

One of the most important achievements of the Mexican Revolution was inscribed in Article 27 of the 1917 Constitution. Article 27 was a radical step in the regulation of the property rights and land-tenure system in Mexico, calling for the nationalisation of strategic economic sectors, such as oil and utilities, and the reinstatement of the institution of collective land-ownership (*ejidos*). Furthermore, it devised an active role for the state in implementing land reform. Article 27 also included significant legal mechanisms to protect the *ejidos*. Accordingly, those who are members of these collective properties (*ejidatores*) have the right to use their parcel and their heirs can inherit it. But under no circumstances could the *ejidatores* sell, mortgage, lease or transfer the ownership of their parcels. All such concessions, deals and sales were declared null and void according to Section VIII of Article 27. In short, the revolutionary 1917 Constitution of Mexico included measures to create an egalitarian land-tenure regime through land reform. It aimed to protect collective properties from turning into large commercial estates.

The bedrock of the revolutionary land-tenure system was changed by a critical constitutional amendment in 1992, during the Salinas *sexenio*. The reasoning behind the 1992 amendment is captured in an article in the *Economist*, which, as a bastion of the neo-classical school of economics, cheerfully embraces all pro-market reforms. After declaring the 80-year-long land-reform policies 'an agricultural disaster', the article claims that expropriating lands from big landowners and distributing them to small peasants did not make any economic sense. 'With such small holdings, farmers have not been able to invest in modern technology.'[58] They were at a constant disadvantage against larger producers, who could achieve economies of scale. Moreover, the *ejidatores* also lacked access

---

57. Prominent Harvard economist Dani Rodrik states that subsequent to the debt crisis of the 1980s, professional economists, and certainly the World Bank, lumped together apples and oranges. Developing countries were advised to balance their fiscal accounts but, at the same time, were told to overhaul '*their trade and industrial policies [by][...] undertaking privatization on a major scale. [...][T]hese trade and industrial policies had little to do with instigating crisis, and consequently their reform was not a logical necessity*'. While the most pressing concern was stabilisation of macroeconomic indicators (inflation, budget deficit, exchange rates, etc.), these countries were also told to completely demolish their ISI structures and restructure their industrial and trade policies through privatisation, liberalisation and deregulation. Rodrik criticises the sharp reductions in tariffs under trade liberalisation, which not only causes loss of state revenues but also hurts the domestic industry and distorts demand structure. Writing soon after the 1994 economic crisis, Rodrik clearly laments the choices of Mexico's *técnicos*: 'The recent Mexican debacle could possibly have been avoided, or at least its impact minimized, if the authorities had not removed controls on trade and capital flows so enthusiastically.' (Rodrik, 1996, p. 27).

58. 'Farmed out', *Economist*, 1 April 2000, p. 34.

to formal credit mechanisms because of the legal restrictions (under Article 27) against using *ejidos* as collateral. After the 1992 reforms, they could either sell their very small and economically inefficient plots and move on to other jobs, or pool their small parcels with neighbours, get credit, invest in mechanisation and have a chance to compete with large commercial farms.

The 'modernisation of agriculture' argument was heavily deployed by the Salinas administration. The amendment to Article 27 ended the land-distribution policies, granted individual titles to *ejido* owners and secured property rights in the rural sector. Secure property rights are the *sine qua non* of neo-liberal economic doctrine and this was an important step for the commercialisation of collective properties. The new land-tenure regime established a certification program (PROCEDE – *Programa de Certificación de Derechos Ejidales y Titulación de Solares*). *Ejidatores* who were enrolled in PROCEDE could clearly mark the boundaries of their *ejidos* and demarcate their individual parcels, which could then be sold, rented, sharecropped or mortgaged.[59] While I was conducting fieldwork in rural Guanajuato in 2008 and 2013, it was particularly striking to see that nearly all of the *ejido* lands had been sold and converted to large private commercial farms.

President Salinas was committed to modernising Mexico, first and foremost by getting rid of what he assumed was the out-dated, paternalist and inefficient economic system. Much like other technocratic reformers in different parts of the developing world, including Turkey and its Prime Minister Özal, Salinas packed his cabinet with young, US-trained economists. In his first address to the Mexican people, he summarised his position on the necessity and direction of economic reform in the following way:

> The majority of reforms of our revolution have exhausted their effects and no longer guarantee the new development that our country demands [...] [A] bigger state is not necessarily a more effective state, a property-owning state is not necessarily a just one. The reality is that in Mexico, more government meant less response to the social needs of our people.[60]

The overall impact of Salinas' reforms, which privatised telephone companies, banks and airlines, ended land reform and commercialised rural *ejidos*, amounted to a thorough overhaul of the Mexican economy. President Salinas was well aware of the political repercussions of his economic policies, especially after experiencing a tough electoral race in 1988 against a popular leftist candidate. Thus, he devised measures to alleviate the distress among the hardest-hit sectors. During his own PhD research, Salinas had observed the effectiveness of 'targeted' help to the poor. Typically, the old machine politics of the PRI used large-scale government spending schemes, like subsidies and guaranteed prices, to secure the

---

59. W. Assies, 'Land tenure and tenure regimes in Mexico: an overview', *Journal of Agrarian Change* 2008, 8(1), pp. 33–63.

60. Preston and Dillon, 2004, p.186.

loyalty of the peasantry. These were politically effective measures but they laid a heavy burden on government finances. From his fieldwork in Tlaxcala in the 1970s, Salinas had seen that selective and targeted programmes – which cost much less than the previous ones – could also gain the support of rural communities, without compromising fiscal discipline.[61]

The National Solidarity Program (PRONASOL), was created under the Salinas administration to 'help the hardest hit by the crisis and neoliberal transformation', until the market reforms could mature and begin 'lifting up all the boats'. But the most important concern of the Solidarity Program was raking in electoral support for the PRI. Similar programmes continued under different names under subsequent administrations (PROGRESA during Zedillo, *Oportunidades* during Fox), yet they fell significantly short of alleviating the economic distress of the poor.[62] In agrarian states with large concentrations of *campesinos* – such as Michoacán, Guerrero, Oaxaca, Morelos and Puebla – the opposition candidate, Cuahutemoc Cárdenas, was favoured over the PRI machine. He enjoyed the moral authority of being the son of the most prominent land reformer, President Lázaro Cárdenas.[63]

The main purpose of de-regulation and the liberalisation of investment was to attract large capital flows into the country from foreign investors, particularly from the US. Statistical evidence shows that the efforts of PRI technocrats were largely successful in this. In 1997, there were 130 foreign-owned companies in the top 500 Mexican companies. Of those 130 that were foreign-owned, 70.8 per cent of owners were of US origin and 23 per cent of European origin, mostly from Germany.[64] The tipping-point in intensifying US–Mexican economic relations came in 1994, when the NAFTA between the US, Mexico and Canada went in effect.

NAFTA was the brainchild of President Salinas, who successfully pitched the idea on both sides of the Rio Grande. From his perspective, Mexico could modernise only by opening itself to world markets, by becoming competitive and by joining forces with the stronger economies to its north; sealing itself off from the global capitalist system was not an option. Together with his 'Ivy-Leaguers,' Salinas undertook a massive lobbying effort, arguing that NAFTA would reduce Mexican emigration, take advantage of the complementary nature of the US and Mexican economies and improve the competitiveness of North America *vis-à-vis* the European and Asian trading blocks.[65] Before NAFTA, Mexican exports to the US were equal to the rest of the Latin American countries combined and average annual foreign direct investment (FDI) in Mexico was $3.47 billion. Less than a decade after NAFTA, the average annual FDI had exceeded $13 billion and

61. N. Harvey, *The Chiapas Rebellion*, Durham and London: Duke University Press, 1998, pp.169–70.
62. L. Meyer, 'The second coming of Mexican liberalism: a comparative perspective', in E. Sevin, L. Reina and J. Tutino (eds) *Cycles of Conflict, Centuries of Change: Crisis, reform and revolution in Mexico*, Durham and London: Duke University Press, 2007, pp. 290–1.
63. Preston and Dillon, 2004, p. 200.
64. E. Butler *et al.*, *Mexico and Mexico City in World Economy*, Boulder, CO: Westview Press, 2001.
65. Krauze, 1997, p. 773.

Figure 5.3: Foreign direct investment (FDI) net flows, Mexico and Turkey compared, 1970–2012 (balance of payments, current US$)

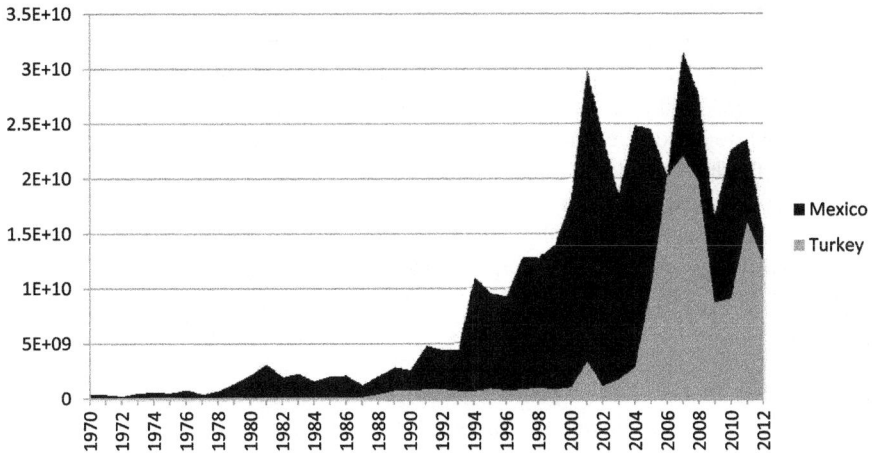

Source: Data from World Bank's World Development Indicators.[67]

'Mexico's exports [to the US] are nearly double those of the rest of the Latin American countries put together.'[66] Figure 5.3, on foreign direct investment, illustrates the significant jump in capital flows to Mexico in the immediate aftermath of the NAFTA in 1994, and its exponential growth since then.

Mexico experienced a significant spike in FDI flows after the inauguration of NAFTA in 1994. Unlike Mexico, Turkey's Customs Union with the EU in 1994 did not cause a similar influx of foreign capital. Overall flow of FDI to Turkey remained rather stagnant until the mid 2000s, and lags consistently behind that of Mexico. In fact, a careful look at the sudden spike since 2004 also reveals a troubling pattern. The sudden jump in FDI flows in Turkey after 2004 is due to the privatisation of Turk Telekom, Tüpraş and few other important utilities and state monopolies. Hence, they came as a result of the acquisition of some of the most profitable sectors by international investors, rather than of new/green investment in novel sectors. In short, Figure 5.3 illustrates a significant gap between Mexico and Turkey in terms of direct foreign investment flows after their economic agreements with their more affluent neighbours.

---

66. J. Serra and E. Espinosa, 'Debate: happily ever NAFTA?' *Foreign Policy*, 2002, 132, pp. 58–65.

67. Long Definition: Foreign direct investment are the net inflows of investment to acquire a lasting management interest (10 per cent or more of voting stock) in an enterprise operating in an economy other than that of the investor. It is the sum of equity capital, reinvestment of earnings, other long-term capital, and short-term capital as shown in the balance of payments. This series shows net inflows (new investment inflows less disinvestment) in the reporting economy from foreign investors. Data are in current US dollars. Online. Available http:// www.databank.worldbank.org (last accessed 09 April 2015).

Social responses to neo-liberal economic restructuring in Mexico

Susan Strange aptly names the post-1980 neo-liberal period as the time of the 'retreat of the state'. She argues that world markets – including private finance, industry and trade – 'are now more powerful than the states to whom ultimate political authority over society and economy is supposed to belong'.[68] With massive financial transactions taking place across national borders in split seconds and global corporations commanding higher net worth than the GDPs of many nations, the power of the state does seem to be diminishing.

While the last decades of the twentieth century were chronicled as the times of drastic economic reforms and state retreat, they were also hailed as the harbingers of new social movements. From the 1980s onwards, social scientists began to observe a profoundly different type of citizen-activism and collective action. During rocky economic times, these popular urban and rural movements were welcomed, for they enriched the social and political arena. As new actors, they created alternative political spaces and contributed to the formation of new (or hitherto neglected) identities, which expanded the realm of civil society. In fact, among the prominent theorists on social movements, Sonia Alvarez and Arturo Escobar highlighted the strong link between these new movements and the democratic progress in the societies in which they were embedded. Alvarez and Escobar stated that the emergence of new social movements in Latin America on a wide range of issues – from indigenous rights to gay rights, from rural poverty and ecological decay to squatter rights – significantly contributed to the democratisation of political cultures and of the day-to-day experiences of citizens in the region.[69]

In the case of Mexico, some analysts maintain a sceptical position in terms of the democratising impact of new social movements. Among them, Judith Hellman argues that despite all the hype over social movements, the Mexican political system continues to depend on persuasion and coercion. She gives the examples of the co-optation and manipulation tactics used by the Salinas administration under the Solidarity Program (PRONASOL), which were not much different from the ones used during the previous Echeverria *sexenio*. According to Hellman, the Mexican state is extremely crafty in the business of clientelism and owes its longevity to this very trait. By selectively delivering the goods, providing concessions and employing the leaders of popular movements in cushy positions, the state can tame even the most autonomous and *luchador* (combative) movements.[70]

Despite the Mexican state's previous success in using the 'iron law of incorporation' to co-opt and tame independent movements, scholars examining the dynamics of state–society relations in Mexico signal certain differences in their

68. S. Strange, *The Retreat of the State: The diffusion of power in the world economy,* Cambridge: Cambridge University Press, 1997, p. 4.

69. S. Alvarez and A. Escobar, *The Making of Social Movements in Latin America: Identity, strategy and democracy*, Boulder, CO: Westview Press, 1992.

70. J. A. Hellman, 'Mexican popular movements, clientelism, and the process of democratization,' *Latin American Perspectives* 1994, 21(2), pp. 124–42.

Figure 5.4: Transition from authoritarian clientelism to semi-clientelism and citizenship in Mexico

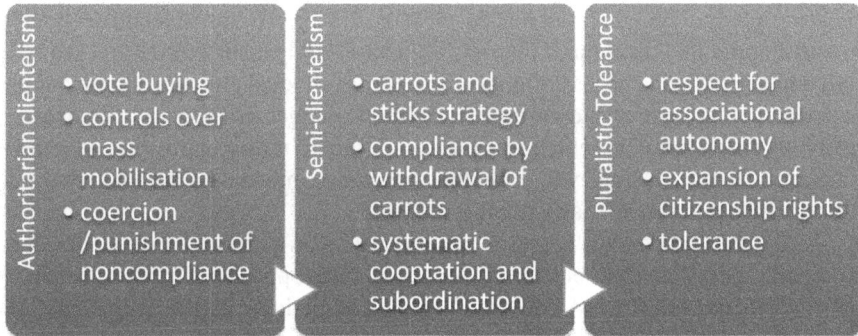

patterns in recent decades. In his well articulated analysis, Jonathan Fox traces the gradual transformation from clients to citizens. Specifically, Fox argues that the stability of the single-party era was built upon an authoritarian form of clientelism. He distinguishes authoritarian clientelism by highlighting the element of 'threat of coercion' along with the exchange of material rewards for votes or political support. According to Fox, Mexico was dominated by 'an authoritarian corporatist brand of electoral machine politics' for a long time. Today, it provides a useful case study of 'transitions from clientelism to semi-clientelism and citizenship'.[71]

Figure 5.4 summarises the dominant characteristics of each pattern of state–society relations. However, Fox warns that this continuum by no means suggests the conclusive extinction of authoritarian clientelism and the triumph of pluralism and greater respect for associational autonomy. On the contrary, Fox argues that all three models of state–society relations can co-exist within the same nation-state, as authoritarian state elites, autonomous social movements and reformist state managers (*técnicos*) go through 'iterative cycles of political conflict'.[72] Yet after nearly three decades of reform, authoritarian clientelism has lost most of its hold in Mexico, save in some of the least developed rural and ethnically diverse enclaves. The 'grey area' of semi-clientelism is also shrinking rapidly, particularly in urban areas, where citizens are progressively becoming more assertive in demanding their rights as citizens and less willing to comply in exchange for material rewards.

The overlapping trends of the increasing autonomous associational activism of Mexican citizenry and the extensive economic reforms, liberalisation and privatisation by the Mexican state are by no means coincidental. Intense privatisation efforts and significant cuts in public spending subsequent to the 1982

---

71. J. Fox, 'The difficult transition from clientelism to citizenship: lessons from Mexico', *World Politics* 1994, 46(2), pp. 151–84 p. 158.

72. Fox, 1994, pp. 156–7.

crisis gradually weakened the Mexican state's ability to run its vast corporatist machine. 'Fiscal discipline' was the mantra of the Washington Consensus era: therefore, the state was compelled to tighten its belt. The technocratic team of Salinas, in particular, found the corporatist network very costly to run and devised cheaper alternatives that connected voters directly to the executive branch, by-passing the PRI machine. This way, Salinas not only centralised his powers but also undermined the success of opposition parties in local elections. For example, he spent 12 per cent of the entire PRONASOL budget in 1992 in Michoácan, a relatively small state but which was the home state of major opposition candidate, Cárdenas. His tactic, however, upset the entrenched interests in the PRI rank-and-file and alienated the old party loyalists.[73]

As the PRI leadership began to de-emphasise its corporatist networks, their patronage ties with the electorate loosened and opposition parties began to score electoral victories. Aside from rising competition at the ballot box, the financial crunch of the state even compromised its ability to respond to national emergencies. The 1985 Mexico City earthquake exposed the relative weakness of the state, which was unable to respond effectively to the mounting problems of its citizens. The failure of the state, in turn, prompted an organised reaction from civil society that took charge of the relief efforts.

It took *thirty-six hours* for President de la Madrid to make his first address[74] to his people, after an earthquake of 8.1 on the Richter scale hit Mexico City on 19 September 1985. The survivors, particularly in the massive public housing projects that were disproportionally affected by the disaster, found no authorities to whom to direct their pleas for help. The slow pace of the rescue operations, grossly incompetent and insensitive attitudes towards the perished (approximately 20,000 dead) and the survivors (nearly 180,000 homeless), invigorated a sense of 'do-it-yourself' politics and a bottom-up movement along with it. Long-time observers of Mexican politics and residents of Mexico City at the time of the quake, *New York Times* correspondents Julia Preston and Samuel Dillon, report the following in order to emphasise the unique nature of the movements that grew out of this devastating event:

> The new force that emerged from the earthquake was civil society. The citizens groups that formed were independent of the PRI, but they had no ties to the opposition parties either. They mobilized Mexicans across class lines. The poorest of the poor, who had lived in decaying tenements in the old city centre, joined with groups from solidly middle-class neighbourhoods. And after the earthquake shattered their homes and lives, many Mexicans were willing to try tactics they had never considered before. Workaday citizens regularly clogged the streets with insolent sit-ins and marches.[75]

73. Fox, 1994, pp. 166–8.
74. Preston and Dillon, 2004, p. 100.
75. Preston and Dillon, 2004, pp. 113–4.

The incompetence of the government fuelled public fury, which was then channelled into creative organisations to fill up the vacuum left by the state. Areas that were previously considered exclusively in the public domain (such as search and rescue and shelter-provision) were penetrated by civil society, which did a much more competent job than the corrupt and inept public authorities.[76] In the reconstruction stage, these civic organisations provided effective monitoring. They also administered the allocation of new homes in a just and fair manner, prioritising the most vulnerable, like widows and single mothers, instead of the best connected. As a result, a vibrant urban social-movement landscape was built upon the debris of the devastating Mexico City earthquake. Cutting across social and class barriers, these bottom-up movements managed to resist the co-opting lure of corporatism and thus contributed to the creation of a new democratic and pluralist political space.

¡Hoy Decimos Basta! *The rise of indigenous movements*

Unfortunately, the rising tide of economic liberalisation did not lift all the boats in Mexico. As successive PRI governments rolled back rights to collectively owned lands, cut social spending in the name of fiscal discipline and welcomed aggressive forms of foreign investment, rural and indigenous communities were further pushed into the margins of society. This time, however, these communities did not acquiesce as the government denied them their most basic rights and corporations destroyed their livelihoods. They by-passed the existing forms of rural representation, which were co-opted, corrupt and subservient and essentially functioned as channels to deliver rural votes for the PRI. Instead, they established autonomous platforms to claim their economic, political and cultural rights from the state.

Probably the most famous of these movements was the rebellion of Mayan peasants in southern Mexico. Not just Mexico but the whole world suddenly became familiar with the *Ejército Zapatista de Liberación Nacional* (EZLN: Zapatista National Liberation Army), after their much-publicised Declaration from the Lacandon Jungle in Chiapas. It came right before Mexico was to celebrate its NAFTA membership on 1 January 1994. The following excerpt from the First Declaration highlights the reasons why these Mayan peasants rebelled, and lists their demands of the government. Moreover, it illustrates how the EZLN perceives itself as part of the centuries-long history of resistance in Mexico, side by side with the revolutionary figures of Pancho Villa and Emiliano Zapata. Their reference to Article 39 of the Mexican Constitution and their explicit call for a democratic regime for Mexico also testify to EZLN's nationalist, pro-Mexican and anti-secessionist sentiments:

---

76. D. Levy and K. Bruhn, *Mexico: The struggle for democratic development*, Berkeley, CA, Los Angeles, London: University of California Press, 2001, p. 70.

To the people of Mexico: Mexican Brothers and Sisters:

We are a product of 500 years of struggle: first against slavery, then during the War of Independence against Spain lead by insurgents, then to promulgate our constitution and expel the French empire from our soil, and later [when] the dictatorship of Porfirio Díaz denied us the just application of the Reform laws and the people rebelled and leaders like Villa and Zapata emerged, poor men like us. We have been denied the most elemental education so that others can use us as cannon fodder and pillage the wealth of our country. They don't care that we have nothing, absolutely nothing, not even a roof over our heads, no land, no work, no health care, no food and no education. Nor are we able freely and democratically to elect our political representatives, nor is there independence from foreigners, nor is there peace nor justice for ourselves and our children.

But today, we say ENOUGH IS ENOUGH!

[...] To prevent the continuation of the above and as our last hope, after having tried to utilize all legal means based on our Constitution, we go to our Constitution, to apply Article 39 which says: 'National Sovereignty essentially and originally resides in the people. All political power emanates from the people and its purpose is to help the people. The people have, at all times, the inalienable right to alter or modify their form of government.'

[...] To the People of Mexico: [W]e ask for your participation, your decision to support this plan that struggles for work, land, housing, food, health care, education, independence, freedom, democracy, justice and peace. We declare that we will not stop fighting until the basic demands of our people have been met by forming a government of our country that is free and democratic.[77]

It is beyond the scope of this book to develop a definitive analysis of the Zapatistas. A colossal body of scholarship from numerous disciplines of social science has emerged since the first declaration of the movement in 1994. However, being the target of so much academic and popular writing may become more of a liability than asset. Because of certain misconceptions and biases against the movement, it might be helpful first to highlight what Zapatistas are *not*, instead of trying to elaborate what they are and what they stand for. 1) They are not like the traditional guerrilla movements in Latin American that take up arms against the state and hope to bring about change through violence. 2) Unlike traditional guerrilla movements, Zapatistas do not have a top-down, hierarchical organisation, nor do they believe in vanguardism. 3) They are not reactionary, 'backwards' Indians trying to block development and progress – as many on the right presume.

---

77. EZLN, *Zapatistas! Documents of the New Mexican Revolution*, New York: Autonomedia, 1994, pp. 35–6. Online. Available http://www.lanic.utexas.edu/project/Zapatistas/Zapatistas_book.pdf (last accessed 10 April 2015).

4) Nor are they 'noble savages' who are heroically resisting the rise of global capitalism – as most on the left idealise the Zapatistas as. 5) EZLN is not an ethnic movement embracing separatist ideas. Although many are from the Mayan communities, they encompass all the poor, not just the indigenous. 6) They do not have a leadership cult. They emphasise collective/communal decision-making procedures and maintain a strongly anti-leader attitude.[78] In fact, in May 2014, they declared that their globally famous spokesperson, Subcomandante Marcos, will 'cease to exist'. Marcos was replaced by Subcomandante Insurgente Galeano, simply because they did not want a single name or personality to overshadow the horizontal and collective nature of the movement.

Although the uprising on New Year's Day in 1994 surprised many in government, for seasoned Mexicanists, Chiapas had certain characteristics that made the state ripe for such a confrontation. On nearly all measures of public welfare and development, Chiapas scored as one of the most underdeveloped states in all of Mexico. Less than half of the indigenous population could speak Spanish, only 11 per cent of households had moderate income (the national average was 24 per cent) and less than 50 per cent of homes had access to clean water (national average, 67 per cent). These miserable conditions became even starker as the resources of Chiapas were being tapped more aggressively during the post-1982 neo-liberal wave. Frequently described as 'a rich land, and a poor people', Chiapas provided 54 per cent of Mexico's hydroelectric power; yet when the rebellion broke out, more than half of the population in Chiapas lacked electricity. All of this neglect and abuse took place despite the overwhelming political support of Chiapas for the ruling PRI. Like many other rural constituents across Mexico, voters in Chiapas were loyal followers of the PRI as well, delivering victories to the party with enormous margins (85–90 per cent).[79]

Aside from the sharp inequalities, deprivation and underdevelopment, a second factor also triggered the emergence of a strong resistance movement. Chiapas was one of the most authoritarian states in Mexico, in terms of social and political power-relations. In certain parts of the state, racist exploitation was practised as if Chiapas was frozen in time. During my fieldwork, I was told that, as late as the 1990s, it was customary and expected for the Indians to step aside and bow, when a white or *mestizo* person was passing by. *New York Times* correspondent Julia Preston mentions even more disturbing forms of racial abuse:

In 1994, at the time of Zapatista uprising, there were still *fincas*, or big farms, in remote Chiapas where the owners exercised *la pernada*, the right to sleep with an Indian bride on her wedding night before her new husband.[80]

---

78. G. Esteva, *Celebration of Zapatismo*, Oaxaca Mexico: Ediciones Basta, 2008, pp. 9–10; G. Collier, *Basta!: Land and Zapatista rebellion in Chiapas*, Oakland, CA: Food First Books, 3rd edn, 2005, pp.1–10.

79. Collier, 2005, pp.16–17.

80. Preston and Dillon, 2004, p. 443.

In the political realm, Chiapas suffered under the iron fists of local and regional *caciques* (bosses) for a very long time. Jan Rus cogently describes how the policies of the much revered Cárdenas era in the 1930s transformed these 'closed corporate communities' in the highlands of Chiapas into 'institutionalized revolutionary communities' that were 'harnessed to the state'. Whilst bringing new rights to the indigenous communities, *Cardenismo* replaced the characteristics of autonomous self-rule and communal solidarity with a centralised bureaucracy that tied the communities directly to the state. In this process, co-opted local strongmen began to serve as the middlemen and monopolised the political and economic power that emanated from the state.[81] In a tragic paradox of revolution, policies that aimed at improving the lot of the impoverished indigenous peoples ended up condemning them to terribly abusive, authoritarian power structures.

Immediately after the rebellion broke out in Chiapas, the Mexican state retaliated with massive military force. Over 15,000 troops were deployed, villages were bombed and captives experienced harsh treatment in the hands of government security forces. Yet shortly after the brutal military campaign, there were high-level negotiations between Mexican authorities and the Zapatistas, during which progressive members of the Catholic Church functioned as mediators. For most analysts, the softening of government strategy was due to the Mexican state's fear of the bad international publicity in the wake of NAFTA, which might have deterred much-sought-after foreign investors. The movement itself also claims credit in this switch from military tactics to politics by stating that the uprising in Chiapas spread like wildfire across the region and that sympathy poured in from around the world, particularly from North America and Europe. All of this support 'tremendously strengthened the hand of the Zapatistas, and forced the government to withdraw to the negotiating table'.[82] A third explanation is the 'elite splintering' argument. According to Fox, the Zapatista rebellion in the remote municipalities of Chiapas 'led to a deep split within Mexico's national political class over whether to respond militarily or politically'.[83] In fact, during my interviews in Mexico City, a prominent Mexican scholar close to the PRI leadership also expressed the strong preference within the party for negotiating its way out of this unexpected blunder on the eve of NAFTA. In the end, the reformists won over the hardliners and the demands of the indigenous communities were brought to the negotiation table.

Even though they were carrying guns and wearing ski masks, the Zapatistas had almost nothing in common with the traditional guerrilla movements of Latin America. Their top priorities were democratisation and the empowerment of

---

81. J. Rus, 'The "Comunidad Revolucionaria Institucional": the Subversion of Native Government in Highland Chiapas, 1936–1968', in G. Joseph and D. Nuget (eds), *Everyday Forms of State Formation*, Durham & London: Duke University Press, 1994, pp. 265–300.

82. Zapatistas, 1994, p. 15.

83. J. Fox, 'How does civil society thicken? The political construction of social capital in rural Mexico', *World Development* 1996, 24(6), pp. 1089–1103, p. 1092.

civil society in Mexico.[84] Both the ideology and the methods of the Zapatistas seemed to have caught conventional political actors by surprise. On the one hand, the EZLN harshly criticised neo-liberal economic policies and the discourse of 'development,' which, in reality, delivered only exploitation and misery for indigenous communities. Therefore, they strongly challenged the universalistic assumptions of this so-called progress and advocated a pluralistic world in which 'many worlds' could fit (*un mundo donde quepan muchos mundos*). Because of this, the EZLN certainly did not make many friends among the centre-right parties, who were trying hard to keep Mexico on the development track with NAFTA and other neo-liberal projects. On the other hand, the EZLN alienated itself from the conventional left in Mexico (represented by the PRD), largely because of its disturbingly horizontal organisation and its open aversion to hierarchy and power-relations.

During my field trip in Mexico in 2008, I had a chance to attend two public lectures by a long-time advisor to the movement. In both those lectures and in our interview, Gustavo Esteva tried to clarify the thorny issue of EZLN–PRD relations. This was a delicate issue, partly because, during the 2006 Presidential elections, the PRD candidate, Andrés Manuel López Obrador lost the election by a very slim margin. Esteva stated that first, EZLN was a *movement* that emerged when the communities felt compelled to say *basta!* (enough!) Second, as a movement, it had very little structure, if any, and this structure was rather horizontal and flexible. In the EZLN, those with the capacity of decision-making lead by obeying the collective preferences of the communities (*mandar obedeciendo*). Third, and related to the second point, the Zapatistas did not share the PRD's goal of capturing state power and implementing its own view of 'good society' in a top-down manner.

In the end, the Zapatistas were able to carve out a distinct space in the socio-political landscape of Mexico independent from the PRI and the conventional leftist parties. In Chiapas, they were able to organise communities in autonomous municipalities, which were then connected to *Juntas de buen gobierno* (councils of good governance). The selection and decision-making procedures in these bodies were on a rotating basis and more than half were staffed with women. Although some are sceptical about the quality of life and basic services (schools, education in local languages, healthcare and so on) in the EZLN-controlled municipalities in the region,[85] the Mexican state seems to have conceded the Zapatistas' right to establish their alternative world in the highlands of Chiapas. Besides, there are state-provided services in the region, should the residents want to opt out of the EZLN system. According to Jonathan Fox, successful alliances of the Zapatistas with national and international civil society organisations (the Catholic Church and human rights organisations) also played an important role in their success.

---

84. C. Gilbreth and G. Otero, 'Democratization in Mexico: the Zapatista uprising and the civil society', *Latin American Perspectives* 2001, 2(4), pp. 7–29, p. 8.

85. Preston and Dillon, 2004, p. 447.

Consequently, the Zapatistas were able to form a 'strictly bottom-up consolidation of civil society in one of Mexico's most remote indigenous regions', despite the entrenched authoritarian clientelism in the region.[86]

The rise of grassroots movements and civil society in rural Mexico is not confined to the southern states that have dense indigenous populations. This phenomenon can be observed all across Mexico, including the urban spaces and the more developed central and northern states. For instance, in 1995 and 1996, activists in the city of Tepoztlán, Morelos successfully organised a grassroots movement to counter a government-imposed development project. The project included the construction of a golf course and a country club and required confiscation of their *ejidos*. On learning about this invasive plan, these communities united in protest and managed to block the initiative.[87]

During my fieldwork in rural Guanajuato, one of the civil-society organisations that I had a chance to interview had an impressive track record. The Center for Development in Agriculture (*Centro de Desarollo Agropecuario*, CEDESA) was established in the 1960s, by a Catholic priest and few young activists from the town of Dolores Hidalgo. The first problems they tried to tackle were illiteracy and the lack of potable water. During this process, they experienced first-hand the brutally repressive face of the Mexican state. The constant battle of CEDESA with the state over the most basic rights of the communities in the region, and its gradual success over the years, is testimony to democratic progress in Mexico. Today, it functions as a vibrant hub of grassroots activism that educates nearly 150 surrounding communities. First and foremost, it advocates a life with dignity and sustainability. Their environmental consciousness and stewardship is particularly praiseworthy.

Guanajuato is an important agricultural state in Mexico and, as such, is dominated by large commercial farms that are mostly owned by American corporations. Because of the dry climate, these commercial operations rely heavily upon underground water to grow the fruit and vegetables that they export. Recently, ground-water levels have become dangerously low but the *campesinos* lack the means to tap down hundreds of meters to find a suitable supply. Here is where CEDESA comes into play. It holds workshops to educate communities about water-conservation techniques, which include pipes to capture rainwater, home-made cisterns, recycling of 'grey' water and reusing it for animals and plants (*see* Appendix A for photos). Most community members who participated in these workshops have implemented these cheap and efficient water-conservation techniques in their households. These simple but novel methods have significantly improved the quality of life in these impoverished communities. In short, they are not sitting idle as the international agro-business encroaches upon the region in the last decades. Instead, they are developing viable collective survival strategies, with the help of CEDESA.

---

86. Fox, 1996, p. 1097.

87. J. Stolle-McAllister, 'What *does* democracy look like? Local movements challenge the Mexican transition', *Latin American Perspectives* 2005, 32(4) pp. 15–35.

CEDESA was also active in improving the economic wellbeing of the communities around Dolores Hidalgo. Its initial efforts to establish producers' co-operatives evolved into successful co-ops of apiculturists, organic jam-makers and corn mills (*molinos de nixtamal*). Each co-op had a 'revolving fund' that provided the capital for the new members. Co-ops and communities organised regional fairs in order to bring local producers and consumers together. These fairs also function as platforms for disseminating knowledge about sustainability, solidarity and the collective strength of the communities. If democratic progress is achieved by 'thickening' the civil society, rural communities in Guanajuato are certainly accomplishing this under the organisational structure of CEDESA.

Organised labour and neo-liberal reforms

There is one important sector of Mexican society that is ominously missing from the discussions of democratic transformation and the emergence of pluralist politics: organised labour. Even though the neo-liberal policies after the 1982 crisis placed a disproportionate burden on the working classes, the largest labour confederation in Mexico (CMT) carefully avoided any serious display of protest. The symbol of co-opted trade unionism, Fidel Velasquez, protected his seat as the Secretary General of CMT for 56 years, until his death in 1997.

Subsequent to the 1982 crisis, Mexico implemented one of the harshest austerity packages in the world, which axed housing, health and most other social expenditures from the budget and earned President Salinas de Gortari the nickname *de Cortari*, with reference to Spanish verb *cortar* (to cut). Making matters worse, the sudden exposure of the Mexican economy to global competition also created downward pressure on wages in order to attract foreign investment. In 1980, the hourly compensation for an average Mexican manufacturing worker was 22 per cent of that of an American worker. However, in 1996, a Mexican worker made only 8 per cent of what the American worker earned.[88]

Most PRI Presidents, particularly Salinas, introduced neo-liberal reforms to the top representatives of organised labour and business first, in order to minimise the potential backlash. Instead of being platforms of genuine give and take, these pacts were functioning as mechanisms through which the PRI would secure the subservience of organised labour. Co-opted union leaders would assist the PRI in 'holding down wages and discontent through one punishing anti-inflation program after another'.[89] Instead of serving the interests of the working classes, the most powerful unions in Mexico functioned as quasi-public bodies 'subordinate to the logic of the state'. Official unions continued to enjoy certain privileges (protection from competing independent unions) and some political clout, in exchange for unwavering support for the PRI. Thus, they maintained the corporatist form of relations with the state, even though in other spheres and

---

88. Preston and Dillon, 2004, p. 474.

89. Preston and Dillon, 2004, p. 247.

towards other sectors the state was adopting less controlling and more pluralist forms of interaction.[90]

Enrique de la Garza articulates a more striking observation regarding the persistence of corporatism in state-organised labour relations well into the twenty-first century. He argues that after the historic transfer of power to PAN in 2000, the general expectation was of the dismantling of corporatist traditions, precisely because PAN was the quintessential pro-market, neo-liberal party that had very little to do with old-style corporatist meddling in industrial relations. Yet, corporatism survived into the PAN era as well. First, President Fox and the entrepreneurial class realized that corporatism is a very efficient and historically effective mechanism for controlling workers' demands. At the same time, it served to eliminate dissidents and labour activism. Second, given the intense competitive pressure from the world markets to keep prices down, it would be a very risky adventure to open up the labour unions to democratic and pluralistic forms of organisation. The author points to some attempts by workers, particularly in the very exploitative *maquiladora*[91] sector, to break away from entrenched corporatism. But even now, organised labour remains far from what a pluralistic civil-society model would require.[92] Adding insult to injury, the leader of the largest teachers' union in Mexico, Elba Esther Gordillo (known as *La Maestra*), was thrown in jail in 2013 for embezzling millions.

In the last two decades of the twentieth century, Mexico made great progress in terms of organising its democracy. Capitalising upon critical institutional reforms (such as an independent federal election commission (IFE), lower electoral thresholds and empowered federal units), opposition parties both on the left and right built up significant power: enough to finally dislodge the PRI in 2000. No less significant than these institutional reforms and changes in the party system is the radical democratic transformation at the societal level.

Subsequent to drastic secular changes in the economic and socio-political realms, corporatist venues of representation in Mexico were gradually replaced by a vibrant civil society. Citizens began to articulate their demands, concerns and criticisms more effectively and frequently than usual. At times, social movements could emerge after a single spontaneous incident, as in the case of *Soy 132*. *Soy 132* (I am 132) emerged when the presidential candidate from the PRI was visiting the Iberoamericana University in 2012 during his election campaign. 131 students who protested against him identified themselves with their university IDs, which generated a chain of protests across the country in solidarity with the original 131 protestors. These solidarity protestors claimed to be the 132nd student,

---

90. E. de la Garza Toledo, 'Manufacturing neoliberalism: industrial relations, trade union corporatism and politics', in G. Otero (ed.), *Mexico in Transition*, London & New York: Zed Books, 2004, pp.104–20.

91. These are the foreign-owned assembly plants, mostly concentrated in northern Mexico, along the US border. They take advantage of the tax-free status, low wages and lax enforcement in Mexico. Production is mostly geared towards the exporting to the US and global markets.

92. E. de la Garza Toledo, 2004, p. 120.

hence the name, '*I am 132*'. Another important feature of these new grassroots movements is that they cut across geographic and class divides. As seen in the *Soy 132* movement, they can emerge rather spontaneously. Students and peasants, indigenous communities and women reclaim the political space to articulate their democratic demands. This dense network of autonomous civilian initiatives is critically important, in terms of advancing the democratic credentials of Mexico in the twenty-first century.

Neo-liberalism under praetorian guidance: Economic reforms in Turkey

Similarly to the policy shift in Mexico, the economic direction of Turkey moved in a neo-liberal direction in the 1980s after the famous '24 January Decisions'. As the head of the State Planning Organisation (DPT), Turgut Özal had crafted the 24 January Decisions, marking a watershed moment in the liberalisation of the Turkish economy. When the military took power on 12 September 1980, it culled nearly all of the existing political and bureaucratic cadres but kept one of the key architects of the 24 January Decisions, Turgut Özal. As the economy deteriorated, the coup leaders became more inclined to defer economic decisions to a technocratic team.[93] This marked the beginning of Prime Minister Turgut Özal's ascendance in economic policy-making. In their analysis, Öniş and Webb categorise Turkey as a typical case of 'adjustment from above', in which 'a small group of technocrats outside the traditional bureaucracy, organized under a strong leader, can play a key role in initiating and implementing structural adjustment policies'.[94] In this regard, Turkey's technocratic team, referred as the 'princes of Özal', shows strong similarities with the *técnicos* of Mexico.

Until the late 1980s, Özal and his team had a free hand to restructure the Turkish economy according to the logic of the free market. The politically repressive nature of this era certainly came in handy for their task. The Turkish military ruled directly until the end of 1983 and exerted strong covert control until 1988. Two critical policies during this interregnum in democracy made things relatively easy for Özal's new economic team. First, the military adopted a strongly anti-labour stance. Independent and radical wings of the labour movement were suppressed heavy-handedly. Many unions, including the Revolutionary Trade Unions' Federation or DİSK (*Devrimci İşçi Sendikaları Konfederasyonu*), were shut down and most of the leaders and activists imprisoned.[95] Second, the military curbed

---

93. A. Feroz, *Bir Kimlik Peşinde Türkiye*, İstanbul, Bilgi University Publications, 2007, p. 181, [published in English as *Turkey: The Quest for Identity*], transl. Cem Karadeli, Oxford: Oneworld, 2003.

94. Z. Öniş and S. Webb, 'Turkey: democratization and adjustment from above', *State and Market*, Istanbul: Bogazici University Press, 1998, p. 323, reprinted from: S. Haggard and S. Webb (eds), *Voting for Reform*, Oxford: Oxford University Press, 1998, pp. 128–84.

95. K. Boratav, 'Economic history, 1981–2002', in Sina Akşin *et al.* (eds), *Today's Turkey 1980–2003 History of Turkey volume 5*, Ankara: Cem Publications, 2007, pp. 189–245.

electoral political competition by closing down all political parties and banning their leaders from politics. Turkish generals established a new system of parties and hand-picked their leaders. Turgut Özal's Motherland Party (*Anavatan Partisi* – ANAP) was the only one not directly created by the military. Özal, who was a charismatic civilian leader, and his party, which claimed to unite four dominant currents in Turkish politics – left, right, nationalist and conservative – achieved significant electoral victory (45.14 per cent) at the ballot box.[96] Thus, having discarded all political opposition with the help of repressive military measures, Özal and his team enjoyed the 'honeymoon period' of structural reform. Some of the critical reforms implemented during this era included:

- Liberalisation of banking sector; establishing floating exchange rates and convertibility of Turkish lira.
- 7 per cent to 12 per cent decline in real wages; significant cuts in agricultural subsidies.
- Tax breaks for corporations; implementation of VAT in 1985 to compensate for lost tax revenues.
- Liberalisation of foreign capital movements.
- Promotion of exports through rebates and subsidies.
- Gradual reduction and elimination of import quotas and tariff barriers.
- Establishing new bureaucracies under direct supervision of executive branch to co-ordinate privatisation.[97]

When we look at the overall balance sheet after the structural-adjustment reforms, what seemed to be advantageous for Turkey in the early stages of reform later turned out to be major handicaps. As mentioned above, the reforms were imposed under military tutelage and were handled by small and insulated cadres. While this aspect helped Turkey implement reforms in a speedy fashion, the exclusion of major parties from the process, and the lack of social pacts (*à la* Mexico) to negotiate the distribution of burdens, generated a popular backlash against the reforms. Additionally, the executive-dominant, top-down economic policy-making process eventually became highly conducive to patronage politics and rent-distribution. Despite all the emphasis on the efficiency of private sector as the engine of economic growth, the public sector still maintained its lion's share of the national economy. State economic enterprises (SEEs), public banks, extra-budgetary funds (directly at Prime Minister's discretion) and government contracts became huge reservoirs of resources to be distributed as rents to friends and allies.[98] Ayşe Buğra's seminal work on state–business relations in Turkey is full of testimonies from businessmen during the Özal era, who explain how

---

96. Ahmad, 2007, p. 190.
97. Boratav, 2007, pp. 189–96.
98. Öniş and Webb, 1998, pp. 366–9.

they secured significant concessions and favours from the state through personal connections. All of these experiences display the highly arbitrary and even corrupt nature of economic decision-making during this period, under the cloak of rational, technocratic rule.[99]

Aside from the executive-dominant and *rentier* aspects of the neo-liberal era, Boratav highlights another repercussion for the Turkish economy after the hasty liberalisation era. He argues that the main macroeconomic indicators in Turkey (inflation, budget deficit, public indebtedness, interest rates and so on) worsened despite all the stabilisation measures. Inflation and interest rates soared, which created the *least* favourable environment for long-term investments in industry and manufacturing. For those who had the capital, it was a lot less risky and a lot more profitable to operate in the financial markets. Hence, the liberal economy in Turkey was born with a major birth defect: vulnerability to short-term speculative capital flows at the expense of long-term productive investments.[100] This vulnerability resulted in multiple economic shocks in the following decades, when sudden capital flights created havoc in the financial system and caused sizable contractions in the national economy (-5% GDP growth rate in 1994, -3% in 1999 and -6% in the 2001 crisis).[101]

Aside from capital flights that created periodic economic turmoil, a second structural handicap in the Turkish economy was the constant underperformance of exporting sectors. Political economist Öniş aptly defines the ISI period as 'inward oriented, export dependent'. Figure 5.5 verifies this by illustrating the poor performance of Turkish exports *vis-à-vis* imports during the peak decades of ISI. In fact, one of the most important arguments *for* the neo-liberal reforms was that they would cure the ills of the ISI era, by boosting the performance of exports through competition and by eliminating the chronic dependence on imports through liquidating inefficient domestic industries.

The paradigmatic shift in the economy towards an export-led growth model notwithstanding, the ills of the ISI era remained largely uncured in the Turkish case. Exports continued to lag behind imports, causing a chronic trade-deficit problem. As seen in Figure 5.5, both exports and imports increased significantly after the 1980 reforms. However, despite all the incentives for the private sector to boost exports (such as tax breaks and rebates), the export performance of the country could never keep up with its appetite for imports. Consequently, the economy could not recover from import-dependence. In the three decades since Turkey adopted the export-led growth plan and opened up its economy, its exports surpassed imports only five times (in 1988, 1994, 1998, 2001 and 2002). In fact, on average, Turkey imports 3–5 per cent more

99. A. Buğra, *Devlet Ve İşadamları* [*State and Business in Modern Turkey: A comparative study*], New York: SUNY Press, 1994.

100. Boratav, 2007.

101. World Development Indicators, various years.

Figure 5.5: Import–export performance of Turkey, as % of GDP, 1960–2012

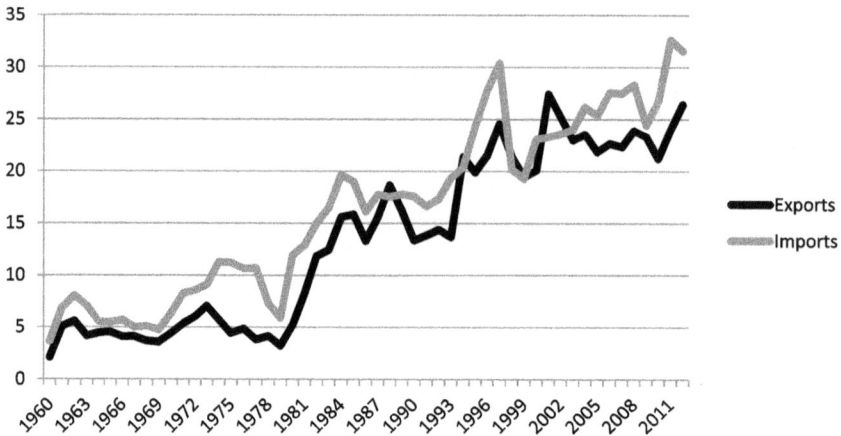

Source: World Bank Economic Indicators, 1968–2012.

than it exports. As of 2012, exports remain at 26 per cent of GDP while imports reach 31.5 per cent.

In terms of the balance between imports and exports, Mexico managed a slightly more positive performance. Mexico, too, showed the typical symptoms of import-dependence during the ISI decades (*see* Figure 5.6). However, after the reforms of the 1980s, Mexican exports managed to outpace imports. While imports seem to have surpassed exports since 2000, unlike Turkey, Mexico seems to have kept the trade deficit consistently around 1–2 per cent. In this regard, one can argue that Salinas and his team was more successful than Özal's in terms of realizing the neo-liberal goal of export-led growth. In both figures (Figure 5.5 and 5.6) we can observe significant jumps after 1994, when Mexico signed NAFTA with the US and Turkey entered into a customs union with the EU. However, while Mexico managed to keep its imports on a par with exports after this critical free-trade agreement, Turkey experienced an ever increasing trade-deficit *vis-à-vis* the EU.

International neo-liberal circles welcomed the liberalisation of the Turkish economy, especially after the customs union with the EU in 1994. The 2005 Report on Turkey by the IMF Mission Chief praised the increase in the trade openness of the Turkish economy (measured by the sum of exports and imports as a percentage of GDP, Table 5.2). Yet this is a tricky variable by which to assess the overall export achievements of an economy. Unlike Mexico, Turkey became a *net importer* with a massively growing trade deficit after these reforms. Robust flows of foreign investment from the EU did not materialise, despite the elimination of structural barriers. In fact, the very same report by the IMF states that despite the increasing openness of the Turkish economy, 'investment shares in

Figure 5.6: Import–export performance of Mexico, as % of GDP, 1968–2012

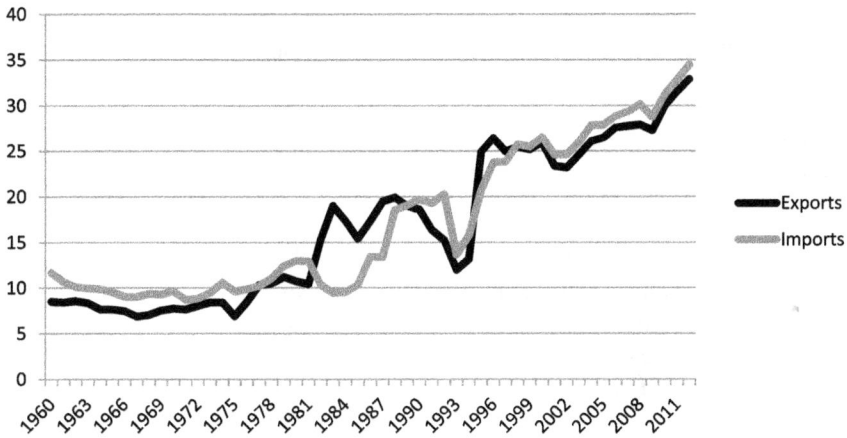

Source: World Bank Economic Indicators, 1960–2012.

Turkey remained relatively low, especially compared with East Asian and OECD economies'.[102]

Unlike the Turkish-EU case, closer economic relations with the US (and, to a lesser extent, with Canada) brought significant foreign investment to Mexico. It generated thousands of jobs in the manufacturing sector (500,000 between 1994 and 2002) and increased the productivity of the Mexican labour-force.[103] In the case of Turkey–EU relations 'some of the expected benefits of the Customs Union, such as the increased foreign direct investment flows or easier access to EU markets […] has not really occurred'.[104] Furthermore, the adjustment aid promised by the EU was either halted due to a Greek veto, or suspended by the European Parliament on political grounds. From a comparative perspective, while Turkey received *four* euros *per capita* in EU aid, Central and East European countries

---

102. R. Moghadam, *Turkey at the Crossroads: From crisis resolution to EU accession*, IMF Occasional Paper # 242, IMF, Washington DC, 2005 p. 8.

103. The downside is, jobs created in the manufacturing sector were not sufficient to match the loss of jobs in the agricultural sector due to NAFTA. Furthermore, the peso crisis in 1994 and 1995 caused a major setback for real wages in Mexico, so that an increase in productivity in the following years due to NAFTA did not translate into higher wages for Mexican workers. In short, NAFTA delivered a mixed bag of results, most of them not predicted by the parties in 1994: see J. Audley *et al.*, *NAFTA's Promise and Reality*, Carnegie Endowment Report, 2004, pp. 6–7.

104. M. Eder, 'Implementing the economic criteria of EU membership: how difficult is it for Turkey?', in A. Çarkoglu and B. Rubin (eds), *Turkey and the European Union: Domestic politics, economic integration and international dynamics*, London: Frank Cass, 2003, p. 228.

Table 5.2: Trade openness of Turkey, 1961–2000

	Region	1961–80	1981–2000
Trade openness (sum of imports and exports, as % of GDP)	Turkey	11.4	37.7
	Latin America	46.0	53.9
	OECD	51.1	64.1

Source: Reza Moghadam, *Turkey at the Crossroads*, IMF Occasional Paper # 242, Washington DC: IMF, 2005, p. 7.

received between 10 and 45 euros aid *per capita*.[105] The miniscule amount of European investment and structural funds headed for Turkey underline the fact that Turkish economic integration with the EU remained on a much limited scale when compared to the Mexican partnership with the US and Canada. While the northern border of Mexico rapidly transformed into an industrial belt after joining NAFTA, one cannot talk about similar regional concentrations of investment and economic activity in the case of Turkey. This is a critical point of divergence between the two cases, which significantly fuels the progress of many secular trends such as urbanisation and industrialisation, as well as the expansion of the middle and working classes.

Despite being the largest trading partner of Turkey,[106] the extent of integration with Europe after the customs union did not reach the levels achieved in the US–Mexico collaboration. Sweeping economic reforms in Mexico ushered in significant political changes, the most famous of which being the PRI's defeat in 2000. Economic liberalisation and integration with North American markets increased the competitive pressures on the Mexican economy. The success of Mexican businesses was no longer heavily dependent upon political connections.[107] Joint ventures, franchises and other forms of partnership with international capital provided leverage and made Mexican businesses less vulnerable to the whims of their own state. Naturally, businesses had little use for the old corporate networks. Moreover, they were progressively becoming more resentful of state involvement, which, from their perspective, was wasteful and corrupt. According to Bellin, it was at this stage that the new class of economic entrepreneurs 'discovered democracy'. Aside from economic freedoms, they

---

105. Eder, 2003, p. 231.

106. Top 10 destinations for Turkish exports in 2013: January–November: Germany, Iraq, UK, Italy, US, France, Russian Federation, UAE, Spain, and Iran. Top 10 countries Turkey imported from in 2013: Russian Federation (mostly petroleum and gas), China, Germany, US, Italy, Iran, France, South Korea, India, and the UK/Spain. *Source*: Turkish Ministry of Economy Statistics. Online. Available http://www.tuik.gov.tr/ (last accessed 10 December 2014).

107. There are some exceptions to this. Privatisation of the telecom sector as a monopoly created the behemoth of Carlos Slim, for example. However, after much public criticism, the PRI government began to work on telecom reform in 2014, in an effort to increase competition and protect Mexican consumers.

aspired to political liberalisation and transformed themselves into political entrepreneurs.[108]

Ultimately, the activities of these entrepreneurs resulted in the bankrolling of the centre-right *Partido Accion Nacional*, PAN. The electoral success of Vicente Fox, an ex-CEO of Coca Cola in Mexico, is a great testament to the ascendance of this new entrepreneurial class in Mexican politics. Post-election surveys after the pivotal 2000 elections revealed that PAN voters had the highest levels of education, were economically better off, lived in an urban areas and were the youngest partisans, in comparison to the PRI or PRD voters.[109] However, to give all the credit to PAN for advancing Mexican democracy would be only a partial explanation. Simultaneously to the increasing political clout of the neo-liberal entrepreneurs and middle classes under PAN, there was also a significant challenge against the PRI from the left of the political spectrum, by the PRD.

Neo-liberal reforms and NAFTA have been detrimental for the urban and rural poor. They sharpened the already deep fissures between the haves and have-nots in Mexico. Although it splintered from the mainstream PRI, the PRD had a solid intellectual basis. It was composed of students and urban intelligentsia, unified by the principles of freedom, democracy and social justice. Moreover, the PRD's emphasis on social justice resonated strongly with *campesinos* in agrarian states. As such, the PRD managed to be the voice of those left behind by the liberal-market train. Therefore, it is no surprise that the supporters of PRD also came both from the non-industrialised regions of Southern Mexico, as well as from the high-literacy areas of urban centres.[110] In the end, while PAN besieged the PRI from the right of the political spectrum, PRD did the same from the left, which ultimately brought the seventy-year-old 'Goliath' down. [111]

In the Turkish case, however, the limited scope of economic integration with the EU could not render such clearly demarcated economic and class interests, which could then be translated into political preferences. Unlike the consolidated party system in Mexico, which reflects the main economic cleavages in the society (centre-right PAN, centrist PRI, centre-left PRD), in the Turkish case, multiple military coups, party closures and partial neo-liberal transformation prevented strong class-based constituencies and strong identification with political parties.

108. E. Bellin, 'Contingent democrats: industrialists, labour, and democratization in late developing countries', *World Politics* 2000, 52(2), pp. 175–205, p. 195.

109. J. Klesner, 'The structure of the Mexican electorate: social, attitudinal and partisan basis of Vicente Fox's victory', in J. Dominguez and C. Lawson (eds), *Mexico's Pivotal Democratic Election*, Palo Alto, CA: Stanford University Press, 2004, pp. 91–122.

110. Klesner, 2004, pp. 102–5.

111. July 2000 Presidential election results: PAN 42.5%; PRI 36.1%; PRD 16.6%. In his analysis of the Mexican elections during the 1990s, Klesner argues that, despite the existence of three major parties in Mexico, only 20 per cent of the districts had genuinely competing three-party systems. PAN and PRD could not challenge the PRI in all parts of the nation. In 80 per cent of the districts (219 districts) the competition was a bipartisan one: either PAN challenging PRI, mostly in the North, or PRD challenging PRI, mostly in the south (Klesner, 2004, pp. 92–5).

The Turkish electorate seems to be more receptive to ideology, ethnicity and religiosity when determining its party choice. Eminent scholars on Turkish voting behaviour broadly agree that pocketbook concerns and economic conditions have either no impact on party choice,[112] or have only a small, secondary impact.[113] The last two general elections in the country (2007 and 2011) seem to have consolidated the identity-ideology-dominant voting preferences of the Turkish electorate: coastal cities prefer the secular/modernising CHP; inland regions strongly opt for the conservative/Islamist AKP; there are some pockets of support for the ultra-nationalist MHP; and the east and south-east remain strongholds for the pro-Kurdish BDP.

Turkey experienced political changes of great magnitude as its relations with the EU intensified. Capital punishment was abolished, the linguistic rights of Kurds were recognised and the military became increasingly subordinate to the civilian authorities, to name a few. However, this pattern of relationship sets Turkey apart from the Mexico-NAFTA affair, wherein economic aspects of the engagement were predominant. In the Turkish–EU case, the political domain was undoubtedly predominant over the socio-economic one. In terms of democratic consolidation, these two different modalities of engagement (intense economic and restricted political engagement in the Mexico-NAFTA case and intense political and restricted socio-economic engagement in the Turkish-EU case) seem to have yielded rather different outcomes. The following section will argue that the intense political and limited socio-economic engagements between the EU and Turkey fits into the *coercive* and *conditional* types of international influence in Schmitter's categorisation. And, as such, they seem to be less effective in assisting democratic consolidation in Turkey than the *consensual* pattern of democratic diffusion in the US–Mexican case.

The conundrum of Turkish-European relations

Ever since the Ottoman Empire realized its relative decline *vis-à-vis* the European powers, Westernisation has been a central concern on the Turkish political agenda. The Ottoman rulers of that time initiated the *Tanzimat* Reforms (1839–76) largely in an effort to close the widening gap between the declining empire and the West. The gist of these reforms was to modernise both state and society by centralising the administration. At the same time, these reforms provided for diverse subjects

---

112. Y. Esmer, 'At the ballot box: determinants of voting behaviour', in S. Sayarı and Y. Esmer (eds), *Politics, Parties and Interest Groups in Turkey*, UK: Lynne Reinner Publishers, 2002, pp. 91–114. Esmer quotes from his Turkish Values Survey data that '40 per cent of those in the highest income group placed themselves to the left of the [political] scale, whereas the figure was only 16 per cent for the lowest income group. It is clear that in Turkey, leftism is not the ideology of uneducated lower classes', p. 108. This 'anomaly' is largely because ideological factors (i.e. secularist modernism *vs* religious conservatism) are a lot more salient in definitions of left and right in Turkey, than class status and redistributive concerns.

113. E. Kalaycıoğlu and A. Çarkoğlu, *Turkish Democracy Today*, London: I. B. Tauris, 2007, p. 169.

of the Sultan certain mechanisms of representation – albeit limited – in order to maintain their allegiance to the Ottoman Empire.[114] These attempts at political opening were too little and too late to hold together the ageing empire. Yet, for the purpose of our argument, they signal two important points: first, political reforms of a progressive nature have a very long history in Turkey, going all the way back to the final decades of the Ottoman Empire; and, second, these reforms are significantly tied to relations with the Western European powers.

For modern Turkey, the crown jewel of westernisation was formal membership in the highly prized European club. The first official agreement between Turkey and Europe was the 1963 Ankara Agreement.[115] The Ankara Agreement aimed at Turkey's full-membership of the European Economic Community (EEC) and established a three-phase customs-union arrangement. Even though Turkey signed up to become a member of an *economic* union and the subsequent relations between the parties tried to hammer out the details of a customs union before full economic integration, the first stumbling block in relations appeared after the military coup in Turkey in September 1980. In January 1982, the European Community decided to freeze its relations with Turkey and suspended the Ankara Agreement. The European Parliament took punitive measures that could be lifted only after Turkey held general elections and established a new parliament.[116] During the 1970s and early 1980s, there were no official talks on the political parameters or criteria for Turkish membership but the strong reaction from Europe after the military coup clearly demonstrated that the EEC would not consider close economic relations with an authoritarian Turkey.

The military interregnum (12 September 1980–7 December 1983) was a dark episode in Turkish politics. During this period, 650,000 people were arrested and 230,000 were prosecuted. Claims of torture, disappearances and summary executions skyrocketed: 300 citizens died in detention and 171 of them were proved to have died from torture. More than 7,000 people were tried in military courts with the possibility of the death penalty being imposed, of whom 49 were executed. Over 30,000 sought political asylum abroad and left the country, while more than 388,000 were denied passports. Another 30,000 lost their jobs, including many teachers, academics and judges.[117] A short visit to the prison-turned-museum Ulucanlar in Ankara illustrates the brutality of this era. Probably

---

114. S. Shaw, *History of the Ottoman Empire and Modern Turkey, Volume II: Reform, Revolution, and the Republic–The Rise of Modern Turkey, 1808–1975*. Cambridge: Cambridge University Press, 1976–7, p. 55 (accessed through History E-Book Project, University of Michigan).

115. For a detailed chronology of Turkish–EU relations, *see*, Chronology of Turkish-EU Relations, official website of the Republic of Turkey, Ministry of EU Affairs. Online Available http://www.abgs.gov.tr/index.php?p=112&l=2 (last accessed 10 April 2015).

116. O. Erdemli, 'Chronology: Turkey's relations with the EU', in B. Rubin and A. Carkoglu (eds), *Turkey and the European Union: Domestic politics, economic integration and international dynamics*, UK, Frank Cass, 2003, p. 4–5.

117. B. Tanör, 'Political history, 1980–1995', in S. Akşin *et al.* (eds), *Today's Turkey 1980–2003 History of Turkey*, Volume 5, Ankara: Cem Publications, 2007, pp. 95–6.

among the saddest incidents was the execution of 17-year-old Erdal Eren by the military on trumped-up charges. For years, incarceration in Ulucanlar, Metris or one of the many other prisons became a rite of passage for journalists, intellectuals and academics in Turkey.

Military rule did not become permanent, as Turkey adopted a new constitution in 1982 and restored its electoral democracy. However, the 1982 Constitution itself was crafted by a few scholars hand-picked by the military. Kalaycıoğlu describes the 1982 Constitution and the institutions it created as a backtracking of Turkish democracy, when compared to the more liberal outlook of the 1961 Constitution.[118] Despite the hollowness of democracy due to the highly restrictive framework drawn by the military, Turkish politics was on its way to normality with new parties and electoral races. Economic relations with Europe were resuscitated in the 1980s as Turkey endorsed an export-oriented model of economic growth.

In June 1993, the Copenhagen European Council announced three criteria for the then candidate states in Central and Eastern Europe: Cyprus, Malta and Turkey. Politically, candidate states must have 'stable institutions guaranteeing democracy, rule of law, human rights and respect for minorities'. Economically, candidates were to establish functioning market economies that could cope with the competitive pressures of European and global markets. Finally, candidates were expected to successfully incorporate the *acquis communautaire*, the body of law the EU had accumulated thus far, into their legal systems. These criteria for accession were confirmed in the December 1995 meeting of the Madrid European Council and the Union clarified the point that membership was not automatic and that it reserved the right to make the final decision. Subsequently, the Union would evaluate compliance with the Copenhagen Criteria in annual reports.[119]

The political conditions put forward in the Copenhagen Criteria included the thorniest issues in Turkish politics. As discussed in detail below, these political requirements touch upon almost every aspect of the Turkish polity, including its long-established state tradition, its justice system, civil-military relations and the political rights and civil liberties of citizens. The Union demands solid credentials as a liberal, pluralist democracy from aspiring candidates. Yet it was not easy to recalibrate post-coup Turkey according to these criteria.

The framers of the 1982 Constitution deliberately increased the tutelary powers of the military, which formalised their 'Praetorian' role as guardians of the state and republican ideology. The Turkish military already had a strong, self-appointed duty to safeguard the founding principles of the republic, in particular its secular and unitary aspects. In the new constitution, the military enjoyed a numerical majority in the National Security Council, whose decisions had to be 'prioritised' by the Cabinet. The military was also granted financial autonomy and judicial immunity, since none of their expenditures or military court decisions could be brought under

---

118. E. Kalaycıoğlu, *Turkish Dynamics: Bridge across troubled lands*, New York: Palgrave Macmillan, 2005, pp. 127–8.

119. Compiled from the official EU website on enlargement.

civilian oversight. In contrast, the military had the right to meddle in civilian affairs in numerous ways. It could make appointments to critical bureaucratic positions, such as the Secretariat of National Security Council, national radio and television (TRT), and the Higher Educational Board, which regulated *all* of the universities in Turkey (better known by its Turkish acronym, YÖK).[120]

The EU accession process was probably the most effective catalyst to increased scrutiny of the role of military in Turkish politics. Despite occasional complaints from the media and a few academics about the anti-democratic nature of the 1982 Constitution, for almost two decades there was no significant effort to democratise the constitutional order. Successive weak and short-lived coalition governments combined with periodic economic crises destabilised both the political and economic climates in Turkey. Similar to the 1980s in Mexico, the 1990s became the 'lost decade' for Turkey. Given the intensity of economic turmoil, democratic reforms were put on the back burner.

Praetorian politics in Turkey reached yet another peak when the military intervened indirectly in politics on 28 February 1997, forcing the Islamist-leaning coalition leader, Necmettin Erbakan, to step down.[121] With such strong political assertions by the military over elected civilians, grave conditions in south-eastern Turkey regarding the basic rights and liberties of Kurdish citizens and mounting complaints to the European Human Rights Court, the EU excluded Turkey from its formal candidate list in December 1997. The European Union Commission prepared annual progress reports for each of the candidates. Its 1998 Report on Turkey's Progress Towards Accession drew a rather grim portrait of reforms and democratic progress in Turkey:

> On the political side, the evaluation highlights certain anomalies in the functioning of the public authorities, persistent human rights violations and major shortcomings in the treatment of minorities. The lack of civilian control of the army gives cause for concern. This is reflected by the major role played by the army in political life through the National Security Council. A civil, non-military solution must be found to the situation in south-eastern Turkey, particularly since many of the violations of civil and political rights observed in the country are connected in one way or another with this issue.[122]

Indeed, democracy was rationed extremely tightly in Turkey well into the 1990s. The Turkish Armed Forces had a dominant role in determining the acceptable

---

120. S.Yazici, *Turkey in the Process of Democratization*, Istanbul: Bilgi University Press, 2009, pp. 35–7.

121. For the full text of the 28 February decisions of the National Security Council, *see* S. Aydin and Y. Taskin, *1960 'tan Günümüze Türkiye Tarihi*, [*Turkey's History Since 1960*], Istanbul: Iletisim Publications, 2014, Appendix/Ek 9, pp. 519–20.

122. Quoted in *1999 Regular Report from the EU Commission on Turkey's Progress Towards Accession*, p. 8, Online. Available http://www.europa.eu.int/comm/enlargement/report_10_99/ (last accessed 10 April 2015).

political discourse in the country. It unilaterally imposed the 'red lines' around some of the most critical issues, such as the Cyprus conflict, the Kurdish problem and relations with neighbours, including Armenia and Greece. The 1982 Constitution itself was written under military tutelage, with an authoritarian spirit. Some 18 political parties (mostly socialist, communist, Islamist-leaning and pro-Kurdish parties) were closed on the grounds that they violated the main provisions of the 1982 Constitution.[123] Because of its rigid interpretation of secularism and intolerant attitude towards cultural differences, Turkey increasingly 'came to be seen by the EU as an illiberal country fighting its own ethnic and religious identity'.[124]

The harsh tone of the Eurocrats, as well as the sanctions imposed by the EU in late 1990s, eventually paid off. Subsequent governments in Turkey began to take political reforms seriously, which were referred as EU Harmonization Packages. Below is a summary of these critical reforms that were accomplished by a series of constitutional amendments:

- Abolishing death penalty and courts with extraordinary powers, called State Security Courts (Turkish acronym, DGM);
- Expansion of political rights, individual liberties and freedom of expression with emphasis on their *fundamentally inviolable* nature;
- Improvements in detention practices (right to lawyer, shorter time in detention) and prison conditions;
- Explicit bans on use of torture and inhumane behaviour;
- Increasing number of civilian members in the National Security Council (NSC) and transfer of the Secretariat to civilian authorities;
- De-prioritising importance of NSC decisions for the Cabinet by modifying the status of NCS to a *consulting* body;
- Bringing expenses of the Turkish Armed Forces under the judicial control of the Court of Accounts;
- Improvements in gender equality by eliminating discriminatory laws and regulations;
- Expanding cultural rights of different ethnicities and legalisation of publications and broadcasting in Kurdish.

The Turkish Parliament passed most of these reforms that were drafted by the EU in annual progress reports in several EU Harmonization Packages. A seemingly infinite number of EU officials travelled to the troubled Kurdish areas in the south-east to observe the heavy-handed measures taken by the state and back to Ankara to suggest requisite reforms and monitor the pace of democratic progress. In one incident, the President of the European Parliamentary Assembly, Rene van der Linden, gave a speech on the floor of the Turkish Parliament. His speech

---

123. O. Can, *The Constitution and Party Closures in the Process of Democratization*, Ankara: Seckin Publications (in Turkish), 2006, p. 162.

124. H. J. Barkey and O. Taspinar, 'Turkey: on Europe's verge?', p. 3. Online. Available http://www.brookings.edu/research/articles/2006/02/07europe-barkey (last accessed 10 December 2014). Print version appeared in *Great Decisions 2006*, a briefing book published by Foreign Policy Association 2006.

was largely dedicated to the steps Turkey needed to undertake, which included elimination of the 10 per cent national threshold for gaining seats in the legislature in general elections, guarantees to Kurdish citizens to freely exercise their rights, establishment of an ombudsman system and further measures for the protection of minority languages.[125] Most nationalist politicians in Turkey considered these rather detailed plans for democratic reform by the European bureaucrats, and their frequent visits to majority Kurdish regions, as 'meddling' and sinister acts. However, mainstream politicians came to realize that 'the road to join Brussels was going through Diyarbakır'.

This type of micromanagement of the democratic-reform process by EU officials sets the Turkish case distinctly apart from the Mexican experience of democratic deepening. It is important to note that the incidents in Chiapas, for example, were taking place when the Clinton administration had endorsed 'Democratic Enlargement' as the cornerstone of its foreign-policy doctrine.[126] Moreover, as Wiarda clearly demonstrates in his analysis, *democracy-promotion* in Latin America has been one of the most consistent foreign-policy choices of US administrations over time, Democratic and Republican alike.[127] But this pro-democracy foreign policy posture of the US towards Latin America notwithstanding, the US government remained remarkably silent during gross violations of democratic principles by its next-door neighbour. Neither during the scandalously fraudulent presidential elections in 1988, nor when President Salinas deployed thousands of the armed forces to suppress the Zapatista rebellion in Chiapas, did US administrations make any official statements condemning the Mexican government. Despite mounting criticisms of the Mexican government by civil-society organisations, NGOs and academics in the US, Washington did not openly comment on the situation in Mexico. Unlike the European reaction to the Kurds in Turkey, the US did not urge Mexico to grant cultural and linguistic rights to its indigenous peoples.[128]

The nature and terms of integration between the US and Mexico differ from the Turkish–EU case. The former has an advanced form of *economic* integration with little or no direct impact on the political regimes of the partners. Mexico did undertake important legislative reforms because of NAFTA. It harmonised some policies with its northern partners in certain areas, in relation to capital movements and the environment. Unlike the Turkish case, however, Mexico did not address issues of human rights as a condition for its relations with the US. Overall, the

---

125. 'Kürsüden AB Ödevleri' ['EU gives homework from the floor'], *Milliyet*, 10 November 2005.

126. D. Brinkley, 'Democratic enlargement: the Clinton doctrine', *Foreign Policy* 1997, 106, pp. 110–27.

127. H. J. Wiarda, 'US Policy and democracy in Latin America and the Caribbean', *Policy Papers on the Americas*, 1995, Volume VI, Study 7, CSIS Americas Program.

128. J. Preston and S. Dillon, *Opening Mexico: The making of a democracy*, New York: Farrar, Straus and Giroux, 2004.

changes in Mexico were far from altering the nature of Mexican state. The reforms were limited in scope and addressed explicitly economic issues.

Wiarda offers a plausible explanation for the relative prudence of the US, in terms of political engagement and democracy-promotion in Mexico. According to the author, the 2000-mile border with Mexico made the US rather wary of any kind of turmoil in this 'large, poor and populous southern neighbour'.[129] As such, political stability became the first and foremost objective of the US in its relations with Mexico. Having a single hegemonic party that ruled Mexico for decades was probably the best way to guarantee stability. This political apathy, however, did not impede close economic co-operation under the rubric of NAFTA, which engendered significant socio-economic changes in Mexico.

While the US preferred not to rock the PRI boat for the sake of political stability in Mexico, and made no overt efforts at democracy-promotion, the EU followed the reverse strategy in Turkey. Intense political engagement between Turkey and the EU had the explicit aim of shaking up the Turkish political *status quo* and improving the lot of pro-democracy sectors in Turkey. On the economic side, however, the amount of co-operation between Turkey and the EU fell far short of anticipated levels, hampering prospects for comprehensive industrialisation, technology-transfer and socio-economic development, as achieved in the case of Mexico. While the EU provided highly restricted incentives and failed to fulfil its commitments as a strong anchor, Turkey also wavered in showing concerted effort and solid political credibility during the accession process.[130] Mixed signals from certain European leaders that questioned the fundamentals of the accession process with Turkey, lack of strong and steady socio-economic connections and, most recently, the changing political priorities of the Turkish regime have further weakened the prospects of accession. Nevertheless, important political reforms were also achieved during the process. The next section will discuss the limited progress in the EU-sanctioned democratisation agenda in Turkey.

Democratic reforms in Turkey

Democratisation and political parties

In the early stages of the democratic reforms, Turkish citizens showed strong support for the EU. Public opinion polls hovered around 75 per cent in favour of EU membership. However, as the political reforms progressed, these numbers started to dwindle and dropped below 60 per cent in 2009.[131] In 2012, popular

---

129. H. J. Wiarda, 'Beyond the pale: the bureaucratic politics of United States in Mexico', *World Affairs* 2000 162(4), pp. 174–91.

130. M. Uğur and N. Canefe, 'Turkey and European integration: introduction', in M. Uğur and N. Canefe (eds), *Turkey and European Integration: Accession prospects and issues*, London: Routledge, 2004, pp. 1–16.

131. TEPAV Survey, presented by G. Sak, TEPAV: Ankara, 2009.

support for EU membership reached a historic low of 36 per cent.[132] There is still no sign of recovery from these numbers at the time of writing. According to most analysts, the main reason for this fading enthusiasm is the limited public knowledge about the overwhelmingly complex and technical nature of the EU-accession process. As a result, public opinion easily falls prey to manipulation by nationalists and euro-sceptic political elites.[133]

The direct involvement of high-ranking EU officials in the democratic-reform process in Turkey has further complicated the issue. Increasingly, the top-down attitude of the EU fuels a nationalist backlash in Turkish society. Reforms that addressed the Kurdish issue, minority rights or the role of military in politics awakened fears of the disintegration of the Republic along ethnic lines, also known as the 'Sèvres syndrome'.[134] Consequently, each handshake between a European bureaucrat and a Turkish Minister is portrayed as yet another concession to Europe and each visit by an EU official to south-east Turkey is interpreted as another plot to agitate the Kurds and weaken national solidarity.[135] More recently, a hubristic criticism of Europe has been added to the repertoire of Turkey's nationalist, euro-sceptical discourse. The 2008 economic crisis and the eurozone's subsequent struggle to pull itself out of a long recession feeds the rhetoric of 'Europe in decline'; and Turkish euro-sceptics ask why Turkey should try to join a club that itself is in such difficulties.

Ironically, the *banderistas* of democratisation and the EU-accession process in Turkey from 2002 on were the 'reformed Islamists' of the Justice and Development Party (*Adalet ve Kalkınma Partisi*, AKP), under the leadership of Prime Minister Erdoğan. Despite the relatively conservative nature of its constituents, the AKP has been vigorously pushing the reform agenda, thanks to the solid parliamentary majority it has enjoyed since the 2002 general elections. The largest opposition party in the Parliament, the 'centre-left' CHP, is squarely against almost every reform attempt. The leadership cadres of the CHP are composed largely of high-level bureaucrats and retired diplomats.[136] Many of their public speeches and publications portray the accession process as a zero-sum game between Turkey and the EU. From the CHP's perspective, complacent Turkish governments keep

---

132. Eurobarometer 2012, 78. pp. 47–8.

133. A. Carkoglu, 'Who wants full membership? Characteristics of Turkish support for EU membership', in A. Çarkoglu and B. Rubin (eds), *Turkey and the European Union: Domestic politics, economic integration and international dynamics*, London: Frank Cass, 2003, p. 187.

134. B. Oran, 'Minority concept and rights in Turkey: the Lausanne Peace Treaty and current issues', in Z. K. Arat (ed.), *Human Rights in Turkey*, Philadelphia: University of Pennsylvania Press, 2007, pp.35–56, p. 52 and F. M. Göçek, *The Transformation of Turkey: Redefining state and society from the Ottoman Empire to the modern era*, London: I. B. Tauris, 2011, pp. 109–10.

135. K. Kirisci and G. Winrow, *The Kurdish Question and Turkey*, London: Frank Cass Publishers, 1997, p. 121 and p. 187.

136. O. Öymen, *Ulusal Çıkar: Küresellesme Çağında Ulus-Devleti Korumak (National Interest: Protecting the nation-state in the age of globalization)*, Istanbul: Remzi Kitabevi, 2005.

giving 'concessions' to Europe in the name of reform, which, in fact, undermine Turkey's national interests, independence and unitary state structure.[137]

Political parties of various shades of right (ranging from the centre-right DYP to the nationalist right MHP) were also critical of the democratic reforms passed by the Parliament on the way to EU accession. These parties also embraced the 'concession' discourse. Their hardliner stance on the Kurdish issue and uncompromising attitude on the Turkish military presence in Northern Cyprus made them rather hostile to intense diplomatic negotiations with the EU. Moreover, the electoral base of these parties came from some of the most conservative regions in Turkey. In terms of their democratic attitudes, these voters were the most sceptical about 'democracy's ability to resolve pressing problems in Turkey'. According to public opinion polls, they were the most likely to approve the 'curtailing of basic rights and freedoms' in some circumstances.[138] Given such a voter profile, it is rather unlikely that right-wing leaders would advocate a pro-democracy and pro-European platform to appeal their core constituencies.

The interesting question, then, is the following: how could the AKP – certainly a right-wing party with solid Islamic credentials – be the leading voice for the pro-EU camp? Figure 5.7 attempts to display the 'family tree' of political parties in Turkey subsequent to the 1980 coup. Contrary to the stability and durability of the Mexican system, the Turkish party system of this period of just over three decades looks like an alphabet soup of parties. Both internal splintering and external political repression systematically cause premature party deaths. When analysing pro-EU and anti-EU coalitions in the Parliament, this political and ideological landscape is of critical importance.

Two of the most vocal advocates of democratisation and explicit supporters of EU membership were the Islamist-leaning Justice and Development Party (AKP) and the pro-Kurdish Democratic People's Party (DTP). As Figure 5.7 demonstrates, the Constitutional Court had banned the predecessors of both parties multiple times. Yet these movements managed to reincarnate themselves under different names after each such blow. Because of this, it would not be a mistake to consider both parties as 'outsiders'. The mainstream political establishment of Turkey had systematically excluded the overtly religious AKP and the pro-Kurdish BDP. These two parties would be the most immediate beneficiaries of a more liberal and democratic Turkey.

From 2000 on, the AKP tried to avoid the fate of its predecessors by embracing two mutually reinforcing strategies. On the one hand, it tried to change its radical image by remaking itself as the new standard-bearer of the centre-right in Turkey. With the rapidly evaporating electoral support for the two established parties of the centre-right (ANAP and DYP/DP), the AKP made a strategic move to fill the

---

137. I. Turan, 'Old soldiers never die: the Republican Peoples Party of Turkey', *South European Society and Politics* 2006, 11(3–4), pp. 559–78, p. 565.

138. Carkoglu, 2003, p. 183.

Figure 5.7: Political party landscape in Turkey after 1980 coup

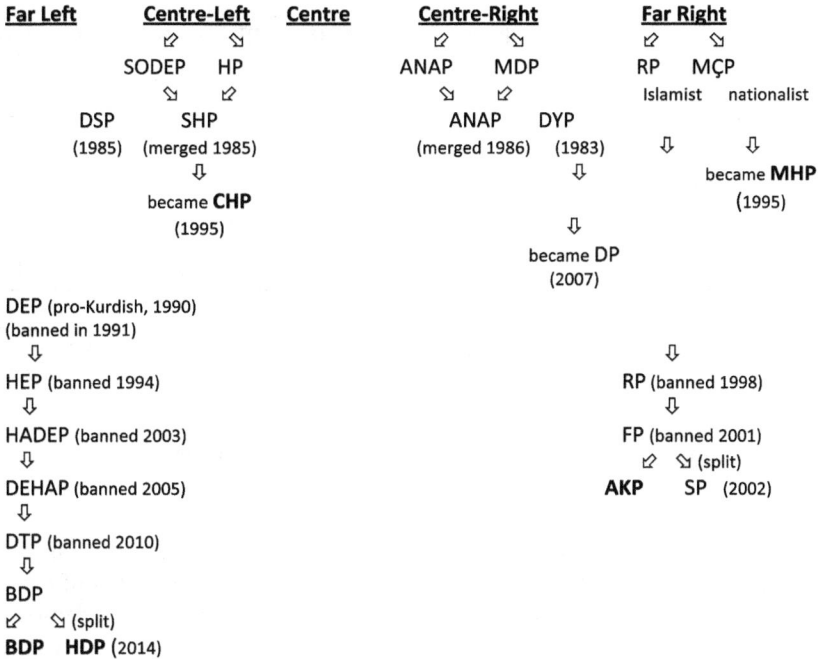

Far Left	Centre-Left	Centre	Centre-Right	Far Right
	↗ ↘		↗ ↘	↗ ↘
	SODEP HP		ANAP MDP	RP MÇP
	↘ ↗		↘ ↗	Islamist nationalist
DSP	SHP		ANAP DYP	
(1985)	(merged 1985)		(merged 1986) (1983)	⇩ ⇩
	⇩		⇩	became **MHP**
	became **CHP**			(1995)
	(1995)		⇩	
			became DP	
			(2007)	

DEP (pro-Kurdish, 1990)
(banned in 1991)
⇩   ⇩
HEP (banned 1994)   RP (banned 1998)
⇩   ⇩
HADEP (banned 2003)   FP (banned 2001)
⇩   ↗ ↘ (split)
DEHAP (banned 2005)   **AKP**   SP   (2002)
⇩
DTP (banned 2010)
⇩
BDP
↗   ↘ (split)
BDP   HDP (2014)

Notes:

- Dates in parenthesis without any explanation show the year the party was founded.
- Parties in bold are represented in Parliament in 2014.
- MDP and HP were the 'military stooges', created by the military to compete in the first post-coup elections. Of the three parties that competed in the 1983 elections, ANAP was the only non-military sponsored party.
- Politically insignificant (less than 1 per cent) and one-hit-wonder parties (like the populist Genç Party of Cem Uzan) are excluded from the diagram in order not to complicate the already busy ideological spectrum of the Turkish party system.

vacuum. Claiming to be the flagship party of the centre-right,[139] party leaders made more frequent references to past figures of the mainstream right, such as Adnan Menderes, rather than the more pious Necmettin Erbakan. When asked about his

139. T. Bora, 'AKP: The new Center-Right' and Yüksel Taşkın, 'Succession fights in center right as nationalist conservatism disintegrates', in Ü. Kurt (ed.), *Is AKP the New Centre-Right?*, Ankara, Dipnot Publications, 2009; E. Özbudun, 'From political Islam to conservative democracy: the case of the Justice and Development Party in Turkey', *South European Society and Politics* 2006, 11(3–4), pp. 543–57.

Table 5.3: Results of 2007, 2011 and 2015 general elections and distribution of seats in Turkish parliament

		DTP/BDP	HDP	DSP	CHP	DP	AKP	SP	MHP
2007	% votes	5.2	–	–	20.8	5.4	46.5	2.3	14.2
	# seats	21	–	8	97	1	338	–	69
2011	% votes	6.5	–	0.25	25.9	0.65	49.9	1.25	12.9
	# seats	2	27	–	130	–	313	–	52
2015	% votes	–	12.96	0.19	25.13	0.17	40.66	2.07	16.45
	# seats	–	80	–	132	–	258	–	80

Source: Government election institute, www.ysk.gov.tr for the percentage of votes; official website of the Turkish Parliament, www.tbmm.gov.tr for the number of seats.

background in the Islamist movement under Erbakan's leadership, Recep Tayyip Erdoğan bluntly stated that 'he had shed that shirt', meaning he was no longer affiliated with the old-style political Islam.

The AKP, on the other hand, tried to diminish the role of the military-bureaucratic establishment in Turkey, in order to avoid future threats of closure. Thus, it appealed to the democratic anchor of the EU. By undertaking democratic reforms and trying to secure the rule of law in the country, the AKP was trying to sideline the bureaucratic establishment that has been – from the AKP's and many other populist centre-right parties' point of view – stifling the 'will of the people'. When one considers the fact that the AKP had hitherto experienced three party closures and its leader, Recep Tayyip Erdoğan, had served jail time for reciting a poem with Islamic sentiments, their efforts to counterbalance the entrenched bureaucratic interests in the country with international pressure seems quite reasonable. Seen through the prism of a power clash between the elected and the appointed, the enthusiastic pro-EU stance of the AKP should not be puzzling for keen observers of the centre-periphery division in Turkish politics.[140]

Democratisation and the military-bureaucratic elites

Through out the 1990s and the first half of the 2000s, Turkey undertook significant legal reforms to improve its democratic and human-rights credentials. However, as leading human-rights scholar Richard Falk notes, the jury is still out on whether 'these reforms and governmental rhetoric in Turkey during the last decade has been effectively and irrevocably translated into consistent patterns of practice'.[141] Other

---

140. Ş. Mardin, 'Centre-periphery relations: a key to Turkish politics?', *Daedalus* 1973, 102(1), pp. 169–90.

141. R. Falk, 'Foreword', in Z. K. Arat (ed.), *Human Rights in Turkey*, Philadelphia: University of Pennsylvania Press, 2007, p. xvi.

scholars who trace the evolution of human rights in Turkey highlight the long list of legislative achievements of recent years. According to these, Turkey is party to most of the international human rights regimes. However, the same authors also warn about the gap between reforms signed on paper and actual practice. Arat, for instance, gives the example of the slogan chanted by the police during a Police Day parade, 'Damn Human Rights!'.[142]

Decades after the reforms, the Gezi protests of 2013 were a litmus-test of Turkey's democratic progress, which the government did not pass. Massive deployments of riot police, excessive use of tear gas and high-pressure water cannons, the deaths of nearly a dozen activists and the complete impunity of police paint a rather grim picture. Popular demands for more green space and environmentally friendly urban development triggered an extremely illiberal reaction from the state authorities. Even the established international press was not spared this fury. During the first anniversary of the Gezi movement, in 2014, Ivan Watson, CNN's resident reporter in Istanbul, was detained in the midst of a live broadcast from Taksim Square. Subsequently, the Prime Minister referred to him as a 'foreign agitator' and 'spy'. This and many other incidents would dampen the spirits of even the most hopeful about Turkey's human-rights progress. While Mexican authorities are largely indifferent to celebrations, demonstrations or protests at the Zocalo in Mexico City, Turkish authorities heavy-handedly deter May Day celebrations or any protest attempts in Taksim Square in Istanbul.

A democratic political culture does not emerge overnight: it takes a long time for laws and formal codes to be internalised by the bureaucracy and law-enforcement agencies. Testifying to the difficulty of internalising democratic reforms, surveys of Ministry of Justice personnel, including many public prosecutors, revealed some disturbing opinions. Both in surveys and interviews, more than half the public prosecutors interviewed stated that their foremost job is to 'serve the interests of the state' even at the expense of individual rights. Put differently, in disputes between the state and the individual, they expressed a clear preference for protecting the state.[143] This kind of a statist predisposition in the judiciary can hardly be compatible with a liberal-democratic political regime, as the primacy of individual rights is a central tenet of liberal-democracy itself.

As indicated in the list of reforms above, another sticking point in the Turkish democratisation process was reforming the military. By insisting upon democratic control of the armed forces, the EU was 'attacking the holiest of sacred cows' in

---

142. During the Police Day Parade in Istanbul during the 1990s, riot police in full gear used the following slogan '*Kahrolsun insan haklari!*' (Z. K. Arat, 'Conclusion: Turkey's prospects and broader implications', in Z. K. Arat (ed.), *Human Rights in Turkey*, Philadelphia: University of Pennsylvania Press, 2007, p. 277.

143. M. Sancar and E. Ümit, *Yargıda Algı ve Zihniyet Kalıpları*, (*Perception and Mentality Patterns in Judiciary*) Istanbul: TESEV, 2007, p. 9.

Turkey. Matthews and Kohen describe the enormous difficulty of this issue in following words:

> In Turkey, the military is more than just a national defence force – it's the backbone of the state. The military is, according to virtually every opinion poll, the single most trusted and respected institution in the country.[144]

The military in Turkey occupies two important and privileged positions in the political system, which, arguably, places the Turkish Armed Forces (TAF) above and beyond every other political institution in the nation. The importance of the role of Atatürk and his military cadres cannot be overestimated in the establishment of an independent, modern and secular Turkey. This historical fact fortifies the vanguard role of the military in terms of determining the direction and future of the nation. Secondly, the military enjoys the self-appointed role to protect its accomplishment, that is, the secular Turkish nation-state. Article 35 of the Military Internal Service Code openly states that it is the duty and responsibility of the military 'to protect and safeguard the Turkish motherland *and* the Turkish Republic as defined by the Constitution'.[145] Thus, democratic reforms at some level need to confront this historic sense of mission and guardianship.

As late as the mid 2000s, the TAF identified four major security threats against Turkey: 1) terrorism; 2) the spread of weapons of mass destruction and long-range missiles; 3) fundamentalist/reactionary activities; and 4) regional conflicts.[146] Among the four, two were predominantly domestic threats (Islamic fundamentalism and Kurdish separatism) but were still included in the TAF list, for they were seen as threats to the secular nature of the Republic. For the longest time, TAF had successfully included both issues under its jurisdiction, which resulted in significant military intrusion in domestic politics.

Ümit Cizre, a prominent name in Turkish civil–military relations, argues that the military managed to expand its influence in politics by monopolising and redefining the concept of 'national security'. 'Islamic activism and Kurdish nationalism were singled out as internal security threats and given primacy over the external ones.' By redefining the internal problems of the country – which are essentially political in nature – 'in the language of internal *security threats*', the military excluded civilian activists from being part of the debate.[147] Particularly

144. O. Matthews and S. Kohen, 'Strong-arm democracy', *Newsweek*, 4 November 2002.

145. E. Ozbudun, *Contemporary Turkish Politics: Challenges to democratic consolidation*, Boulder, CO and London: Lynne Reiner Publications, 2000, p. 110.

146. Defence Policy of Turkish Armed Forces. Online. Available http://www.tsk.tr/1_TSK_HAKKINDA/1_4_Savunma_Politikasi/savunma_politikasi.htm (last accessed 22 November 2009).

147. Ü. Cizre, 'Problems of democratic governance of civil-military relations in Turkey and the European Union enlargement zone,' *European Journal of Political Research* 2004, 43, pp. 107–25, p. 108.

in the case of the Kurdish problem, insisting on the 'military solution' –which itself is an oxymoron, according to Cizre – and addressing it through emergency military measures in the region, the military was 'responsible for the decline of democratic discourse and its replacement by repackaged conservative nationalist reactionism'.[148]

Tanel Demirel eloquently analyses this Turkish political deference to the military in critical issues. According to Demirel, despite numerous military coups in Turkey, in neither case did the military stay long enough to completely discredit itself as an institution. Unlike the Greek, Spanish or Chilean cases, the periods of direct military rule in Turkey 'have hardly been seen by a significant number of civilians as highly repressive, nor have they been conceived as failures in political, economic, or military terms'. This was probably the reason why both public opinion and the political parties perceived military solutions as a 'quick, clear-cut and less costly' way out of a crisis, rather than perceiving them as gross violations of the constitutional order and detrimental blows to the democratic progress of the nation.[149] While Demirel's analysis might explain several issues, it falls short of explaining the delegation of the Kurdish problem to the hands of the military. The fight against the separatist PKK has been going on since 1984, making the military option far from a quick, clear-cut or less costly one.

Theoretically, the ultimate goal of joining the EU should not conflict with the modernisation and westernisation ideals of the Turkish military. In a *Foreign Affairs* article – penned by one active and one retired member of the TAF – the authors argue that up to a certain point, the military accepted the reforms because they perceived EU membership as 'the final stage of a modernisation process they have supported for nearly a century'. Nonetheless, as the reforms intensified, the military started to have second thoughts about its unreserved support for Turkey's EU membership. In particular, the military disapproved of the concessions made to Greek Cypriots. Moreover, from the perspective of the military, the reforms on the Kurdish issue were beginning to get in the way of fighting secessionist terrorists. In short, the authors argued that the goal of EU membership and the goals of the military were starting to diverge and one *should not expect a happy ending* in the membership process when there is resistance from such a pivotal institution of the Turkish polity.[150]

The fact that important institutional changes in civil–military relations have taken place at the top levels under the auspices of the EU by no means guarantees the end of the Turkish state's heavy-handed treatment of certain sensitive issues. An

---

148. C. Ümit, 'The emergence of the government's perspective on the Kurdish Issue', *Insight Turkey* 2009, 11(4), p. 3.

149. T. Demirel,'Lessons of military regimes and democracy', *Armed Forces and Society* 2005, 31(2), pp. 245–71, p. 246.

150. E. Aydinli *et al.*, 'The Turkish military's march toward Europe', *Foreign Affairs* 2006, January/February (*author*).

important stumbling block on the path to normalisation of civil–military relations in Turkey is the reluctance of political parties to whole-heartedly embrace the reforms. Due to solid historical, political and social legacies, as well as immediate electoral concerns, political parties in Turkey avoid what they consider a head-on collision with the military.

However, things took an unexpected turn in 2009, tilting the civilian–military balance in favour of the civilians. Hundreds of active and retired military officers, including the top brass, were prosecuted in criminal courts for attempting to overthrow the government. In the *Ergenekon* and *Balyoz* ('Sledgehammer') cases, officers scattered throughout the branches of the military at various ranks were accused of engaging in a broad conspiracy (with alleged connections to organised criminal elements) aimed at destabilising the government and its allies in civil society. Those who support the criminal cases against the officers draw parallels with the alleged destabilisation efforts of the military prior to the 1980 coup. They argue that the republican rallies in 2007 (*Cumhuriyet mitingleri*) organised by Ataturkist civil-society organisations (*Atatürkçü Düşünce Derneği*, ADD) were concrete examples of how the Turkish military takes advantage of the staunchly Kemalist and modernist *civilian* sectors to put pressure on elected governments. During the rallies, frequent chants from the protestors included 'We are the soldiers of Mustafa Kemal' (*Mustafa Kemal'in Askerleriyiz*) and 'Military back to duty' (*Ordu Göreve*), which, in no uncertain terms, was a plea for direct military rule in Turkey.

Aside from instigating civil society to destabilise elected governments, military officers were also accused of drawing up coup plans during their annual war games. Among the accusations was of black ops bombings of mosques to create havoc in society and compel martial law. Needless to say, these prosecutions became highly divisive and politicised, both at the elite and mass levels. The supporters of the prosecutions cited the long track record of Turkish military intervention in politics, either directly or indirectly through strong-arming the judiciary or making intimidating Internet statements (*e-muhtıra*). For instance, during the infamous 367 decision, the military coached members of the Constitutional Court to decide that the Parliament needed a super-majority to be able to elect the president. Likewise, it published a rather ominous message on its web site (*e-muhtıra*) that emphasised the military's self-appointed role as the guardians of secularism, alarming the conservative government. On the other hand, the families of the officers and pro-military circles emphasised the mounting counter-evidence that significantly challenged the authenticity of the evidence used by the courts. Either way, the prosecution has been dragging for years like a soap opera, with unexpected twists and turns.

In the summer of 2013, some of the high-profile detainees were released, including the Baskent University Rector and transplant surgeon, Mehmet Haberal. A second wave of detainee-releases came when the Constitutional Court of Turkey ruled that five years is long enough time for the courts to reach a verdict. If the courts could not reach a conviction after five years, they could no longer keep people behind bars. However, probably the most interesting twist to the plot came after the 17 December 2013 corruption scandals in Turkey. From that day on, a series of video and voice recordings flooded the media and rocked the nation. The recordings accused top members of the cabinet and the prime minister's family of conducting illicit deals of dramatic proportions. A single watch allegedly presented to a cabinet member as a gift was worth over $300,000. The Prime Minister's instant reaction to these tapes was that they were a plot to overthrow his administration by the Gulenist movement. According to Erdoğan, this Islamic-influenced movement, with its leader in a self-imposed exile in Pennsylvania, has infiltrated the judiciary and security system in Turkey. Claiming that this was not the first time the movement had instigated a plot, the Prime Minister referred to the organisation as 'those who *framed* our military!' (*ordumuza kumpas kuranlar!*) Essentially, this statement severely undermined the integrity of the on-going judicial proceeding against the military. Because of the enormous controversy surrounding the case, it is too early to conclude if this could be a positive step on the way to normalisation of civil–military relations in Turkey.

Could a thousand flowers blossom? Democratic reforms and civil society in Turkey

In Turkey's EU-guided democratisation process, perhaps one of the most important sectors to look at is civil society. Did Turkey witness a boom in civil society and social movements, as Latin America, Mexico and many parts of the Global South did? How did civil-society actors respond to the on-going democratisation process in Turkey? Could Turkey tilt the power balance away from corporatist forms of interest-organisation in favour of more autonomous and democratic civil-society structures?

An important aspect of globalisation since the 1980s has been the dramatic increase in civil society organisations, particularly in the Global South. Both the pull and push factors for voluntary and autonomous civil organisations increased during this era. Large sectors of society that had long been deprived of an independent voice started to organise, articulate their demands and seek collective solutions to their common problems. In the case of Mexico, most of these grassroots organisations were issue-based, either addressing specific political problems, such as electoral fraud or indigenous rights, or socio-economic problems such as rural-sector reforms under NAFTA. They managed to organise across class and ethnic lines and became a strong counterweight against the centralist and corporatist elements of the Mexican state. Non-indigenous joined in the fight for indigenous rights; urban students joined rural *campesinos* to campaign for land rights and so on. In short, vibrant civil society at the grassroots level significantly helped to improve the nature of Mexican polity, moving it towards a more participatory, liberal and pluralistic model.[151]

Compared to recent developments in Mexico, the characteristics of civil society in Turkey show significant differences. While a detailed analysis of the

---

151. Otero, 2004; Preston and Dillon, 2004.

development of civil society in Turkey is beyond the scope of this book, it is important to summarise the central elements for the purpose of grasping the similarities and differences in the two contexts of democratisation. Leading authors on civil society concur that the strength of state and its nationalist and secular discourse significantly hinders the prospects for the development of a robust and autonomous civil society in Turkey. On the one hand, the relative strength of the state *vis-à-vis* society stifles incentives to organise autonomous and critical civilian initiatives. On the other hand, the existence of deep cultural divisions within Turkish society creates an environment of mutual suspicion, low interpersonal trust and low levels of tolerance towards differences. Again, this is hardly an atmosphere conducive to the burgeoning of pluralistic civil society.[152]

According to Keyman and İçduygu, religious and ethno-nationalist organisations use and abuse the concept of civil society in order to advance their essentialist and anti-democratic claims in Turkey. Because of the deep cultural divisions in the country, there emerges a collision of essentialist identity-claims in the so-called civilian arena. Under these circumstances, Islamist organisations confront ultra-secular civil-society organisations and Pan-Turkish nationalist youth organisations clash with Kurdish nationalist groups.[153] When minority rights are already threatened in a society, organisations that try to boost the dominant religious (Sunni) or ethnic (Turkish) identities can be detrimental for a pluralist democracy. In the end, organisations based on such ascriptive and exclusionary categories tend to corrode the democratisation process in the country rather than fostering an atmosphere of pluralism and mutual respect.

Despite these setbacks, civil initiatives in Turkey gained some impetus since the United Nations Conference on Housing and Urban Development (Habitat II) of 1996 in Istanbul. However, probably the most significant spike came after the earthquake of 17 August 1999, which caused significant damage in north-eastern Marmara, including parts of Istanbul. According to the official statistics, around 17,000 citizens died as a result of the earthquake. However, other estimates put the numbers at least twice this. There are several reasons for this major discrepancy: First, the earthquake happened in the hottest days of summer and hit the most densely populated parts of the country. The search and rescue efforts were too little and too late, so bodies under the rubble began to decompose rapidly. Once they located the bodies, many citizens decided to bury their loved ones, particularly babies and young children, and did not bother informing the authorities. Secondly, delayed response by the authorities and their negligence and incompetence once they arrived, gave survivors little incentive to inform the authorities. The smell

152. N. Gole, 'Authoritarian secularism and Islamist politics: the case of Turkey', and B. Toprak, 'Civil society in Turkey', both in A. R. Norton (ed.), *Civil Society in the Middle East*, Leiden: Brill Academic Publishers, 1996.

153. F. Keyman and A. Icduygu, 'Globalization, civil society and citizenship in Turkey: actors, boundaries and discourses', *Citizenship Studies* 2003, 7(2), pp. 219–34.

of dead bodies had already reached overwhelming levels on the second day of the earthquake.[154] Unless the deceased family member had property that required paperwork for inheritance purposes, people spared themselves the trouble of bureaucratic red tape at a time of grave tragedy.

Governors, police and all representatives of public authority were in disarray in the severely hit urban centres, such as Gölcük, Yalova and Sakarya. Record-keeping was either non-existent or sketchy at best. Relief efforts were late and disorganised and information-flow about the survivors (their names, which hospitals they were sent to and so on) was atrociously inaccurate. When the gross incapacity of the state authorities in responding to the plight of the survivors was broadcast on national media around the clock, it fuelled an amazing wave of voluntary activism. Civilian organisations were the first to come to the aid of survivors in places like Gölcük and Yalova. They received a steady supply of volunteers and relief packages, largely coming from Istanbul.[155]

From a distance, the 1999 earthquake and subsequent mushrooming of civil society and NGO activism in Turkey might resemble the Mexican experience after the devastating 1985 Mexico City earthquake. However, a closer analysis reveals some important differences. First, in the case of Mexico, civil-society organisations emerged from among the survivors themselves. Various apartment projects (particularly the publicly constructed ones, like the one in Tlatelolco) and neighbourhoods, both rich and poor, decided to organise to fill the vacuum created by the government's inaction or incapacity. Hence, it was a more *organic* form of social activism, directly emerging from the grassroots. However, in the case of Turkey, civilian organisations and NGOs from the developed metropolitan areas were largely 'transplanted' to the earthquake-hit areas. While urban legends of cool, bike-riding young men with pierced ears hopping on their bikes and selflessly coming to the aid of earthquake survivors exist, others who participated in the relief efforts raise an important point by asking whether voluntarism and civil initiatives would still be this strong, had Istanbul and not Gölcük been the major site of the earthquake.[156]

Similarly to Mexico, government authorities in Turkey were almost completely paralysed after the earthquake. As many volunteers and civil-society activists expressed, the earthquake *humbled* the state authorities and made them more accommodating towards civil society. However, in the case of Turkey, the performance of one state institution markedly differed from the rest. The military, despite suffering great loss in the quake at the Gölcük naval base, did a remarkable job in its rescue and aid operations. As a member of the 'Civilian Coordination' at the time, author and journalist Ümit Kıvanç admits that, strangely enough, they had the most smooth and co-operative relations not with the civilian bureaucracy

---

154. I was living in Istanbul during the 1999 earthquake and travelled to Yalova in search of a friend's parents on August 18th. Unfortunately, they could not have escaped. Excavation teams reached their bodies on the fourth day. The information here is largely based on my personal observations.

155. U. Kıvanç, 'State and the civilians after the earthquake: the tremble', in S. Yerasimos *et al.* (eds), *Civil Society and Nationalism in Turkey*, Istanbul: Iletisim, 2002, pp.599–607.

156. Kıvanç, 2002, p. 603.

but with the military. While the civilian authorities were paralysed by bureaucratic minutia and hierarchy, and were a lot less willing to collaborate with civilian initiatives, young military personnel were a lot more flexible in making quick decisions and getting the job done.[157]

Despite the positive momentum gained after the 1999 earthquake, civil society in Turkey is still faced with significant problems. Empirical studies on the profile of members and leaders of civil society organisations reveal their highly skewed socio-economic origins. One such study conducted by the sociology department at the Middle East Technical University[158] displays the following demographic characteristics: two-thirds of the members are male; more than half of them have at least university or post-graduate degrees; most of them have lived in urban, metropolitan centres for most of their lives; and most of them come from middle- and upper-income groups.[159] Clearly, these findings do not present an evenly dispersed civil-society network in Turkey that encompasses a diverse cross-section of the general society. Typically, civil-society activism seems to be an upper class and largely male endeavour in Turkey. This highly skewed nature of social activism in terms of its class and gender is also articulated as a problem by many organisers from within these movements. Numerous factors are listed as the reasons for this problem (for example, the impact of 1980 coup, legal restrictions on civic activism, young generations' apathy towards politics, sexism, endemic poverty and bread- and-butter concerns), all of which are valid and important.[160] However, from a comparative perspective, if we take a snapshot of both Turkey and Mexico, there is not a huge variation in terms of the levels of socio-economic development and sexism in both societies. Yet, civil society in Turkey is not as advanced as it is in Mexico. Civic activism and social movements emerge from all sectors of society in Mexico, including urban and rural residents, indigenous movements, environmentalists, students, white-collar professionals, women and gay-rights activists. Collectively, they claim a central role in deepening the democratic experience of Mexico. Unfortunately, this process is at a much earlier stage in the case of Turkey.

Pioneering authors of democratisation studies in Turkey focus on the state structure and underline the necessity of constitutional reforms,[161] the nature of elections and party politics,[162] requisite reforms in civil–military relations and,

---

157. Kıvanç, 2002, p. 606.

158. The study includes in-depth interviews with 139 NGO leaders of 79 organisations in 10 cities and 896 questionnaires conducted with activists in four cities. *Sivil Toplum Kuruluşları, Yerelleşme ve Yerel Tönetimler* (Civil Society Organisations, Localisation and Local Governments), Symposium Proceedings, 21–22 June, 2002, Economic and Social History Foundation of Turkey, Istanbul Technical University, p. 136.

159. Sivil Toplum Kuruluşları, Yerelleşme ve Yerel Tönetimler, 2002, pp. 136–40.

160. Sivil Toplum Kuruluşları, Yerelleşme ve Yerel Tönetimler, 2002.

161. Ozbudun, 2000; S. Yazici, *Turkey in the Process of Democratization*, Istanbul: Bilgi University Press, 2009.

162. E. Kalaycıoğlu and A. Çarkoğlu, *Turkish Democracy Today: Elections, protest and stability in an Islamic society*, London and New York: I. B. Tauris, 2007.

most recently, political culture and the values of the citizens[163] as obstacles on the way to democratic deepening. In terms of the predominant concerns, current research on Turkey's democratic consolidation distinguishes itself from that of Mexico. In the Mexican case, there is a burgeoning literature on the role of societal forces, new social movements and collective citizen action as the driving forces of consolidation. These movements place bottom-up pressures on the political system in their active pursuit of democratic deepening. However, in the Turkish case, democratic consolidation is still top-heavy, focusing mostly on reforming the state and the main political institutions. Grassroots activism is still in the embryonic stages and does not involve a large cross-section of Turkish society, as illustrated by the Middle East Technical University survey results.

Canonical studies on democracy and civil society highlight the importance of *interpersonal trust* and *tolerance* as crucial values for a democratic polity. In general, high levels of interpersonal trust and tolerance for diversity are strongly associated with strong democracy and healthy associational life.[164] For a more quantitative comparison of Mexico and Turkey on interpersonal trust and tolerance, we can look at the findings of the World Values Survey, which brings together prominent researchers from more than 70 countries and supplies social scientists with critical information that spans decades and is comparable across many countries.[165]

The questions on tolerance for diversity (Table 5.4) do not portray a broad-minded society in the Turkish case. Nearly one-third of Turkish respondents seem to be disturbed by having someone of a different race as their neighbour and this percentage seems to have declined only slightly (from 33 per cent to 28 per cent) over a period of one and a half decades. However, in Mexico, there seems to be a more or less steady decline in the same number, down to 8 per cent in 2005, which indicates gradually improving racial tolerance among Mexican citizens. Similarly, Turkish respondents show much higher levels of intolerance towards immigrant or foreign worker neighbours (29 per cent), which is rather unfortunate since the number of immigrant labourers from the Caucasus, Africa, Central Asia, Ukraine, Moldova and most recently from Syria seems to be ever increasing. Intolerance against an immigrant workforce, however, has decreased in a steady fashion in Mexico. Here, the extensive experience of Mexican citizens as immigrant labourers in the US might also have played some role in the softening of attitudes towards foreign workers within Mexico. Lastly, there is the issue of homophobia. Clearly, the numbers here reveal a harsher and more intolerant attitude in Turkey than in Mexico (87 per cent and 29 per cent respectively).

---

163. Y. Esmer, *Revolution, Evolution and Status Quo: Social, political and economic values in Turkey*, Istanbul: TESEV, 1999.

164. R. Putnam, *Making Democracy Work*, Princeton, NJ: Princeton University Press, 1993.

165. R. Inglehart, *Human Values and Social Change: Findings from the values survey*, Leiden and Boston: Brill Academic Publishers, 2003.

Table 5.4: Tolerance for diversity

	Country	1990	1996	2000–1	2005
% that would have problem with neighbour of different race	Mexico	16	26	14	8
	Turkey	33	30	28	28
% that would have problem with immigrant/foreign worker as neighbour	Mexico	17	26	13	9
	Turkey	28	34	36	29
% that would have problem with homosexual neighbour	Mexico	60	36	42	29
	Turkey	91	86	88	87

Source: World Values Survey, 1990–2005. Online. Available http://www.worldvaluessurvey.org (last accessed 10 April 2015).

Robert Putnam's classic work *Bowling Alone*[166] establishes a compelling link between high levels of interpersonal trust and high levels of civic activism in democratic societies. When we look at the World Values Survey findings on levels of interpersonal trust in Turkey and Mexico, they reveal comparatively higher rates of interpersonal trust in Mexico than Turkey. On average, more than half of the Mexicans think that their fellow citizens would *not* try to take advantage of them. Whereas in Turkey, less than half of the respondents declare confidence in their fellow citizens (Table 5.5). Certainly, higher levels of mistrust in society makes it harder for citizens to pool their resources and seek collective solutions to their shared problems. Finally, the last question in Table 5.5 reveals another interesting aspect of both societies. In terms of having freedom of choice and control over one's life, Turkish respondents seem to exhibit somewhat more passive and fatalistic attitudes than their Mexican counterparts. Such fatalistic attitudes are, hardly conducive to collective can-do spirits, or vibrant civic activism.

The results of the World Values Survey display higher levels of interpersonal trust, tolerance, and personal sense of control and efficacy in the Mexican case. These findings seem to complement the conclusions of the qualitative analysis above, regarding the obstacles and relative underdevelopment of grassroots activism and civil-society organisations in the Turkish case. In fact, the levels of social intolerance in Turkey are increasingly being viewed as alarming by social scientists. In 2007, Şerif Mardin coined the expression 'neighbourhood pressure' (*mahalle baskısı*) to describe the increase in communitarian forces that compelled individuals to conformity. This small statement quickly became a media sensation, with columnists, pundits and talking heads filling in the concept as they wished.[167]

---

166. R. Putnam, *Bowling Alone: The collapse and revival of American community*, New York: Simon & Schuster, 2001.

167. For a collection of the interviews with Mardin when he first coined the term, and subsequent debates in the media and academic circles, *see* R. Çakır, *Mahalle Baskısı* (*Neighbourhood Pressure*), İstanbul: Doğan Publications, 2008.

Table 5.5: Interpersonal trust and sense of personal empowerment

Survey questions	Country	1990	1996	2000–1	2005
Q: Do you think most people can be trusted? % of respondents who say most can be trusted	Mexico	33	31	21	15
	Turkey	9	5	15	4
Q: Do you think most people would try to take advantage of you? (1 to 10 scale, 1 = would take advantage; 10 = most would be fair)	Mexico	n/a	n/a	*	6.3
	Turkey	n/a	n/a	*	4.6
Results are country averages					
Q: How much freedom of choice and control you feel you have over the way your life turns out? (1 = no control; 10 = a great deal of control) Results are country averages	Mexico	7.2	7.4	8.2	8.3
	Turkey	n/a	4.8	5.4	7.4

Notes: *The same question was asked but a different scale was used in 2000–1 survey (1 = most people would take advantage; 0 = most would try to be fair). Percentage of those who agreed that most people would try to take advantage was 69% in Mexico and 80% in Turkey.

Secular commentators employed it to describe the 'Islamist neighbourhood pressure', for which they gave the examples of pressures on women in small towns to cover up, stricter limitations on alcohol consumption and similar restrictions on modern/secular lifestyles; conservatives also deployed Mardin's term to describe their suffering at the hands of the secular establishment, most notably citing the headscarf ban in universities.[168]

Before Mardin's term 'neighbourhood pressure' exploded in public debate, studies mostly focused on the plight of the more religious and conservative sectors in such a staunchly secular state.[169] However, after political Islam increased its electoral appeal and began to take part in coalition governments, and particularly since the AKP's landslide victories in the 2002 and 2007 elections, this sense of victimisation seems to have diminished. In a national survey on religiosity in Turkey conducted in 1999, 42 per cent of the respondents stated that religious

---

168. For a comprehensive analysis of the recent debacle on the issue, which started with constitutional amendments to lift the headscarf ban on campuses and led to a paralyzing case in front of the Constitutional Court for the closure of the AKP, *see* E. C. Wiltse, 'The Gordian Knot of Turkish politics: regulating headscarf use in public', *South European Society and Politics* 2008, 13(2), pp.195–215.

169. N. Göle, 1997, 'Secularism and Islamism in Turkey: the making of elites and counter-elites', *Middle East Journal* 1997, 51(1), pp. 46–58.

citizens were repressed in Turkey. However in the 2006 round of the same survey, the numbers dropped to 17 per cent for the same question.[170]

While it certainly is welcome news that citizens who espouse strong religious identities are feeling less persecuted in modern-day Turkey, a reverse sense of persecution seems to be growing recently. Toprak and her team tried to capture this new phenomenon and flesh out Mardin's controversial concept when they initiated their research project titled 'Being Different In Turkey.' This qualitative study yielded rather disturbing findings about the degree of social hostility towards expressed signs of difference and non-compliance, particularly in the smaller cities and towns of Anatolia. Testimonies of university students, Kurds, Alevis (a heterodox sect of Islam), teachers, nurses, officers, and many other individuals reveal an intolerant social atmosphere in most cities of Turkey. Some of the students admit that they have to send in their 'normal' friends as dummies (ones who speak without a Kurdish accent, do not have tattoos or, for males, long hair) to negotiate with landlords, otherwise they could never find rentals. Public employees and professionals who are appointed to these cities mention strong pressure from the locals to join in religious rituals (such as Friday prayers or fasting during Ramadan) and report experiences of retribution if they do not comply. Women teachers and nurses report very close monitoring of their outfits (short skirts and sleeves are not welcome) and their consumption habits (buying alcohol causes immediate stigmatisation).[171]

The signs of this social intolerance towards different identities, ethnicities and lifestyles also find their expression in organised forms. There is a growing visibility of organised, illiberal civilian activism in Turkey, which has manifested itself in a number of high-profile incidents. In 2005, an important international conference on Ottoman Armenians at Bogazici University was postponed by court order. It was the first time in the country that an academic conference was suspended by court intervention. Globally appreciated Turkish author Orhan Pamuk (awarded the Nobel prize in 2006) and numerous writers, journalists (among them Perihan Mağden and Elif Şafak, whose books have been translated into more than ten languages) were taken to court for 'insulting Turkishness' under the controversial Article 301 of the Turkish penal code. All of these cases were initiated by a group of nationalist lawyers who belonged to a 'civic' organisation called The Jurists' Union.[172] In a perverse fashion, increasing organised citizen activism in Turkey seems to be bullying universities and hauling intellectuals and writers into courthouses. Probably the most tragic victim of the Article 301 and this public bullying was the Turkish-Armenian journalist Hrant Dink.

---

170. A. Çarkoğlu and B. Toprak, *Religion, Society and Politics in Changing Turkey*, Istanbul: TESEV, 2000, p. 69; A. Çarkoğlu and B. Toprak, *Religion, Society and Politics in Turkey*, TESEV, 2006, p. 30.

171. B. Toprak *et al.*, *Being Different In Turkey*, Istanbul: Metis, 2009.

172. M. Belge, 'Trials of free speech', essay published in *Open Democracy* 2006, 2 February. Online. Available http://www.opendemocracy.net/democracy-turkey/belge_3241.jsp.

While his highly publicised trial was in process, Dink was assassinated on 19 December 2007. A young gunman from Trabzon killed him in front of his office in Şişli, İstanbul, in broad daylight. Unfortunately, Dink's assassination has been handled with gross negligence by the judiciary, causing further grief to his family and loved ones. Since the assassination, each year thousands gather in front of the newspaper for which Dink worked (*Agos*) and chant 'We are All Hrant Dink, We are All Armenians!' (*Hepimiz Hrant Dink'iz, Hepimiz Ermeniyiz!*) to commemorate him.

Despite all these difficulties, genuinely democratic, issue-oriented and grassroots-based civil-society organisations have emerged in Turkey over the last decade. Business organisations lobbying for EU membership, environmental organisations resisting the construction of dams and power plants, women's movements and urban activists confronting forced gentrification projects are all chiselling progressively deeper marks on the civil-society landscape of Turkey. Among these, women's organisations particularly stand out for their remarkable achievements. Organisations like KAMER and Mor Çatı have been successful in raising awareness on domestic violence and honour killings. They have reached thousands of women across the country and initiated strong civilian incentives to empower women in the least fortunate circumstances. Feminist civil society organizations successfully pushed for legal reforms to criminalise domestic violence and have provided shelters for abused women and children.[173] All of these certainly contributed to the emergence of a more assertive and pluralistic civil-society sector in the case of Turkey.

Post-reform state–society relations in Turkey: Persistence of corporatism and clientelism

The radical shift in the dominant economic paradigm in the 1980s generated an avalanche of socio-political changes in the world. The election of staunch free-market advocates like Ronald Reagan and Margaret Thatcher in the US and the UK respectively, was accompanied with the hegemonic ascendance of neo-liberal Washington Consensus policies in the Global South. In most cases, this transition to free-market-dominant capitalism dislodged existing corporatist forms of state–society relations. As the state gradually lost its economic clout, it could no longer cater to its costly corporatist network. The Mexican case discussed in the first half of this chapter was a prime example of this trend. After the 1980s, corporatist

---

173. There is a sizeable literature on the women's organisations in Turkey. For a selected overview, *see* A. G. Altınay and Y. Arat, *Violence Against Women in Turkey: A nationwide survey*, Istanbul: Punto, 2009; Y. Arat, 2008. 'Contestation and Collaboration: Women's struggles for empowerment in Turkey', in R. Kasaba (ed.), *The Cambridge History of Turkey, Vol IV: Turkey in the Modern World*, Cambridge: Cambridge University Press, pp. 388–418; A. Bora and A. Günal (eds), *Feminism in Turkey in the 1990s*, Istanbul: Iletisim, 2002.

Figure 5.8: Co-existence and hierarchy of multiple forms of state–society relations in Turkey

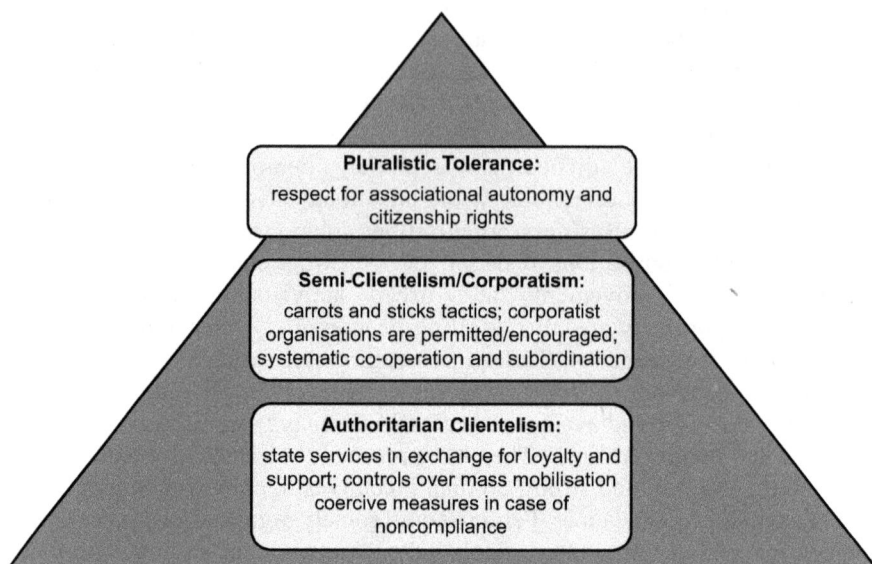

Pluralistic Tolerance:
respect for associational autonomy and citizenship rights

Semi-Clientelism/Corporatism:
carrots and sticks tactics; corporatist organisations are permitted/encouraged; systematic co-operation and subordination

Authoritarian Clientelism:
state services in exchange for loyalty and support; controls over mass mobilisation coercive measures in case of noncompliance

structures in Mexico gradually receded, giving way to more competitive and pluralist forms of interest-representation in state–society relations.

The Turkish case, however, sets itself slightly apart from these trends on state–society relations on various accounts. Instead of a steady decline of corporatist forms of representation in favour of more liberal and democratic ones, Turkey displays a perplexing co-existence of multiple forms. Jonathan Fox describes the Mexican experience as an evolution of the predominant model of state–society relations. Progressively, the country is moving from authoritarian clientelism to semi-clientelism and then to a pluralistic society one based on citizenship rights. Unfortunately, this trend can only be partially observed in Turkey. Instead of the horizontal flowchart of the Mexican case, with comparatively equal brackets in each stage, (*see* Figure 5.4), a pyramid would be more apt to capture state–society dynamics in the Turkish case (Figure 5.8). The pyramid is also symbolic in terms of the relative weight of each stage. Civil society organisations with significant autonomy from the state are still a rare phenomenon in Turkey, whereas carrot-and-stick tactics and systematic co-optation of semi-corporatist organisations still remain common.

In order to see the resilience of both authoritarian clientelistic relations and corporatist structures in the neo-liberal era, the healthcare sector in Turkey provides ample evidence for researchers. According to the leading analysts, social-policy structures in Turkey have a dualistic character. On the one hand, there is 'a well-developed *corporatist social protection system* excluding large segments of the population', according to Buğra.[174] This corporatist social-security system includes the formal sector, particularly public employees in Turkey. On the other hand are the *informal social-security networks* – most often the family – which assist individuals at times they are vulnerable. In sum, the characteristics of this dual social-policy regime are as follows: 1) paid work is not completely based on formal contracts: employment in the *informal sector* and *peasant agriculture*, not bound by any formal contract, remain significant; 2) *family* is an important risk-absorber; 3) *clientelism* is an important mechanism of social inclusion, along with the formal mechanisms. When possible, even the state tends to avoid legally spelling out its rights and duties.[175]

This dual structure (corporatist/formal versus clientelistic/informal) is not a peculiarity of Turkey, for it exists in many other regions that lack well established, mature welfare states. In Latin America and, up until their integration with the EU, in many Southern European states, all three of the above mentioned characteristics (informality, role of family, clientelism) exist to various degrees.[176]

With greater emphasis on the private sector, decentralisation and the diffusion of the state, the conventional understanding of social policy was also modified in the neo-liberal era. The World Bank in its *1997 World Development Report* promoted the role of civil society and philanthropic associations in sharing the responsibilities of social-protection and -inclusion. Buğra and Adar state that the current rise of Islamic charities addressing many forms of poverty-alleviation fully comply with the new international regime of mixed welfare systems, wherein the state no longer assumes the sole responsibility of redistributive action.[177]

Other scholars also link the emergence of strong Islamic movements, which provide not only authenticity and group identity but also tangible benefits to their members, to the dismantling of welfare regimes under the pressures of global capitalism. This perspective articulates a critical political-economic analysis in assessing the causes and conditions of the recent resurgence of political Islam. Consequently, the rise of political Islam is no longer conceptualised as an anomaly to classic modernisation theories, which predicted religion would have become obsolete a long time ago.[178] On the contrary, political Islam is largely a 'modern' phenomenon, directly linked to the precariousness of social safety nets under neo-liberal globalisation.

---

174. A. Buğra and S. Adar, 'Social policy change in countries without mature welfare states? The case of Turkey', *New Perspectives on Turkey* 2008, 38, pp. 85–106, p. 85.

175. Buğra and Adar, 2008.

176. M. Ferrera, 'The 'southern model of welfare in social Europe', *Journal of European Social Policy* 1996, 6(1); A. Barrientos, 'Latin America: towards a liberal-informal welfare regime', in I. Gaugh and G. Wood (eds), *Insecurity and Welfare Regimes in Asia, Africa and Latin America*, Cambridge: Cambridge University Press, 2004.

177. Buğra and Adar, 2008, p. 102.

178. H. Gülalp, 'Globalisation and political Islam: the social basis of Turkey's Welfare Party', *International Journal of Middle East Studies* 2001, 33, pp. 433–48.

Economic policies during the neo-liberal era increased the role of market forces in the healthcare sector. In a paradoxical fashion, while the US – arguably the most advanced capitalist country – is trying to reform its market-based healthcare system by increasing the public's share (the Affordable Healthcare Act), the World Bank and the IMF have been advising the opposite strategy for developing countries. Structural adjustment programmes imposed by these institutions diminish the public role in healthcare provision, and cause detrimental outcomes in countries struggling with serious epidemics like AIDS.[179] This perspective disregards healthcare as a public good and a basic citizenship right. Rather, it views the healthcare sector just like any other economic activity on the market, where the 'clients' purchase the services they want based on the heftiness of their pocket books.

Current and previous administrations in Turkey have done their fair share to undermine the public's role in the health sector as well. By gradually shifting to a premium-based system, underfunding the public hospitals, decreasing the number of healthcare staff and encouraging private investment in this sector, they are certainly in the process of radically changing the nature of the healthcare regime in Turkey.[180] The paradox of the Turkish case is that, while centre-right governments are implementing these market reforms in the name of efficiency, they are simultaneously creating populist networks in healthcare to rake in political support and loyalty. Eder provides an astute discussion of how this seemingly paradoxical development takes place. She argues that neo-liberalism can lead to populism instead of market efficiency, particularly in the hands of right-wing parties.[181] The *Yeşil Kart* (Green Card) practice in Turkey, designed to provide health coverage for the poor, is a fine example of this type of neo-liberal populism.

Turkey has a fractured health insurance regime. Public employees and their dependents are covered under *Emekli Sandığı* (Retirement Pension Fund). Workers are covered by *Sosyal Güvenlik Kurumu* (SGK –Social Security Institution) and the self-employed are organised under *Bağ-Kur*. In general, *Emekli Sandığı* is the most generous and comprehensive of all three retirement and healthcare programmes. As the market reforms intensified, however, there was a growing pool of poor and uninsured who could not be protected by any of these three programmes. In 1992, the Green Card policy was initiated in order to provide health coverage for uninsured, low-income (defined as earning less than one-third of the minimum wage) citizens. The centre-right candidate, Tansu Çiller, was the leading figure behind the Green Card initiative and she was pictured during the 1991 election campaign joyfully waving Green Cards with the promise of free

---

179. P. Lurie *et al.* 'Socioeconomic obstacles to HIV prevention and treatment in developing countries: the roles of the International Monetary Fund and the World Bank', *AIDS* 1995, 9(6), pp. 539–46.

180. For a detailed analysis of the healthcare forms in Turkey from a comparative perspective, *see* Keyder, Çağlar *et al.* (eds) *Health Policies in Turkey and Europe*, Istanbul: Iletisim, 2007.

181. M. Eder, 'Populism as a barrier to integration with the EU: rethinking the Copenhagen criteria', in M. Uğur and N. Canefe (eds), *Turkey's Europe: An internal perspective on EU-Turkey relations*, London: Routledge, 2004, pp. 49–74.

access to healthcare. Even though her performance was mediocre in implementing this new healthcare regime for the poor, subsequent governments found greater opportunities to realise her goal.

As the economy recovered from the 2001 crisis, it gave ample opportunity to the AKP government to boost the dormant Green Card policy. Instead of expanding health coverage on the basis of equal citizenship rights and universalistic principles, the leaders of the AKP preferred the means-tested Green Card model. This way, the party could establish direct patron–client links with voters. Those lucky enough to be Green Card holders would certainly not bite the hand that delivered then free healthcare, hence, would show their loyalty to the AKP at the ballot-box.

As of 2009, nearly ten million citizens (one of every seven in the population) are active Green Card holders.[182] However, the geographic distribution of the beneficiaries illustrates a highly skewed pattern, as shown in in Tables 5.6 and 5.7. The cities with the highest percentage of Green Card holders are located in the east and south-east, whereas cities with the least number of recipients are located in the western and coastal regions. Nearly half of the population in the east and south-east is poor enough to qualify for these benefits whereas in the west the number drops to single digits. This enormous geographic discrepancy is telling on so many levels. Yet, it is also informative in terms of reflecting the strength of clientelism in Turkey.

In Table 5.6, we can see phenomenal levels of electoral support for the ruling AKP (71.5 per cent in Bingöl), which is much higher than the party's national average of 46 per cent. However, in the provinces with fewer Green Card holders (Izmir and Muğla), the opposition seem to have achieved more limited electoral success (*see* Table 5.7). This political strategy – using healthcare as a 'carrot' to attract votes – resembles the *semi-clientelistic* pattern in Jonathan Fox's categorisation (Figure 5.4). However, one should note that, at times, it could just as easily slide into *authoritarian clientelism*. After some teenagers threw stones at the security forces in Adana during a demonstration, the governor of Adana promptly threatened to annul the Green Cards of the families whose children took part in the protest.[183]

The healthcare sector has been going through significant changes in recent years. While the AKP is implementing radical reforms which, they claim, will expand the choices of the publicly insured by providing them access to private hospitals and university hospitals, progressively increasing co-payments (from 10 per cent to 30 per cent and recently to 70 per cent of the treatment cost) make

---

182. The official number is 9,709,006 according to the Ministry of Health. However, the actual number is much larger, closer to 15 million. Green Card holders need to prove their eligibility each year, which is referred as 'renewing the visa'. This is a process to verify their income status. Those who have not renewed their visas are inactive cardholders. In practice, many cardholders tend to avoid going through a bureaucratic hassle each year. When they absolutely need to receive medical care, they activate their cards by renewing their visas. Thus, aside from the nearly 10 million active Green Card holders, there are some 5 million dormant ones, making it one of the largest healthcare plans in the country.

183. *Milliyet*, 22 December 2008.

Table 5.6: Provinces with highest % of Green Card holders in 2009

Rank	City	Green Card holders %	2007 AKP votes %
1	Ağrı	58	63.3
2	Van	55	53.3
3	Bitlis	53	58.7
4	Bingöl	51	71.5
5	Şırnak	48	27.9
6	Hakkari	48	33
7	Muş	46	38.5
8	Batman	46	46.2
9	Siirt	46	48.7
10	Adıyaman	42	65.1
	National average		46.4 %

Table 5.7: Provinces with lowest % of Green Card holders in 2009

Rank	City	Green Card holders %	2007 AKP votes %
1	İstanbul	2.7	45.8
2	Ankara	3.6	47.5
3	Kocaeli	3.7	49.2
4	Bursa	3.8	50
5	Bolu	4.3	54.8
6	Muğla*	4.4	26.3*
7	İzmir *	4.8	30.5*
8	Eskişehir	5.1	44.4
9	Zonguldak	5.1	41
10	Karabük	5.2	54.6
	National average		46.4 %

Notes: * The main opposition party, CHP, won in Izmir and Muğla. In all the others, AKP won.
Sources for both tables: Per cent of card holders calculated by the author with the help of Ministry of Health data. Online. Available http://www.ykart.saglik.gov.tr/ykbs/ykbs_ilaktif.jsp. and Turkish Statistics Institute data on population of provinces based on the 2008 Census, http://www.tuikapp.tuik.gov.tr/adnksdagitapp/adnks.zul (last accessed 11 November 2009).

it nearly impossible for most to enjoy this new 'choice'. On the other hand, public hospitals are systematically undermined, diminishing the appeal of public healthcare services for citizens. When we look at social reaction to these troubling trends, unfortunately, those who will be the worst affected by them show almost no outward signs of discontent. Despite the sizable increase in co-payments and marketisation of health services, the gap between the ruling party and the opposition remain wider than ever. Here, the authoritarian clientelism strategy seems to have paid off in silencing millions of poor and vulnerable citizens. The fear of losing the bare minimum coverage they have is a serious concern for these sectors: hence, they tend to avoid serious confrontations with the state.

Interestingly, the most vocal resistance to the current healthcare reforms come from the corporatist organisations that represent pharmacists and doctors. In December 2008, the pharmacists' association of Turkey (*Türk Eczacılar Birliği*, TEB) managed to gather more than 20,000 of its members from across the country at a massive public rally in Ankara to protest against the reforms. This event was extremely telling in terms of the relative significance of corporatist organisations in Turkey, as well as their legitimacy in the eyes of state actors and the public. A critical question is, why was it the pharmacists' association that organised the largest public protest on healthcare reform and not another civil-society group representing the more vulnerable groups of poorer citizens?

First, the TEB was able to draw such large crowds because all the pharmacists in the country are compelled to be members. The quintessentially corporatist nature of state–business relations in Turkey grants a monopoly of representation to similar organisations of doctors (TTB), veterinarians (TVHB), engineers and architects (TMMOB) and merchants and business-owners (TOBB). Thus, TEB enjoys a vast network of members in all 81 provinces of the country that it can mobilise easily from its headquarters in Ankara. Second, being a state-sanctioned institution grants significant legitimacy to these organisations. This makes a huge difference, should they decide to publicly express their dissent. While the security forces can be extremely rough when handling workers, students and other civilian demonstrators, they seem to be a lot more reserved and respectful when it is the professional associations taking their cause to the streets. During the December 2008 pharmacists' rally in Ankara, police officers were using the formal 'you' in Turkish (*siz*), when they addressed the demonstrators at checkpoints. Their manners were polite, no pushing or shoving people, no clubs pulled, which was remarkably different from the way they handled, for instance, demonstrating students.

The pattern of state–society relations in the healthcare sector is not atypical of the general patterns in the country. At the bottom of the pyramid, authoritarian clientelistic practices are dominant. These establish vertical links between individuals and the state, without leaving much room for the emergence of horizontal connections between citizens. At the second tier, there is some level of social organisation among the citizens but this too is sanctioned, regulated and closely monitored by the state. These corporatist organisations are more assertive than the clients at the bottom of the pyramid. Yet this by no means implies a sense of autonomy from the state. In fact, in the 2007 elections, the then-President of TEB was awarded a seat in the Parliament from the AKP ranks, after signing a contract with the state that had a devastating impact on pharmacists.[184] While the parliament is full of MPs who were presidents of unions or federations, desperate working conditions in unionised mines, shipyards and construction sites continue to claim the lives of the workers by the dozens. The Soma mine blast in May 2014, which left 301 miners dead, is a sufficient indicator of the highly compromised and co-opted nature of interest-representation in Turkey.

Finally, at the top of the pyramid, there are the autonomous civil-society organisations. These are voluntary organisations whose establishment is not directly sanctioned by the state. They are also able to secure independent revenue sources through donations and grants, hence are less dependent on the state for funding purposes. Most of the women's, human-rights, environmentalist, pro-education and urban-neighbourhood organisations fall into this category. Probably the most influential ones are the voluntary business associations, such as TUSIAD, MUSIAD and TUSKON. The economic clout of their members make these business associations slightly more privileged compared to the rest of the civil-society organisations. TUSIAD members, for example, include Turkey's top industrialists. Collectively, TUSIAD members account for approximately 50 per cent of all private-sector employment, 65 per cent of industrial production and 80 per cent of Turkey's foreign trade. Moreover, they provide 85 per cent of the private-sector tax revenues.[185]

Given the importance of civil-society organisations as the building blocks of a pluralist and democratic polity, their relative weakness in terms of scale and scope in the Turkish case should be a serious cause for worry. Since its landslide referendum victory on 12 September 2010 that brought about major changes to the judiciary branch and removed the immunity of perpetrators of the 1980 coup, the government and the security forces under its control seem to have handled civil-society activism extremely heavy-handedly. When the Gezi protests erupted in May 2013, to defend the only remaining green space in downtown Istanbul, authorities responded by burning the tents of the protestors, the deployment of riot squads and massive amounts of tear gas and water cannons.[186] Over the course of the summer, dozens of citizens were either killed or blinded by direct police fire. Criminal charges against peaceful protestors were pressed for such trivial reasons as wearing a red scarf or carrying swimming goggles or dust masks. Medical professionals, hotel-owners and even imams who tried to alleviate the pain of desperately wounded people seeking refuge were later reprimanded by

---

184. The state is the largest purchaser of drugs in Turkey because of the extensive public coverage in healthcare. On behalf of all the pharmacists, TEB has the right to sign the contracts with the state that determine the terms of the commercial transactions between the state and the pharmacies.

185. http://www.tusiad.org, TUSIAD by Numbers (as of May 2014).

186. T. Arango and S. Yeginsu, 'Turkey moves to silence dissenters, but with one eye on its image abroad', *New York Times*, 14 November 2013.

the government. Doctors who tried to improvise help for the wounded were handcuffed and taken into custody. The owners of the luxury hotel, Divan Otel in Taksim, the Koc Family, which has multiple family members both in the top-ten richest and highest tax-payers list in Turkey faced a swift tax audit after their much-publicised hospitality to desperate gassed and soaked protestors. The imam of the Dolmabahce Mosque, which was used as a makeshift infirmary to treat the wounded, lost his post and was relocated multiple times within a month. The following excerpts from reports of international Medical Associations and Human Rights organisations describe police reaction during the protests:

> Turkish riot squads fired enormous amounts of tear gas, often at close range in confined spaces, and used other types of disproportionate force in their tactics to crush the antigovernment protests […]

> Our investigation in Turkey confirmed that the government has been engaged in the excessive and unnecessary use of force – including using tear gas as a weapon of mass scale – which has claimed several lives and led to thousands of injuries […]

> [E]vidence compiled by the Turkish Medical Association […] documented more than 8,000 injuries attributed to tear gas, rubber bullets, water cannons, beatings and live ammunition. Four people died in the mayhem, and 11 victims who were struck by tear-gas canisters lost eyes.[187]

Unfortunately, the Gezi events were only a single episode in Turkey's long drama of democratic regress. The failure to establish institutional solutions to pressing political problems has gradually set Turkey apart from the Mexican case. The lack of an agreement on basic rights and liberties as described in a new constitution; the persistence of corporatist forms of representation; extremely tight restrictions of freedoms of expression and organisation; the overly centralised state power, which impedes democratic participation at local levels; and the lack of institutional autonomy and transparency at key levels of government all continue to undermine Turkey's democratic progress.

Compared to Turkey's performance, recent developments gradually set the Mexican case apart from Turkey. Unlike their Turkish counterparts, Mexican politicians seem to have reached consensual and institutional solutions to some of their most taxing problems. After years of tainted elections, they have established the IFE (which recently changed its name to INE) to make elections at all levels more just, fair and transparent. They have revitalised the federal system by increasing the fiscal and political autonomy of the states. These and other measures have expanded the cultural and linguistic rights of indigenous citizens. Even for the most controversial reforms, such as the energy and telecom, governments

---

187. R. Gladstone, 'Rights groups accuse Turkish police of excessive force against protesters', *New York Times*, 12 July 2013.

have tried to bring the opposition to the negotiating table to establish lasting, collective solutions. Despite being a presidential system and having a legacy of larger-than-life presidents in the past, Mexican politics today is much less dominated by individual personalities. The executive branch needs the blessings of multiple institutions in order to pursue its policy agenda. There are effectively functioning checks and balances and term limits are strictly enforced at all levels of government. All of these features, which largely emerged in the last decade, significantly differentiate the democratic progress of Mexico from that of Turkey.

Despite moving up to the 'Free' category in the Freedom House rankings in 2000, Mexico eventually faced a whole other set of problems that began to threaten its democratic gains. Unlike Turkey, probably the most significant challenge to Mexican democracy today stems not from domestic political conflicts or polarisation. Rather, it is the devastating impact of the 'war on drugs'. The global drug trade that seems to have latched on to Mexico as a convenient port of entry to the massive US market.[188] Incredibly high profit margins, insatiable demand from the US market and the 2000-mile long US-Mexican border place tremendous stress on the shoulders of Mexican authorities and law enforcement.

The global war on drugs is not solely a Mexican problem; nor can it be resolved solely by Mexican efforts. Therefore, calling Mexico a 'failed state' or simply focusing on the most notorious acts of narco-traffickers and condemning Mexico would miss the complete picture. It is important to note that the US and the Organisation of American States (OAS) are carefully trying to address this hemispheric predicament. Drug-prevention, rehabilitation and legalisation programmes are gradually taking hold in the US. Moreover, bilateral and multilateral attempts at collaboration against drug-trafficking are also important steps in the right direction.

Conclusion

This chapter focused on the post-1980 democratic progress in Mexico and Turkey. After a brief theoretical section, it highlighted the reasons behind Turkey's 'Partly Free' categorisation by the Freedom House Survey, as opposed to the 'Free' status, which Mexico enjoyed for almost a decade after the 2000 presidential elections. The first conceptual tool used to analyse both cases was corporatism. Compared to Mexico, corporatist structures of interest-representation seemed to be more resilient in Turkey. They continue to enjoy significant power and legitimacy, despite radically changing socio-economic structures as a result of neo-liberal reforms. While autonomous civil society is still at an infant stage in Turkey, corporatist structures, such as the chambers of commerce (TOBB), professional associations of doctors (TTB), pharmacists (TEB) and engineers (TMMOB) assert themselves as significant social actors, despite their quasi-public status as state-sanctioned

---

188. D. A. Shirk, *The Drug War in Mexico: Confronting a shared threat*, Council on Foreign Relations: Centre for Preventive Action, Council Special Report No 60, 2011.

organisations. The strength of corporatism as well as its legitimacy in the eyes of the public diverts significant potential from independent civil society organisations. Voluntary civil society organisations have a difficult time asserting their autonomy and even the most powerful business associations remain vulnerable to the whims of the state. This, in turn, undermines the consolidation of a pluralistic democratic regime in the country.

Secondly, there seems to be a growing gap of institutionalisation between Turkey and Mexico in terms of democratic consolidation. Pressing problems in the Turkish case are still not resolved through institutional means. Despite on-going efforts by the parliament and by civil-society organisations, the country could not shed the straitjacket of the military-inscribed 1982 Constitution. All of the tutelary institutions it created, as well as its authoritarian spirit, remain intact. Even the blatantly unjust and undemocratic 10 per cent national electoral threshold has prevailed, despite decades-long bloodshed in the predominantly Kurdish regions. After much hype about the EU-sanctioned reforms in civil–military relations, there is miniscule progress in terms of making the military more transparent and accountable to civilian authorities. On the principle of checks and balances, Mexico displays a better performance as well, by curbing the powers of the executive and strengthening the autonomous institutions. In the Turkish case, however, instead of strengthening the institutional autonomy of the judiciary branch, what we observe is increase in the powers of the executive over the judiciary. High turnover rates amongst judges and public prosecutors, slow and ineffective legal proceedings and the politicisation of Constitutional Court decisions all end up eroding the rule of law in Turkey.

The third important factor affecting the democratic gap between Turkey and Mexico has to do with the patterns of their respective international connections. In the Mexican case, relations with the US resembled the *contagion* and *consent* categories in Schmitter and Whitehead's classification of international influences on democratisation. This meant diffusion of democratic norms and practices via the close interaction of both societies at various levels (economic, social, cultural). In the end, relatively higher levels of democratic consolidation in Mexico today testify to the efficacy of the contagion model. The case of Turkey–EU relations, however, has closer similarities to Schmitter and Whitehead's *coercion* and *conditionality* categories. Turkey's democratisation process is formally negotiated with the EU under the highly regulated accession process. However, despite the ever-lengthening list of conditions, which would have seemingly compelled Turkey to improve its democratic performance, this coercively patterned relationship has yet to deliver the desired outcome of full EU membership with a fully consolidated and ever-deepening liberal democracy.

Chapter Six

Conclusion

> We might be tempted to go to the small and familiar. But the only way to make
> sense of the reality is to put it in a larger context. (Immanuel Wallerstein)[1]

'Making the world safe for democracy' has been a central concern in international
politics since President Woodrow Wilson coined the phrase in the aftermath of
World War I. Even though democracy-promotion abroad was placed on the back
burner during the Cold War years, it resurfaced with stronger momentum when
the Soviet bloc so unexpectedly fell apart. Many countries in Central and Eastern
Europe and in Latin America moved away from authoritarianism and began their
transit towards democracy. The EU and the US became key international actors
in assisting democratisation globally. Since 2011, hopes of a fourth democratic
wave in the Middle East went up after the authoritarian regimes in Egypt, Tunisia
and Libya fell successively, almost as if there had been a chain reaction. Except
for Tunisia, however, subsequent episodes of internal strife, sectarian violence,
military coups and civil wars in the region have made it clear that the so-called
Arab Spring is still a long way from rendering a genuine democratic transition.

Once the third-wave democracies completed the transition phase, they
encountered a new set of good-housekeeping measures necessary to move
their democratic systems beyond mere electoralism. The process of deepening
or consolidating this new generation of democracies was not an easy task. As
the Freedom House data demonstrates, there is still ample room for democratic
progress in the world. The 2014 *Freedom in the World Report* states that less than
half of the global population (40 per cent) lives in free and democratic societies.
The rest live in *Partly Free* and *Not Free* regimes, according to the Freedom
House classification.

The critical question this book tried to tackle is related to a group of countries
that occupy a half-way position between full-fledged democracy and closed,
authoritarian regimes. These *Partly Free* societies, which amount to 59 countries
and account for 25 per cent of the world's population, pose an interesting
challenge to social scientists. These are not blatantly authoritarian regimes, yet
their democratic politics suffer from significant flaws. This book tried to tackle
the following questions: what are the conditions for democratic consolidation?
How do societies with some degree of democratic opening widen their horizons

---

1. Speech by Immanuel Wallerstein delivered at a special conference on World-Systems School and
    Faruk Tabak, March 7, 2008, Bilgi University, Istanbul.

and create free and open regimes based upon citizen consent? Which types of institutional structures and state–society relations foster democratic consolidation? What factors help this process; which developments hinder it? Which forms of international engagement enhance the prospects of democratic consolidation at home and which ones undermine it?

This book focused on two pivotal countries in its analysis of the dynamics of democratic consolidation from a comparative historical perspective: Mexico and Turkey. The main purpose of the book was to illustrate *how* and *why* these two countries – very much on a par with each other on many accounts until the 1980s (corporatist, semi-democratic, clientelistic polities with state-centric economies) – gradually began to part ways by the end of the 1990s. Most strikingly, after the momentous presidential race in 2000, Mexico's status improved significantly in democratic rankings. Despite some temporary setbacks in Mexico due to international drug-trafficking problems, overall, the major institutional parameters of democracy seem to have improved significantly. To the contrary, Turkey's democratic progress seems to have stalled, with serious concerns that the country is, in fact, backsliding.

After decades of political and economic reforms, democratic progress in Mexico has surpassed that of Turkey. For most scholars of democratisation, Mexico's relative success *vis-à-vis* Turkey should have been *less likely*, given the fact that the former was saddled with the seven-decade-long authoritarian legacy of a single party, the PRI. However, Mexico seems to have beaten its structural odds, while Turkey has underperformed despite its long experience with competitive multi-party elections *and* despite its close engagement with the EU – a quintessentially democratic union. This book attempted to grasp the mechanisms behind the apparent performance gap in the democratic deepening of Mexico and Turkey. It tried to do so by looking at both domestic (state–society relations) and international (Mexico–US and Turkey–EU relations) dynamics.

Mexico and Turkey are usually treated as exceptions in regional studies on Latin America and the Middle East respectively. Furthermore, they are rarely placed next to each other as comparable cases, given the territorial rigidity of conventional area studies. Yet, a closer analysis of the historical legacies, political cultures and basic patterns of state–society relations of both countries reveal a vast number of similarities, some of which are vividly captured by eminent authors such as Fernand Braudel and Octavio Paz. While Braudel approaches the issues from a political-economic perspective and closely connects the economic destinies of these seemingly distant Empires, Paz articulates the socio-cultural links by highlighting the strength of Iberian, Mediterranean and Muslim elements in the Mexican political culture and psyche. Due to its emphasis on structural variables, this book is probably closer to Braudel in style.

After laying out the main premises of the book in the first chapter, the second chapter highlighted the importance of strong imperial legacies in both the Mexican and Turkish contexts. Despite having potent revolutionary traditions that tried to break from their respective pasts, neither of these countries managed an absolute disconnect. Religious, cultural and political legacies of these dominant imperial legacies lingered on. While most countries in the Global South wrestle with the problems of establishing functioning states and effective bureaucracies, Mexico and Turkey shared high degrees of *stateness*, strong central administrations and deep-rooted structures of state–society relations, thanks to the formidable legacies of the Spanish and Ottoman Empires. The predominant patterns of bureaucratic and administrative systems, as well as the economic policies and land-tenure regimes of both the Spanish and Ottoman Empires were discussed in detail in Chapter Two.

This discussion of the two imperial legacies underlines some of the more outstanding administrative and economic characteristics of both the Spanish and Ottoman Empires. Strikingly enough, a distinct class of state elites (*letradores* and *Devşirmes*), who came from humble origins and were fiercely loyal to the Crown or Sultan – at least during the golden ages of these empires – can be observed in both cases. Braudel praises the effectiveness of the central administration and the tax-collecting capabilities of both empires in an age when the rest of Europe lacked such levels of political unity. In both the Spanish and Ottoman Empires, political authority was organised in a top-down, hierarchical manner and there was little room for administrative autonomy, self-rule and town-council-type participatory practices. While these hierarchical structures proved to be handy during the age of empires, facilitating the flow and concentration of political power in the centre, they came to be important roadblocks when Mexico and Turkey tried to modernise their political regimes.

Another critical issue raised in the chapter on imperial legacies is the intimate connection between political office and economic fortune. The particular kind of land-tenure system in Spanish and Ottoman Empires (*encomienda* and *timar*, respectively) articulated distinct forms of capital-accumulation that set the Spanish and Ottoman cases apart from feudal Europe. Conquest and military success by the elites were rewarded with huge land-grants in both Empires. While the Crown or Sultan remained as the ultimate title-holder, the grantees had the right to use these huge estates, which included the labour of the native residents as well. In a sense, this land-tenure regime concentrated the political and economic power in the same hands, while limiting the opportunities for any autonomous economic sector to emerge. The prevalence of mercantilism, corporate group privileges and the late awakening to the fruits of free trade eventually hampered the economic progress of both empires. Undoubtedly, the economic structures and political culture inherited from this medieval imperial past had lasting impacts on the institutions and political cultures of modern-day Mexico and Turkey.

Chapters Three and Four discussed the modernisation efforts of Turkey and Mexico during the twentieth century. The new century started with a radical break from the past as Mexico became embroiled in a decade-long popular revolution in 1910. Turkey also fought a devastating War of Independence and, in 1923, managed to create a new Republic from the ashes of the deceased Ottoman Empire. The national goals Mexico and Turkey sought were largely similar: establishing *modern*, *secular* and *republican* regimes. The new constitutions highlighted these goals by establishing representative forms of government, curbing the powers of religious authorities and expanding those of the secular state. Among their modernisation efforts, both nations initiated massive public-education campaigns in order to generate an enlightened citizenry. The fact that both Mexico and Turkey faced religiously inspired counter-revolutionary uprisings during the 1920s (the *Cristeros* and *Şeyh Said* rebellions, respectively) is a curious reminder of the strength of secularism as well as the resistance to it in both contexts.

The role of the state in the economy was revised significantly in the modern republican era as well. Having experienced rather exploitative periods of liberal economic policy, particularly in the second half of the nineteenth century, both countries undertook massive nationalisation programmes during the 1920s and 1930s. They reclaimed rights over national infrastructure, utilities, railroads and subsoil riches. With foreign capital expelled and a national bourgeoisie only at an infant stage, the state became the locomotive of economic growth. This developmentalist role of the state in Mexico and Turkey fitted in nicely with the post-depression international climate and subsequent ascendance of the import-substitution industrialisation (ISI) strategy in the developing world. Both countries endorsed this state-led development model. The ISI strategy nicely complemented the corporatist forms of state–society relations that the new republics had created under their single-party regimes in the first half of the twentieth century.

Corporatism proves to be a significantly superior analytical category in terms of explaining state–society relations in the early modern periods of Mexico and Turkey. While the concept carries some notoriety due to its popularity in 1930s Europe, corporatism in Mexico and Turkey does not have much in common with these models. Rather, it emerges as a sociological and historical artefact and an organic outcome of the political cultures in these nations. Neither too liberal and individualistic, nor too repressive and communistic, corporatism represented the 'happy medium', in Parla and Davison's words,[2] for Turkish elites who wanted to keep all social sectors neatly organised under the watchful eye of the state. Likewise, in Mexico, the predominance of Augustinian political tradition, scepticism towards liberalism and autonomous interest-group activism and the post-revolutionary Mexican state's desire to collect all the relevant sectors of the society under a single great umbrella (thanks to the ingenuity of President Calles in 'institutionalising' the revolution in the form of a single party) created the perfect environment for a corporatist regime that lasted seven decades.

The last substantive chapter (Chapter Five) picks up the story of democratisation in Turkey and Mexico from the 1980s and analyses the last three decades, which saw profound changes in the economic and political realms in both countries. The 1980s started with major economic overhauls in Mexico and Turkey as they tried to switch from an inward-oriented development model (ISI) to an export-oriented, neo-liberal one. This new economic model, which was largely implemented by groups of young technocratic elites, carried significant implications in terms of

---

2.   T. Parla and A. Davison, *Corporatist Ideology in Kemalist Turkey: Progress or order?*, New York: Syracuse University Press, 2004.

a new distribution of socio-political and economic power in these societies. In both nations, the state gradually receded and gave way to the private sector as the engine of economic growth. Undoubtedly, the social and economic role of the state diminished due to extensive cuts in public spending and privatisation. In both countries, the neo-liberalisation process was further accelerated by free-trade agreements with advanced neighbouring economies. Mexico joined the North American Free Trade Agreement (NAFTA) in 1994 and, likewise, Turkey signed and put into effect a customs-union agreement with the EU in the same year.

Despite the 'rising tide lifts all boats' premise of neo-liberalism, the new economic model generated distinct sets of winners and losers. It placed significant strain on the old corporatist coalition, which finally crumbled and gave way to a relatively competitive and pluralistic regime in the case of Mexico. From the mid 1980s on, both the pro-business PAN, which represented the winners' camp in the neo-liberal era, and the leftist PRD, which was critical of the neo-liberal project, had become formidable competitors of the corporatist PRI at the ballot box. Intense exposure to neo-liberal market mechanisms and subsequently sharpening class cleavages engendered a neatly compartmentalised party spectrum in Mexico. PAN consolidated the votes on the centre-right, the PRD claimed the centre-left and the traditional, centrist position remained in the hands of the PRI.

A comparative analysis of Turkish and Mexican politics since the 1980s thus reveals a divergence between the two cases. While integration with the US economy under NAFTA triggered a large-scale socio-economic transformation in Mexico, Turkey's lacklustre customs union with the EU and its prolonged period as a potential membership candidate fell short of catalysing a similar socio-economic transformation. The flow of direct foreign investment from the EU to Turkey was modest, help from the structural funds was almost non-existent and economic, social and cultural interaction between the Union and Turkey was, at best, limited. While Mexican immigrants to the US (both formal and informal) amount to nearly 12 million and create a formidable constituency that drives both nations ever closer, nearly 4 million Turkish citizens working in the EU are more like a liability, jeopardising Turkey's accession. When economic co-operation is limited and socio-cultural interaction is even hostile, it becomes next to impossible to speak of a natural, consensual flow of democratic norms between the EU and Turkey.

A second important handicap for Turkish democratisation lies in the structure of its party system. Unlike Mexico's party system, in which party cleavages are largely delineated along the bread-and butter-issues, highly divisive questions of identity dominate the political agenda in Turkey. In a society as diverse as Turkey's, identity-oriented politics chops up the political parties into ever-smaller and mutually antagonistic units. It has created a complicated political-party spectrum, wherein parties oppose each other not over substantive policy agendas but in terms of their essentialist identity claims (seculars *versus* Islamists, moderate Islamists *versus* radical Islamists, secular centrists *versus* conservative centrists, Turkish nationalists *versus* Kurdish nationalists and so on). Needless to say, all these divisions and the mutual distrust they engender make it harder to reach a consensus over the necessary democratic reforms.

The pattern of US–Mexican relations reveals a stark contrast with Turkish–EU relations as well. The customs union agreement in 1994 notwithstanding, Turkish–EU relations had an explicit political goal of Turkey's eventual entry into the Union as a mature democracy. Thus, the EU developed significant political engagement with Turkey and had been carefully coaching and monitoring the democratic-reform process in its candidate country for decades. In fact, Turkey faced frequent repercussions, particularly after the coups and military interventions, because of the conditionality measures regulating its affairs with the EU. As a result, the predominant characteristics of Turkish–EU relations tended to be extensive political engagement based upon conditionality at the top level, with limited economic and socio-cultural integration at the societal level.

In stark contrast with the EU–Turkish model, the US government displayed no explicit signs of taking on a democratising mission in its large and populous neighbour. However, there has been extensive economic integration between the two countries and inevitably, this intimate economic interaction has spilled over into the socio-cultural and political realms as millions work and invest on both sides of the Rio Grande. Subsequently, it has acted as a catalyst for the transformation of the Mexican polity. Among the more important consequences of this transformation is the weakening of corporatist and clientelist forms of interest-articulation and the growing resilience of autonomous civil-society organisations and social movements in Mexico. Today, Mexico boasts a vibrant civil society that includes world-class human-rights organisations, women's organisations, indigenous movements, environmentalists, independent thinktanks and student movements. The state has to reckon with them, especially when important reforms are on the negotiation table.

Democratic-consolidation in Mexico was an important achievement on the political front. Yet it was also heavily influenced by the rapid secular changes in the socio-economic realm that took place as a result of intense economic engagement with the US. On the one hand, it weakened the corporatist establishment's ability to co-opt large sectors of the society, by diminishing the economic clout of the state. On the other, it sharpened class divisions, due to severe cuts in social spending, stimulating those on the losing end of the bargain to raise their voices and reclaim their rights in a democratic polity. If PAN was the voice of the winners of the neo-liberal reforms, the PRD certainly represented the disempowered. Finally, in 2000, Mexico joined the premier league of democratic nations after successfully replacing its acquiescent masses with participatory citizens, and establishing a vibrant civil society and a genuinely competitive electoral regime.

The recent democratic gap between the Turkish and Mexican cases can be informative, especially regarding the efficacy of different forms of international engagement. Particularly in large countries with significant socio-cultural and political heritage, conditionality and coercion may not always yield the desired outcome. A narrow focus on the political realm and top-down imposition of democratic reforms may even generate a nationalist or reactionary backlash. However in the long run, a consensual diffusion of democratic norms and practices *via* close societal interaction may have a greater chance of consolidating semi-democratic regimes.

Table 6.1: Summary of findings on Turkish and Mexican cases

	State versus markets	State–society relations	Relations with superpower neighbours	Consolidation of democratic institutions
Mexico	Role of state decreased significantly; extensive integration with global economy; increasing transparency.	Weakened corporatism; vibrant, more autonomous civil society; collective expressions of dissent considered legitimate.	Intimate/strong socio-economic and cultural ties; limited political interaction; 'contagion' of democratic norms across the border.	Little dispute on fundamentals of democratic institutional framework; strong checks over executive; no pending signs of democratic relapse.
Turkey	State still a formidable power in economy; public sector remains dominant; patronage, clientelism rampant.	Corporatism maintained alongside fledgling civil society; collective expressions of dissent harshly repressed.	Limited socio-economic and cultural ties; intense political engagement; 'conditional' endorsement of democratic norms.	No consensus over the Constitution, party laws, basic rights and liberties; no effective checks and balances; serious warning signs of democratic regress.

Current challenges to democratic consolidation in Turkey and Mexico

While this book concludes on a relatively positive note regarding the Mexican case, the situation in the country is far from being rosy. In the last few years, Mexico had the misfortune to confront a devastating 'war on drugs'. Narco-trafficking and related human-security problems pose significant challenges to the less-than-perfect law-enforcement system in the country. Due to high levels of corruption and ineptitude in the police, the military is increasingly drawn into the fight against narco-traffickers. Even if we discard sensationalist stories in the popular media, there remain significant risks. Summary executions on both sides and widespread impunity might undermine the integrity of the justice system, due process and rule of law in the long run. Sadly enough, the conclusion of this book coincided with the disappearance of 43 students near Iguala, Guerrero, which revealed the chilling ties between the police, local administrators and the drug cartels.[3]

However, as most analysts of the matter concur, both the reasons of the drug problem, as well as its solutions lie mostly outside the borders of Mexico. Domestic drug-use in Mexico is much lower than in its more affluent northern neighbours. The drug problem in Mexico is largely driven by seemingly insatiable

3. R. Archibold, '43 missing students, a mass grave and a suspect: Mexico's police' *New York Times*, 6 October 2014.

international demand. However, the tide is turning on that front as well. Many states in the US are shifting their policies away from harshly punitive measures. A growing number of states are endorsing policies to legalise milder substances, while addressing the health dimensions of substance abuse problem as well.[4] Hopefully, these realistic policy changes will eliminate the incredible price mark-ups in the drug business and make its trade less lucrative and deadly. Most studies show that between 40 and 70 per cent of marijuana in the US is imported from Mexico. Studies by Mexican thinktanks argue that legalisation in the US can significantly curb the profits of narco-traffickers and organised crime in Mexico.[5] Certainly, Mexico would be among the first to benefit from such pragmatic shifts in drug policies across North America.

The Turkish picture painted here of the prospects for Turkish democratic consolidation may seem rather gloomy but there remains significant potential for improvement. The country has managed to confront two of its taboo subjects, the role of the military and the Kurdish issue, head-on in the last few years. As discussed in detail in Chapter Five, probably the biggest problem for Turkey is its inability to find institutional solutions to these chronic problems. Political debates seem to get bogged down either on personalities or in essentialist identity claims. Unlike the consensus-forging negotiations and pacts in the Mexican legislature, futile debates and shouting matches in the Turkish Parliament hamper the possibility of genuinely democratic political reforms. In fact, in February 2015, during the discussions of a new security bill, a mass fight broke out and five parliamentarians (all of them from the opposition ranks) were severely injured. The gavel from the speaker's desk was used to slash open the head of an MP.

In the absence of democratic patterns and institutions of reconciliation, the old corporatist and semi-authoritarian frameworks continue their reign. When this book was going into press, the Turkish public was getting ready for another round of elections in June 2015, in an extremely polarised atmosphere. The issues of religious education and compulsory religion classes, the equal status of women in society, Kurdish resistance across the border in Kobane, the barbaric attacks of the Islamic State of Iraq and al-Sham (ISIS), the costs of the new presidential palace (which has more than 1000 rooms) and the pros and cons of a transition to presidentialism were all among the hotly debated topics. As such, the Turkish political landscape was bogged down with issues of religion, gender, ethnic conflict, regime-type and the personality of its President.

---

4. For a state-by-state breakdown of marijuana policies (i.e. reduced penalties, legalisation of medicinal use or legalisation of recreational use) as of November 2014, *see* J. Harkinson, 'Map: the United States of legal weed', *Mother Jones*, 5 November 2014. Online. Available http://www. motherjones.com/politics/2014/11/map-united-states-legal-marijuana-2014–2016 (last accessed 10 January 2015).

5. Mexican Institute for Competitiveness, *Posible impacto de la legalización de la marihuana en Estados Unidos* [*Possible impact of legalization of marijuana in United States*], 31 October 2012. Online. Available http://www.imco.org.mx/seguridad/posible_impacto_de_la_legalizacion_de_ la_marihuana_en_estados_unidos// (last accessed 10 January 2015).

Nonetheless, one should not underestimate the dynamism of Turkish politics. Turbulent politics in the Middle East compels Turkey to finally settle its pending democratic deficits, particularly regarding its very own Kurdish citizens. Even if the EU might have underperformed in terms of shepherding Turkish democratic progress, the Arab Spring and the subsequent political uncertainty in its southern borders might give Turkey an urgent democratic jolt. In the twenty-first century, an absolute ban on Kurdish as a language of education and a high electoral threshold (10 per cent) aimed at keeping Kurdish parties out of Parliament are unacceptable. Given its sophistication in terms of socio-economic development and decades-long experience with elections, moving to the premier league of democracies remains within the reach of Turkish polity.

The findings of this book attest, first, to the effectiveness of more horizontal and consensual links between established democracies and the countries that are in the process of organising their democracy for further consolidation. Consequently, neutral and unintended flows of democratic experience turn out to be better catalysts for democratic consolidation than explicit democracy-promotion through positive or negative sanctions. Secondly, the research conducted throughout this book addresses an important gap in the democratic-consolidation literature: Most studies on consolidation are either quantitative works with large sample sizes (large-N studies), or they are in-depth qualitative analyses of single cases. Though both approaches have definite advantages, the former tends to provide aggregate information at the expense of detail on individual countries while the latter tends to offer too-intricate explanations, which make it harder to observe general trends.

The method of intensively comparing two cases, as applied throughout this book, allows sufficient degree of substance as well as generalisation. Moreover, the two cases function as benchmarks for each other, making it easier to gauge the degree of democratic progress and consolidation in either one. Thirdly, the selection of the cases in this study, namely Turkey and Mexico, poses a challenge to the classic boundaries of area studies. Addressing these two countries together highlights the necessity and viability of seeking comparative cases across conventional regional borders. Further comparative research that attains a global perspective rather than a tight regional focus might reveal important clues for democracy scholarship. It might help translate the findings from one region to another. Moreover, cases that seem like exceptions or regional outliers may not necessarily be so when placed in a larger context.

The ever-increasing levels of global security threats since 9/11 and the subsequent chain of bombings in Istanbul, Bali, Madrid, London and Boston, also illustrate the profound scale and scope of global interconnectedness. Dysfunctional countries no longer seem to be solely the problem of unfortunate citizens who happen to live there. Nor do these countries abide by the Westphalian rules of international politics, by keeping their domestic predicaments within their territorial boundaries. Authoritarian regimes in Egypt, Syria or Venezuela are no longer the concern only of their own citizens. Recent atrocities in Syria and Iraq, the flight of millions of refugees from region, as well as the brutal executions of minorities and journalists that have been broadcast in real time are all testimonies to progressively diminishing barriers in global politics. As a result of global turmoil and elevated security concerns in the international system, there is a resurgence of the democratising mission *à la* Wilson in the west. Problematic regimes in the Global South appear on the radar of advanced democracies more intensely than ever. Before dashing into these troubled regions and trying to induce elections and democracy as a panacea, it might be prudent to look at prior experiences. In this regard, the Turkish and Mexican cases can offer significant insights on different modalities of international engagement and, as such, can be illustrative of the ways in which democratic progress can be helped or hindered.

Appendices

Appendix A

Freedom in the World based on Freedom House Data

Table A1: Political Regimes in 2010 and 2015 according to the Freedom House Rating System

FREE			PARTLY FREE			NOT FREE		
Name	*Freedom Status*		*Name*	*Freedom Status*		*Name*	*Freedom Status*	
	2010	*2015*		*2010*	*2015*		*2010*	*2015*
Argentina	F	F	Albania	PF	PF	Afghanistan	NF	NF
Australia	F	F	Armenia	PF	PF	Algeria	NF	NF
Austria	F	F	Bangladesh	PF	PF	Angola	NF	NF
Bahamas	F	F	Bhutan	PF	PF	Azerbaijan	NF	NF
Barbados	F	F	Bolivia	PF	PF	Bahrain	NF	NF
Belgium	F	F	Bosnia & Herzegovina	PF	PF	Belarus	NF	NF
Belize	F	F	Burkina Faso	PF	PF	Brunei	NF	NF
Benin	F	F	Colombia	PF	PF	Burundi	PF	NF
Botswana	F	F	Ivory Coast	**NF**	PF	Cambodia	NF	NF
Brazil	F	F	East Timor	PF	PF	Cameroon	NF	NF
Bulgaria	F	F	Ecuador	PF	PF	Central African Republic	**PF**	NF
Canada	F	F	Fiji	PF	PF	Chad	NF	NF
Cape Verde	F	F	Georgia	PF	PF	China	NF	NF
Chile	F	F	Guatemala	PF	PF	Congo, Dem. Rep.	NF	NF
Costa Rica	F	F	Guyana	**F**	PF	Congo, Rep of	NF	NF
Croatia	F	F	Guinea-Bissau	PF	PF	Cuba	NF	NF
Cyprus	F	F	Haiti	PF	PF	Djibouti	**PF**	NF
Czech Rep.	F	F	Honduras	PF	PF	Egypt	NF	NF
Denmark	F	F	Hong Kong*	PF	PF	Equatorial Guinea	NF	NF
Dominica	F	F	Indian Kashmir*	PF	PF	Eritrea	NF	NF
Dominican Rep.	F	F	Indonesia	**F**	PF	Ethiopia	**PF**	NF
El Salvador	F	F	Kenya	PF	PF	Gabon	NF	NF

Table A1 (*continued*)

FREE			PARTLY FREE			NOT FREE		
Name	*Freedom Status*		*Name*	*Freedom Status*		*Name*	*Freedom Status*	
	2010	*2015*		*2010*	*2015*		*2010*	*2015*
Estonia	F	F	Kosovo	PF	PF	Gambia	**PF**	NF
Finland	F	F	Kuwait	PF	PF	Gaza Strip*	NF	NF
France	F	F	Kyrgyzstan	**NF**	PF	Iran	NF	NF
Germany	F	F	Lebanon	PF	PF	Iraq	NF	NF
Ghana	F	F	Liberia	PF	PF	Jordan	NF	NF
Greece	F	F	Macedonia	PF	PF	Kazakhstan	NF	NF
Grenada	F	F	Madagascar	PF	PF	Laos	NF	NF
Guyana	F	F	Malawi	PF	PF	Libya	NF	NF
Hungary	F	F	Malaysia	PF	PF	Mauritania	NF	NF
Iceland	F	F	Maldives	PF	PF	Myanmar/ Burma	NF	NF
India	F	F	Mali	**F**	PF	N.Korea	NF	NF
Ireland	F	F	*Mexico*	**F**	PF	Oman	NF	NF
Israel	F	F	Moldova	PF	PF	Pakistani Kashmir*	NF	NF
Italy	F	F	Morocco	PF	PF	Qatar	NF	NF
Jamaica	F	F	Mozambique	PF	PF	Russia	NF	NF
Japan	F	F	Nagorno-Karabagh*	PF	PF	Rwanda	NF	NF
Kiribati	F	F	Nepal	PF	PF	Saudi Arabia	NF	NF
Latvia	**PF**	F	Nicaragua	PF	PF	Somalia	NF	NF
Liechtenstein	F	F	Niger	PF	PF	South Ossetia*	NF	NF
Lithuania	F	F	Nigeria	PF	PF	South Sudan	n/a	NF
Luxemburg	F	F	Pakistan	PF	PF	Sudan	NF	NF
Malta	F	F	Papua New Guinea	PF	PF	Swaziland	NF	NF
Micronesia	F	F	Paraguay	PF	PF	Syria	NF	NF
Monaco	F	F	Philippines	PF	PF	Tajikistan	NF	NF
Mongolia	F	F	Seychelles	PF	PF	Thailand	**PF**	NF
Namibia	F	F	Sierra Leone	PF	PF	The UAE	NF	NF
Netherlands	F	F	Singapore	PF	PF	Tibet*	NF	NF
New Zealand	F	F	Solomon Islands	PF	PF	Turkmenistan	NF	NF
Northern Cyprus*	F	F	Somaliland*	PF	PF	Uganda	**PF**	NF
Norway	F	F	Sri Lanka	PF	PF	Uzbekistan	NF	NF
Palau	F	F	Tanzania	PF	PF	Vietnam	NF	NF
Panama	F	F	Togo	PF	PF	West Bank*	NF	NF

Table A1 (*continued*)

FREE			PARTLY FREE			NOT FREE		
Name	*Freedom Status*		*Name*	*Freedom Status*		*Name*	*Freedom Status*	
	2010	*2015*		*2010*	*2015*		*2010*	*2015*
Peru	**PF**	F	*Turkey*	PF	PF	Western Sahara*	NF	NF
Poland	F	F	Ukraine	**F**	PF	Yemen	NF	NF
Portugal	F	F	Venezuela	PF	PF	Zimbabwe	NF	NF
Puerto Rico*	F	F	Zambia	PF	PF			
Romania	F	F						
Samoa	F	F						
San Marino	F	F						
Senegal	**PF**	F						
Serbia	F	F						
Slovakia	F	F						
Slovenia	F	F						
South Africa	F	F						
South Korea	F	F						
Spain	F	F						
Suriname	F	F						
Sweden	F	F						
Switzerland	F	F						
Taiwan	F	F						
Tunisia	**NF**	F						
UK	F	F						
US	F	F						
Uruguay	F	F						
Total # of FREE in 2015	*76*		*Total # of PARTLY-FREE in 2015*	*58*		*Total # of NOT-FREE in 2015*	*57*	

Source: Freedom House Table of Country Ratings. The ratings reflect global events from 1 January 2014 to 31 December 2014. Available on-line at https://www.freedomhouse.org/report/freedom-world-2015/table-country-ratings (last accessed 18 June 2015).

* indicates territories, as opposed to independent countries.

Bold entries indicate change of democratic status between 2010 and 2015.

According to the 2015 findings:

- 40% of the world population (2,826,850,000 people) lives in FREE countries.
- 25% of the world population (1,822,000,000 people) lives in PARTLY FREE countries.
- 35% of the world population (2,467,900,000 people) lives in NOT FREE countries.

Table A2: Freedom House Individual Country Ratings and Status for Mexico and Turkey (1972–2014)

Edition	Jan–Feb 1973			Jan–Feb 1974			Jan–Feb 1975			Jan–Feb 1976			Jan–Feb 1977			1978			1979		
Year(s) covered	1972			1973			1974			1975			1976			1977			1978		
	PR	CL	Status	PR	CL	Status	PR	CL	Status	PR	CL	Status	PR	CL	Status	PR	CL	Status	PR	CL	Status
Mexico	5	3	PF	4	3	PF	4	3	PF	4	3	PF	4	4	PF	4	3	PF	4	4	PF
Turkey	3	4	PF	2	4	PF	2	3	F	2	3	F	2	3	F	2	3	F	3	3	F

Edition	1980			1981			1982			1983–84			1984–85			1985–86			1986–87		
Year(s) covered	1979			1980			Jan 1981–Aug 1982			Aug 1982–Nov 1983			Nov 1983–Nov 1984			Nov 1984–Nov 1985			Nov 1985–Nov 1986		
	PR	CL	Status	PR	CL	Status	PR	CL	Status	PR	CL	Status	PR	CL	Status	PR	CL	Status	PR	CL	Status
Mexico	3	4	PF	3	4	PF	3	4	PF	3	4	PF	3	4	PF	4	4	PF	4	4	PF
Turkey	2	3	F	5	5	PF	5	5	PF	4	5	PF	3	5	PF	3	5	PF	3	4	PF

Table A2 (*continued*)

Edition	1987–88			1988–89			1989–90			1990–91			1991–92			1992–93			1993–94		
Year(s) covered	Nov 1986–Nov 1987			Nov 1987–Nov 1988			Nov 1988–Dec 1989			1990			1991			1992			1993		
	PR	CL	Status	PR	CL	Status	PR	CL	Status	PR	CL	Status	PR	CL	Status	PR	CL	Status	PR	CL	Status
Mexico	4	4	PF	3	4	PF	4	3	PF	4	4	PF	4	4	PF	4	3	PF	4	4	PF
Turkey	2	4	PF	2	4	PF	3	3	PF	2	4	PF	2	4	PF	2	4	PF	4	4	PF

Edition	1994–95			1995–96			1996–97			1997–98			1998–99			1999–2000			2000–01		
Year(s) covered	1994			1995			1996			1997			1998			1999			2000		
	PR	CL	Status	PR	CL	Status	PR	CL	Status	PR	CL	Status	PR	CL	Status	PR	CL	Status	PR	CL	Status
Mexico	4	4	PF	4	4	PF	4	3	PF	3	4	PF	3	4	PF	3	4	PF	2	3	F
Turkey	5	5	PF	5	5	PF	4	5	PF	4	5	PF	4	5	PF	4	5	PF	4	5	PF

Edition	2001–02			2003			2004			2005			2006			2007			2008		
Year(s) covered	2001			2002			2003			2004			2005			2006			2007		
	PR	CL	Status	PR	CL	Status	PR	CL	Status	PR	CL	Status	PR	CL	Status	PR	CL	Status	PR	CL	Status
Mexico	2	3	F	2	2	F	2	2	F	2	2	F	2	2	F	2	3	F	2	3	F
Turkey	4	5	PF	3	4	PF	3	4	PF	3	3	PF	3	3	PF	3	3	PF	3	3	PF

Table A2 *(continued)*

Edition	2009			2010			2011			2012			2013			2014			2015		
Year(s) covered	2008			2009			2010			2011			2012			2013			2014		
	PR	CL	Status	PR	CL	Status	PR	CL	Status	PR	CL	Status	PR	CL	Status	PR	CL	Status	PR	CL	Status
Mexico	2	3	F	2	3	F	3	3	PF	3	3	PF	3	3	PF	3	3	PF	3	3	PF
Turkey	3	3	PF	3	3	PF	3	3	PF	3	3	PF	3	4	PF	3	4	PF	3	4	PF

Source: Freedom House Individual Country Ratings and Status Dataset (1972–2015), available online at http://www.freedomhouse.org (last accessed 18 June 2015).

Key:
PR = Political Rights **CL** = Civil Liberties **F** = Free **PF** = Partly Free
Political rights include: questions on 1) Electoral Process, 2) Political Pluralism and Participation, and 3) Functioning of Government.
Civil liberties include questions on 1) Freedom of Expression and Belief, 2) Associational and Organizational Rights, 3) Rule of Law, and 4) Personal Autonomy and Individual Rights.
In the Freedom House rating system, 1 represents the most free and 7 the least free rating.
Free: 1.0 to 2.5
Partly Free: 3.0 to 5.0
Not Free: 5.5 to 7.0
For details on the Methodology of Freedom House Ratings, please see https://www.freedomhouse.org/report/freedom-world-2015/methodology#.VYSdKtyJlg0

Notes:

- Both Turkey and Mexico were mostly rated as Partly Free by the Freedom House from 1973 to 2015.
- Turkey was rated as Free from 1974 to 1979.
- Mexico was rated as Free from 2000 to 2009.

Appendix B

Photos from Mexico

Water-saving techniques displayed at CEDESA

Models of micro-tunnels that help grow *nopales* year round, alongside a drip irrigation system that uses significantly less water than conventional irrigation methods, and recycles grey water. Photo by the author, taken in Dolores Hidalgo.

A small workshop at CEDESA

This large room accommodates up to 100 participants and provides hands-on teaching in vital topics such as sustainable agriculture and irrigation techniques; economic self-sufficiency and regional co-operation in fairs; basic health; sanitation; and childcare information. The workshops draw demographically diverse crowds, including young and old men, women and children from nearly 150 communities and villages around Dolores Hidalgo. CEDESA is particularly accommodating to women with small children. After the long workshop sessions, participants are provided with a mid-afternoon meal (*la comida*). There are dormitories on the premises for those who came from long distances. The format of the workshops is rather horizontal, facilitating the flow of information among the participants themselves as well as between the CEDESA staff and participants. Nearly all participants report that what they learn from these sessions at CEDESA makes significant improvements to their day-to-day lives. Photo by the author.

Regional fair at Dolores Hidalgo, Guanajuato

One of CEDESA's founders

Left to right, Graciela (Chela) one of CEDESA's founders is pictured here with a young workshop participant and the author.

CEDESA participants' stand at a loal fair

CEDESA teaches various ways to make use of local produce – in marmalades, pickles, liquors and soaps – and helps communities participate in local fairs.

Photos from Turkey

Summer 2013 protests, reflected in graffiti

Posters of a minor left-wing political party calling for a rally on 9 June, below which is the spray-painted slogan *Boyun Eğme* (Do Not Bow), widely used by protestors across the country. Photo taken by the author in Batıkent, Ankara.

Protestors made extensive use of popular culture and humour. 'Winter is coming' is a well-known line from the HBO Series *Game of Thrones*. Photo by the author taken in Kızılay, Ankara

Protestors at Kuğulu Park

While the Gezi Park in Istanbul was undoubtedly the main location in which protests sprang up, similar occupation efforts took place in other metropolitan centres. This photo shows the tents of protestors at Kuğulu Park in Ankara. Subsequently, tents were torn down and taken away by the municipal authorities. Photo by the author.

Protesting Beşiktaş fans

Fans of leading soccer clubs also took part in the protests. Here, Beşiktaş fans build a barricade to block police vehicles on Kennedy Street, right across from the US Embassy in Ankara.

Justice and Development Party rally

Simultaneously with the protests, the ruling Justice and Development Party held rallies across the country. This photo was taken during Ramadan 2013, at an *iftar* rally where the then Prime Minister, Recep Tayyip Erdoğan, delivered a speech. Photo by the author, Altinpark, Ankara.

Appendix C – Websites

Full text of constitutions: https://www.constituteproject.org (last accessed 16 February 2015).

- Mexican constitution: https://www.constituteproject.org/constitution/ Mexico_2007?lang=en (last accessed, 25 November 2014).
- Sabancı Holding: http://www.sabanci.com.en (last accessed 16 February 2015).
- Organization of American States (OAS): http://www.oas.org (last accessed 16 February 2015).
- Freedom House: http://www.freedomhouse.org (last accessed 16 February 2015).

Bibliography

Acemoglu, D. and Robinson, J., *Why Nations Fail? The origins of power, prosperity and poverty*, New York: Random House, 2012.

Ahmad, F., *Bir Kimlik Peşinde Türkiye* [*Turkey: The quest for identity*], Cem İstanbul: Bilgi University Publications, 2007.

— *Demokrasi Sürecinde Türkiye 1945–1980*, [*Turkey in The Process of Democratization*], Istanbul: Hil Publications, 1996.

— *The Making of Modern Turkey*, London: Routledge, 1993.

Aksin, S., (ed.) *Çağdaş Türkiye 1908–1980*, [*Modern Turkey 1908–1980*], İstanbul: Cem Publications, 1997.

Almond, G. and Verba, S., *The Civic Culture: Political attitudes and democracy in five nations*, Princeton, NJ: Princeton University Press, 1963.

Altinay, A. G. and Arat, Y., *Violence against Women in Turkey: A nationwide survey*, Istanbul: Punto, 2009.

Alvarez, S. and Escobar, A., *The Making of Social Movements in Latin America: Identity, strategy and democracy*, Boulder, CO: Westview Press, 1992.

Anderson, L., 'Demystifying the Arab Spring', *Foreign Affairs* 2011, 90(3), pp. 2–54.

Anon., *Koçi Bey Risalesi*, (Original 1654) Ankara: Akçağ Publications, 1998.

Arat, Y., 'Contestation and collaboration: women's struggles for empowerment in Turkey', in Kasaba, R. (ed.) *The Cambridge History of Turkey, Volume IV: Turkey in the Modern World*, Cambridge: Cambridge University Press, 2008.

Arat, Z. K., (ed.) *Human Rights in Turkey*, Philadelphia: University of Pennsylvania Press, 2007.

Arango, T. and Yeginsu, S., 'Turkey moves to silence dissenters, but with one eye on its image abroad', *New York Times*, 14 November 2013.

Archibold, R. A., '43 missing students, a mass grave and a suspect: Mexico's police' *New York Times*, 6 October 2014.

Assies, W., 'Land tenure and tenure regimes in Mexico: an overview', *Journal of Agrarian Change* 2008, 8(1), pp. 33-63.

Ataturk, M. K., 'Atatürk's opening remarks at Izmir economy congress', 17 February 1923, accessed online through the historical archives of Izmir Economy University, Research Institute For Izmir Economy Congress, tbs no: 2006/01. Online. Available http://www.ieu.edu.tr/en (last accessed 10 April 2015).

Audley, J. *et al., Nafta's Promise and Reality*, Carnegie Endowment Report, 2004.

Ayata, A. G. 'The Republican People's Party', in Rubin, B. and Heper M. (eds) *Political Parties in Turkey*, London: Frank Cass, 2002.

Aydin, S. '*Amacımız Devletin Bekası*' *Demokratikleşme Sürecinde Devlet Ve Yurttaşlar* [*'Our Goal in the Longevity of the State' State and Citizens in the Democratization Process*], İstanbul: TESEV Publications, 2006.

Aydin, S. and Taskin, Y., *1960'tan Günümüze Türkiye Tarihi* [*Turkey's History Since 1960*], Istanbul: Iletisim Publications, 2014.

Aydinli, E., Ozcan, N.A. and Akyaz, D., 'The Turkish military's march toward Europe', *Foreign Affairs* 2006, Jan–Feb, 85(1), p. 77.

Babb, S., *Managing Mexico: Economists from nationalism to neoliberalism*, Princeton, NJ: Princeton University Press, 2004.

Bantjes, A., 'Burning Saints, Molding Minds: Iconoclasm, civic ritual, and the failed cultural revolution', in Beezeley, W. *et al.* (eds), *Rituals of Rule, Rituals of Resistance: Public celebrations and popular culture in Mexico*, Lanham, MD: Rowman & Littlefield, 1994.

Barkan, O. L., *Türkiye'de Toprak Meselesi. [The Land Issue in Turkey]* Istanbul: Gözlem Publications, 1980.

Barkey, H. J., *The State and the Industrialization Crisis in Turkey*, Boulder, CO: Westview Press, 1990.

— 'State autonomy and the crisis of import substitution', *Comparative Political Studies* 1989, 22(3), pp. 291–314.

Barkey, H. J. and Taspinar, O., *Turkey: On Europe's Verge?* 2006. Online. Available http://www.brookings.edu/research/articles/2006/02/07europe-barkey (last accessed 10 December 2014).

Barkey, K., *Bandits and Bureaucrats: The Ottoman route to centralization*, Ithaca, NY: Cornell University Press, 1994.

Belge, M., 'Trials of free speech', *Open Democracy*, 2 February 2006. Online. Available http://www.opendemocracy.net/democracy-turkey/belge_3241.jsp (last accessed 10 December 2014).

Barrientos, A., 'Latin America: towards a liberal-informal welfare regime', in Gough, I. and Wood, G. (eds), *Insecurity and Welfare Regimes in Asia, Africa and Latin America*, Cambridge: Cambridge University Press, 2008.

Beckman, B., 'Explaining democratization: notes on the concept of civil society', in Ozdalga, E. and Persson, S. (eds) *Civil Society and Democracy in the Muslim World*, Istanbul: Swedish Research Institute, 2002, pp. 1–7.

Bellin, E. R., 'Contingent democrats: industrialists, labor, and democratization in late developing countries', *World Politics* 2000, 52(2), pp. 175–205.

Benjamin, H., 'Revolutionary education in Mexico', *Annals of the American Academy of Political and Social Science* 1935, 182, pp.181–9.

Bethell, L. (ed.), *Mexico since Independence*, New York: Cambridge University Press, 1991.

Bianchi, R., *Interest Groups and Political Development in Turkey*, Princeton, NJ: Princeton University Press, 1984.

Boix, C., *Democracy and Redistribution*, Cambridge: Cambridge University Press, 2003.

Bora, A. and Gunal, A. (eds), *Feminism in Turkey in the 1990s*, Istanbul: Iletisim Publications, 2002.

Bora, T., 'AKP: the new center-right', in Kurt, U. (ed.), *Is AKP the New Center-Right?* Ankara: Dipnot Publications, 2009.

Boratav, K., 'Iktisat Iarihi 1908–1980; 1981–2002' [Economic history 1908–1980; 1981–2002'], in Aksin, S. *et al.* (eds), *Türkiye Tarihi Cilt 4-5* [*History of Turkey*], Istanbul: Cem Publications, 9th edn, 2007.

—   *Türkiye İktisat Tarihi 1981–2002* [*Turkish Economic History 1980–2002*], İstanbul: İmge Publications, 2004.

Braudel, F., *The Mediterranean and the Mediterranean World in the Age of Philip II*, trans. S. Reynolds, London: Harper Collins Publishers, 1992.

—   'History and social science', in Burke, P. (ed.), *Economy and Society in Early Modern Europe: Essays from Annalles*, New York: Harper & Row, 1972.

Brinkley, D., 'Democratic enlargement: the Clinton Doctrine', *Foreign Policy* 1997, 106, pp. 110–27.

Bugra, A., *Devlet Ve İşadamları* [*State and Business in Modern Turkey*] İstanbul: İletişim Publications, 2nd edn, 1997.

—   *State and Business in Modern Turkey: A comparative study*, New York: Suny Press, 1994.

Bugra, A. and Adar, S., 'Social policy change in countries without mature welfare states? The case of Turkey', *New Perspectives on Turkey* 2008, 38, pp. 83–106.

Bugra, A. and Keyder, C., 'The Turkish welfare regime in transformation', *Journal of European Social Policy* 2006, 16(3), pp. 211–28.

Bulmer-Thomas, V., *The Economic History of Latin America Since Independence*, Cambridge: Cambridge University Press, 2003.

Burkholder, M., 'An empire beyond compare', in Meyer, M. and Beezely, W. (eds), *Oxford History of Mexico*, New York: Oxford University Press, 2000.

Butler, E. *et al.*, *Mexico and Mexico City in the World Economy*, Boulder, CO: Westview Press, 2001.

Cakir, R., *Mahalle Baskısı* [*Neighborhood Pressure*] İstanbul: Doğan Publications, 2008.

Calles, P. E., 'A nation of institutions and laws', speech delivered to Congress 1 September 1928, quoted in G. Joseph *et al.* (eds), *The Mexico Reader: History, culture, politics*, Durham and London: Duke University Press, 2002, pp. 422–3.

Camp, R.A., *Mexico's Military on the Democratic Stage*, Westport, CT: Praeger and Washington, DC: CSIS, 2005.

—   *Politics in Mexico*, New York and Oxford: Oxford University Press, 1996.

—   *Generals in the Palacio: The military in modern Mexico*, New York: Oxford University Press, 1992.

Can, O., *The Constitution and Party Closures in the Process of Democratization*, Ankara: Seckin Publications, 2006.

Caneque, A., *The King's Living Image: The culture and politics of viceregal power in colonial Mexico*, New York: Routledge, 2005.

Cardoso, F. H., 'On the Concentration of Authoritarian Regimes in Latin America', in Collier, D. (ed.) *New Authoritarianism in Latin America*, Princeton, NJ: Princeton University Press, 1979.

Carkoglu, A., 'Who Wants Full Membership? Characteristics of Turkish support for EU membership', in Carkoglu, A. and Rubin, B. (eds), *Turkey and the European Union: Domestic politics, economic integration and international dynamics*, London: Frank Cass, 2003.

Carkoglu, A. and Toprak, B., *Religion, Society and Politics in Turkey*, Istanbul: Tesev Publications, 2006.

— *Religion, Society and Politics in Changing Turkey*, Istanbul: Tesev Publications, 2000.

de las Casas, B., *An Account of the first voyages and discoveries made by the Spaniards in America: Containing the most exact relation hitherto publish'd, of their unparallel'd cruelties on the Indians, in the destruction of above forty millions of people: with the propositions offer'd to the King of Spain to prevent further ruin of the West-Indies*, London, printed by J. Darby for D. Brown, 1699. Accessed online through the University of Massachusetts Libraries, EEBO-Early English Books On-line service.

Cavdar, T., *Türkiye'nin Demokrasi Tarihi: 1950'den Günümüze* [*Democratic History of Turkey: From 1950s On*], 3rd edn, Ankara: İmge Publications, 2004.

— *Türkiye Ekonomisinin Tarihi (1900–1960)* [*The History of the Turkish Economy 1900–1960*], Ankara, İmge Publications, 2003.

Cesarini, P. and Hite, K. (eds), *Authoritarian Legacies and Democracy in Latin America and Southern Europe*, South Bend, IN: University of Notre Dame Press, 2004.

Chase-Dunn, C., *Global Formation: Structures of the world-economy*, Cambridge, MA: Basil Blackwell, 1991.

Cizakca, M., 'Fiyat tarihi ve bursa ipek sanayii: Osmanlı sanayiinin çöküşü üzerine bir inceleme' ['Price history and the silk industry in Bursa: a study of the decline of Ottoman industry], *Toplum Ve Bilim* [*Society & Science*], 1980, 11, pp. 89–114.

Cizre, U., 'The emergence of the 'government's perspective on the Kurdish issue', *Insight Turkey*, 2009, 11(4), pp.1-12.

— 'Problems of democratic governance of civil-military relations in Turkey and the European Union enlargement zone', *European Journal of Political Research* 2004, 43(1), pp. 107–25.

Cline, H., 'Mexico: a matured Latin-American revolution', *Annals of the American Academy of Political and Social Science* 1961, 334, pp. 84–94.

Coatsworth, J. H., *Growth against Development: The impact of railroads in Porfirian Mexico,* Dekalb, IL: Northern Illinois University Press, 1981.

Colasan, E., *24 Ocak: Bir Dönemin Perde Arkası* [*January 24th: Behind the Scenes of a Period*], İstanbul: Milliyet Publications, 1983.

Coles, P., *The Ottoman Impact on Europe*, London: Thames & Hudson, 1968.

Collier, G., *Basta! Land and Zapatista Rebellion in Chiapas*, Oakland, CA: Food First Books, 3rd edn, 2005.

Cornelious, W. and Myhre, D. (eds), *The Transformation of Rural Mexico: Reforming the Ejido sector*, La Jolla, CA: Centre for U.S.-Mexican Studies, University of California, San Diego, 1998.

Dahl, R. *et al.*, *The Democracy Sourcebook*, Cambridge, MA: MIT Press, 2003.

Defence Policy of Turkish Armed Forces, on official web site of TAF. Online. Available http://www.tsk.tr/1_tsk_hakkinda/1_4_savunma_politikasi/savunma_politikasi.htm (last accessed 22 November 2009).

de la Garza, E., 'Manufacturing Neoliberalism: Industrial relations, trade union corporatism and politics', in Otero, G. (ed.), *Mexico in Transition*, London and New York: Zed Books, 2004.

Demirel, M., '"Oybirlikli Demokrasi" Açısından 1920–1945 Arasında Tbmm'deki Oylamalar' ['TGNA votes from 1925–1945 from the "unanimous democracy" perspective'], in M. Alkan, T. Bora, and M. Koraltürk, (eds), *Mete Tunçay'a Armağan* [*Tribute To Mete Tunçay*], İstanbul: İletişim Publications, 2007.

Demirel, T., 'Lessons of military regimes and democracy', *Armed Forces and Society* 2005, 31(2), pp. 245–71.

Deringil, S. *Turkish Foreign Policy during the Second World War: An 'active' neutrality*, New York: Cambridge University Press, 1989.

Diamond, L., *Developing Democracy: Towards consolidation*, Baltimore, MD: Johns Hopkins University Press, 1999.

Dogan, M. and Pelassy, D., *How to Compare Nations: Strategies in comparative politics*, Chatham, NJ: Chatham House Publishers, 1990.

Dominguez, J., Lawson C. H. and Moreno, A. (eds), *Consolidating Mexico's Democracy: The 2006 presidential campaign in comparative perspective*, Baltimore, MD: Johns Hopkins University Press, 2009.

Dornbusch, R. and Werner, A., 'Mexico: Stabilization, reform and no growth', *Brookings Papers on Economic Activity* 1994, 1, pp. 253–315.

Doyle, M., 'Kant and Liberal Internationalism' in Kant, I., *Towards Perpetual Peace and Other Writings on Politics, Peace and History*, New Haven, CT: Yale University Press, 2006.

Economist, 'Farmed out', 1 April 2000, p. 34.

Eder, M., 'Populism as a barrier to integration with the EU: rethinking the Copenhagen criteria', in Ugur, M. and Canefe, N. (eds), *Turkey's Europe: An internal perspective on EU–Turkey relations,* London: Routledge, 2004.

— 'Implementing the economic criteria of EU membership: how difficult is it for Turkey?', in Carkoglu, A. and Rubin, B. (eds), *Turkey and the European Union: Domestic politics, economic integration and international dynamics*, London and Portland, OR: Frank Cass, 2003.

Edwards, A. C., 'The impact of the war on Turkey', *International Affairs* 1946, 22(3), pp. 389–400.

Elliot, J. H., 'The Spanish conquest', in Bethel, L. (ed.), *Colonial Spanish America*, Cambridge: Cambridge University Press, 1987.

Erdemli, O., 'Chronology: Turkey's relations with the EU', in Carkoglu, A. and Rubin, B. (eds), *Turkey and the European Union: Domestic politics, economic integration and international dynamics*, London and Portland, OR: Frank Cass, 2003, pp. 4–5.

Escalante Gonzalbo, F., *El Crimen Como Realidad Y Representación* [*Crime as Reality and Representation*], Mexico D. F: El Colegio De Mexico, 2013.

— 'Homicidios 2008–2009: la muerte tiene permiso', *Nexos* 397, 1 January 2011.

Esmer, Y., 'At the ballot box: determinants of voting behavior', in Sayari, S. and Esmer, Y. (eds), *Politics, Parties and Interest Groups in Turkey*, Boulder, CO: Lynne Reinner Publishers, 2002, pp. 91–114.

— *Revolution, Evolution and Status Quo: Social, political and economic values in Turkey*, Istanbul: Tesev Publications, 2002.

Esteva, G., *Celebration of Zapatismo*, Oaxaca, Mexico: Ediciones Basta, 2008.

Eurobarometer no.78, 2012 http://ec.europa.eu/public_opinion/archives/eb_arch_en.htm (last accessed 10 December 2014).

European Commission, *1999 Regular Report from the EU Commission on Turkey's Progress Towards Accession*. Online. Available http://ec.europa.eu/enlargement/archives/pdf/key_documents/1999/turkey_en.pdf (last accessed 10 December 2014).

Evans, P., 'State structures, government–business relations and economic transformation', in Maxfield, S. and Schneider, B. R. (eds), *Business and State in Developing Countries*, New York: Cornell University Press, 1997.

EZLN, *Zapatistas! Documents of the new Mexican revolution*, New York: Autonomedia, 1994, pp.35–6. Online. Available http://lanic.utexas.edu/project/zapatistas/zapatistas_book.pdf (last accessed 10 September 2014).

Falk, R., 'Foreword', in Kabasakal, Z. A. (ed.), *Human Rights in Turkey*, Philadelphia: University of Pennsylvania Press, 2007.

Ferrera, M., 'The "southern model" of welfare in social Europe', *Journal of European Social Policy* 1996, 6(1), pp. 17–37.

Fox, J., 'How does civil society thicken? The political construction of social capital in rural Mexico', *World Development* 1996, 24(6), pp. 1089–1103.

— 'The difficult transition from clientelism to citizenship: lessons from Mexico', *World Politics* 1994, 46(2), pp.151–84.

Freedom House, *Map of Freedom in the World 2014*. Online. Available http://www.freedomhouse.org/report/freedom-world/freedom-world-2014#.uuqw0hz6gy4 (last accessed 25 January 2014).

Frey, F., *The Turkish Elite*, Cambridge, MA: MIT Press, 1965.

Fuentes, C., *The Buried Mirror: Reflections on Spain and the New World*, New York: Houghton Mifflin Company, 1999.

Gerber, H., *State, Society and Law in Islam: Ottoman law in comparative perspective*, Albany, NY: State University of New York Press, 1994.

Gerschenkron, A., *Economic Backwardness in Historical Perspective*, Cambridge, MA: Harvard University Press, 1962.

Gilbert, J. *et al.* (eds), *The Mexico Reader: History, culture, politics*, Durham and London: Duke University Press, 2002.

Gilbreth, C. and Otero, G., 'Democratization in Mexico: the Zapatista Uprising and the civil society', *Latin American Perspectives* 2001, 28(4), pp. 7–29.

Gladstone, R., 'Rights groups accuse Turkish police of excessive force against protesters', *New York Times*, 12 July 2013.

Göçek, F. M., *The Transformation of Turkey: Redefining state and society from the Ottoman Empire to the modern era*, London: I. B. Tauris, 2011.

Goffman, D., *The Ottoman Empire and Early Modern Europe*, Cambridge: Cambridge University Press, 2002.

Göle, N., 'Secularism and Islamism in Turkey: the making of elites and counter-elites', *Middle East Journal* 1997, 51(1), pp. 46–58.

—   'Authoritarian secularism and Islamist politics: the case of Turkey', in Norton, R. (ed.), *Civil Society in the Middle East*, vol. II, Leiden: Brill Academic Publishers, 1996.

Gomez Tagle, S., 'Elections in Mexico: what's the use?', *NACLA Report On the Americas* 2008, 41(5), pp. 12–18.

Gore, C., 'The rise and fall of the Washington Consensus as a paradigm for developing countries', *World Development* 2000, 28(5), pp. 789–804.

Gulalp, H., 'Globalisation and political Islam: the social basis of Turkey's Welfare Party', *International Journal of Middle East Studies* 2001, 33, pp. 433–48.

Haber, S. *et al.*, *Mexico Since 1980*, 2nd edn, New York: Cambridge University Press, 2011.

Haerpfer, C. W. *et al.* (eds), *Democratization*, New York: Oxford University Press, 2009.

Hale, C., 'Frank Tannenbaum and the Mexican Revolution', *The Hispanic American Historical Review* 1995, 75(2), pp. 215–46.

Haring, C. H., *The Spanish Empire in America*, Oxford: Oxford University Press, 1947, available online through ACLS History E-Book Project.

Harkinson, J. 'Map: the United States of legal weed', *Mother Jones*, 5 November 2014. Online. Available http://www.motherjones.com/politics/2014/11/map-united-states-legal-marijuana-2014-2016 (last accessed 10 April 2015).

Hart, J. M., 'The Mexican Revolution', in Meyer, M. and Beezley, W. (eds), *The Oxford History of Mexico*, New York: Oxford University Press, 2000.

Harvey, N., *The Chiapas Rebellion*, Durham and London: Duke University Press, 1998.

Hellman, J. A., *Mexican Lives*, New York and London: New Press, 1995.

—   'Mexican popular movements, clientelism, and the process of democratization', *Latin American Perspectives* 1994, 21(2), pp. 124–42.

Heper, M., 'The Ottoman legacy and Turkish politics', *Journal of International Affairs* 2000, 54(1), pp. 63–82.

—   'The strong state as a problem for the consolidation of democracy: Turkey and Germany compared', *Comparative Political Studies* 1992, 25(2), pp. 169–94.

— *The State Tradition in Turkey*, Walkington: Eothen Press, 1985.

Hernandez-Rodriguez, R., 'The renovation of old institutions: state governors and political transition in Mexico', *Latin American Politics and Society* 2003, 45(4), pp. 97–129.

Herr, R., *Spanish History*, Libro, the Library of Iberian Sources Online. Available http://libro.uca.edu/herr/essay.htm (last accessed 10 December 2014).

Hirschman, A., *A Bias for Hope: Essays on development and Latin America*, New Haven, CT: Yale University Press, 1971.

Hobsbawm, E., *The Age of Extremes: The short twentieth century, 1914–1991*, London: Michael Joseph Ltd, 1994.

Hourani, A., *A History of the Arab Peoples*, Cambridge, MA: Belknap Press of Harvard University Press, 1991.

Huber, E., 'The role of cross-regional comparison' (Letter from the President), *APSA-CP: Newsletter of the APSA Organized Section in Comparative Politics* 2003, 14(2), pp. 1–6.

Huntington, S. P., 'American ideals versus American institutions', in Ikenberry, J. (ed.), *American Foreign Policy*, 5th edn, NY: Pearson, 2005; and also in *Political Science Quarterly* 1982, 97(1), pp. 1–37.

— *The Third Wave: Democratization in the late Twentieth Century*, Norman, OK: University of Oklahoma Press, 1991.

— *The Soldier and the State: The theory and politics of civil-military relations*, Cambridge, MA: Harvard University Press, 1964.

Imber, C., *The Ottoman Empire, 1300–1650: The structure of power*, Basingstoke and New York: Palgrave Macmillan, 2002.

Inalcik, H., *From Empire to Republic: Essays on Ottoman and Turkish social history*, Istanbul: Isis Press, 1995.

— *The Ottoman Empire: The classical age, 1300–1600*, trans. N. Itzkowitz and C. Imber, London: Weidenfeld & Nicolson, 1973.

— 'Capital formation in the Ottoman Empire', *Journal of Economic History* 1969, 1, pp. 98–106.

Inalcik, H. and Quataert, D. (eds), *An Economic History of the Ottoman Empire, 1300–1914*, New York: Cambridge University Press, 1994.

Independent Commission on Turkey, *Turkey in Europe: The imperative for change*, Third report of the Independent Commission on Turkey, March 2014. Online. Available http://www.independentcommissiononturkey.org/pdfs/2014_english.pdf (last accessed 10 December 2014).

Inglehart, R., *Human Values and Social Change: Findings from the values survey*, Leiden and Boston, MA: Brill Academic Publishers, 2003.

Iversen, T., 'Capitalism and democracy', in Goodin, R. E. (ed.), *Oxford Handbook of Political Science,* New York: Oxford University Press, 2009, pp. 841–2.

Kafadar, C., *Between Two Worlds: The construction of the Ottoman state*, Berkeley, CA: University of California Press, 1996.

Kalaycioglu, E., *Turkish Dynamics: Bridge across troubled lands*, New York: Palgrave, 2005.

Kalaycioglu, E. and Carkoglu, A., *Turkish Democracy Today: Elections, protest and stability in an Islamic society*, London and NY: I. B. Tauris, 2007.

Kant, I., *Towards Perpetual Peace and Other Writings on Politics, Peace and History*, New Haven, CT: Yale University Press, 2006.

Karakoyunlu, Y., *Salkım Hanımın Taneleri*, Istanbul: Simavi Yayınları, 1990.

Karpat, K., *Türkiye'de Siyasi Sistemin Evrimi 1876–1980* [*The Evolution of the Political System in Turkey 1876–1980*], Istanbul: Imge Publications, 2007.

Katz, F., 'Labor conditions on haciendas in Porfirian Mexico', *Hispanic American Historic Review* 1974, 54(1), pp.1–47.

Keyder, C., *Türkiye'de Devlet Ve Sınıflar* [*The State and Classes in Turkey*], 6th end, İstanbul: İletişim Publications, 2000.

Keyder, C. *et al.* (eds), *Health Policies in Turkey and Europe*, Istanbul: Iletisim Publications, 2007.

Keyder, C. and Pamuk, S., 'Çiftçiyi Topraklandırma Kanunu Üzerine Tezler' [Thesis on the Land Reform Law], *Yapıt*, 1984–85, 8, pp. 52–63.

Keyman, F. and Icduygu, A., 'Globalization, civil society and citizenship in Turkey: actors, boundaries and discourses', *Citizenship Studies*, 2003, 7(2), pp. 219–34.

Kirisci, K. and Winrow, G., *The Kurdish Question and Turkey*, London: Frank Cass Publishers, 1997.

Kıvanç, U., 'State and civilians after the earthquake: the tremble', in Yerasımos, S. *et al.*, (eds) *Civil Society and Nationalism in Turkey*, Istanbul: Iletisim Publications, 2002.

Klesner, J., 'The structure of the Mexican electorate: social, attitudinal and partisan basis of Vicente Fox's victory', in Dominguez, J. and Lawson, C. (eds), *Mexico's Pivotal Democratic Election*, Stanford, CA: Stanford University Press, 2004, pp. 91–122.

Knight, A., 'Rise and fall of Cardenismo', in Bethell, L. (ed.), *Mexico Since Independence*, New York: Cambridge University Press, 1991.

Koçak, C., 'Siyasal Tarih (1923–1950)', ['Political history (1923–1950)'], in S. Aksin (ed.), *Çağdaş Türkiye 1908–1980*, [*Modern Turkey 1908–1980*], İstanbul: Cem Publications, 1997, pp. 98–9.

Köker, L., *Modernizm, Kemalizm Ve Demokrasi*, [*Modernism, Kemalism, and Democracy*], İstanbul: Iletişim Publications, 1995.

Krauze, E., *Mexico: Biography of power 1810–1996*, trans. H. Heifetz, New York: Harper Collins Publishers, 1997.

Kryzanek, M., *U.S.–Latin American Relations*, Westport, CT: Praeger, 1996.

Kuran, T., *The Long Divergence: How Islamic law held back the Middle East*, Princeton, NJ: Princeton University Press, 2010.

Levy, D. and Bruhn, K., *Mexico: The struggle for democratic development*, Berkeley, CA and London: University of California Press, 2001.

Lewis, B., *The Emergence of Modern Turkey*, 3rd edn, New York: Oxford University Press, 2002.

Linz, J. and Stepan, A., *Problems of Democratic Transition and Consolidation*, Baltimore, MD: Johns Hopkins University Press, 1996.

Lockhart, J., *Of Things of the Indies*, Stanford, CA: Stanford University Press, 1999.

Luciani, G., 'Allocation vs. production states: a theoretical framework', in Luciani, G. (ed.), *The Arab State*, London: Routledge, 1990.

Lurie, P. *et al.*, 'Socioeconomic obstacles to HIV prevention and treatment in developing countries: the roles of the International Monetary Fund and the World Bank', *Aids* 1995, 9(6), pp. 539–46.

Lustig, N., *Mexico: The remaking of an economy*, 2nd edn, Washington, DC: Brookings Institution Publications, 1998.

Lynch, J., 'Review of Jean Meyer: the Cristero Rebellion', *Journal of Latin American Studies* 1978, 10(2), pp. 365–6.

Madrid, R. L., 'Labouring against neoliberalism: unions and patterns of reform in Latin America', *Journal of Latin American Studies* 2003, 35(1), pp. 53–88.

Magaloni, B., 'The demise of Mexico's one-party dominant regime', in Hagopian, F. and Mainwaring, S. (eds), *The Third Wave of Democratization in Latin America*, New York: Cambridge University Press, 2005.

Mainwaring, S. and Perez-Liñan, A., *Democracies and Dictatorships in Latin America: Emergence, survival, and fall*, New York: Cambridge University Press, 2013.

Makal, A., 'Türkiye'de tek parti dönemi ve korporatizm tartışmaları' ['The single party era and corporatism debates in Turkey'], *Toplum Ve Bilim* [*Society and Science*], 2002, 93, pp. 173–99.

Mardin, S., *Religion, Society and Modernity in Turkey*, Syracuse, New York: Syracuse University Press, 2006.

— *Türkiye'de Toplum Ve Siyaset – Makaleler 1.* [*Society & Politics in Turkey –Articles*], İstanbul: İletisim Publications, 1994.

— *Jon Türklerin Siyasi Fikirleri 1895–1908* [*The Political Ideas of the Young Turks 1895–1908*], İstanbul: Iletişim Publications, 1983.

— 'Center-periphery relations: a key to Turkish politics?', *Daedalus* 1973, 102(1), pp. 169–91.

Matthews, O. and Kohen, S., 'Strong army democracy', *Newsweek International* 2002, 140(3), p. 30.

Mendez-Vigota, A., 'Post-revolutionary regimes in Mexico and their influence on Mexican public architecture 1920–1952', in Burian, E. (ed.), *Modernity and the Architecture of Mexico*, Austin, TX: University of Texas Press, 1997.

Mexican Institute for Competitiveness, *Posible impacto de la legalización de la marihuana en Estados Unidos* [*Possible impact of legalization of marijuana in United States*], 31 October 2012. Online. Available http:// imco.org.mx/seguridad/posible_impacto_de_la_legalizacion_de_la_ marihuana_en_estados_unidos// (last accessed 10 April 2015).

Meyer, J. A., 'Revolution and reconstruction in the 1920s', in Bethell, L. (ed.), *Mexico Since Independence*, New York: Cambridge University Press, 1991.

—   *The Cristero Rebellion: The Mexican people between church and state 1926–1929*, trans. R. Southern, Cambridge and New York: Cambridge University Press, 1976.

Meyer, L. 'The second coming of Mexican liberalism: a comparative perspective', in Servin, E., Reina, L. and Tutino, J. (eds), *Cycles of Conflict, Centuries of Change: Crisis, reform and revolution in Mexico*, Durham and London: Duke University Press, 2007.

Middlebrook, K. J., *The Paradox of Revolution: Labour, the state and authoritarianism in Mexico*, Baltimore, MD and London: Johns Hopkins University Press, 1995.

Milliyet, 'Kürsüden Ab Ödevleri' ['EU gives homework from the floor'], 10 November 2005.

Moghadam, R. 'Turkey at the crossroads: from crisis resolution to EU accession', IMF Occasional Paper No. 242, Washington, DC: IMF Publications, 2005.

Moore, B. *Social Origins of Dictatorship and Democracy*, Boston, MA: Beacon Press, 1967.

Muck, G. and Snyder, R., 'Debating the directions of comparative politics: an analysis of leading journals', *Comparative Political Studies*, 2007, 40(1), pp. 5–31.

Needler, M. C., 'Metaphors, models, and myths in the interpretation of Mexican politics', *Mexican Studies/Estudios Mexicanos*, 1991, 7(2), pp. 347–57.

New York Times, 'Turkey is advancing toward western democracy: President Inönü spearheading the campaign', 29 March 1950, p. 24.

Obama, B., 'Remarks by the President on a new beginning', speech delivered at Cairo University, 4 June 2009. Online. Available http://www.whitehouse.gov/the_press_office/remarks-by-the-president-at-cairo-university-6-04-09 (last accessed 23 April 2014).

O'Donnell, G., *Bureaucratic Authoritarianism: Argentina 1966–1973 in comparative perspective*, Berkeley, CA: University of California Press, 1988.

O'Donnell, G. *et al.* (eds), *The Quality of Democracy: Theory and applications*, Notre Dame, IN: University of Notre Dame Press, 2004.

OECD, *Decentralisation & Local Infrastructure in Mexico*, OECD Publications, 1998.

Önis, Z., 'Sharing power: Turkey's democratization challenge in the age of the AKP hegemony', *Insight Turkey* 2013, 15(2), pp. 103–22.

Önis, Z. and Webb, S., 'Turkey: democratization and adjustment from above', in Haggard, S. and Webb, S. (eds), *Voting For Reform*, Oxford: Oxford University Press, 1994.

Oran, B., 'Minority concept and rights in Turkey: the Lausanne peace treaty and current issues', in Arat, Z. K. (ed.), *Human Rights in Turkey*, Philadelphia: University of Pennsylvania Press, 2007.

Ortayli, I., *İstanbul'dan Sayfalar* [*Pages from Istanbul*], İstanbul: İletişim Publications, 1995.

Otero, G., (ed.) *Mexico in Transition*, London and New York: Zed Books, 2004.

Owen, R., *State Power and Politics in the Making of the Modern Middle East*, London: Routledge, 2000.

Oymen, O., *Ulusal Çıkar: Küreselleşme Çağında Ulus-Devleti Korumak* [*National Interest: Protecting the nation-state in the age of globalization*], Istanbul: Remzi Kitabevi, 2005.

Özbudun, E., 'From political Islam to conservative democracy: the case of the Justice and Development Party in Turkey', *South European Society and Politics* 2006, 11(3–4), pp. 543–557.

— *Contemporary Turkish Politics: Challenges to democratic consolidation*, Boulder, CO and London: Lynne Reiner Publications, 2000.

— 'The Ottoman legacy and the Middle East state tradition', in Brown, C. (ed.), *Imperial Legacy: The Ottoman Imprint on the Balkans and the Middle East*, New York: Columbia University Press, 1996.

Ozdemir, H., 'Siyasi tarih 1960–1980', in *Türkiye Tarihi 4* [*History of Turkey Volume 4*], Sina Akşin et al. (eds), 9th edn, İstanbul: Cem Publications, 2007, pp. 260–7.

Pagden, A. (ed. and trans.), *Hernan Cortes: Letters from Mexico*, New Haven, CT: Yale University Press, 2001.

Pamuk, S., 'Dünyada ve türkiyede iktisadi büyüme' ['Economic growth in the world and in Turkey'], *Uluslararası Ekonomi Ve Dış Ticaret Politikaları* [*International Economic and Trade Policies*], 2007, 1(2), pp. 3–26.

— 'The evolution of financial institutions in the Ottoman Empire, 1600–1914', *Financial History Review*, 2004, II(1), pp. 7–32.

— 'The evolution of fiscal institutions in the Ottoman Empire, 1500–1914', paper presented at the 13th International Economic History Congress, Buenos Aires, 2002.

— *A Monetary History of the Ottoman Empire*, Cambridge: Cambridge University Press, 2000.

Parla, T., *Ziya Gökalp, Kemalism and Corporatism in Turkey*, Istanbul: İletişim Publications, 1989.

Parla, T. and Davison, A., *Corporatist Ideology in Kemalist Turkey: Progress or order?*, New York: Syracuse University Press, 2004.

Paz, O., *Labyrinth of Solitude*, New York: Grove Press, 1985.

— 'Introduction' in Poniatowska, E., *Massacre in Mexico*, New York: Viking Press, 1975.

Pekin, F., 'Farklı Olmanın Adı: Disk' ['The name of being different: disko], *Sosyalizm Ve Toplumsal Mücadeleler Ansiklopedisi 1960–80* [*Encyclopedia of Socialism and Popular Resistance Movements*], 1988, 7, Istanbul: İletişim Publications.

Preston, J. and Dillon, S., *Opening Mexico: The making of a democracy*, New York: Farrar, Straus and Giroux, 2004.

Przeworski, A., Alvarez, M., Cheibub, J. A. and Limongo, F., *Democracy and Development: Political institutions and well-being in the world, 1950–1990*, New York: Cambridge University Press, 2000.

Przeworski, A. *et al.*, 'What makes democracies endure?', *Journal of Democracy* 1996, 7(1), pp. 39–55.

Putnam, R., *Making Democracy Work*, Princeton, NJ: Princeton University Press, 1993.

— *Bowling Alone: The collapse and revival of American community*, New York: Simon & Schuster, 2000.

Quataert, D., *The Ottoman Empire 1700–1922*, New York: Cambridge University Press, 2000.

Quataert, D., Inalcik, H., and Zurcher, E. (eds), *The Ottoman Empire: Society and economy 1300–1914*, New York: Cambridge University Press, 1994.

Republic of Turkey, Ministry of EU Affairs, *Chronology of Turkish-EU Relations*. Online. Available http://www.abgs.gov.tr/index.php?p=112&l=2 (last accessed 10 December 2014).

Rice, C., 'Remarks at the American University in Cairo', 20 June 2005. Online. Available http://2001-2009.state.gov/secretary/rm/2005/48328.htm (last accessed 28 January 2014).

Rodrik, D., 'Understanding economic policy reform', *Journal of Economic Literature*, 1996, 34(1), pp. 9–41.

Rosenberg, J., 'Mexico: end of party corporatism?', in Thomas, S. C. (ed.), *Political Parties and Interest Groups: Shaping democratic governance*, Boulder, CO: Lynne Reinner Publishers, 2001.

Rother, L., '20 years after a massacre, Mexico still seeks healing for its wounds', *New York Times*, 2 October 1988.

Rus, J., 'The "Comunidad Revolucionaria Institucional": the subversion of native government in highland Chiapas, 1936–1968', in Joseph, G. and Nuget, D. (eds), *Everyday Forms of State Formation*, Durham and London: Duke University Press, 1994, pp. 265–300.

Rustow, D., 'Atatürk as a founder of a state', *Daedalus* 1968, 97(3), pp. 793–828.

Samstad J. G., 'Corporatist and democratic transition: state and labor during the Salinas and Zedillo Administrations', *Latin American Politics and Society* 2002, 44(4), pp.1–28.

Sancar, M. and Umit, E., *Yargıda Algı Ve Zihniyet Kalıpları* [*Perception and Mentality Patterns in the Judiciary*] Istanbul: Tesev Publications, 2007.

Sayari, S., 'The changing party system', in Sayari, S. and Esmer, Y. (eds.), *Politics, Parties and Elections in Turkey*, Boulder, CO and London: Lynne Reinner Publishers, 2002.

Sayari, S. and Esmer Y. (eds), *Politics, Parties and Elections in Turkey*, Boulder, CO and London: Lynne Reinner Publishers, 2002.

Schedler, A., 'What is democratic consolidation?', *Journal of Democracy* 1998, 9(2), pp. 91–107.

Schmitter, P. C., 'The influence of international context upon the choice of national institutions and policies in neo-democracies', in Whitehead, L. (ed.), *The International Dimensions of Democratization: Europe and the Americas*, Oxford and New York: Oxford University Press, 1996, pp. 26–54.

—   'Still the century of corporatism?', in Schmitter, P. C. and Lembruch, G. (eds), *Trends Toward Corporatist Intermediation*, Thousand Oaks, CA: Sage Publications, 1979.

Schneider, B. R., 'Why is Mexican business so organized?', *Latin American Research Review* 2002, 37(1), pp. 77–118.

Serra, J. and Espinosa, E., 'Debate: happily ever after NAFTA?', *Foreign Policy* 2002, 132, pp. 58–65.

Shaw, S. J., *History of the Ottoman Empire and Modern Turkey, Volume I*, Cambridge: Cambridge University Press, 1976–77.

—   *History of the Ottoman Empire and Modern Turkey, Volume II: Reform, revolution, and the republic –the rise of modern Turkey, 1808–1975*, Cambridge: Cambridge University Press, 1976-77.

Sherman, J., 'The Mexican "Miracle" and its collapse', in Meyer, M. and Beezeley, W. (eds), *The Oxford History of Mexico*, Oxford and New York: Oxford University Press, 2000.

Shirk, D. A., *The Drug War in Mexico: Confronting a shared threat*, Council on Foreign Relations: Center for Preventive Action, Council Special Report No: 60, 2011.

Sil, R., 'Area studies, comparative politics and the role of cross regional small-N comparison', *Qualitative & Multi-Method Research* 2009, 7(2), pp. 26–32.

Sivil Toplum Kuruluşları, Yerelleşme ve Yerel Tönetimler, [Civil Society Organisations, Localisation and Local Governments], Symposium Proceedings, 21–22 June 2002, Economic and Social History Foundation of Turkey, Istanbul Technical University.

Skidmore, T. and Smith, P., *Modern Latin America*, 5th edn, New York: Oxford University Press, 2001.

Smith, P., 'Mexico since 1946: Dynamics of an authoritarian regime', in Bethell, L. (ed.), *Mexico since Independence*, New York: Cambridge University Press, 1991.

Sönmez, M., *Türkiye Ekonomisinde Bunalım [Depression in the Turkish Economy]*, İstanbul: Belge Publications, 1980.

Sosyalizm ve Toplumsal Mücadeleler Ansiklopedisi [Encyclopedia of Socialism and Popular Resistance Movements], vol. 7 (1960–1980), İstanbul: İletişim Publications, 1988.

Stolle-Mcallister, J., 'What *does* democracy look like? Local movements challenge the Mexican transition', *Latin American Perspectives* 2005, 32(4), pp. 15–35.

Story, D., 'Policy cycles in Mexican presidential politics', *Latin American Research Review* 1985, 20(3), pp. 139–61.

Strange, S., *The Retreat of the State: The diffusion of power in the world economy*, Cambridge: Cambridge University Press, 1997.

Sülker, K., *15–16 Haziran: Türkiye'yi Sarsan İki Uzun Gün [June 15–16: Two Long Days That Shook Turkey]*, 3rd edn, İstanbul: İleri Publications, 2005.

Sunar, I., *State Society and Democracy in Turkey*, İstanbul: Bahçesehir University Publications, 2004.

Tachau, F., 'An overview of electoral behavior: toward protest or consolidation of democracy', in Sayarı, S. and Esmer, Y. (eds), *Politics, Parties and Elections in Turkey*, Boulder, CO and London: Lynne Reinner Publishers, 2002.

Tanör, B., 'Political history, 1980–1995', in Aksin, S. *et al.* (eds), *Today's Turkey 1980–2003, History of Turkey, Vol.5,* Ankara: Cem Publications, 2007.

Tarrow, S., 'The strategy of paired comparison: toward a theory of practice', *Comparative Political Studies* 2010, 43(2), pp.230–59.

Taskin, Y., 'Succession fights in center right as nationalist conservatism disintegrates', in Kurt, U. (ed.), *Is AKP the New Center-Right?*, Ankara: Dipnot Publications, 2009.

Tenenbaum, B., *Mexico and the Royal Indian: The Porfiriato and the national past*, College Park, Latin American Studies Centre, University of Maryland, 1994.

TEPAV Survey, 2009, presented by Sak, G. TEPAV, Ankara. Online. Available http://www.tepav.org.tr/tr/ (last accessed 16 February 2015).

Tepe, S., 'The perils of polarization and religious parties: the democratic challenges of political fragmentation in Israel and Turkey', *Democratization* 2013, 20(5), pp. 831–56.

Therborn, G., 'Beyond Civil Society: Democratic experiences and their relevance to the Middle East', in Ozdalga, E. and Persson, S. (eds), *Civil Society and Democracy in the Muslim World*, Istanbul: Swedish Research Institute, 2002.

Tilly, C., *Democracy*, New York: Cambridge University Press, 2007.

Tocqueville, A. de, *Democracy in America*, trans. A. Goldhammer, New York: Library of America, distributed to the trade in the US by Penguin Putnam, 2004.

Today's Zaman, 'Interview with the Mexican Ambassador in Turkey, Hon. Salvador Campos Icardo', 4 September 2007.

Toledo, E. G., 'Manufacturing neoliberalism: industrial relations, trade union corporatism and politics', in Otero, G. (ed.), *Mexico in Transition*, London and New York: Zed Books, 2004.

Toprak, B., *et al., Being Different in Turkey*, Istanbul: Metis Publications, 2009.

—— 'Civil society in Turkey', in Norton, R. (ed.), *Civil Society in the Middle East, Volume II*, Leiden: Brill Academic Publishers, 1996.

—— *Islam and Political Development*, Leiden: Brill Academic Publishers, 1981.

Tuncay, M., *Türkiye'de Tek Parti Doneminin Kurulması 1923–1931 [Establishment of the Single Party Era in Turkey 1923–1931]*, İstanbul: Cem Publications, 1989.

Turan, I., 'Old soldiers never die: the Republican Peoples Party of Turkey', *South European Society and Politics* 2006, 11(3–4), pp. 559–78.

Türkes, M., *Kadro Hareketi [The Kardo Movement]*, İstanbul: İmge Publications, 1999.

TUSIAD (Turkish Association of Industrialists and Business People). Online. Available www.tusiad.org, TUSIAD by numbers (last accessed 25 May 2014).

Tutino, J., *From Insurrection to Revolution in Mexico: Social bases of agrarian violence, 1750–1940,* Princeton, NJ: Princeton University Press, 1986.

Uğur, M. and Canefe, N. 'Turkey and European Integration: Introduction', in Uğur, M. and Canefe, N. (eds), *Turkey and European Integration: Accession prospects and issues,* London: Routledge, 2004.

Ümit, C., 'The emergence of the government's perspective on the Kurdish Issue', *Insight Turkey* 2009, 11(4), p. 3.

USAID (2011) *US Overseas Loans & Grants, FY2011.* Online. Available http://gbk.eads.usaidallnet.gov/data/fast-facts.html (last accessed 05 February 2014).

Vachudova, M. A., *Europe Undivided: Leverage and integration after communism,* Oxford: Oxford University Press, 2005.

Vali, F. A., *The Turkish Straits and Nato,* Stanford, CA: Hoover Institution Press, 1972.

Van Young, E., *Hacienda and Market in Eighteenth-Century Mexico,* Berkeley, CA: University of California Press, 1981.

Veliz, C., *The Centralist Tradition of Latin America,* Princeton, NJ: Princeton University Press, 1980.

Wallerstein, I., Speech delivered at a special conference on World-Systems School and Faruk Tabak, 7 March 2008, Bilgi University: Istanbul.

Weber, M., 'The types of legitimate domination', in Roth, G. and Wittich, C. (eds), *Economy and Society: An outline of interpretive sociology, Volume I,* Berkeley, CA: University of California Press, 1978.

Whitehead, L., 'Three international dimensions of democratization', in Whitehead, L. (ed.), *The International Dimensions of Democratization: Europe and the Americas,* Oxford and New York: Oxford University Press, 1996.

Wiarda, H. J., *Civil Society: The American model and third world development,* Boulder, CO: Westview Press, 2003.

—   *The Soul of Latin America: The cultural and political tradition,* New Haven, CT: Yale University Press, 2001.

—   'Beyond the pale: the bureaucratic politics of the United States in Mexico', *World Affairs* 2000, 162(4), pp.174–91.

—   *Non-Western Theories of Development,* Fort Worth, TX: Harcourt Brace College Publications, 1999.

—   *Corporatism and Comparative Politics: The other great 'ism',* New York and London: M.E. Sharpe, 1997.

—   'US policy and democracy in Latin America and the Caribbean', *Policy Papers on the Americas,* VI(7), CSIS Americas Program, 1995.

Wiarda, H. J. and Guajardo, C. C., 'Mexico: the unravelling of a corporatist regime', *Journal of Interamerican Studies and World Affairs* 1988–9, 30(4), pp. 1–28.

Wiltse, E. C., 'The Gordian Knot of Turkish politics: regulating headscarf use in public', *South European Society and Politics* 2008, 13(2), pp. 195–215.

Woldenber, J., *La Transición Democrática En México* [*The Democratic Transition in Mexico*], México D. F.: El Colegio De México, 2012.

World Bank, *World Development Report 2002*, New York: Oxford University Press.

— World Development Indicators. Online. Available http://data.worldbank. org (last accessed 10 April 2015).

Yazici, S., *Turkey in the Process of Democratization*, Istanbul: Bilgi University Press, 2009.

Yesilkaya, N., 'Halkevleri' ['People's houses'] in *Modern Türkiye'de Siyasi Düşünce: Kemalizm (II)*, [*Political Thought in Modern Turkey: Kemalism*], İstanbul: İletişim Publications, 2001.

Yilmaz, H. (ed.), *Placing Turkey on the Map of Europe*, Istanbul: Bogazici University Press, 2005.

— 'External-internal linkages in democratization: developing an open model of democratic change', *Democratization* 2002, 9(2), pp. 67–84.

— 'Democratization from above in response to the international context: Turkey 1945–1950', *New Perspectives on Turkey* 1997, 17, pp. 1–37.

Zarakol, A., 'Revisiting second image reversed: lessons from Turkey and Thailand', *International Studies Quarterly* 2013, 57(1), pp. 150–62.

Zarembo, A., 'Second coming: Vicente Fox's religion', *Newsweek International* 8 January 2001, p. 48. Online. Available http://www.newsweek.com/ second-coming-150873 (last accessed 25 November 2014).

Zavala, S., *New Viewpoints on the Spanish Colonization of America*, New York: Russell & Russell, 1968.

Zürcher, E. J., 'Institution building in the Kemalist Republic: the role of the People's Party', in Atabaki, T. (ed.), *Men of Order: Authoritarian modernization under Ataturk and Reza Shah*, London: I. B. Tauris & Co, 2004.

Index

Afghanistan 3, 4, 140
Ağaoğlu, A. 70–1
Alemán, M. 100, 105, 115, 117,
    121–2, 127–8
    agrarian 'Green Revolution' of
        122–5
    and 'Mexican Miracle' 121–2
Arab Spring 4, 213, 221
    democracy promotion, use in 140
    and regional generalisations 6
Argentina 17, 121, 141, 146, 154
Atatürk, M. K. 57, 58, 59, 61–2, 70,
    84, 190
    economic policy of 68, 70
    People's Houses and Rooms, use of
        64–6
        ideological agenda of 65–6
    'six arrows of Kemalism' 60, 62–4,
        77
        and republicanism 62–3
        and nationalism 63
        and populism (*halkçılık*) 63, 64,
            65
        revolutionarism 63
        secularism 63
        statism 63
    see also Turkey
Augustine, St. 15, 51, 52, 216
authoritarian regimes
    and democratisation xix, 9, 45–6,
        142, 213, 221
        consolidation stage in 142
    legacies of 45–6, 142, 144
    and MENA region 4, 213
    in 1930s Europe 61, 76
    see also democratic consolidation;
        democratic progress analysis
Aztecs 8, 13

Bayar, C. 70, *84*
Bolivia 141, 146, 154
Brazil 11, 146
Bulgaria 22, 146
Bull, H. 146
Byzantine Empire 14, 22

Calderón, F. 137
Calles, P. E. 61, 100 n.10, 104–5,
    108–10, 112, 114–15, 216
    Maximato period of 105
Camacho, M. A. 126–7
Canada, Mexican partnership 175, 176
    NAFTA agreement 139, 158
capitalism 51, 53, 149
Cárdenas, C. 158
Cárdenas, L. 115, 116–17, 118, 120,
    122, 126, 127, 158, 166
Carranza, V. 102, 103
CEDESA organisation 168–9, 227–30
    grassroots activism of 168
    teaching areas of 230, 231
Chile 121, 141, 146, 191
Çiller, T. 204–5
civic activism 150, 196, 198
    and grassroots organisations 193
    and interpersonal trust 198
    and new social movements 160, 196
civil society xix, 48, 49, 55, 141,
    148–9
    definition/concept of 140, 149–50
        Anglo-American model of 150
        difficulties in use of 149–50
    and democratic consolidation
        148–9, 197
    and globalisation 193
    and grass-roots movements 193,
        197

www.ingramcontent.com/pod-product-compliance
Lightning Source LLC
Chambersburg PA
CBHW072057020426
42334CB00017B/1541